Forensic Investigation and Management of Mass Disasters

Compiled and edited by

Matthias I. Okoye
Cyril H. Wecht

Contributors

Steven C. Batterman
Larry R. Bedore
John J. Buturla
Bruce W. Dixon
Annette Doying
Bassel El-Kasaby
John Filippi
L. Sue Gabriel
Timothy E. Huntington
Erin Kimmerle
Henry C. Lee

Christopher Long
David McCann
Edmund J. C. Nwana
John O. Obafunwa
Roberta Chizoma Opara
Timothy Palmbach
Mark W. Perlin
Mark Roper
Michael Welner
Thomas Young

 Lawyers & Judges
Publishing Company, Inc.

 **Lawyers & Judges
Publishing Company, Inc.**

P.O. Box 30040 • Tucson, AZ 85751-0040
(800) 209-7109 • FAX (800) 330-8795
e-mail: sales@lawyersandjudges.com
www.lawyersandjudges.com

Library of Congress Cataloging-in-Publication Data

Forensic investigation and management of mass disasters / compiled and edited by Matthias I. Okoye, Cyril H. Wecht.
    p. cm.
  Includes index.
  ISBN-13: 978-1-933264-41-7 (hardcover : alk. paper)
  ISBN-10: 1-933264-41-1 (hardcover : alk. paper)
  1. Disasters. 2. Forensic sciences. 3. Emergency management. I. Wecht, Cyril H., 1931- II. Okoye, Matthias I.
  HV8080.D5F67 2007
  363.25--dc22

                            2007036692

ISBN 10: 1-933264-41-1
ISBN 13: 978-1-933264-41-7
Printed in the United States of America
10 9 8 7 6 5 4 3 2 1

Dedication

This book is dedicated to the millions of victims and survivors of mass disasters throughout the world, both from natural catastrophies and man-made acts of terrorism.

Table of Contents

Acknowledgements

The editors extend their appreciation to the contributing authors for their excellent manuscripts in this book. We are well aware of the personal sacrifices that they have made even while on vacation with their families during the summer; and we are indebted to them for their dedication of time to write their respective chapters. We are grateful to Professor Donald J. Guter, Dean of the Duquesne University School of Law, for writing the foreword to this book. We would like to acknowledge our many friends and colleagues who encouraged us and aided in the completion of this volume. The staffs of the Wecht Institute of Forensic Science and Law at the Duquesne University School of Law and the the Nebraska Institute of Forensic Sciences, Inc. deserve special recognition for their guidance and assistance throughout the development of this text. Special thanks are given to Ms. Sally Knickman of Nebraska Forensic Medical Services, P.C., and Ms. Eileen Edwards of the Wecht Institute of Forensic Science and the Law for their generous assistance. We are indebted to the staff of Lawyers & Judges Publishing Co., Inc., for their support and excellent work and in guiding us through the publication of this reference book in truly record time. Finally, we extend our sincere thanks to our wives, Cordelia and Sigrid, for their understanding and support in making this project possible.

—Dr. Matthias I. Okoye and Dr. Cyril H. Wecht

Foreword

On any given day, it takes only a glance at the headlines to understand the breadth of the destruction in our world and the disruption in our lives caused by catastrophic events springing from the uncontrollable power of nature and the tyranny of man. More than ever, it seems as though we are increasingly impacted by mass-casualty events - natural disasters, terrorist threats (made and realized), carelessly destroyed ecosystems, environmental hazards, war, tsunamis, earthquakes, hurricanes, floods, wildfires, famine, and disease.

Although we continue to make advances that help us understand, prevent and respond to these conditions, our need to sustain and accelerate our efforts remains unabated by any scientific, social or political success to which we may be tempted to lay claim. Unfortunately, the reality of the worst aspects of both nature and man leave small room for error or contentment.

In the Navy, we have a common expression—"all hands on deck"—that inspires uncommon valor in the face of imminent harm or disaster. Sitting at my desk in the Pentagon on the morning of September 11, 2001, I experienced the best in our people as they mustered their unrehearsed response to a disaster that was once beyond imagination While I have witnessed many "disasters" in my lifetime, none has touched my spirit as did the events on that tragic day.

From Katrina to 9/11 to similarly deplorable conditions throughout the international community, Forensic Investigation and Management of Mass Disasters makes it clear that neither government nor any people is immune from the continuing effect of destructive forces.

The editors and authors of this text, under many conditions and circumstances, have seen the worst and the best that can come from disaster investigation and medicine. Their expertise is unparalleled and the lessons they offer are vital to our national security and to the interests of the international community, as well as to individual lives. I am proud of our close affiliations with Dr. Cyril H. Wecht and Dr. Matthias I. Okoye, and we are grateful for the continuing efforts of both the Wecht Institute at the Duquesne University School of Law and the Nebraska Institute of Forensic Sciences for their efforts to inform and enlighten our lives.

My colleagues understand that we live in a dangerous world where unrehearsed responses to disasters should be the exception, and not the rule. I hope that all readers will take the writers' insights and expertise to heart. In reading this text, it occurs to me that they are issuing their own call for "all hands on deck." I know they share my hope that the reader will come to understand this expanding area of study in medicine, public health, emergency medical services, public safety, and mental health.

—Donald J. Guter
Rear Admiral, Judge Advocate General's Corps, U.S. Navy (retired)
Dean, Duquesne University School of Law
Pittsburgh, Pennsylvania

Introduction

A mass disaster is a catastrophic event that always leads to substantial loss of lives and damage of property. In mass disasters, the resources of the community are usually affected and their capacity to cope or respond to the tragedy may be limited. Such incidents are becoming more common with the increase in terrorism, expansion of travel facilities, larger size of means of passenger transport, and bizarre climatic conditions. Recent disasters such as airplane crashes and transportation accidents, building collapses, explosions, industrial accidents, epidemics and environmental conditions, such as earthquakes, cyclones, and floods and civil riots have shown the need for a multi-disciplinary approach in the management of mass disasters. Because of the frequent tragic disasters in the recent past, many nations and cities all over the world have formulated "Mass Disaster Plans." Such mass disaster plans cover many aspects related to search and rescue services, health care, rehabilitation, reconstruction, and preventive measures. However, despite the availability of disaster plans, the management of mass disasters has always been very difficult in both developed and underdeveloped countries. In many cases, there is a lack of coordination even if there are abundant resources for handling such incidents. Furthermore, many key personnel are unaware of the importance of preservation and examination of the dead, and still continue to harbor age-old casual attitudes, thereby remaining oblivious to the tremendous development and advancements in this new field of medicine and forensic science. The consequences of this grave omission will not only cause untold anxiety and misery to the bereaved families, but also seriously jeopardize the investigation of mass disasters. Sometimes, even diligently prepared plans may become ineffective, as in the case of tragedies where there are several hundred corpses. A plan without any provision for the proper examination of the dead will obviously be found lacking, resulting in a serious crisis in relation to the dead victims. Apathy towards this critical important aspect may be due to lack of insight, logistic constraints, and ignorance. One should not forget that the manner in which a society deals with its dead reflects its attitude to the sanctity of life and the rights of the individual. Our responsibility to the dead is a reflection of our respect for the society in which we live. It is important to realize that examination of the dead is usually for the benefit of the living. There are many social, legal, and health reasons as to why it is important to preserve and properly examine the dead.

The U.S. Department of Homeland Security recently issued a report assessing the country's catastrophic plan capabilities. According to this report, only one in four states in the United States is fully prepared to cope with a terrorist attack or natural disaster. Usually, when multi-casualty incidents occur, different government agencies react and interact. Any conflicts in such interactions or lack of coordination will adversely affect mass disaster investigations and overall management. In the investigation and management of mass disasters, various professionals including forensic pathologists, coroners and medical examiners, forensic anthropologists, forensic odontologists, forensic engineers, health care professionals in the emergency rooms of hospitals, various medical and surgical specialists, forensic entomologists, law enforcement personnel, fire marshals, ambulance professionals, forensic toxicologists, and microbiologists interact to provide needed services. The rescue, search, and recovery efforts are usually very extensive, labor intensive, and time consuming. The roles of forensic pathologists, coroners and medical examiners, forensic dentists and other forensic and medical professionals have been highlighted in this volume for the benefit of government planners regarding mass disaster scenarios.

Firstly, establishment of the identity of the victims is paramount. Identification represents cognizance of the fundamental human right to have an identity both in life and in death. The identification of the dead is essential for the lives of others to proceed and return to normalcy. In all mass disasters, there is an urgent and future need to identify the victims. It usually appears simple to establish the identity of an intact body. However, it is important to recognize the difficulty in recapturing the living appearance of an individual from mutilated, charred, or skeletonized remains that may be partial or intermingled, a situation frequently encountered in mass disasters. In such cases, the forensic pathologist can help in establishing the identity of the victims from the morphology, anatomic features, individual identifying features (i.e., tattoos, old surgical scars, etc.), fingerprinting, DNA profiling, forensic odontologic features and forensic imaging, etc. The importance and necessity of establishing identity is primarily an appropriate endeavor, humanitarian, as well as, being necessary for the legal establishment of death, future settlements of inheritance, returning the bodies to the families who have legal property rights, and for the purposes of any future civil and criminal court actions and litigation.

Secondly, there is a need to reconstruct the mutilated remains for decent presentation and burial by the family. It is also necessary for proper preservation and handling of the remains by skilled professionals such as funeral directors, to prevent crucial loss of evidence and inadvertent introduction of artifacts; to prevent further decomposition and putrefaction, and to facilitate reduction of health hazards.

Thirdly, it is necessary to determine the cause of the disaster by collecting evidence, such as a bomb or detonator fragments that may be embedded in the bodies. Toxicologic analyses of victims is an important aspect of all such deaths. Pathologic evidence to evaluate any disease conditions in key victims that could have contributed to their death is a vital aspect of such postmortem examinations. In the case of a possible epidemic resulting from biologic or chemical terrorism, coroners and medical examiners can help in the detection and diagnosis of the causative agent which in turn enables the concerned authorities to take necessary preventive measures. Finding any trace evidence that could help in the investigation of the tragedy can also be obtained through the assistance of forensic pathologists.

The reconstruction of the cause of the disaster is also very essential. That can be accomplished through the assistance of forensic engineers in air-crashes, building collapses, and transportation accidents. Studying the nature and pattern of injuries sustained by the victims to see whether the injuries demonstrate a pattern that conforms to other similar incidents is very important. Studying the position of the remains in relation to the wreckage at the site of the tragedy is also very important. Forensic pathologists and forensic engineers can assist in such determinations.

Another aspect of the role of forensic scientists, especially forensic pathologists is the establishment of the time of survival of victims of mass disasters. This is a critical determination in cases involving presumption of survivorship. Also, it can helpful to determine whether there was any lapse in the search and rescue operations; and accordingly, lead to recommendations and corrective measures that can be incorporated in future plans. The use of forensic entomologists in determining the time since a victim's death; and forensic toxicologists in the study of poisons have been dramatically demonstrated in some mass disaster cases. The evaluation and analysis of the data during the course of medicolegal investigation can be utilized as a tool in the development and improvement of safety measures including workplace, seatbelts, airbags, head rests, helmets, leg guards, laminated windshields, etc. All of these have been developed and improved over the years by studying such data. Many of these measures have been made mandatory in several countries. Forensic entomologists use flies and maggots for identification purposes, and to extract trace samples of drugs or other toxicologic evidence. Forensic imaging allows investigators in mass disasters to pick up shoe or tire treads that can provide criminal evidence than can lead to the conviction of criminal perpetrators. The application of virtual autopsies employing forensic imaging techniques such as 3D CT-scan that has been developed using mummies and skeletal remains is now in vogue. Such modalities can be useful in the near future to reduce the extensive dissection and anatomic examination by forensic pathologists, coroners, and medical examiners in mass disasters.

The U.S. National Disaster medical system and the disaster mortuary operational response teams (D-MORT) have been very useful in several recent mass disasters such as the September 11, 2001 World Trade Center castastrophy, Hurricane Katrina in New Orleans, Louisana, and in the Guam air plane crash. Many medical examiner and coroners' offices do not have enough storage space for bodies. In such situations refrigerator trucks to store the remains of body subsequent to mass disasters have been found to be tremendously expensive. There is a need for effective and appropriate federal, local, and state coordination for mass disaster plans so that each state will have adequate morgue facilities in order to plan for the handling of corpses after mass disasters. It must be kept in mind the investigation and management of mass disasters are always State and federal governmental functions and responsibilities.

The responsibilities of the police and law enforcement cannot be underestimated in mass disaster cases. Their roles include the saving of lives in conjunction with other emergency services, protection of property, coordination of the emergency services and other support organizations, protection and preservation of the scene, investigation of the incident in conjunction with other investigative agencies where applicable, and correlation and dissemination of casualty information. Their duties also include assistance in the identification of the deceased victims and restoration of normalcy (i.e., law and order) at the earliest opportunity.

Every mass disaster should be considered a potential crime scene. Hospitals and emergency room departments of medical centers are also very important in their role during mass disasters. At around the time of any mass disaster, those working in a designated hospital may also be receiving injured and non-injured survivors. Each hospital in the area should have elaborate emergency procedures and plans to manage a mass disaster event. The plan should be regularly exercised and revised. All potential participants should have read a copy of the plan and ascertained how they fit in. This should enable to develop and process procedures to make the plan work. There should be established lines of communication between hospital emergency room departments and the major incident control room or command center to ensure continuity in documentation of casualties, property, and subsequent victim identification. There is also a need to ensure coordination with the coroner or medical examiner and local forensic pathologist with respect to injured victims who subsequently die. The medical personnel in the hospital should be able to interview those patients who are able to report what has happened to them. Discussion with paramedics, ambulance crews, nurses and doctors to enable reconstruction of the incident and to obtain details of the kinds of injuries sustained are very useful. The hospital personnel should be involved in body recovery, casualty assessment and triage, and also in identification.

Many countries have developed disaster victim identification plans, and there have been standardized identification forms developed by the International Criminal Police Organization (INTERPOL) for use by all member countries. This is most important if the missing persons are from overseas, requiring ante-mortem information to be obtained in other countries. This is usually very important in international aviation mass disasters. The use of Disaster Victim Identification (DVI) teams and procedures is being encouraged in many countries as well. Such teams have sub-groups that are organized to work in a collaborative fashion cohesively. The antemortem identification team undertakes to determine a list of missing persons believed to have been involved in the disaster; establish evidence that such missing persons were likely to be involved; complete disaster victim identification forms for each victim; prepare a file for comparison purposes using the information obtained from the disaster victim identification forms (DVI), prepare a file for comparison purposes and deliberation by the identification commission for presentation to the coroner or medical examiner subject to his or her identification requirements; inform the next-of-kin that all identifications have been completed; and provide a point of contact for the next-of-kin and render them all possible assistance. The postmortem identification sub-team usually is comprised of members of various units forming the mortuary documentation team together with the forensic pathologists who perform postmortem examinations and forensic odontologists responsible for dental comparison. The identification methods usually include fingerprints, DNA profiling, dental characteristics, physical characteristics, radiologic examination, clothing and personal effects, documents, jewelry and visual identification.

Following a mass disaster, it is a certainty that there will be some formal inquiry and subsequent litigation. The various experts who are involved in mass disaster investigation and management should be prepared to testify in courts of law or before governmental commissions about their findings and should also be prepared to inform the public of their findings. The handling of the press and media is very essential in mass disasters. There should be a media or public relations department that will handle all information that is released to the news media and newspaper reporters. This will allow effective streamlining of the information that is published or related to the public.

The aftermath of a disaster is a critical time for all concerned. Judgments and decisions will often be made in error based upon inadequate information. Mistakes will be made. However, it is essential that such errors are minimized as much as possible, and hopefully detected before adverse consequences occur. It is important to make good use of professional colleagues who have the experience that is needed. Every minute spent in preparation will save hours, days and even weeks later on. This will bring increased order that is essential following a major disaster, and necessary for the long term planning. Public expectation is a key factor in making decisions regarding the preparation for mass disasters, as well as, during mass disaster investigation and management.

Today, mass disaster management is considered a formal professional discipline. There is currently a newly established Specialty Board, The American Board of Disaster Medicine, which is a multidisciplinary specialty board approved by the American Board of Physician Specialties (ABPS). It requires the cooperation and coordination of various professions such as government administration, police, medical, and forensic scientific experts, fire service, civil defense, public work services (including water and power supply), transport and telecommunication, (etc)., geologists, non-governmental organizations, and all other disciplines and professions at different levels in the course and management of mass disasters. There is always a need for constant revision of any mass disaster plans. The process of review, rehearsal, and training of necessary personnel should be a continuous one so that disaster plan can be implemented effectively at any time.

The world truly needs a network of experts and clear procedures to deal with mass disasters and psychological trauma in order to improve the response to disasters such as earthquakes and tsunamis that recently claimed more than 200,000 lives in several Indian Ocean countries. The World Health Organization (WHO), the health arm of the United Nations, should play a greater role in mass disasters - directing volunteer doctors and nurses, distributing donated equipment medicines and monitoring the health of affected communities. It has been clearly shown that during mass disasters, uncoordinated needs assessments are counterproductive, and that insufficient support is given to womens' health. Clear roles, responsibilities, and operating procedures need to be worked out so that military and civilian organizations can work together on disaster responses, WHO should establish a pool of forensic pathologists and other forensic scientists to be called upon to deal with mass fatalities and dead bodies in future disasters. Experts should work to agree on standards that can be made available for large scale emergencies. A greater focus on the health threats faced by women and children and the aged who are particularly vulnerable groups, is recommended. Simplified procedures should be agreed upon to deal with psychological trauma and mental health issues related to mass disasters. WHO estimates that around 80 percent of psychological needs are usually addressed in a disaster-stricken community. However, it was found that outside experts were needed to provide additional essential help. More guidance is needed to improve the treatment of those suffering from psychological trauma and other forms of mental illness during mass disasters. There is a need for international assistance through the World Health Organization (WHO) and pooling of resources by multinational efforts to assist the thousands and millions of people who are likely to be displaced in cases of mass disasters in future years.

The chapters in this reference book are authored by eminent international experts in various fields of forensic sciences, and mass disaster medicine and their contributions will be useful to any local, national or international group in formulating adequate and appropriate mass disaster plans.

—Dr. Matthias I. Okoye and Dr. Cyril H. Wecht

Chapter 1

Scene Investigation: The Role of Law Enforcement and Forensic Scientists in Bioterrorism and Mass Disasters

Henry C. Lee, Ph.D., Major Timothy M. Palmbach, M.S., J.D., and Major John J. Buturla

1.1 Introduction

America is at war. A war we are engaged in simply because of the increase in domestic and international terrorist attacks. These attacks have threatened our fundamental American way of living in a free and democratic society with open borders.

This war has necessitated that the front line on American soil is our police, fire departments, emergency medical services, forensic professionals, public health departments, national guard, emergency management and, of course, our citizens. Although the response to an incident will often involve all emergency personnel, the responsibility for preventing and investigating terrorist acts rests primarily with law enforcement personnel.

There is no mistaking that there is a shift in the paradigm for law enforcement in the twenty-first century. Preventing and solving crime had followed traditional roles and methods. Resources remained constant and were easily identified and procured, and were personnel trained. The shift is now away from tradition. To rely on the abilities and experiences of the past would mean a failure in the responsibility of law enforcement and crime scene investigators, today and in the future, to respond to acts of domestic and international terrorism.

This shift in the paradigm is not only warranted, it is overdue. In the twenty-year period between 1981 and 2001, there was an annual average of 369 terrorism related incidents worldwide.1 Although improvised explosive devices are commonplace weapons, law enforcement has faced increasing use of nontraditional chemical and biological weapons. Formerly a concern only for the military, law enforcement must now recognize their vulnerability and the viciousness of these attacks. The use of chemical, biological, or other weapons of mass destruction, and the individual groups or organizations using them have a singular purpose: to cause mass casualties and destroy a peaceful society.

Domestic and international terrorism have become daily events in the modern world. Hundreds and thousands of deaths occur as the result of terrorist actions. Commonly the identity of the suspects is found by determining the type of weapons used in the attack. Therefore, maintaining scene integrity and searching for physical evidence are extremely important for the first responder and investigator. Certainly there are differences in the scene techniques required at rape, robbery, or homicide cases in contrast to a scene involving a terrorist attack. Yet the basic guidelines and procedures are the same.

This chapter addresses some of the most important aspects of scene investigation of terrorist incidents. The first, and most urgent of steps, is establishing a working protocol from the point of initial notification of the incident through the collection and preservation of evidence. All law enforcement, fire, and emergency service personnel should be trained and knowledgeable of these protocols. Second, any successful terrorism investigation needs the cooperation of federal, state, and local agencies. A team and systematic approach of crime scene investigation is essential for all of the participants. See Figure 1.1.

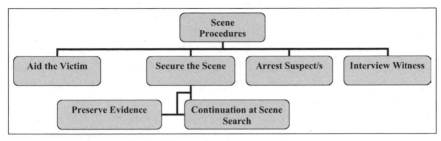

Figure 1.1 *General scene procedures*

A. Initial notification

Reports of an incident of chemical or biological weapon usage may come from several sources. The notification for chemical weapon dispersal will likely be an overt act. This overt act will inundate 911 dispatch centers with reports of noxious odors, and incapacitated or dead people and animals. All operators must have a protocol to follow to insure they are obtaining as much information as possible and disseminating it to all emergency responders as quick as possible. Failure to do so will result in the "blue canary" syndrome. The first responding law enforcement officers will enter the hazardous situation blindly and succumb to the weapon. Responding fire and EMS units will note the "blue canary" and equip themselves accordingly for proper response.

Biological weapons will likely have a covert dispersal and notification of their use will be made through different methods. Emergency dispatchers will be replaced by emergency room physicians and public health disease surveillance systems. The communication between law enforcement and public health officials must be present to insure timely reporting. Biological weapons, with their incubation periods, will require a different response by government officials.

Whether overt or covert, a threat or a hoax, those charged with the protection of our citizenry and investigation of the crime must respond. This response must be coordinated and be by trained and equipped law enforcement, EMS and forensic personnel. All available resources must be used. The scene or potential scene requires thorough examination, documentation, preservation and collection by trained forensic and evidence technicians.

B. Response

The initial report will no doubt yield a significant multidisciplinary response. These responders must work collectively, in a unified command structure, to effectively and efficiently mitigate and manage an event. Although fire departments have long had training, experience and the appropriate equipment to respond to hazardous material calls, law enforcement and emergency medical services must now be on par. All have a role and responsibility and must understand their own and each others functions.

The initial response will quickly establish whether local resources are overwhelmed and county, state and federal assistance may be required. With the implementation of Homeland Security, Presidential Directive 5 (HSPD-5) all responders will understand the importance of a seamless function in the emergency. HSPD-5 establishes the National Response Plan (NRP) and National Incident Management System (NIMS) for adoption and integration by emergency response personnel. It further establishes that any deliberate terrorist act requires an investigation by law enforcement personnel. Although large-scale acts will rest with federal law enforcement, state, county and local law enforcement have jurisdictional authority with the adoption of state terrorism laws. Most states passed legislation after 9/11 to give law enforcement the ability to actively pursue actual, suspected or hoax chemical or biological weapons incidents, in the absence of a federal investigation or with the consent of the United States Attorney.

The response to these incidents must be made in the safest and most effective manner possible.

1. Establish a clear protective zone

These zones, designated as "hot" "warm" and "cold" will be established to determine the required functions within the zones and level of protection required. See Figure 1.2.

The cold zone will function as an area in which protective equipment is available or may be required. The purpose of personnel in this tier of scene management is to provide support to those entering the "warm" or "hot" zones and to insure scene security. The duties will also include triage assistance to the fire and EMS personnel.

The "warm" zone will function as a decontamination area. This area will essentially function as a screening point for law enforcement. As a function of decontamination, exposed victims will be required to remove personal effects that may contain evidence of the chemical or biological weapons or material. Law enforcement personnel, working with fire and EMS personnel, will be required to separate, catalogue, identify, and package potentially hazardous material.

2. Develop protective zones

Protocols identifying these procedures should be established and exercised long before an incident. They must demonstrate a unified approach to patient care, without compromising potential evidence. Trained crime scene personnel should be part of the warm zone team to alleviate the burden of decontamination personnel and insure integrity of belongings.

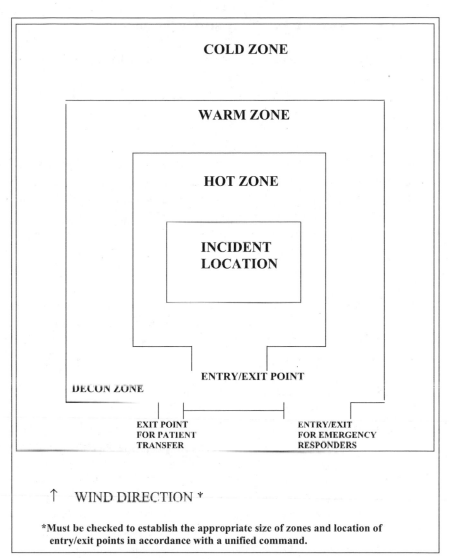

Figure 1.2 Protective zones

3. Develop special protocols related to the following issues

- Allowing citizens to collect their small items of personal belongings, such as wallets, purses, cell phones, and keys
- Segregating and appropriately labeling clothing and personal effects
- Keeping all items in the warm zone until examined or decontaminated
- Removing sensitive law enforcement equipment before entering the warm zone and securing it with supervisory personnel
- Having personnel and clean items sufficient for the duration of the mission
- Securing items that may contain secondary devises or delivery systems
- Rotating crime scene personnel in the area to reduce fatigue associated with wearing personal protective equipment
- Consulting with federal or state prosecutorial authorities regarding search and seizure warrant requirements

C. The crime scene

As discussed, the crime scene may encompass a variety of areas, individuals, items and locations. There are many challenges associated with chemical or biological weapon scenes that must be managed to effectively prosecute responsible parties. One of these challenges is the "hot" zone and the intricacies associated in this area.

The hot zone encompasses the actual incident site. It may be a bus, plane, train, home, mail facility, office building or individual. It is only limited by one's imagination. Therefore, adequate training and exercising is essential for all emergency responders in a variety of conditions in order to improve their safety and that of the public.

The entry will be performed only by trained hazmat or EOD teams. These teams should be trained in scenarios that familiarize them with rules and responsibilities, including that of crime scene and forensic personnel. Crucial steps are taken in the evidentiary process by these teams that greatly influence the criminal investigation. The hazmat or EOD team will be required to obtain initial samples only as part of preliminary screening of the suspected materials. National Guard Civil Support Teams or FBI, ATF, and other specially trained response teams can also be used for this function. Subsequent scene examination must be by trained law enforcement crime scene, forensic laboratory or public health laboratory personnel.

Careful consideration must be given to insure established crime scene procedures are adhered to. These procedures include the following.

- Using appropriate personal protective equipment
- Instructing hazmat teams to only collect quantities required for initial screening

- Using GPS devices to mark locations of evidence for diagram purposes
- Using photographic equipment capable of being decontaminated, such as commercially available underwater equipment, or disposable cameras
- Following chain-of-custody procedures for all samples and evidentiary items
- Securing unknown materials in packaging that is capable of being decontaminated prior to site removal to the laboratory

Following are procedures for general processing of crime scene related to biological and chemical weapon incidents.

1.2 Processing a Crime Scene Containing Biological or Chemical Weapons

Despite other significant health concerns for the general public and investigative personnel a policy and procedure must be in effect that recognizes the critical need to treat incidents that involve hazardous agents as crime scenes. Therefore, fundamental crime scene procedures involving recognition, documentation, collection and preservation of evidence must be followed. Of course modification to routine procedures will be necessary to protect personnel and equipment.

First, the scene must be secured and contained by properly trained and equipped personnel. Many uses or threatened uses of biological or chemical weapons depend on a hazardous deployment device. Thus, personnel trained in handling explosive or hazardous devices are essential. Once that threat is mitigated the suspected agent must be contained and secured. Preliminary field presumptive tests may be conducted to give scene personnel and investigators an idea as to what they are dealing with and how best to proceed. While recent advances in these field tests have occurred it must be emphasized that these are presumptive tests only, susceptible to false negatives and positives. A positive and negative control should be run with each test. Any samples must be handled with all precautions until which time laboratory analysis confirms the preliminary negative test results.

If biological or chemical agents are suspected, the following general sequence should be followed.

A. Containment of affected areas

Containment of potentially infected areas can be best accomplished by multiple levels of access or control zones, as previously described. The scope and configuration of these zones will be determined by the nature of the actual or perceived threat as well as the general structural or topography considerations. Moreover the design and structure of the physical barrier or zone boundary will vary. It may be as simple as blocking access to a roadway with police personnel or as complex as constructing an encompassing physical barrier.

Any citizens in the affected areas should be evacuated to a safe area as soon as practical. However, individuals should not be transplanted from the area until it is determined that they are not potential transport agents. If necessary these individuals will have to undergo a personal decontamination process. The extent of the evacuation plan is dependent on the nature and degree of the chemical or biological agent. Moreover, the manner in which the agent was deployed, and prevailing environmental factors such as wind, will also dictate the evacuation plan. In addition to controlling individual access, the protected area must also be restricted to vehicular and air traffic.

B. Decontamination facility

To protect both people and equipment exposed or potentially exposed to these biological or chemical agents a decontamination area or facility need to be established. The decontamination area must be sufficiently close to the affected areas to prevent further spread or contamination, but removed enough that true decontamination can occur. These facilities are essentially portable and constructed on the selected sites.

The specific design will depend on the magnitude of the event, how many individuals and what equipment will need to be decontaminated. These facilities need to be designed and managed by specifically trained personnel.

C. Scene management

Crime scenes must be properly managed to ensure proper procedures are followed and that the integrity of the scene is preserved (see Figure 1.3). Management needs to be directed through a unified command post. This command center should be located near to the event site or scene, but far enough removed not to interfere with scene functions and integrity, and far enough away so it does not endanger personnel at the command post. It must always be outside of the protective zones. The command post may be established in an available facility or room, or may be a mobile command center brought to the location. Mobile command centers are beneficial in that they are a known entity, stocked in advance with necessary supplies and communications equipment. If it will take significant time to get the long-term command post to the scene, a temporary staging area or command center should be established as soon as possible. This may be as simple as a patrol vehicle with communications capabilities. All information should be processed through the command post. In addition, personnel availability and assignments should be coordinated through the command center.

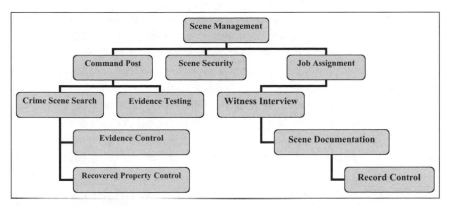

Figure 1.3 General scene management

After the emergency aspects of the scene have been adequately addressed and contamination and decontamination issues resolved, the command center can begin directing the scene activities relevant to processing the crime scene. First, experienced crime scene and forensic personnel should conduct a preliminary scene survey. Essentially this will require a personal inspection or walk-through. With scenes involving the use or potential use of chemical or biological agents, personnel entering the scene must wear adequate protection and undergo decontamination afterward. During this survey, the process of evidence recognition will begin. All forms of evidence should be noted. Types of evidence likely to be encountered include examples of the following five general categories of evidence.

> **Conditional evidence.** This is evidence that is the result of an action or event such as the size or color of the flame, the degree of destruction, and the condition of victims.
>
> **Transient evidence.** This type of evidence is temporary in nature and may be easily lost or destroyed, such as an odor, color, smoke and fire.
>
> **Pattern evidence.** Examples of pattern evidence include fire burn pattern, explosive damage pattern, victim injury pattern, building destruction pattern and glass fracture pattern.
>
> **Transfer or trace evidence.** This type of evidence occurs when objects come in contact with one another and there is a mutual exchange of material between the items such as explosives, gun powder, biological agents, deployment devices, cigarettes, glass, blood, hairs, fingerprints, footprints and tire marks.
>
> **Associative evidence.** This type of evidence helps establish links among the scene, vehicle, device, victim, suspect, and physical evidence associated with the case.

Systematic documentation must occur as soon as the scene process commences and continue throughout the entire process (see Figure 1.4). Documentation can be accomplished in many forms, and often requires the use of these varied formats as each form has its own attributes and weaknesses. These formats include photography, video taping, sketching and diagramming, and general note-taking—written or audio. With contaminated scenes these procedures have many additional challenges. It may be difficult to operate some of this documentation equipment with the protective suits and respiratory equipment. In addition, the equipment used must be capable of operating in the environment and being decontaminated. Generally, that would require the equipment to be in watertight capsules or the use of disposable equipment. Otherwise, the equipment will need to be properly discarded or quarantined until it can be determined that there are no residual biological or chemical agents on it.

After the scene has been thoroughly documented, the collection process can begin. While general collection and packaging procedures establish a basic framework, there will need to be modifications made, because of contamination issues. As with documentation equipment, collection tools will need to be in protective shields capable of decontamination processes, or disposable. Packaging and handling procedures may also have to be modified to prevent contamination. Essentially, packaging containers must be secure and airtight. This type of packaging may conflict with other evidentiary concerns. For example, standard protocol dictates that items containing biological materials should not be placed in airtight containers since that may result in bacterial growth and sample degradation. Despite these additional concerns, special biohazard or chemical explosive labeling and documentation must be done to establish a chain of custody, protecting the integrity of the collected evidence.

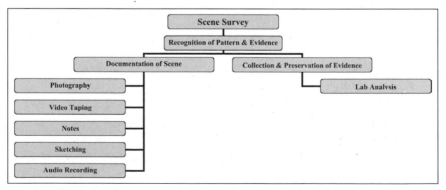

Figure 1.4 A proper scene survey leads to the recognition, documentation, collection, preservation, and analysis of evidence.

Generally, scene investigators should expect to find evidence in one or more of the following general classifications of evidence:

- Bodies or body parts
- Other forms of biological material
- Chemical matter
- Biological, chemical or nuclear-based weapons of mass destruction
- Explosive materials or hazardous devices
- Trace evidence: hair, fibers, tissue, debris and so forth
- Imprint or impression evidence
- Various forms of pattern evidence
- Vehicles or vehicle parts
- Clothing, valuables and personal belongings

Each piece of evidence should be marked on a diagram and photographed. These steps are extremely important for further reconstruction. Based on the nature of the evidence, condition of the evidence, contamination of the evidence, and questions to be resolved the precise collection, preservation, and analysis schemes may vary somewhat.

1.3 The Role of the Forensic Scientist

Successfully preparing for and working through a biological or chemical weapon attack requires collaboration of a diversified team. A key component of that team is the forensic scientist. Forensic science is a broad based discipline and likely will require the assistance of several forensic specialists representing various key subdisciplines. Generally, these scientists will focus on several aspects of the incident involving the use of weapons of mass destruction. Roles include recognition of a biological or chemical attack, victim identification, determination of symptoms and exposure or manner and cause of death, scene analysis and reconstruction, examination of physical evidence, classification and identification of biological or chemical agents or weapons, tracing the chemical or biological fingerprint, and linking suspects to the case.

A. Recognition of a biological or chemical attack

Many times the use or threatened use of a biological or chemical agent will be telegraphed or easily identified. Terrorists who employ these types of weapons thrive on the fear and chaos that accompanies their use, so they clearly mark or identify these agents. Most often the essential task is to confirm the stated threat and scientifically confirm the structure of the agent. However, forensic scientists, emergency personnel, and healthcare workers need to be prepared to rapidly and correctly identify the symptoms and characteristics of these agents in the event that they are used without warning or public knowledge. The diversity of these agents makes this a very daunting mission.

Recognition starts at the scene of a suspicious a substance or package that may be used to contain or disseminate these agents. Next, immediate precautions must be taken to contain the contaminated areas and begin isolation and decontamination of potentially infected individuals and objects. Reliable and sensitive field testing kits or portable testing equipment should be used to screen for the common chemical or biological agents. Finally, the materials must be properly collected, preserved, and transported to a qualified laboratory for additional testing.

B. Identification of victims

Identification of a victim's remains can be challenging under normal settings; potential contamination with biological or chemical agents further complicates the process. Positive identification of the remains is a necessary legal and investigative requirement, and this may be accomplished by a variety of means. Generally, two methods of identification should be used. How identification will be accomplished often depends on the conditions of the remains, and the available resources or alternatives. Use of witnesses who can visually identify the victim is relatively rapid and reliable. However, the state of remains, or difficulty in presenting contaminated remains, may pose a significant hurdle. With contamination issues, use of quality photographic or video images is recommended.

If identification of the actual remains is not possible or practical, it may be possible for an individual closely associated with the victim to effect identification by examination and verification of the victim's personal belongings. These must be sufficiently unique to allow for a reliable identification—such as identification documents, photographs, clothing, jewelry, keys, badges, and other miscellaneous accessories.

External markers also provide a means of identification. Facial characteristics, and anthropological measurements and findings may be obtained by a forensic anthropologist. Computer programs can reconstruct facial features based on anthropological measurements and characteristics obtained from the skull. Careful examination of the remains may also detect birthmarks, birth defects and deformations, or surgical markings. If the friction ridge skin on the fingers and palms is intact it may provide the means of identification. If known inked impressions are not available for the person's fingerprints, they can be entered into a national automatic fingerprint identification system (AFIS) in hope that the individual was fingerprinted in some capacity in his lifetime. Individuals are fingerprinted for a variety of reasons, such as arrests, military or government employment, applications for classified jobs, pistol permits, special licenses or permits and so on. Also, tattoos can be a means of identification through either a friend or family member, or the artist who created it.

As examination of the remains continues internal markings can be studied and documented. Comparison of dentition to dental records is a common means of identification. However, this method depends on the recovery of dental materials and the ability to obtain current quality dental records and X-rays. Other medical records and radiographs can also be used to identify bodies or remains. Surgical records or artificial organs can also provide valuable information.

With advances in DNA typing, the use of genetic markers has become a method for positive identification. The sensitive and discriminating characteristics of STR-based (short tandem repeat) methods can provide a definitive identification even with a very small amount of remains. When only minute body parts are available, or the body is significantly decomposed or degraded, alternate methods such as mitochondrial DNA analysis may be required to provide a genetic profile. However, mitochondrial DNA typing is not as discriminating as STR typing and is only effective for establishing maternity links. DNA samples should be collected from family members and personal belongings of the victim; these samples can be used to create a data bank. Each piece of recovered body part or biological sample should be preserved and typed.

C. Determination of symptoms and exposure: Manner and cause of death

A health professional's first obligation is to the welfare of the patient. However, a timely and proper diagnosis provides investigators and scientists with information that they will use to identify the actual agents used, likely methods of dissemination, and links in the effort to trace the origin of the biological or chemical materials.

For both medical and legal reasons, the manner and cause of death for each victim must be correctly established. Therefore, it is essential to develop early communications with medical examiner's or coroner's offices. Teams of experienced forensic pathologists should be formed to conduct the autopsies. Communication is essential within the medical community so that illness or deaths associated with biological or chemical agents are not inadvertently attributed to normal causations (e.g., pneumonia or influenza).

D. Examination of physical evidence and classification and identification of agents

Examination of physical evidence suspected of being a biological or chemical weapon, or other evidence contaminated with these materials, poses many challenges to a forensic science laboratory. There are two major issues with this type of evidence. First, the material must be identified. While this type of testing can be done with existing laboratory protocols, it must be conducted in a facility that can safely handle these hazardous materials; only qualified laboratories should conduct this type of analysis. Laboratories are classified by levels that delineate what types of materials they may safely handle. The following is the Centers for Disease Control and Prevention's guidelines for laboratory capacity with chemical agents.

> **Level-one laboratories.** These facilities can collect and ship human blood and urine specimens in response to a chemical terrorism incident.
> **Level-two laboratories.** These facilities can analyze human samples for level-two industrial chemicals, selected chemical threat agents (such as heavy metals, lewisite, and cyanide), or their metabolites.
> **Level-three laboratories.** Theses facilities can analyze human samples for chemical threat agents that require a higher level of analytical expertise. Level-three chemical agents include nerve agents, mustards, mycotoxins, and selected toxic industrial chemicals.

Until laboratory testing has deemed the specimen as a nonbiological or chemical threat, stringent laboratory precautions must be followed. Once the material is deemed as a safe or routine material, the sample may be handled with normal precautions. This may facilitate the use of additional instruments or methods, or transferring the sample to another, more analytically sophisticated laboratory that was not capable of conducting examinations for biological or chemical agents.

In addition to identifying the compound there is often the need to conduct a variety of other forensic examinations on the submitted physical evidence. Examples of this analysis would include processing objects for latent fingerprints, examination of machine or tool marks on devices, and visualizing any labels or writings. Collection and analysis of a wide variety of trace evidence on the objects can also provide investigators with leads. Trace components may be biological or chemical in nature, and may include materials suitable for DNA analysis, hair, fibers, or a variety of trace chemical components. This type of laboratory analysis can provide important investigative leads, identify suspects, prove or disprove alibis, or establish links between the victim, suspect, crime scene, and evidence. A real concern is to ensure that the evidence is properly collected and preserved throughout the entire process to prevent its alteration or destruction. This will require a coordinated plan with the scene personnel who will be handling the contaminated materials, as well as with the laboratory that will first examine the evidence.

E. Tracing the chemical or biological fingerprint

Once the material is identified, analytical schemes should be considered that may yield information about the origin of the material. For example, with some biological agents, such as anthrax, a DNA analysis can be conducted to determine the specific genetic fingerprint of that particular strain of bacteria. Thus, that anthrax may be linked with other anthrax samples of known or unknown origins. Even if the origin is unknown, the association of samples from several different cases is invaluable to investigators. This same type of analytical tracing can be conducted on certain chemical agents as well. Manufacturing impurities or additives that can be identified and quantified may help scientists link several samples. Unfortunately, currently there are no worldwide databases that contain this type of information. Therefore, tracing biological or chemical agents will require significant inquiries outside the realm of modern artificial intelligence resources. A global database should be established to trace all traditional chemical and biological weapons.

F. Linking a suspect to the case

Linking a suspect to a specific sample containing a chemical or biological agent can occur by various means. Classification and identification of the storage container or dissemination device should be a priority. The components used, or the manner in which they were assembled, may provide a signature of the individual or group who manufactured the weapon. In a general sense, the overall *modus operandi* (method of operation), if systematically determined, may help associate different events, and provide potential investigative links. In addition, these related objects should be processed for latent prints and trace evidence. It may be possible to obtain trace residues with sufficient material to develop a suspect's DNA profile. This may have occurred as the suspect handled certain components of the device. If envelopes were used, genetic material may have been transferred if the suspect licked the adhesive flap. Hair and trace evidence often will render class characteristics that may assist in including or excluding a certain suspect or provide some genetic trait of the suspect. Moreover, mt-DNA typing can be used on hair samples. If the hair includes a follicle, then traditional STR analysis can be conducted. If there is no follicle then the only option is mitochondrial DNA analysis. If documents were seized during the investigation, then document and handwriting analysis can provide leads to potential suspects.

Document examination may focus on the paper or envelopes, including type of material, watermarks, or other physical characteristics, such as the manner in which the paper was folded. Analysis of the ink or toner used to create the document may also provide leads. In addition the content or language may be evaluated to help determine likely educational, cultural, or other characteristics of the author. As with any type of forensic examination nondestructive methods should be employed first and subsequent destructive methods used only if necessary. Nondestructive methods for document examination include macro and microscopic examination, use of various forensic lighting sources, and ESDA (electrostatic document analysis).

1.4 Scene Analysis and Reconstruction

Despite the concerns and particular issues associated with scenes involving the use or threatened use of these weapons it must be emphasized that these are nothing more than another form of crime scenes. Therefore, all standard precautions and procedures must be considered. Too often there is an emphasis on and panic related to the biological or chemical weapon materials. As a result, traditional evidence is overlooked. This evidence includes transient evidence, conditional evidence, pattern evidence, transfer evidence, and associative evidence. In the final analysis the case will likely be solved and successfully prosecuted only if the basic investigation and crime scene procedures are followed.

Proper crime scene analysis requires the recognition, documentation, collection, and preservation of all types of evidence. Failure to conduct these foundational tasks will greatly restrict, if not totally prohibit, a subsequent crime scene reconstruction.

Reconstruction is the process of establishing or eliminating certain events and actions that occurred at the scene through analysis of scene patterns, the location and position of physical evidence, laboratory examination of physical evidence, and analysis of relevant information. This process is conducted following the basic scientific method (see Figure 1.5) and logical reasoning. The scientific method is comprised of five sequential steps: data collection, conjecture, hypothesis formulation, testing and, finally, theory formation.

The information that is incorporated into the process comes from a variety of sources. These sources include crime scene documentation in all forms, such as notes, photographs, sketches, and video tapes. Relevant investigative reports and documents should also be considered. If appropriate, medical or autopsy reports and photographs should also be evaluated. Reconstruction can be conducted through various levels or means. These levels include direct scene examination, review of records and documents, examination of physical evidence, and a review of documentary materials such as photographs, sketches, and videos. Finally, the ultimate product will depend on the amount of information available as well as the extent of inquiry or unresolved issues. Thus, reconstructions can be partial, limited, or full-scale.

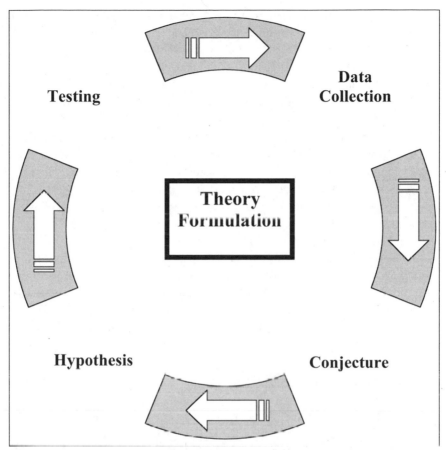

Figure 1.5 *The scientific method*

1.5 Case Example: Oxford Connecticut, Anthrax Incident

Within months of the tragic 9-11 events, the United States was confronted with the need to respond to the threat and actual use of anthrax as a weapon of potential mass destruction. In a short period of time five individuals succumbed to the deadly effects of anthrax inhalation. These individuals consisted of a sixty-three-year-old photo editor from Florida, two Washington D.C. postal workers (forty-seven and fifty-five years old), a sixty-one-year-old postal worker from New York, and a ninety-four-year-old retiree from a small community in Connecticut.

A. Information management and notification procedures

Ottilie Lundgren, a ninety-four-year-old female, retiree, living in Oxford, Connecticut, appeared to be a very unlikely target. On November 14, 2001, she became sick with flu-like symptoms. By November 16th her sickness progressed to the point that hospitalization was required, and she was admitted with pneumonia. The following day, blood tests indicated the possibility of anthrax in her system. Connecticut's Department of Public Health was notified through an existing disease surveillance system. An additional test for anthrax was administered on November 18th, but was inconclusive. However, by November 20 the governor of Connecticut responded with a public announcement regarding Ms. Lundgren's diagnosis, and he ordered her Oxford home quarantined. The following day, November 21, 2001, Ottilie Lundgren died, and the Centers for Disease Control confirmed that she had died as a result of exposure to anthrax. The CDC began its investigation into the matter, and offered Cipro to relatives or associates of Ottilie, as well as to postal workers at the Seymour post office and Wallingford postal facility where the anthrax was suspected of having originated.

An extensive search was initiated to locate the source of anthrax. A background into Ottilie's daily contacts revealed that she led a fairly isolated life and there were only a few potential sources of exposure outside of her residence. After confirming that her local church, hair salon, bakery and grocery store were not likely sources, the search focused on her residence. Moreover, trace amounts of anthrax were identified at the Wallingford postal facility, where Ottilie's mail was routed.

B. Searching the suspected scene

Officials from the CDC and the Connecticut Department of Public Health conducted an extensive search of Ottilie Lundgren's house for trace amounts of anthrax. Samples were taken from both inside and outside the house; these included samples from filters in air ducts located within the residence. Finally, handheld devices were used to obtain air samples. Large fans were brought into the residence to assist in getting any particles airborne during some of the air testing procedures. All the testing failed to detect any anthrax spores.

There came a point in the investigation when it was determined that a traditional crime search of the Lundgren house might provide investigative leads. Thus, trained crime scene personnel were dispatched to the home to conduct a systematic crime scene search and documentation. However, the home was still a potential biological incident location and had to be treated as a hot zone. Personnel conducting the scene search had to wear protective suits and subject themselves and their equipment to decontamination (Figures 1.6–1.8).

C. Investigative efforts

Follow-up investigation into the trace amounts of anthrax detected at the post office indicated that the mail system was the likely source of the anthrax that had resulted in Ottilie Lundgren's demise. Very small amounts of anthrax were associated with mail that was delivered in areas adjacent to the Lundgren residence. A trail of the mail through the sorting facility was determined by postal inspectors.

Figure 1.6 Crime scene personnel conduct an exterior examination of the Lundgren residence. Note that this location is within the hot zone, thus protective equipment is required.

Figure 1.7 Scientists prepare to enter the residence to begin the scene survey process. All items brought into the hot zone must be decontam-inated. A clipboard and pencil are in the large, clear plastic bag.

While it was never conclusively demonstrated where Ottilie Lundgren had been exposed to anthrax, it was determined that most likely she was exposed to a small number of spores on mail that had been tainted at the nearby postal facility and delivered to her residence. Medical experts hypothesized that, because of her age and related health status, she was more vulnerable and so contracted anthrax from the inhalation of a very few spores—too few to detect in the subsequent examination of her residence. These findings, in conjunction with further examination results by FBI and state police forensic laboratories, indicated that this case was an isolated incident. Ms. Lundgren was likely not targeted by an anthrax letter, but was exposed through a secondary contact. Additional DNA testing on the anthrax may provide a genetic profile that can be used to establish associations with other anthrax investigations or known sources of anthrax. This can be accomplished by using DNA testing to identify a particular strain of DNA by its unique DNA profile.

Figure 1.8 *Crime scene personnel and laboratory scientists undergoing decontamination after exiting the residence.*

Bibliography

Bioterrorism: A Guide for First Responders (Springfield, IL: Imaginatics, 2003).

Butler, Jay C. et al. "Collaboration between public health and law enforcement: New paradigms and partnerships for bioterrorism planning and response," *Emerging Infectious Diseases* 8(10), 2002.

Chemical/Nuclear Terrorism: A Guide for First Responders (Springfield, IL: Imaginatics, 2003).

Counterterrorism Office, U.S. Department of State. *Patterns of Global Terrorism 2001* (Washington, DC: U.S. Department of State, 2002).

Lee, Henry C., Timothy Palmbach and Marilyn T. Miller. *Henry Lee's Crime Scene Handbook* (San Diego: Academic Press, 2001).

Sidell, Frederik R., William C. Patrick III and Thomas R. Dashiell. *Jane's Chem-Bio Handbook* (Alexandria, VA: Jane's, 1998).

U.S. Army Soldier and Biological Chemical Command (SBCCOM), *Law Enforcement Officers Guide for Responding to Chemical Terrorist Incidents,* (U.S. Army Soldier and Biological Chemical Command, 2003).

Chapter 2

Mass Casualty Identification through DNA Analysis: Overview, Problems, and Pitfalls

Mark W. Perlin, M.D., Ph.D.

Introduction

When people die in a mass disaster, they leave behind biological material. This biological material may be their entire body, or body parts. One important task of mass casualty identification is to identify these victim remains by associating them with missing people. Identification of victim remains from a mass casualty site is critical for bringing closure to family and loved ones.

A complementary forensic task is to identify the people who are missing after a mass casualty, and associate them with victim remains. These missing people typically leave behind biological material in their homes and with their families. One source of biological material for missing people is their personal effects, such as toothbrushes, hairbrushes and clothing. Another source of biological material is the missing people's family references, since relatives have biological features which are similar to those of the missing person.

The key task of mass casualty identification is to match the biological material from the mass casualty site to the missing people. This is done by identifying the biological features of each of the victim remains found at the mass casualty site. Separately, the biological features of the personal effects and of the family references are analyzed to form a biological profile of each missing person. By comparing the biological features of each of the victim remains against those of each of the missing people, a match may be obtained between a particular victim remain found at the mass casualty site and one of the missing people.

23

DNA Identification

The DNA genetic code contained within each person is ideally suited for mass casualty identification. Each person's genome contains three billion DNA letters spread out over twenty-three pairs of human chromosomes. This genetic code contains features that are unique to each individual, and is therefore is ideal for forensic identification. Moreover, the chromosome pairs come from an individual's parents with one copy coming from the father and one copy coming from the mother. Therefore, an individual's genetic identity can be partially reconstituted from their family DNA.

Forensic identification is best done using distinguishing features that are relatively unique to an individual. In the human genome, there are hundreds of thousands of such highly polymorphic genetic locations or loci which differ greatly between individuals. One type is known as the short tandem repeat (or STR) which is an excellent marker that is now widely used for human identity. At each STR locus, a short DNA phrase comprising about four letters is tandemly repeated about ten to twenty times. At an STR locus, an individual will have two different copies of DNA, each having their own specific length. These pairs of DNA fragment lengths are the features which form the basis for STR genetic identity, as it is currently used in forensics.

STR data is generated from a biological specimen in a molecular biology laboratory in three steps. First, the DNA is extracted from the biological material. Next, ten to fifteen STR loci are amplified simultaneously in one tube one million-fold using the polymerase chain reaction (or PCR). Finally, the amplified PCR product is detected and separated on an automated DNA sequencer. The DNA signal that is produced contains peaks that correspond to the DNA fragments. The peak location on the x-axis corresponds to the length of the DNA fragment, while the peak height on the y-axis corresponds to the amount of DNA present. When an individual has two different STR lengths at the same locus (i.e., heterozygote), two peaks appear. When an individual has two copies of the same STR lenght at a locus (i.e., homozygote), one peak appears in the data.

The DNA profile of an individual is the listing of these pairs of allele lengths at each STR locus. With the ten to fifteen STR loci currently used in forensic practice, these pairs of allele lengths produce a virtually unique digital signature for an individual. Each STR locus provides (on average) a factor of ten of distinguishability from a person who might be randomly selected from the human population. Therefore, twelve STR loci provide (on average) 10^{12}, that is, a 1 followed by twelve 0's, giving a trillion to one relative uniqueness of DNA identifiability for that individual.

In principal then, the task of identifying human remains is arduous, but straightforward. A DNA laboratory produces an STR profile from each of the victim remains, and, separately, produces a DNA profile for each of the missing people. By comparing all the victim remains DNA profiles against all the missing person profiles, matches can be obtained; these matches pair particular victim remains with particular missing people. This approach assumes, however, that perfect DNA profiles can be obtained from victim remains and from missing people.

Uncertain DNA Evidence

The damaged victim remains found at a mass casualty site do not produce pristine biological specimens. Rather, DNA that has been burned, degraded, mixed with other samples, or environmentally decomposed does not amplify well. Instead of producing pristine DNA data, damaged victim remains can produce multiple low level peaks that are not amenable to standard DNA interpretation methods.

This DNA data uncertainty can produce considerable uncertainty in the inferred DNA profile. For example, an ambiguous DNA peak pattern may be consistent with many different allele pair genotype alternatives. The data, however, do contain considerable DNA identification information, and a key forensic objective is to preserve evidence. Given the different DNA interpretation alternatives available, what, then, is the best DNA review method for examining compromised DNA data at a mass casualty site?

Match Information

One approach might be to allow a DNA profile inferred from ambiguous DNA data to match all possible DNA profiles. For example, the inferred profile might be comprised of two wild card alleles that can match any possible reference profile. This DNA profile inference and matching approach is entirely non-specific, and is not at all useful.

This lack of utility is because inferring all genotype possibilities yields no match information. The "all possibilities" genetic profile, comprised of all possible genotypes, matches all other genotypes. Therefore, a match would occur with a 100 percent probability. When the relative frequency of an inferred profile is a 100 percent, the match information is 0 (where match information is the logarithm of one over the relative frequency).

More precisely, match information is defined as the ratio of two probabilities. The numerator is the probability of a specific match of the inferred DNA profile against a particular missing person. The denominator is the probability of a random match between the inferred victim remains profile and a random genotype in the population. This ratio, when used with unambiguous DNA profiles, is often referred to as a random match probability. Taking the logarithm of this ratio measures information. Therefore, match information is defined as the logarithm of the "specific to random" probability match ratio.

Human Review

Conservative review of DNA data is used by human STR analysts to avoid overstating the match results. When applied to uncertain STR data, conservative review can provide more than zero information, but not the full information that is present in the DNA data. This "conservative" interpretation method entails reporting alleles, rather than genotypes. The genotypes are inferred afterwards by forming all possible pairs of these alleles. Wild card alleles are also allowed. For example, when there is one strong peak and other smaller peaks, the analyst would call the one "obligate" allele corresponding to the one tall peak. Then, any genotype allele pair that contains this tall peak allele, as well as any other allele, would be considered part of this genotype set.

Comparing a genotype that contains one allele and a wild card allele against a known or referenced genotype that also includes that allele will produce a match. Therefore, the numerator of the match ratio information ratio is 1, because the probability of a match is 1. The denominator of the match ratio is determined by the relative frequency of the inferred profile. In conservative review, for this example that would include all possible genotypes that contain this one allele, as well as any other allele. With a common allele, that possibility of all combinations which include this allele may encompass half (or 50 percent) of the genotypes in the population for that locus. Therefore, the match information (which is the base 10 logarithm of 1 over 0.50) increases from 0 to a small number such as 0.3.

Aggressive human review is a more informative approach to inferring STR profiles. The goal here is to try ruling out unlikely combinations of genotypes from the set of all possible allele pairs. Suppose that the uncertain STR data at the locus is comprised of a small peak 'a' and a large peak 'b'. Then the analyst might designate the genotype possibilities [a b], as well as [b b], thereby producing just two of the possible genotypes. The inferred profile would be reported out as a list of the possible allele calls.

When this shorter list of inferred profiles from the victim remains sample is compared against a profile from a known missing person, there are fewer match possibilities. Therefore, when there is a match, the numerator (which is the probability of the match) is 1. However, the denominator contains a smaller number which reflects the reduced relative frequency of this more specific DNA feature. For example, a small set of human genotypes may only match 20 percent of the random population. Therefore, the match information would be the logarithm of 1 over 0.20. This increased specificity in the inferred genotype would therefore increase the match information value to 0.7.

Genetic Profile—Victim Remains

A more scientific review of the STR data would infer DNA profiles in a way that preserves all the match information. This is done by assigning each candidate genotype a probability. Probabilistic genotypes have been used in genetics for over a century. When parent genotypes are known, Mendel's Laws dictate the possible genotypes of the offspring, as well as the probability of each candidate. For example, when a heterozygote father is combined with a homozygote mother having a different allele, there are exactly two genotype possibilities for the child, each having a probability of one half.

Just as there is genetic uncertainty in human inheritance, there can be data uncertainty in the STR peak information. The conservative and aggressive human review methods create lists of genotypes that assign each candidate on the list the same uniform probability. A scientific review of the data also creates a list of genotype candidates, but instead using the same probability for every genotype, it assigns an individualized probability to each genotype based on the data. The result is that more likely genotypes will have a higher probability than less likely genotypes.

When an inferred victim remain genetic profile is compared against a known missing person reference, the more probable genotypes in the genetic profile will have greater weight in the match. This increased weighting will cause the relative frequency of the true genotype to predominate in the match statistic. The result is that the match information will reflect the relative frequency of the true matching inferred profile, instead of a composite that is less specific. For example, if the relative frequency of the true genotype is 10 percent, that will lead to a match information of equal to the logarithm of 1 over 10 percent (i.e., $\log 10(1/(1/10))$ $= \log 10(10) = 1$), which equals 1 match information unit. In this way, we see that using probabilities of genotypes to represent a genetic profile will tend to preserve match information, and therefore produce a greater match association statistic between victim remain biological specimens and missing people.

Genetic Profiles—Missing People

The genetic profiles of missing people can be formed using family DNA reference material. Geneticists have long been able to reconstruct the genetics profiles of individuals from their family members. For every mother-father-child relationship triple, there is potentially useful genetic information. The resulting genetic profile is a probability distribution over genotypes. These genetic profiles of missing people can be compared against victim remain genetic profiles to produce matches. When personal effects are not available for an individual, such kinship derived genetic profiles may be the only way to establish a match with victim remains.

As with victim remains, personal effects from missing people can also produce compromised biological material, such as DNA mixtures. These materials can therefore produce uncertain data which similarly requires a scientific review. By assigning probabilities to the genotypes at a locus, such as 90 percent for one possibility and 10 percent for another possibility, a more specific genetic profile is produced. Comparing a more specific missing person genetic profile against a victim remains genetic profile can produce more match information. Whereas approximate DNA profile inference using conservative or aggressive human methods tends to reduce match information with damaged personal effects, scientifically inferred profiles can preserve this match information.

DNA Mixtures

DNA mixtures occur when a biological specimen contains material from more than one individual. Such DNA mixtures can produce uncertain data that contains more than two allele peaks at each locus. In particular, human identification of the individual component contributors may not be possible from this data. DNA mixture analysis has been a longstanding limitation of human review. However, in mass casualty DNA analysis, DNA mixtures are found both among the victim remains, as well as in the personal reference material. For example, a missing person's toothbrush may have been used by that person and by their spouse.

Fortunately, mathematical and computer solutions have been developed to resolve mixed DNA samples. One such approach is linear mixture analysis,[1] which can represent known and unknown genetic profiles using coupled linear equations. Computer solution of these mathematical equations can produce the genetic profiles of the contributors. At each contributor locus, the genetic profile is represented by a probability distribution of genotypes. These inferred mixture genetic profiles can then be used to match victim remains against missing people.

Computer based mixture resolution is about a thousand times more informative than conventional human review methods.[2] This has been demonstrated in scientific studies that have compared dual human review versus computer interpretation on the same data.[2] In addition to being more informative than human review, computer mixture interpretation with linear mixture analysis is more reproducible than human review.[3] Whereas human analysts can often generate different genetic profiles from the same mixture data, this variation is much less with computer implementation with appropriate mathematical models.[3]

Inferred contributor profiles from DNA data can be matched just like any other genetic profile. When a victim remains biological specimen contains two contributors, two contributor profiles may be produced instead of one. Similarly, when the personal effects from a missing person contain more than one contributor, distinct genetic profiles for that individual can be produced. The matching comparison then proceeds by comparing one or more inferred profiles from the victim remains against the one or more genetic profiles that have been inferred from the missing person. A match between the genetic profiles in this case indicates that some component of a biological specimen matches some component of another biological specimen.

Scientific Calculator

It would be helpful to have a scientific calculator that could assist the human DNA analyst in examining evidence for a mass casualty. A typical scientific calculator permits a DNA analyst to add, subtract, multiply, divide and perform other straightforward operations. However, three functionalities are missing from this quantitative device. The first is a button to interpret DNA by conducting a scientific review of the original quantitative STR data. A second useful button would be one which matches DNA by comparing two different profiles. Third, it would be helpful to have a button for a database engine that could record the results of all these profile interpretations and the matches between them. We shall discuss the development of such a scientific calculator device in the next chapter.

Conclusion

Uncertain DNA data does not pose a problem for computer based massed casualty analysis. The proper scientific approach is to use DNA profiles with probability. These probability based genetic profiles contain more human identification information than profiles produced with conventional human review. These general DNA profiles permit informative DNA analysis of damaged victim remains, damaged personal effects, integrated family references, DNA mixture samples, and multiple sources of DNA data. Using more informative DNA profiles produces a more informative DNA match between victim remains and missing people that preserves the DNA evidence.

References

1. Perlin MW, Szabady B. Linear mixture analysis: a mathematical approach to resolving mixed DNA samples. Journal of Forensic Sciences 2001;46(6):1372-1377.

2. Perlin MW. Real-time DNA investigation. In: Promega's Sixteenth International Symposium on Human Identification; Dallas, TX; 2005.

3. Perlin MW. Scientific validation of mixture interpretation methods. In: Promega's Seventeenth International Symposium on Human Identification; Nashville, TN; 2006.

Chapter 3

Identifying Human Remains Using TrueAllele® Technology

Mark W. Perlin, M.D., Ph.D.

Introduction

The DNA laboratory transforms biological specimens into STR sequencer data. To accomplish this task automatically, the laboratory applies a series of DNA analysis instruments. These instruments include a DNA extraction robot, a DNA quantitation device, a PCR DNA amplifier, and a fluorescent DNA sequencer. But the resulting DNA data must then be further transformed into human identification information: genetic profiles and matches. This information can be obtained automatically using a DNA interpretation instrument - the TrueAllele® Scientific Calculator (TASC™). The TASC™ instrument is a small supercomputer specifically designed for transforming DNA sequencer data into genetic profiles and matches.

TrueAllele® System

The TrueAllele® Casework system[1] consists of an analysis workstation, a TASC™ supercomputer, and visual DNA review software for forensic analysts. The analysis workstation reads the laboratory's DNA sequencer data, and performs a number of automated quality checks. A human operator then visually checks the data in the context of the computer's quality information. Questionable data is routed back to the laboratory for reanalysis, while acceptable data is further quantitated and uploaded to the TASC™ database. The entire human interaction takes about one minute for each plate of 96 DNA samples and controls.

The TASC™ database holds the DNA data and interpretation requests for specific case questions. Once all the data has been uploaded for an interpretation request, the request is ready for processing by one of the many parallel TASC™ interpretation computers. (For example, the TASC™-16 model runs 16 parallel interpretation processes.) An interpretation process statistically examines all the data and their uncertainty in the context of a mathematical model of the STR process. After inferring genetic profiles from the data, the interpretation computer uploads its results to the database. Another TASC™ computer then automatically matches the inferred profiles on the database against one another, according to the lab's specific application requirements. For example, with mass disasters, victim remains profiles are compared against personal effects profiles.

Forensic scientists use the TrueAllele® visual user interface client software to review the inferred genetic profiles and matches in the context of their original DNA data. Information is displayed both visually and textually, and the presented visualizations dynamically adapt to the user's focus of interest. From the TrueAllele® interface, the user can annotate the data and initiate additional TrueAllele® interpretation.

TrueAllele® Science

The TrueAllele® casework science broadly encompasses three areas: data quality, genetic profiles, and genetic matches. Data quality is quantified by statistical modeling that determines the relative confidence in each data component. In mass disasters, this is important, since the DNA data can be highly uncertain, even when data quality is high. For example, damaged victim remains may contain little DNA and produce peaks that are below the validated human detection threshold. However, these data can be highly informative when analyzed by a TrueAllele® computer.

To preserve the genetic identity information that is present in uncertain STR data, forensic scientists often generate lists of genotype possibilities, and give them an equal weighting. However, the data may strongly suggest that some genotype candidates are more probable than others. Therefore, TrueAllele® Casework represents the genetic profile of a contributor at a locus as a probability distribution of genotype possibilities, assigning more probable genotypes a higher probability.

Quantitative DNA match information is obtained by comparing the probability of the genetic profile matching a specific target, relative to the probability of that profile matching a random person in the population. With straightforward single source DNA profiles, the specific match probability (numerator) is 1, and the random match probability (denominator) is the frequency of the genotype in the population. TrueAllele® matching generalizes this match ratio concept in order to compare genetic profiles that are described using probability distributions. This mathematical refinement was specifically designed for handling uncertain DNA data. Therefore, it is not surprising that TrueAllele® match can preserve more human identity information than the current DNA match statistics, since these older methods originated from comparisons based on unambiguous pristine DNA data.

TrueAllele® Technology

The TrueAllele® casework technology is highly useful in the challenging DNA interpretation problems found with mass disasters. Victim remains are often damaged by heat and moisture, which degrade the DNA molecules and produce low signals. Personal effects (e.g., toothbrushes) often contain a mixture of DNA contributors, such as the missing person and a spouse. A missing person's family references can be used to combine relatives' profiles to infer a genetic profile. In all these situations, the DNA data are highly uncertain and genetic profiles with refined probability representation are needed to preserve identification information.

TrueAllele® Workflow

The sexual assault DNA identification problem is quite similar to identification issues in a mass disaster.[2] In a mass disaster, unknown genetic profiles from victim remains are matched against the missing person reference profiles from personal effects and kinship DNA. Similarly, in a sexual assault case, the unknown assailant's genetic profile is inferred from uncertain DNA data that contains a mixture of the victim and the assailant. This unknown inferred profile is then matched against reference profiles, such as a particular suspect or a database of known criminal convicted offenders.

The DNA process workflow for sexual assault or mass disaster begins with a selection of relevant biological specimens. The specimens go through the DNA laboratory process, are entered into a Laboratory Information Management System (LIMS), and ultimately produce DNA sequencer data. The TrueAllele® Analysis workstation conducts a quality control check, followed by a rapid human review; this check provides laboratory feedback to the LIMS database, and uploads quality checked DNA peaks to the TrueAllele® database on the TASC™ instrument. A case's interpretation request specifies which DNA mixture evidence and victim reference to use. A TrueAllele® interpretation process examines the data indicated by this request, inferring the unknown genetic profile and uploading this profile to the TrueAllele® database. TrueAllele® can then match the inferred profile against a suspect database.

A forensic scientist thus has the original DNA data, the inferred genetic profiles, and the DNA matches as an organizing foundation for their review. This computer-inferred information is available to the examiner from the TrueAllele® database throughout their own visual review. The scientist can specify interesting data subsets for the TrueAllele® scientific calculator to solve with new DNA interpretation and matching.

The property crime (burglary, car theft, etc.) DNA identification process is also similar to the mass disaster task.[2] Here, the unknown profiles come from

DNA left by the criminal at the crime scene, and the reference profiles are largely derived from a suspect database of known criminal offenders. Property crime DNA data is often uncertain due to the low levels of biological material left behind by the perpetrator. Since burglars are serial offenders who often progress to more violent crimes (e.g., sexual assault), it is important to match their unknown crime scene genetic profiles to a criminal database so that they can be identified and apprehended by the police before they commit more crimes.

In both mass disasters and property crime, much of the crime scene DNA evidence produces genetic profiles that do not match any reference profile. It is therefore useful to modify the genetic analysis and interpretation workflow to maximize the utility of the human scientist's time. This can be done by screening the DNA information so that a forensic scientist only needs to look at STR data and genetic profile after a DNA match has already been found. In the TrueAllele® Casework system, this workflow is implemented by having the computer automatically generate interpretation requests, and match computer-inferred genetic profiles to the reference DNA database. The first human look at the DNA data (plus genetic profiles and match results) can then occur for just the DNA evidence that has a known match.

So Much Data, So Little Time

With the advent of automated laboratory instrumentation, the DNA lab has witnessed an exponential increase in its data generation capability. Robotic and computer systems for DNA extraction, amplification, detection, and database organization have also improved the reproducibility of the STR experiment. However, most DNA data review is still done manually without the aid of scientific calculation for inferring and matching genetic profiles. So DNA data review only scales linearly: to double the capacity, a lab must double the number of people. In order to meet the DNA data challenge of a mass disaster, the data review must scale exponentially along with the vast amounts of DNA data.

The goal of every forensic scientist and their laboratory director is to do the best job possible in making a human identification with DNA evidence. This entails (1) looking at all the good data, (2) ignoring the bad data, (3) considering every possibility, and (4) obtaining the most match information for human identification. The number of interpretation possibilities and interactions between data grows much faster than the amount of data. This increase in interpretation difficulty is even greater with the highly uncertain data often found in a mass disaster.

TASC™ Instrument - A Scientific Calculator

For rapid DNA identification in a large-scale mass disaster, another DNA instrument is required after the DNA sequencer. This "scientific calculator" instrument is needed to interpret STR data and generate genetic profiles by doing the best job possible. The TASC™ instrument performs the necessary functions of this scientific calculator. First, it interprets DNA evidence and generates genetic profiles by considering every possibility and preserving match information using probability representations. Second, it matches genetic profiles (e.g., between victim remains and personal effects or kinship profiles) using genotype probabilities in order to retain match information. Third, the supercomputer instrument maintains a database for storing and retrieving DNA information.

The TASC™ engine interprets DNA data through repeated application of the scientific method. Specifically, at each decision it forms a new hypothesis about one of its statistical modeling parameters. These parameters include genotypes, mixing weights, PCR artifacts, DNA amounts, background noise, data uncertainty, and parameter uncertainty. Combining these parameters, the computer generates a hypothetical data pattern, which it compares against the STR data in order to form a probability value. The statistical decision process prefers higher probabilities to lower probabilities, and is therefore able to compute the probability distribution of each parameter. The end result is that the TrueAllele® interpretion assigns higher probabilities to those genotypes which best fit the observed DNA data.

Solving a DNA mixture problem simply entails considering additional parameters. These parameters include the number of contributors, the genetic profile at each locus of a new contributor, and the mixing weight between the contributors. The hypothesized data patterns are more complex, because they include alleles for more than one contributor. However, the basic mechanism (of comparing hypothesized patterns against the actual data in order to form probabilities and make decisions) is the same.

In the process of converging to an answer, the computer probabilistically searches the values of a parameter. This random variation captures the statistical variation of that parameter, and can be represented by a histogram. The center value of the histogram estimates the mean value of the unknown parameter, while the width of the histogram describes its standard deviation. In this way, the statistical TrueAllele® engine determines both the values of genetic parameters (e.g. genotypes, mixing weights) and the scientific confidence in those values based on the data uncertainty.

Forensic Review

The TrueAllele® database contains the genetic profiles of each interpreted mass disaster sample, and the appropriate matches between them. These results can be viewed by accessing the database via a local computer network to their own lab's in-house TASC™ instrument, or by Internet to a remote TASC™ server.

Either way, a user connects to a TASC™ database by logging on to their secure TrueAllele®.net account. A web browser client provides complete access to the genetic profiles, matches and data for each interpreted request. The browser window presents in table form the genotypes and probabilities for each locus of each contributor, along with discriminating power and match information statistics. All of the original data peaks are also viewable as tables.

A separate TrueAllele® database client for viewing results is provided by a Windows-based visual user interface. After logging in to their TASC™ database, and selecting a case to review, the user sees all of their original DNA sequencer data signals in an easily navigable graphical interface. With one or two mouse clicks, the user can zoom in on the sequencer lanes and genetic loci of greatest interest. Another window shows the genetic profiles (including genotypes and probabilities) in an intuitive visual form. Focusing on information in one window will automatically zoom in on comparable information in the other windows. The result is a user experience entirely determined by the immediate genetic information interests of the visual user.

The visual user interface also provides the capability for the forensic scientists to conduct "what if...?" scenarios. The user can submit requests for interpretation and matching that include additional samples. The forensic scientist has complete control over which samples should be used in reinterpretations of the evidence, and can ask questions like "Is there too much data?" or "Should low-quality data be discarded?" The forensic user can combine or separate low signal data in order to obtain the most statistically reliable answer to their forensic DNA identification questions.

Mass Disaster DNA Identification

The DNA mass disaster process[2] begins by obtaining three sets of biological specimens: victim remains from the mass disaster site, personal effects from the missing people, and family references from their immediate relatives and spouse. These biological specimens are transformed by the DNA laboratory into DNA signals, where each signal peak has a size (in base pair units) and an amount (in relative frequency units).

True Allele interpretation requests are organized by biological specimen, so that all of the DNA sequencer lanes developed from one biological specimen will be interpreted together. This grouping together of all related data for a specimen provides far greater statistical power than analyzing each sequencer lane separately, and having a person try to subjectively reconcile multiple genotypes across the multiple experiments. With joint data interpretation, a single hypothesized genotype pattern must match well at all of the experiments for that specimen at a locus. Consistent use of mathematical probability functions that represent these pattern comparisons and their statistical uncertainty can be rigorously performed by a computer.

For each biological specimen, all the DNA peak data are examined together in order to infer a genetic profile. When there is no ambiguity about the genotype at a locus of the contributor to the DNA sample, the genetic profile at that locus has only one feasible genotype. However, in mass disasters, damaged victim remains will typically yield uncertain DNA data, and so the genetic profile at such a locus will contain multiple genotypes, each with an associated probability derived from the data. The inferred genetic profiles are organized into groups, depending on their role in the DNA identification process (e.g., victim remains, missing people).

As each genetic profile is inferred, it is compared against the previously determined profiles in other profile groups. For example, a victim remains profile will be compared against all the personal effects profiles and all of the kinship derived profiles. Similarly, when a new personal effects genetic profile is inferred, it is compared against all of the victim remains profiles. In this way, all of the victim remains DNA information is matched against the missing person DNA information, as new genetic profiles become available. The use of multiple coordinating computers to infer and match genetic profiles, and communicate via a central database, enables such real-time dynamic updating of DNA match information.

When a forensic scientist examines a candidate DNA match between a victim remain and a missing person, the TrueAllele® casework system provides all the relevant information for assessing the validity of that candidate match. The inferred genetic profile of the victim remain is shown, along with its discriminating power. The same genetic information, in both tabular and visual forms, is similarly provided for the missing person. The match information is represented numerically and graphically, along with the individual locus hits and misses. Ready access to the original DNA sequencer data signals also helps the scientist during forensic examination. Since the TrueAllele® scientific calculator is merely an aid to human decision-making, all final decisions are made by forensic scientists and their supervisors.

World Trade Center TrueAllele® System

The TASC™ supercomputer that we are using to analyze the World Trade Center data has a central multiprocessor TrueAllele® database computer, 20 DNA interpretation processors, and a DNA match computer. In its current configuration, optimized for extensive analysis of damaged victim remains STR data, the system can automatically infer and match a new genetic profile every two minutes. Doubling the number of interpretation processors would halve this instrument turnaround time.

We are currently working with New York City's Office of the Chief Medical Examiner to help identify more World Trade Center victim remains. They anticipate that the use of the TrueAllele® technology on the World Trade Center effort will yield additional results. We are currently well along in the process of providing DNA decision-support to their forensic scientists using the TrueAllele® Casework System.

Conclusion

The TrueAllele® Casework system is being used to identify human remains. The heart of its speed and accuracy is the TASC™ supercomputer, a multiprocessor instrument specifically designed for inferring and matching DNA profiles. The primary goal of the TrueAllele® Casework system is to preserve DNA evidence. When inferring genetic profile and match information, the TrueAllele® system considers every possibility, has high automated capacity, and produces rapid results, relative to conventional human review. Applying dedicated DNA statistical support to mass disasters can accelerate and improve human decision-making in identifying human remains.

References

1. Perlin MW. Simple reporting of complex DNA evidence: automated computer interpretation. In: Promega's Fourteenth International Symposium on Human Identification; Phoenix, AZ; 2003.

2. Perlin MW. Real-time DNA investigation. In: Promega's Sixteenth International Symposium on Human Identification; Dallas, TX; 2005.

Chapter 4

Dental Identifications in Mass Disaster Investigations

John Filippi, DDS, D-ABFO

Forensic dentistry and the formation of dental identification teams has been an instrumental part of the mass fatality incident response plans for many years. Dental identification has been proven to be a valuable forensic tool for the families of these unfortunate victims in obtaining a positive identification and assisting with the grieving process. With the development of regional and local identification teams, strides have been made using computers and imaging programs to compare antemortem and postmortem dental records for positive identification. The role of forensic dentistry can be structured to be a significant component for the Coroner/Medical Examiner systems when managing a mass disaster investigation.

Summary of a Mass Fatality Incident (MFI)

A "disaster" can be defined as a sudden occurrence that exceeds or overwhelms the resources and capabilities available for a community to manage. A mass fatality incident (MFI) is an occurrence that causes loss of life that exceeds the resources of the Medical Examiner or Coroner system of that community. A disaster contingency plan develops and utilizes resources that will be required to address these investigations.[1] The dental identification team is a good example of such a forensic resource because these teams can be formatted and trained as a unit, some with an equipment cache, to meet the needs of the community.

Teamwork and extensive planning are two important components when developing a disaster plan. Many communities, counties, and state agencies have developed a disaster contingency plan. These plans can be segregated into the Emergency Medical System (EMS) of the operation, which includes police, fire, and medical assistance. The other part of the plan can be classified as a resolution phase or mortuary operation, which consists of many forensic specialties that assist the Medical Examiner and Coroner offices. These specialties can include forensic pathologists, forensic anthropologists, forensic odontologists, DNA specialists, fingerprint specialists, funeral directors and licensed embalmers, medical legal investigators, mental health specialists, security, and administrative and support personnel.

History of Forensic Dentistry (Odontology)

Forensic dentistry is that branch of dentistry which deals with the proper handling and examination of dental evidence and the proper evaluation and presentation of dental findings in the interests of justice. The study of the history of forensic dentistry is more than collecting dental evidence, but also how it applies to the questions of law and developing legal codes. Dental evidence is only of value in societies that have laws.[2]

Some benchmark cases date back to 2500 B.C. in Egypt, where the first evidence of forensic dentistry as a profession was performed to identify a skull at the pyramids of Giza, Egypt. In 45–70 A.D. a mistress of Emperor Nero of Rome was identified by a discolored tooth and malocclusion. Other famous names that were identified through forensic dentistry include William the Conquer (1066), Charles the Bold (1477), and the first case in the United States in 1776, when Paul Revere identified General Joseph Warren, at the Battle of Bunker Hill. Other people identified include John Wilkes Booth (1868), Adolf Hitler (1945), and Lee Harvey Oswald (exhumation 1981). Some current day forensic examinations where dentistry was utilized, in conjunction with other forensic sciences, were of Saddam Hussein and also the confirmation of identity of his sons Qusay Hussein and Uday Hussein (2003).

The Role of Forensic Dentistry (Odontology)

With the help of the media and the proliferation of CSI-type television programs, the activities of forensic odonotolgy throughout the United States and international communities have seen an upsurge of interest. This interest has always been in the background, but is now somewhat glamorized by the media and the advent of one-hour crime solving through "forensics." There has always been a dissemination of interest by a core of forensic dentists (odontologists) in such organizations as The American Academy of Forensic Sciences (www.aafs.org), The American Society of Forensic Odontology (www.newasfo.com), and the American Board of Forensic Odontology (www.abfo.org). These organizations are of key importance in developing and updating standardizations, guidelines, protocols and peer review that forensic odontology should follow.

The forensic odontologist may be requested by many agencies to assist in the following type of investigations:

A. Routine Dental Identification: The identification of unknown remains in various stages of decomposition.
B. Mass Disasters: Previously defined and the main focus of this chapter.
C. Bite Mark Evidence and Analysis.

D. Child and Elderly Abuse.
E. Civil Litigation: Oral trauma occurrences via accident, negligence, or malpractice.

The scope of the forensic odontologist is as varied as the cases and problems presented. The field is demanding, challenging, and intriguing as it attempts to assist the victims and their families that it serves.[2] The true value of the science is often commingled with other forensic scientific experts and modalities towards the common goals of discovering the truth, and providing service to the community in times of dire need.

The Role of Forensic Dentistry in Mass Disasters

On June 23–24, 1986, the First National Symposium on Dentistry's Role and Responsibilities in Mass Disaster Identification was convened at the American Dental Association Headquarters in Chicago, Illinois. The discussions at this symposium charged state dental associations with the development, organization and planning of state dental identification teams. In 1988, President Ronald Regan supported the goals of the symposium.

Forensic dental expertise has been utilized in past mass disasters, or MFI, such as the Tenerife, Canary Islands, air crash (1977), PSA air crash in San Diego (1978), Jonestown Guyana massacre (1978), Las Vegas MGM Hotel fire (1980), and Flight 232 air crash in Sioux City, Iowa (1989).

In 1979, the Coast Guard established a Casualty Assistant Response Team Plan (CART). In 1980, and concurrent with the U.S. Public Health Service (USPHS), the National Funeral Directors Association (NFDA) aided with the formation of a team to assist in a MFI. This federally funded team was called the Disaster Mortuary Operation Team (DMORT) and became part of the National Disaster Medical System (NDMS). The DMORT teams were made up of multiple types of forensic and support specialists to assist the Coroner/Medical Examiner System in times of mass disaster crisis.

DMORT arose out of concern for the families of victims of aviation disasters.[7] The Family Assistance Act of 1996 (Public Law 104-264, Title VIII) mandated family and victim support tasks for the National Transportation Safety Board and other agencies. The DMORT mission is directed under this law.[1] Through the Emergency Support Function (ESF#8) directive, the National Response Plan charges NDMS (through the DMORT teams) with responsibility to provide victim identification and mortuary services in MIFs.

In 1996, after the troubled experiences of the TWA 800 crash (Figure 4.5) and under President Bill Clinton, the law now mandated the federal government provide special teams to help provide a family assistance support center. Within that support center came the additional capabilities of the forensic identifications teams.

Although the final result numbers vary for positive identifications obtained through forensic dentistry in a mass fatality incident, it remains a very viable option for rapid identification responses early in the morgue operations. Dental records are stored and obtained relatively quickly from the family dentist or dental clinics. The dentition can often resist high impact trauma and the heat created by these types of mass disasters. Certainly forensic dentistry is not the only scientific analyses utilized, but it is an invaluable identification option early in the investigation of many aircraft disasters.

In 1998, the DMORT teams and their forensic specialists were sent on an international mission to assist with the investigation of Korean Airline Flight #801 in Guam. The Korean Air Flight 801 in Guam marked the first time that federal teams (DMORT) were deployed out of the continental United States to provide forensic identification services.

Figure 4.1 *Tenerife Air Crash (1977)*

Figure 4.2 PSA Crash, San Diego, CA (1978)

Figure 4.3 Flight 232, Sioux City, Iowa (1989)

Figure 4.4 *Debris Field, Flight 232 Sioux City, Iowa*

Figure 4.5 *TWA Flight 800 Boeing 747-100 (July 1996)*

Figure 4.6 *PSA Crash, San Diego, CA (1978)*

Figure 4.7 KAL Flight 801 (1989)

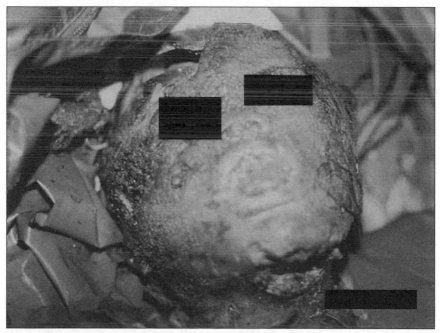

Figure 4.8 Recovered victim KAL Flight 801

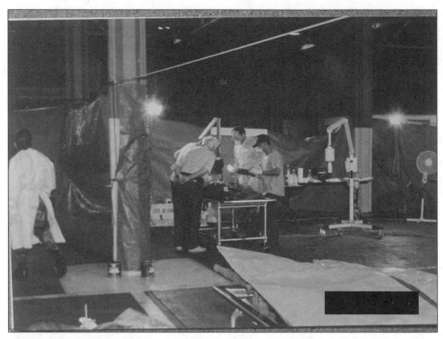

Figure 4.9 Postmortem dental section, Flight 801

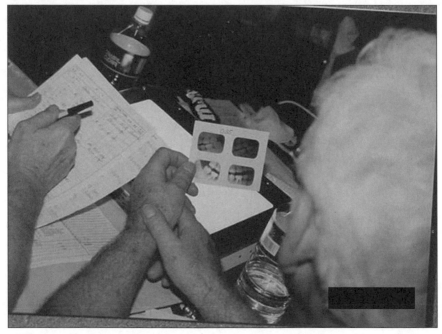

Figure 4.10 Antemortem dental X-ray comparisons

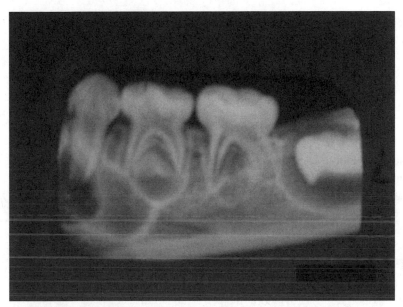

Figure 4.11 Dental X-rays assist with chronological aging

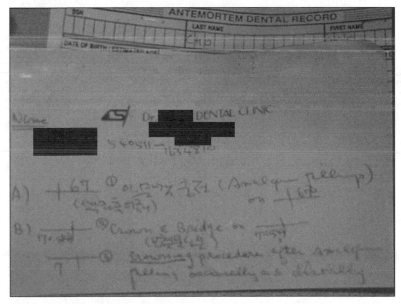

Figure 4.12 Language barriers in dental records challenge the dental team at Korean Air Flight 801

The National Incident Management System

The National Incident Management System (NIMS) was developed as a result of the 9/11 World Trade Center terrorist attacks. The Homeland Security Presidential Directive (HSPD-5) was signed by George W. Bush in 2003, mandating the utilization of NIMS in disaster management. The overall objective of NIMS is to coordinate government agencies, non-government organizations and the private sector to resolve incidents of national significance.

Under NIMS, the concept of Incident Command was utilized. This chain of command listed in Figure 4.13 is the best organizational practice that forensic identification teams should follow to maintain operational structure during a mass fatality incident.

In morgue operations and victim identification, the Coroner or Medical Examiner is the Incident Commander. She oversees the support functions, family services, media contact, and mortuary services. The forensic dental team falls under the Operations side of the below diagram (Figure 4.13).

As the human remains are recovered, they are transported to the identification center (morgue) as provided in the pre-arranged disaster plan. The identification center processes the remains for identification and returns those remains to the family, through the chain of command. All authority is maintained by the Coroner or Medical Examiner, whether the operation is staffed by federal or local forensic specialist teams.

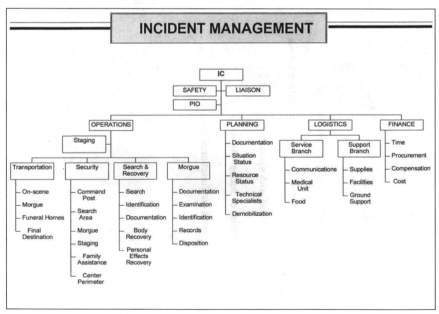

Figure 4.13 *Incident Command System (ICS)*

Morgue Operations

The morgue is divided into multiple forensic stations to record and document information for eventual comparison to antemortem information. The log entry, or the processing, area (shown in Figure 4.14) maintains the chain of custody and begins the tracking of the remains throughout the morgue operations.

As the human remains move through the morgue processing system (Figure 4.14), a forensic photographer documents these remains as they are received and assigned identification tracking numbers. These tracking numbers are key and must remain fixed and consistent throughout the operation. Full body medical X-rays are conducted on each victim to locate any prosthetic devices, objects or personal effects that could aid with identification. Fingerprints will be obtained, if possible, by the FBI Team. The pathology section will then perform an autopsy to confirm the manner of death and samples will be taken for DNA or by a team from The Armed Forces DNA ID Lab (AFDIL). The dental section will then initiate the postmortem examination, using digital or convention X-rays, and a complete dental charting. A physical anthropologist will examine and obtain information regarding age, sex, racial origin and skeletal abnormalities. Once all the information is recorded and the body has been examined by all the forensic stations, the mortuary section prepares the remains for repatriation to the family. Documentation, systematic log entry, and a specific tracking number of all remains and personal effects is maintained throughout the morgue operation. The disaster planning should include provisions for additional storage of the remains using refrigerated trucks or containers.

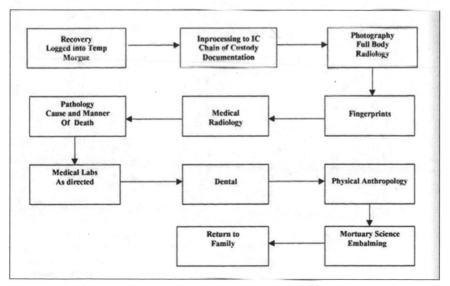

Figure 4.14 *Morgue Processing Protocol and flow chart[1]*

Figure 4.15 Morgue facility, St. Gabriel, LA (Katrina 2005)

Figure 4.16 Morgue station: St. Gabriel, LA (Katrina 2005)

The forensic teams, particularly the forensic dental identification teams, require special equipment availability or a mobile cache. Because mass disasters overwhelm the community, they also overwhelm the resources required to deal with the incident. The morgue is usually set up in a warehouse, airplane hangar or portable structure that can adapt to specific requirements. The cache or equipment is portable and has to be transported and set up in a prompt and expeditious fashion. The federal DMORT teams have a DPMU (Disaster Portable Morgue Unit). Local or state teams may have access to state-funded equipment or portable morgues as designated. (See Figures 4.17–22.)

Figure 4.17 The Disaster Portable Morgue (DPMU)

Figure 4.18 *Off loading the portable morgue (2004)*

Figure 4.19 *Palletized packaging*

Figure 4.20 Individualized containers

Figure 4.21 Morgue computer equipment

Figure 4.22 Morgue operations

Figure 4.23 Personal Protective Equipment (PPE).

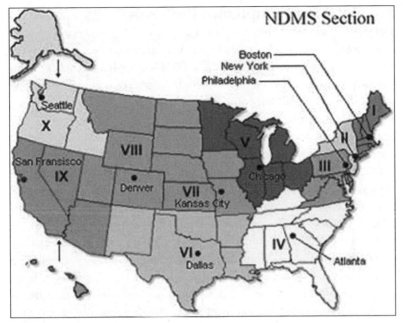

Figure 4.24 Personal Protective Equipment (PPE)

Figure 4.25 Members of various disciplines of a DMORT response team. Flight 5966 Kirksville, Missouri (2004)

Morgue Safety and Compliance Protocols

The importance of safety during the operation should be understood by all morgue personnel. A safety officer has the overall responsibility to ensure the use of personal protection equipment (PPE), OSHA compliance and accountability. Forensic and support personnel should have proper immunizations and vaccinations for influenza, MMR, polio, tetanus diphtheria, varicella, hepatitis A and B, and TB skin tests.

In the event of a bioterrorism incident, epidemic crisis, or chemical, biological, radioactive, or nuclear agents, specific government agencies, in conjunction with the CDC, will provide scene assessment and guidelines prior to all identification operations.

Morgue protocols during a mass disaster must also include proper identification badges, clearance and security authorization for secure protection of the operation. The use of a Public Information Officer (PIO) is important regarding the release of any information during the disaster operation. Protocols regarding the HIPPA Act should also be addressed. The taking of photographs while on the premises is restricted to a specific designated photographer. In this day of internet access and rapid information availability, the protection of privacy for the decedents and their families are mandated and respected.

The Forensic Dental Team Organization

The dental team is divided into three sections during a mass disaster:

- The Postmortem section
- The Antemortem section
- The Comparison section

The postmortem team is designed and split into groups of three. They have the responsibility of maintaining proper body identification tracking numbers, examining the human remains and dental structures, intra-oral charting, taking conventional or digital radiographs, and providing digital oral photography. There are two dentists who record the data and re-verify, and one dentist or auxiliary who scribes the data onto a log sheet or in computer format utilizing the proper dental codes.

Specific numbering systems are utilized. If the disaster occurs in the United States, the Universal Numbering System is the standard format of choice (Figure 4.26). The Palmer Notation system and the Federation Dentaire Internationale (FDI) are used in international communities. Forensic odontologists should be familiar with all these different dental charting codes.

Permanent Teeth

Universal Numbering System
upper left

16	15	14	13	12	11	10	9	8	7	6	5	4	3	2	1
17	18	19	20	21	22	23	24	25	26	27	28	29	30	31	32

lower left   lower right   upper right

Palmer Notation

8	7	6	5	4	3	2	1	1	2	3	4	5	6	7	8
8	7	6	5	4	3	2	1	1	2	3	4	5	6	7	8

FDI Two-Digit Notation

28	27	26	25	24	23	22	21	11	12	13	14	15	16	17	18
38	37	36	35	34	33	32	31	41	42	43	44	45	46	47	48

Figure 4.26 Dental charting numbering systems

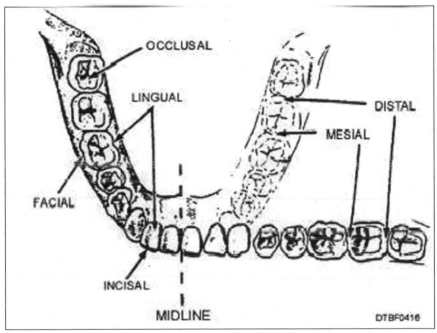

Figure 4.27 Surfaces of teeth

The dental team must be consistent in using the charting system codes when examining both adult and pediatric dentitions. Also, specific terminology of tooth surfaces must be maintained when dealing with dental restorations and their proper locations. Human remains are sometimes fragmented or commingled when recovered from the crash or disaster site and delivered to the morgue for a forensic dental examination. The use of a three man postmortem team provides the re-verification and detailed accountability during examination and creation of the postmortem dental record (Figures 4.27 and 4.28).

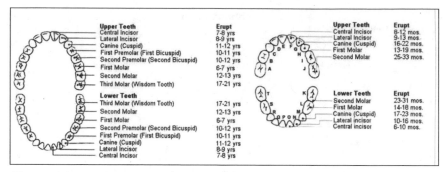

Figure 4.28 *Permanent and primary dental tooth charts*

The postmortem dental team may also contribute age estimation of the mass disaster victim by utilizing the chronological tooth eruption sequences. Forensic dentistry can be a valuable tool in age estimation, particularly in children, adolescents and young adults. The specific presence or absence of certain teeth, along with tooth eruption sequence, root apex formation, and closure, can be a fundamental guideline for age determination. Dental maturity between the ages of 18–20, when the final set of molars (wisdom teeth or third molars) complete their development.[4] (See Figures 4.29 and 4.30 by Schour and Massler.)

In multiple fatality disasters, dental age estimation may include or exclude some victims or fragmented remains in the profile and also provide support data in assisting, but not determining, the positive identification.

The postmortem dental team can document their dental findings in either a paper log entry form as shown in Figures 4.33 and 4.34, or in the computer generated software Program WINID3 (Figures 4.35 and 4.36).

State-of-the-art formats—the entry of postmortem data directly into the WINID3 software programs—were used in the Hurricane Katrina deployment (2005). Utilizing specific dental codes, a digital postmortem record can be created and stored in a designated database.

Dental charting must be accompanied by a complete series of postmortem X-rays. The advent of digital X-rays, portable X-ray units, and digital photography has expedited the process for the postmortem dental team. The unique design of the WINID3 software allows the merger with the DEXIS Digital X-ray system and has created an excellent combination of quality and efficiency for capturing postmortem forensic dental information.

The postmortem dental team must work as a cohesive unit during mass fatality operations. Many of the human remains that are examined can be in various stages of decomposition, fragmented or severely charred. This can create numerous challenges for the dental team.

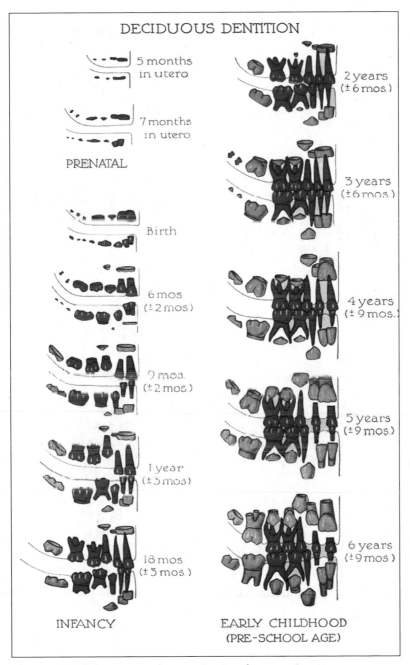

Figure 4.29 *Primary tooth eruption and age estimates*

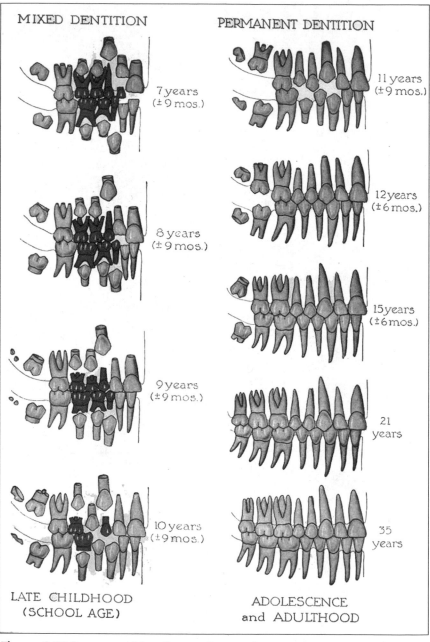

Figure 4.30 Permanent tooth eruption and age estimates

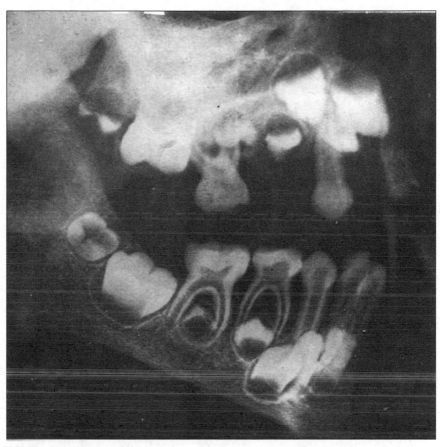

Figure 4.31 Postmortem X-ray of five-year-old male[4]

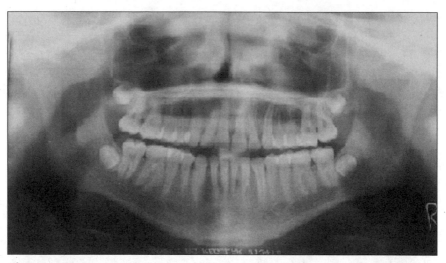

Figure 4.32 *Postmortem panoramic radiograph. Age estimate: 15 plus or minus one year[4]*

Depending on the magnitude of the operation and the number of deceased in the MFI, morgue operations may operate with two 12-hour shifts, 24 hours a day, 7 days a week. The staff per shift may be up to 18 to 20 dental members per shift. Fatigue and mental stress must be monitored by the mental health specialists.

Specific identification guidelines and protocols have been established by the American Board of Forensic Odontology (ABFO), in conjunction with the inter-agency agreements between the National Transportation Safety Board (NTSB) and DMORT. These guidelines should be reviewed prior to morgue start up, and during daily morgue briefings. The ability to adapt and adjust guidelines to fit the mission specific needs is paramount to the identification process, if so approved by the section leader and Coroner or Medical Examiner.

If state or local teams are selected to staff the morgue, they may also elect to follow these guidelines when so directed and authorized by the Coroner or Medical Examiner in charge of the operation.

Teamwork, chain of command, accountability, and accuracy are just some of the many coordinated efforts required to obtain an accurate postmortem dental record.

Figure 4.33 *Postmortem chart*

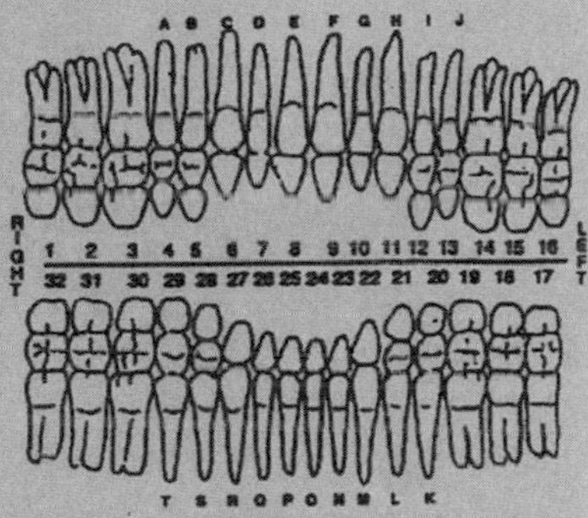

Antemortem Dental Record   ID#: _____

Last: _____   First: _____   MI: _____

Date: _____   Sex: _____   Race: _____   Age/DOB : _____

Height: _____   Weight: ____   Eye: _____   Hair: _____   Blood Type: _____

Team Member: _____

Confirm by: _____

Type, Date and Number of X-Rays _____

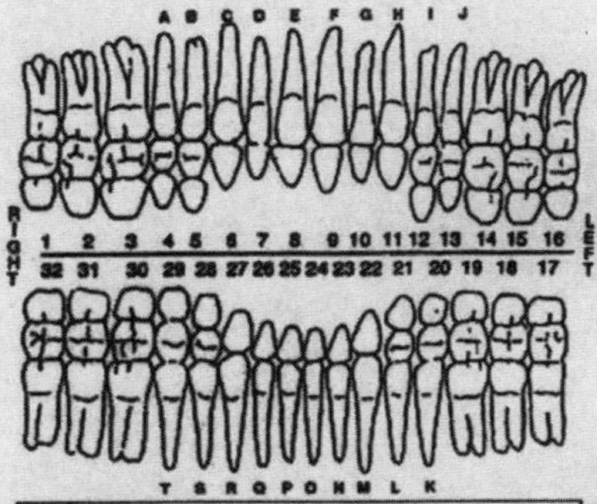

				Description	Code
1	18				
2	17				
3	16				
4	15	A	55		
5	14	B	54		
6	13	C	53		
7	12	D	52		
8	11	E	51		
9	21	F	61		
10	22	G	62		
11	23	H	63		
12	24	I	64		
13	25	J	65		
14	26				
15	27				
16	28				
17	38				
18	37				
19	36				
20	35	K	75		
21	34	L	74		
22	33	M	73		
23	32	N	72		
24	31	O	71		
25	41	P	81		
26	42	Q	82		
27	43	R	83		
28	44	S	84		
29	45	T	85		
30	46				
31	47				
32	48				

Codes

Primary Codes	Secondary Codes
M – Mesial	A – Annotation
O - Occlusal	B – Deciduous
D – Distal	C - Crown
F – Facial	E - Resin
L – Lingual	G - Gold
I – Incisal	H - Porcelain
U – Unerupted	N - Non-Precious
V – Virgin	P - Pontic
X – Missing	R - Root Canal
J – Missing Cr	S - Silver Amalgam
I - No Data	T - Denture Tooth
	Z - Temporary

A: _____
B: _____
C: _____

ID As: _____

Comments: _____
_____
_____

Figure 4.34 Antemortem chart

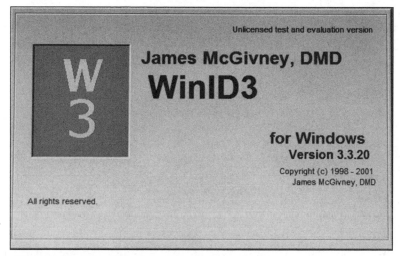

Figure 4.35 WINID3 forensic software

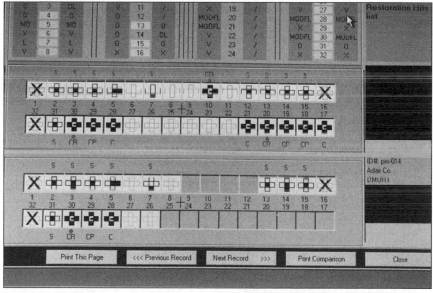

Figure 4.36 WINID3 Computer odontogram dental chartings

Figures 4.37-39 The DEXIS Digital X-ray system and the Nomad portable X-ray unit

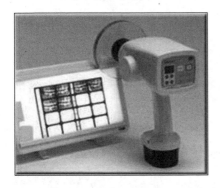

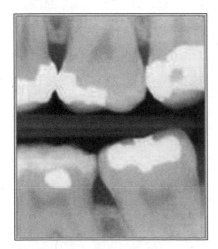

Fatality Management Considerations for the Dental Team

1. Number of fatalities
2. Decedent populations (open or closed)
3. Availability of an antemortem dental record
4. Conditions of the remains (complete or fragment)

These factors drive the following: the number of dental personnel needed, how long the identification process will take, and the necessary adjunct methods to make positive identifications. In general, as the number of decedents increases, the resources needed to manage and process them increases.[3]

There are two types of decedent populations: closed and open. In a closed population the number of the victims and their names are known. An example would be an aircraft accident, where an accurate manifest can be generated and trusted.[3]

Conversely, an open population is one in which neither the victims nor their names are known. The response personnel must sort those who are reported missing (by friends and relatives) from those who are actually missing.[3] This sorting process can take time. Once a decedent is known to be missing, then the process of obtaining and examining antemortem data can begin. An example of an open population occurred in 2001 at the World Trade Center disaster. Initial media reports indicated as many as 10,000 dead. In the following days, the reported missing persons fluctuated between 3,950 and 6,450.[9] The total missing was actually 2,749 and total identified were over 1,590 (NTSB Reports June 2005).[3]

Another example of an open population disaster was with Hurricane Katrina and Rita. There were over 1,400 storm-related deaths from the Gulf Coast disaster. There were over 900 victims recovered and examined at the morgue facilities in St. Gabriel and Carville, Louisiana, by state and local agencies and the DMORT teams. Over 870 individuals have been identified through the coordinating efforts of the coroner's office and multiple forensic science modalities (LFAC August 2006).[8]

Obtaining positive identifications requires comparing postmortem information to the antemortem data. As mentioned previously in this chapter, some of the requirements for obtaining the postmortem data is tedious but can rapidly be analyzed when the remains become available from the scene. However, locating and obtaining accurate and current antemortem data is more time consuming and complex. For families that know the dentist or physician of the decedent, these records can be obtained quickly. Such factors as age, socioeconomic status, cultural practices, and religious beliefs of the victims and the family can impact the antemortem record availability.

Victims of low socioeconomic status may not have dental work, and subsequently no dental record on file.[3] Other forensic sciences struggle with similar issues. Many people may not be fingerprinted, and some families may be unwilling to provide DNA samples for identification purposes.

Another obstacle in obtaining antemortem records is that many of the decedents are not from the location where the accident occurs, such as an aircraft disaster. Delays in obtaining the dental records can complicate the dental investigation. With the Hurricane Katrina disaster, much of the infrastructure was damaged surrounding these communities. Many dental offices were destroyed or severely affected by storm damage rendering the dental records and X-rays unsalvageable.

Experience shows that obtaining accurate antemortem records in a timely fashion is a critical factor in completing the identification process and the return of the remains to the family. The same level of attention and resources provided to the postmortem dental section processes should be awarded to the antemortem dental data collection process.

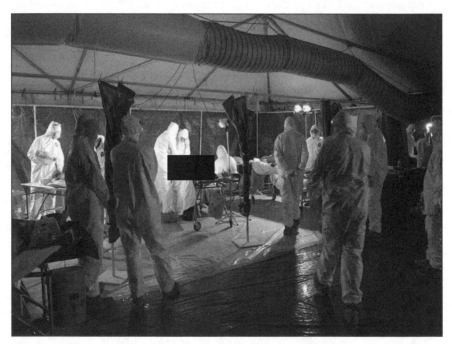

Figure 4.40 DMORT postmortem dental identification teams in St. Gabriel, LA, morgue (Katrina 2005)

Figure 4.41 Fire victim in an aircraft accident

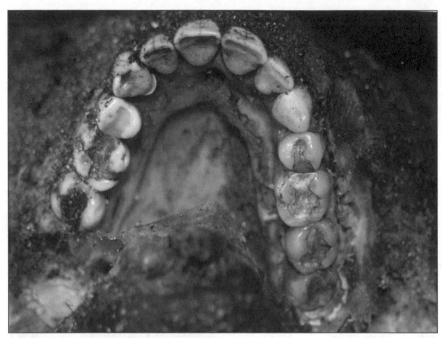

Figure 4.42 Dental structures intact

Figure 4.43 Flight 232, Sioux City, Iowa (1989)

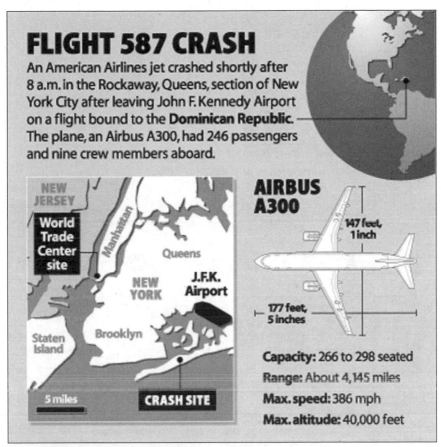

FLIGHT 587 CRASH

An American Airlines jet crashed shortly after 8 a.m. in the Rockaway, Queens, section of New York City after leaving John F. Kennedy Airport on a flight bound to the **Dominican Republic.** The plane, an Airbus A300, had 246 passengers and nine crew members aboard.

AIRBUS A300

147 feet, 1 inch

177 feet, 5 inches

Capacity: 266 to 298 seated
Range: About 4,145 miles
Max. speed: 386 mph
Max. altitude: 40,000 feet

NEW JERSEY

World Trade Center site

Manhattan

Queens

NEW YORK

J.F.K. Airport

Staten Island

Brooklyn

5 miles

CRASH SITE

Figure 4.44 *Flight 587, Queens, New York (2001)*

Figure 4.45 *World Trade Center (2001)*

Figure 4.46 *Superdome Hurricane Katrina (2005)*

Figure 4.47 *Hurricane Katrina Morgue Operations, Carville, Louisiana (2005)*

Figure 4.48 *Hurricane Katrina Morgue Operations, Carville, Louisiana (2005)*

Antemortem Dental Section

The antemortem dental section is made up of a section leader and his alternate with at least three members, consisting of two dentists and an auxiliary or dental student as the third member.[5] The number of dental antemortem teams required is dependent on the size of the incident and the number of fatalities.

The antemortem section and its team members are stationed in close proximity to the postmortem dental morgue operation. The antemortem section requires different parameters and logistical requirements from that of the postmortem team and must be positioned in an area that is kept clean and dry. These requirements include special power needs for computers, scanners, printers, X-ray view boxes, storage file cabinets, and internet connection. The area must have access to multiple phone lines with toll free capabilities, along with a fax machine and dedicated lines. The ability to store multiple antemortem dental records in file cabinets in an organized fashion is mandatory. The utilization of dental auxiliary is paramount, since they can possess the ability to manage incoming phone calls, dental records, charting, accurate filing and secretarial skills.

The antemortem team works closely with the Family Assistant Center (FAC) team (Figure 4.49) in obtaining the dental records from the decedent's family. Funeral directors and others trained to deal with families utilize the Victim Identification Profile (VIP) Program to obtain pertinent identification and contact information regarding the victim's profiles. This information, along with the disaster manifest, is continually updated, referenced and verified between the antemortem dental and FAC teams. Other resources for dental records can be searched: dental schools, clinics, employer dental insurance carriers, or the military depository.

Figure 4.49 *FAC team interview family member*

Once the antemortem dental records are received, that dental data is entered into the WINID3 Program. This dental information can then be searched against postmortem dental data, entered similarly by the dental team in the morgue. As the dental records (ante- and postmortem) begin to accumulate in the database of the WINID3 Program, algometric search functions can be initiated to begin the comparison and matching of dental records and X-rays (Figure 4.50). The use of computer software dental programs like WINID3 can be invaluable in managing large disaster operations, as was seen in Hurricane Katrina (2005) and with the World Trade Center (2001).

Antemortem
dental record →

Postmortem
dental record →

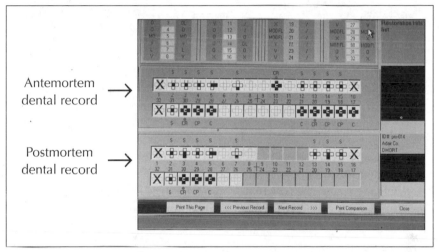

Figure 4.50 Computer comparison results (antemortem/postmortem) dental

The comparison of antemortem and postmortem dental X rays is utilized to confirm the positive identification. Through the comparison of dental restoration size and location, missing and present teeth, root and pulp morphology, and other congruent dental findings, the final match can be determined (Figures 4.51 and 4.52). The computer can rank hundreds of possible candidates, which can be confirmed or rejected by the comparison team. The final conclusion on whether a positive identification is to be rendered is not determined by the computer, but by the dental team, through visual comparison of appropriate dental X-rays and dental evidence.

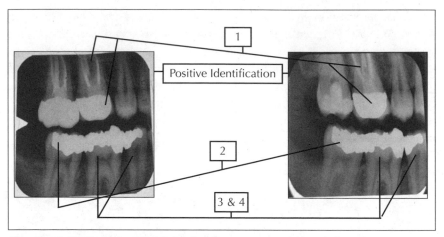

Figures 4.51 (left) and 4.52 (right) *Postmortem X-ray taken in morgue (left) and Antemortem X-ray of descedent (right)*

The final dental comparison opinion is based on the following dental guidelines:[6]

Positive Identification:
The antemortem and postmortem data match in sufficient detail to establish that they are from the same individual. In addition, there are no irreconcilable discrepancies.

Possible Identification:
The antemortem and postmortem data have consistent features, but due to the quality of either the postmortem remains or the antemortem evidence, it is not possible to positively establish dental identification.

Insufficient Evidence:
The available information is insufficient to form the basis for a conclusion.

Exclusion:
The antemortem and postmortem data are clearly inconsistent. However, it should be understood that identification by exclusion is a valid technique in certain circumstances.

Figure 4.53 *Dental team member confirms the identification*

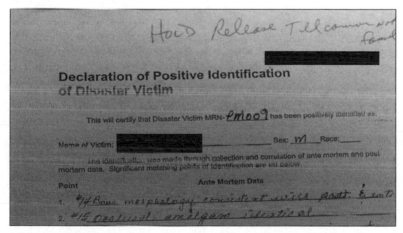

Figure 4.54 *Declaration of Positive Identification Form*

Once the final opinions are determined regarding the dental identification, they are released to the Coroner or Medical Examiner in charge of the operation (Figure 4.54).

They will then determine how this information will be cross referenced with the other forensic science experts and modalities, which can include fingerprints, DNA, pathology, anthropology, medical radiology, photography, and personal effects. The Coroner or Medical Examiner will then determine the protocols for final preparation, release, and transportation of the remains along with the notification to next-of-kin.

Summary

The process of dental identification for a mass disaster incident has many unique aspects when compared with that of a routine dental identification, outside of the increase in numbers of victims and responders.[9] The utilization of the incident command system applies to the dental team as well as the entire disaster operation. Following an approved set of guidelines and protocols is mandatory for the forensic dentist as well as the entire disaster response team. The adhesion to these specific standards maintains the chain of evidence, credibility and accuracy in the investigation.

The respect and dignity for the victims and the repatriation of those human remains back to family members is paramount to the grieving process and assisting families with final closure.

The past and future service of forensic odontology to the victims of a mass disaster and their families is an excellent example of how dentistry can contribute as a valuable service to the community in times of special need.

Disclaimer

It is the intent of this chapter and its author to offer personal opinions for education purposes regarding the association of forensic dentistry as it relates to past mass fatality disasters. The information provided is the personal opinion of the author and not that of any mentioned professional organization, government agency, product, or website.

References

1. Fixott RH. Dental Clinics of North America. Forensic Odontology. W.B. Saunders Company 45 pp 221-290 (2001)

2. Cottone JA. Standish, SM. Outline of Forensic Dentistry. Yearbook Medical Publisher. Chicago, Ill. (1981)

3. DMORT Standard Operating Procedures for National Transportation Safety Board Activations pp12(May 2006)

4. Forensic Dentistry Online. (www.forensicdentistryonline.org)

5. Manual Forensic Odontology, Publication of American Society of Forensic Odontology (2006)

6. American Board of Forensic Odontology Inc, Diplomates Reference Manuals- Section III Policies, Procedures, Guidelines, &Standards (2007) www. abfo.org

7. Johnson LT: Evolution of recovery and identification of aviation disasters fatalities 1980-1998 17 4-5 (1998)

8. Louisiana Family Assistance Center (LFAC). "Reuniting the families of Katrina and Rita. Final Report of the Louisiana Family Assistance Center (August 2006) p6.

9. DMORT Standard Operating Procedures for National Transportation Safety Board Activations (May 2006) pp 12. Referencing (Simpson and Stehr, 2003, "Victim management and identification after World Trade Center Collapse," in Beyond September 11th: An Account of Post- Disaster Research, Center Collapse.

Chapter 5

The Role of the Forensic Pathologist in a Mass Disaster

Thomas W. Young, M.D. and Matthias I. Okoye, M.D., J.D.

Mass disasters come unexpectedly. When they do come, they often come in a fashion that is not foreseen. In the aftermath, confusion reigns. Multiple agencies, even in jurisdictions where there is a mass disaster plan, are initially off balance. Each agency's role may not be clear at the outset. After the initial search and rescue phase of the disaster response finishes, multiple agencies are left with the large task of searching for and recovering the dead. This phase of the response is critical, and there are major consequences for not doing this well. Where can people turn to make sure that this important phase is handled correctly? Only one person—the trained, credentialed and experienced forensic pathologist—possesses the experience and knowledge to lead successfully in the recovery, identification and investigation of the dead during a mass disaster.

Who is a forensic pathologist?

In order to discuss the role of the forensic pathologist in a mass disaster, we must first be clear about who a forensic pathologist is and what he or she does.

Pathology is the study of disease. It is not only a course taught in medical schools, but also a specialty in the practice of medicine. Pathologists use their knowledge of disease most often in the hospital setting. Trained in the appearance of disease, the pathologist receives samples of tissues—some small and some large—and identifies the disease process found in the tissues. The information gleaned from pathologists allows medical doctors to treat their patients. Additionally, pathologists are also trained in laboratory methods and usually manage the clinical laboratories in hospitals and clinics.

Pathologists for centuries have performed autopsies. An autopsy is a systematic examination of a dead person to discover what caused the death and to identify any evidence of disease or injury in the body. Because of this training in autopsy pathology, the pathologist is uniquely trained to investigate deaths.

Pathologists frequently subspecialize into areas of greater expertise. One important subspecialty of pathology is forensic pathology. Forensic pathologists

81

are trained to investigate deaths that occur due to violence, that are suspicious for foul play, that occur suddenly and unexpectedly, or that occur under circumstances that are not well understood. The forensic pathologist is an expert in the autopsy as applied to these investigations. Rather than practicing solely in the hospital setting, the forensic pathologist is essentially a "community" pathologist who practices outside of the hospital. Various agencies and interests—law enforcement, prosecutors, attorneys, public health agencies, insurance companies and others—rely on the data and opinions generated by the forensic pathologist as violent deaths occur within a community over time.

The forensic pathologist serves in coroner and medical examiner systems

In accordance with state law, the responsibility of death investigation may fall on the shoulders of a coroner or medical examiner. Although the definitions of these roles may vary from state to state, the job is essentially the same. Both investigate violent and unexpected deaths within a jurisdiction. Both are charged with filing death certificates for these deaths.

A death certificate is a document required by law that states, among other items, the name of the dead person, the date, time and location of the death, and the cause and manner of death. A cause of death represents a disease or injury that sets into motion a chain of events that lead to death. A manner of death is a one-word description of the circumstances surrounding the death. Manners of death include natural (a death from disease), homicide (a death intentionally caused by another person or persons), suicide (an intentionally self-inflicted death) or accident (a violent death that is unforeseen). The cause and manner of a death represents the stated opinion of the coroner or medical examiner; and other agencies rely upon that opinion and the results of the investigation to perform their needed legal functions.

In more populous jurisdictions, forensic pathologists play a key role in the death investigation process. Most medical examiners—both deputy medical examiners and chief medical examiners—are forensic pathologists in more populated jurisdictions. Coroners may not be forensic pathologists, but the larger offices utilize the expertise of forensic pathologists in performing their death investigation roles. Also, even in coroner jurisdictions, it is the forensic pathologist who appears in court, relating to judge and jury his or her findings at autopsy and expressing his or her opinions about the death.

The role of the forensic pathologist is distinct from law enforcement

Although forensic pathologists often work closely with law enforcement, they themselves are not law enforcement officers. Although they may interact at the same death scene, the roles of both are separate and distinct. Essentially, the forensic pathologist serving in a coroner or medical examiner system is interested in what happened to cause the death. Law enforcement is essentially interested in who is responsible for what happened, particularly under circumstances in which laws may have been violated.

To do their respective missions, forensic pathologists and law enforcement officers have to work together and to rely on each other. Both provide items of information essential for the understanding of what happened and who is responsible. Both are involved in the acquisition of evidence. The forensic pathologist acquires evidence from the body mostly, and law enforcement acquires evidence from the scene mostly, but there is overlap in this. Also, law enforcement provides security for the scene of death in order for the scene to remain intact and not subject to the predations of meddlers and onlookers.

The forensic pathologist prepares to answer future questions

How does a forensic pathologist perform the work of medicolegal death investigation from day to day? What is the process?

First, the forensic pathologist relies on an investigation of the scene of death and the circumstances surrounding the death. Usually, investigators employed by the coroner or medical examiner visit the scene. Along with law enforcement personnel, the coroner or medical examiner investigator obtains witness and scene information, anticipating the questions asked of him or her by the forensic pathologist.

The forensic pathologist on the basis of this initial information anticipates the questions to be asked in the future. The questions not only include the cause and manner of death but also any question that may be asked of the forensic pathologist about the death.

On the basis of this anticipation, the forensic pathologist then plans how to obtain the physical evidence. The forensic pathologist may examine the external surface of the body and the clothing. He or she may perform an autopsy and submit specimens from the body for other laboratory evaluations. Some of these laboratory evaluations may include toxicology (the analysis for drugs and poisons), DNA analysis, or vitreous chemistry (analysis of eyeball fluid).

As the physical evidence develops in a case, the forensic pathologist correlates this evidence with the witness and scene investigation. From these correlations, he or she forms an opinion for cause and manner of death. Also, the forensic pathologist prepares to answer other questions about the death that may be asked in the future.

The forensic pathologist performs each step in the process in a painstaking manner. Because of the effects of time on memory and on the degradation of physical evidence, the investigation must be performed properly from the very beginning or vital information will be lost forever.

What are the important questions?

There are questions that are basic and critical to any death investigation. Probably the most important question about a death has to do with identity: Who is this person?

Proper identification of remains is critical. The loss of a loved one is one of the most profound tragedies of life. To be mistaken on the identity of a dead body can lead to serious and severe consequences, not only to the bereaved family but also to those responsible who had the misfortune to make the critical error.

When a body is visually identifiable, the identification is less problematic. When the remains are no longer visually identifiable because of disfigurement by injury, fragmentation or decomposition, identification becomes much more problematic. Although identity may be presumed by associated personal effects, such as a wallet with a driver's license, a proof-positive means of identification requires the comparison of a unique, biological characteristic in the remains with that same characteristic from the individual when he or she was alive. For example, the fingerprints of a dead body — unique identifying characteristics not shared by others — may be compared with a set of fingerprints taken from the victim before he or she died or a latent fingerprint developed from an object known to be held by the victim when he or she was alive. Dental restorations, DNA from blood or bone, and unique skeletal characteristics seen on an X-ray are other unique identifying characteristics that can be compared from before and after death. Without these, identity can only be presumed by using other evidence such as personal effects, the process of elimination, and the circumstances surrounding the death.

Other important questions involve the circumstances of the death: What happened? When did it happen? How did it occur? Was there pain and suffering? Could the death have been prevented? Who is responsible? Frequently, these questions require the performance of an autopsy. Frequently, these questions are addressed in the courtroom, and the answers may put at stake large sums of money.

Much is at stake in the answering of these very important questions. A community should employ experienced and properly trained forensic pathologists — people accustomed to answering these questions — to ensure the best possible outcomes.

The role of the forensic pathologist in the mass disaster

A mass disaster involving numerous deaths occurring from a cataclysmic event is also a death investigation. The same questions asked above will be asked in the aftermath of a mass disaster. The forensic pathologist uses the same pain-staking methods and approach for this critical death investigation that he or she uses day after day.

Although the questions and the approach remain the same, there are some notable unique features brought about by a mass casualty event.

One feature is the number of deaths. A disaster by definition exceeds the ability of the death investigation system in its usual day-to-day function. The number of dead bodies in a disaster exceeds the refrigerated storage capacity of the office. Also, the number and the nature of the remains exceed the capacity of the office facility and personnel to process them in a timely fashion. The coroner or medical examiner must request additional materiel and personnel to cope with the crisis.

Most disasters also have other elements that render the situation more difficult. Many mass casualty events involving high-energy impacts may lead to fragmentation of the remains, rendering visual identification impossible. Also, the passage of time for recovery of the remains introduces the element of decomposition, also rendering visual identification impossible. The combination of these factors along with the numerous deaths adds to the complexity and challenge of identification and increases the chances for identification error.

Depending on the scope of the disaster and the size of the death scene, security of that scene provided by law enforcement also becomes more extraordinary. For similar reasons, documenting the recovery of remains from the scene—the obtaining of evidence, the gridding of the scene, the charting of the location of the remains, the photography of the scene and the remains—are also challenges.

The high media and public profile of a mass disaster also complicates the process. Information release, although critical, is time consuming. Also, mistakes made in the provision of information can add to the confusion and stress of the bereaved and those responding to the disaster.

Finally, the event brings about severe psychological stress to both the community and people working on the disaster. The potential consequences of psychological stress require the application of additional resources.

In spite of the complexities and the need to rely on others for needed services and expertise and in spite of the pressures of the moment, the overall approach, the professionalism, and the leadership of the forensic pathologist must remain intact. The forensic pathologist must continue to rely on the same approach, methods and techniques that he or she uses for day-to-day death investigation.

The mass disaster plan

The forensic pathologist who serves as a medical examiner must communicate her or his approach and methods of death investigation in the setting of a mass disaster. This is best done through the promulgation of a mass disaster plan.

The National Association of Medical Examiners (NAME) has written a sample mass disaster plan. Although the chief medical examiner of each jurisdiction should write or supervise the writing of a plan that fits his or her jurisdiction, the NAME plan contains most of the needed elements. A copy of the NAME plan accompanies this reference book as Appendix A.

The mass disaster plan is not only useful for reminding office personnel how to function in a mass casualty incident but it also serves another very important purpose. The plan informs other agencies of the role and responsibilities of the medical examiner office during a cataclysmic event, and it informs them of what they can do to support that function. It communicates to the many others who will assist the chief medical examiner what the needs of the office are. For example, the medical examiner office cannot support the recovery of the remains by itself. It must rely on others in law enforcement, for example, to grid the disaster scene, to document graphically and photographically the location of each body or body fragment and associated personal effects, to assign the appropriate unique accession number, and to transport each uniquely labeled body bag. A mass disaster plan helps to stem some of the initial chaos frequently seen in a disaster response.

With each plan, the office should maintain a list of vendors who can provide various and sundry items needed on short notice for a disaster. Items such as refrigerated trucks, paint, stakes, and body bags need to be thought of in advance. Although it may not be practical to maintain items before the onset of a disaster in large quantities, there should be a plan and a way to obtain these items on short notice. Also, potential locations for housing and a Family Assistance Center should be part of this same contingency list.

Although a plan is important, such a plan cannot foresee the needs of all possible disasters. The chief medical examiner—the forensic pathologist in charge—must be willing to modify the plan to meet the requirements brought about by a particular disaster. For that reason, the chief medical examiner must visit the disaster scene prior to the recovery. She and others within a select team delineated by the plan must assess the situation to determine what is required for the recovery and the operation.

The forensic pathologist and DMORT

In the event of a disaster, the federal government provides multiple teams of professionals to support the local effort. The federal teams available to the chief medical examiner or the coroner are the Disaster Mortuary Operations Response Teams (DMORT). Each DMORT team, designated by numbers corresponding to geographic regions of the country, deploys in accordance with the needs of each disaster and the location of the disaster within the country. A DMORT team contains mortuary personnel, forensic dentists, forensic anthropologists, X-ray technologists, forensic pathologists, and many other personnel who support the Family Assistance Center and the DPMU (Disaster Portable Morgue Unit). In addition to DMORT, the federal government also provides a team of fingerprinting specialists from the Federal Bureau of Investigation (FBI).

The DMORT team does not run the medical examiner operation during a disaster. Rather, it supports the chief medical examiner and follows his or her lead. Its role can be as great or as minimal as that prescribed by the chief.

Much of the usefulness of DMORT is the provision of the portable morgue, the DPMU. This allows the morgue operation to occur outside of the medical examiner office, thereby allowing the office to function as usual for day-to-day, non-disaster operations. Within the DPMU, teams of forensic specialists receive the accessioned remains in assembly-line fashion and add data to a computer database set up in the morgue.

Although there are forensic pathologists on DMORT teams, their role in the team is limited. Much of the strength in DMORT lies in the identification of remains, and the pathologists in the team are of limited use in that function, particularly if the remains are extensively fragmented. If there are remains with minimal fragmentation, the pathologists may examine them for characteristics suitable for identification, if that is needed. The chief medical examiner may also elect to utilize DMORT forensic pathologists to perform autopsies as needed for the operation, or the chief may elect to utilize other forensic pathologists familiar to him or her

It is the responsibility of the chief medical examiner—ideally a board certified forensic pathologist—to make sure the work of the DMORT team and others is done according to standard. Although DMORT team members should double check any identifications, the chief should also make sure the identifications are correct. The chief also is the one who signs the death certificates. Although these functions are frequently delegated in more normal settings, the high media profile and the potential for confusion from misidentification in a disaster is sufficiently high to require personal involvement by the chief.

The forensic pathologist has an executive role in a disaster

The role of the forensic pathologist, particularly as the chief medical examiner, is to serve in an executive capacity, delegating his or her work to others. Additionally, the chief needs to interact with other agencies, both governmental and volunteer, that serve in the disaster response. The expertise of this executive forensic pathologist aids in the decisions made by others as he or she interacts in a cooperative fashion. Although the chief may utilize the services of a public information officer, he or she should be available to answer questions and concerns from the public and the media. The chief is also responsible for the safety and well being of those who work in the stressful setting of a disaster response.

In spite of the confusion that may reign during a disaster and the response following it, the forensic pathologist should make sure to utilize the same approach to death investigation that he or she would use in a less stressful time. The forensic pathologist/chief medical examiner should remain calm and clearly assess the situation, making sure the response is in accordance with the highest of professional standards for death investigation. Although he or she may cooperate with many other agencies, the chief needs to articulate clearly and convincingly the approach needed for a successful outcome and, having done that, to execute that approach with the help of many others.

Accompanying reference

NAME Mass Fatality Plan. www.thename.org. Accessioned August 3, 2007.

References

1. Wisner B, Adams J. Environment health in emergencies and disasters: a practical guide. Geneva. World Health organization, 2002: 198.

2. Hsu CM, Huang NE, Tsai LC, Kao CH, Linacre A, Lee JC. Identification of victims of the 1998 Taoyuan Airbus crash accident using DNA analysis. Int J Legal Med 1999; 113: 43-6.

3. Leclair B, Fregqau CJ, Bowen KL, Fourney RM. Enhanced kinship analysis and STR-based DNA typing for human identification in mass fatality incidents; the Swissair flight 111 disaster. J. Forensic Sci 2004; 49: 1-15.

4. Budimlija ZM. World Trade Centre Human Identification Project: experiences with individual body identification cases. Croation Med J 2003; 44: 259-63.

5. Clayton TM, Whitaker JP, Maguire CN. Identification of bodies from the scene of a mass disaster using DNA amplification of short tandem repeat (STR) loci. Forensic Sci Int 1995; 76: 17-25.

6. Ian WE, Weir BS. Parentage testing. In: Interpreting DNA Evidence. Statistical Genetics for Forensic Scientists. Massachusetts: Sinauer Associates Inc. 1998: 163-87.

7. Vardon-Smith G. Mass disaster organization In: Payne-James J. Busuttil A, Smock W, editors. Forensic Medicine - Clinical and Pathological Aspects. London: Greenwich Medical Media Ltd, 2003, 565-78.

8. Saukko P, Knight B. Mass disasters - the role of pathologist. Knight's Forensic Pathology. 3rd ed. London: Arnold, 2004: 41-51.

9. Herdson PB, Mason JK. The role of pathology in major disasters. In: Mason JK, Purdue BN, editors. The Pathology of Trauma. 3rd ed. London. Arnold, 2000: 30-46.

10. Black S, Vanezis B. The forensic investigation of mass graves. In: Payne-James J, Busuttil A, Smock W, editors. Forensic Medicine - Clinical and Pathological Aspects. London: Greenwich Medical Media Ltd, 2003: 67-78.

11. Southwick G, Pethick AJ, Thalayasingam P, et al. Australian doctors in Bali: the initial medical response to the Bali bombing, Med J Aust 2002; 177: 624-626. (Reprinted in ADF Health 2003; 4: 16-18).

12. Hampson GV, Cook SP, Frederiksen SR. Operation Bali Assist. The Australian Defence Force response to the Bali bombinb, 12 October, 2002, Med J Aust 2002, 177: 620-623. (Reprinted in ADF Health 2003; 4: 12:15).

13. Association of Chief Police Officers of England and Wales and Northern Ireland General Policing Committee, standing sub-committee on Emergency Procedures. Emergency Procedures Manual 1999.

14. Home Office Publication Dealing with Disaster. 3rd Edition, 2000.

15. Webb B 2000 Paddington Recommendations from the Paddington Review group of Casualty Bureau, identification process and Family Liaison arrangements. Lord Justice Clarke's Enquiry: The ID of Victims following mass transportation incidents. HSE 2001.

Chapter 6

The Role of the Coroner/ Medical Examiner After a Mass Disaster

Cyril H. Wecht, M.D., J.D.

Disasters typically occur without warning and can strike anywhere and at any time. Whether the disaster is natural like a flood or earthquake, or man-made like a fire or terrorism attack, the primary roles of the Coroner/Medical Examiner's (C/ME) office are essentially the same.

The three primary roles of the C/ME are: (1) examination of samples of tissues and bones to determine if they are human remains; (2) positive identification of such human remains; and (3) determination of the cause and manner of death. The C/ME also has three important secondary functions. These include: (1) provide data and evidence collected from the scene and victims to local, state, and federal investigative agencies; (2) provide epidemiological summary of the victims of the disasters; and (3) develop information to prevent or diminish future fatalities.

After a flood or a bombing, the scene contains a large amount of debris, consisting of pieces of building materials, papers, clothing, vegetation, and human and animal remains. The first role of the death investigators at the scene is to locate and differentiate human remains from other materials. Once human remains have been identified, their original locations must be marked and documented by photographs. Next, the human remains must be positively identified. The method used for identification is dictated to a great extent by the physical state of the remains. The methods at the disposal of the C/ME include tattoos, fingerprints, dental comparisons, medical implants, and DNA analysis. The third role of the C/ME is to determine the cause and manner of death in order to issue the certificate of death. In case of a terrorist attack, obviously the manner of death will be homicide. In non-criminal situations, it is conceivable that the manner of death could be ruled natural—or rarely suicide—although, undoubtedly, deaths occurring in such instances will almost always be categorized as accidental.

Once the identified remains have been located and the death certificate (DC) issued, the forensic epidemiologist would provide a detailed breakdown of the age, sex, race, cause of death, and also specify the methods used to identify the victims. A post-disaster analysis of the location and actions of the victims may offer meaningful and feasible suggestions designed to prevent similar types of deaths in the future.

The final role of the C/ME is to provide statistical and epidemiological data regarding physical evidence recovered during the postmortem investigation to various governmental investigative agencies. In non-criminal matters, similar information would be made available to private attorneys, insurance companies, and appropriate entities acting with the permission and legal authorization from the victims' families.

The following plan represents a suggested overall outline for C/MEs that could be implemented immediately after the occurrence of a disaster. All necessary planning and arrangements should be in place for rapid implementation and deployment.

Preamble

Current societal trends lend themselves to clustering of large groups of people whether it be in cities, buildings, or various modes of transportation, such as airplanes and trains. It is this frequent clustering that increases the probability of mass disasters.

When disasters occur involving multiple deaths, the C/ME must rapidly and accurately identify and determine a cause of death for all victims. These disasters are often complicated by fire, high-impact force, and the scattering of victims and their possessions. Accordingly, preplanned protocols for the recovery and processing of disaster fatalities are important and necessary to help relieve the extent to which a community's resources are strained during such situations.

Every metropolitan C/ME should have a plan that provides a high level of preparedness for their office to respond to disasters with fatalities within their jurisdiction and surrounding communities that may require assistance.

Section I. OPERATIONAL STRUCTURE

A. Administrative Division

The administrative component of the C/ME Office is responsible for the activation and overall coordination of office disaster activities.

1. The C/ME has overall administrative authority and responsibility. In addition, the C/ME has the following specific duties and responsibilities:

a. Acts as a direct liaison between the C/ME Office and the other responding agencies.

b. Makes personnel staffing assignments based on the size and location of the disaster.

c. Authorizes all C/ME Office press releases and interviews.

d. Serves as a member of the Human Factors Group for any transportation accident investigated by the National Transportation Safety Board.

e. Delegates any of the foregoing functions deemed appropriate.

2. The CHIEF DEPUTY (CD) assists the C/ME in the overall administration of that office. Additionally, this person has the following specific duties and responsibilities:

a. Discharges the duties of the C/ME in instances where he/she is unable to perform in his/her capacity.

b. Serves as Coordinator of the Disaster Operations Division.

c. Assumes any other duties and responsibilities which the C/ME deems necessary.

3. The SENIOR FORENSIC PATHOLOGIST has authority over all autopsy operations. Additionally, the Senior Forensic Pathologist has the following specific duties and responsibilities:

a. Discharges the duties of CD in instances where he/she is unable to perform in his/her capacity.

b. Makes staffing assignments for both the morgue and the temporary forensic area.

c. Assumes any other duties and responsibilities which the C/ME deems necessary.

4. The FISCAL/ADMINISTRATIVE ASSISTANT has general authority over the financial affairs of the C/ME Office, subject to the C/ME's approval. In addition to this financial authority, the Fiscal/Administrative Assistant has the following specific duties and responsibilities:

a. Maintains an account of the disaster expenditures and receipts of the C/ME Office

b. Maintains a record of the hours worked by all C/ME Office personnel during a disaster response.

c. In conjunction with the Chief Forensic Photographer, arranges for photographic and video documentation of disaster response activities. Note: This photography is for educational documentation and is independent of normal evidence photography.

d. Assumes any other duties and responsibilities which the C/ME deems necessary.

5. The PUBLIC INFORMATION SPOKESPERSON assists the C/ME in the preparation of press releases and interview information. In addition, the spokesperson has the following specific duties and responsibilities:

a. Prepares a media information sheet which describes the C/ME Office's role in a mass disaster and contains the names and titles of certain key contact officials in charge of various aspects of the C/ME's response (i.e., C/ME, CD, Senior Pathologist, Odontologist, and Anthropologist, and other ancillary forensic scientists).

b. Coordinates and compiles positive identification information for the C/ME.

c. Issues any press releases as directed by the C/ME.

d. Assumes any other duties and responsibilities which the C/ME deems necessary.

6. The Office or County SOLICITOR advises the C/ME on all legal matters which may arise in a disaster response by the C/ME's Office. Additionally, the Solicitor has the following duties and responsibilities:

a. Assists in the acquisition of antemortem medical and dental records when outside the jurisdiction of a C/ME's subpoena powers.

b. Evaluates specific methods employed in the disaster response to determine if proper chain of custody and documentation for all evidence is maintained.

c. Assumes any other duties and responsibilities which the C/ME deems necessary.

B. Disaster Operations Division

This division is responsible for handling all aspects of the C/ME's investigation for all fatalities resulting from a disaster.

1. The CD serves as coordinator of the Disaster Operations Division and has administrative responsibility over this division.

2. One Senior CD should serve as the office liaison.

3. The BODY RECOVERY SECTION is responsible for documenting the location of disaster fatalities and supervising their removal to the morgue facility.

a. Staffing for this section includes:

1.) One forensic pathologist or forensic anthropologist serves as section chief.

2.) RECOVERY TEAMS comprised of:

a.) 1 forensic pathologist.

b.) 1 forensic anthropologist.

c.) 1 forensic odontologist.

d.) 1 deputy.

e.) 3 military search and rescue personnel.

f.) 1 photographer.

b. Additional staff may be called in, as appropriate for the situation.

4. The SECURITY SECTION is responsible for providing controlled access to the morgue building, the temporary forensics area and the triage morgue.

Also, this section provides constant security over all personal effects obtained from disaster victims. Further, this section is responsible for scene security prior to the removal of fatalities.

    a. Staffing for this section includes:

        1.) Deputy Sheriffs.

        2.) County Police Officers with dog patrols (for scene security).

        3.) 1 CD serves as credentialing liaison.

    b. Additional staff may be called in, as appropriate and necessary for the situation.

5. The EXAMINATION AND IDENTIFICATION SECTION is responsible for obtaining antemortem and postmortem identification information and determining cause of death for all disaster fatalities.

    a. Staffing for this section includes:

        1.) The Senior Forensic Pathologist serves as section chief.

        2.) BODY TRACKING TEAMS comprised of:

            a.) 1 tracker for each 5 bodies.

        3.) PERSONAL EFFECTS TEAMS comprised of:

            a.) 1 senior deputy CD (team leader).

            b.) 1 deputy CD

            c.) 1 deputy sheriff.

        4.) IMAGING TEAMS comprised of:

            a.) 1 forensic photographer (chief photographer - head, photography unit).

            b.) 1 radiologist (head, radiology unit).

            c.) 1 autopsy radiology technician (radiology unit).

            d.) 1 radiation health specialist (for monitoring radiation exposure levels).

        5.) FINGERPRINT TEAMS comprised of:

            a.) 1 latent fingerprint examiner.

            b.) Federal Bureau of Investigation (FBI) Fingerprint Disaster Squad and/or State Police Latent Fingerprint Unit.

        6.) FORENSIC DENTISTRY TEAMS comprised of:

            a.) The chief forensic odontologist (team leader).

        7.) FORENSIC PATHOLOGY TEAMS comprised of:

            a.) The senior forensic pathologist (team leader).

            b.) 3 autopsy technicians.

        8.) FORENSIC ANTHROPOLOGY TEAMS comprised of:

            a.) 2 forensic anthropologists.

        9.) FORENSIC LABORATORY TEAMS comprised of:

            a.) 2 laboratory sample "runners".

> b.) Members of the County Department of Forensic Laboratories.
>
> Note: All lab tests will be performed in the usual Department of Forensic Labs facility.

b. Additional staff may be called in, as appropriate for the situation.

6. The RECORDS AND COMPUTER SERVICES SECTION is responsible for maintaining orderly files of all identification and pathololgic examination information. This section is also responsible for coordinating the status of all identification information for a given victim, as well as the preparation of all disaster victim death certificates

> a. Staffing for this section includes:
>> 1.) 1 senior deputy CD serves as section chief.
>> 2.) 1 deputy CD.
>> 3.) 1 computer operator.
>> 4.) 2 medical secretaries.
>
> b. Additional staff may be called in, as appropriate for the situation.

7. The FUNERAL DIRECTOR RELATIONS SECTION is responsible for coordinating the embalming and casketing of all disaster victims, and the proper release and shipping of victims from the temporary forensics area.

> a. Staffing for this section includes:
>> 1.) 1 senior deputy DC serves as section chief.
>> 2.) 2 deputy CD.
>
> b. Additional staff may be called in, as appropriate for the situation.

C.   Standard Operations Division

This division is responsible for handling all aspects of the C/ME's Office normal functions, while the office is occupied with a disaster response.

1. The ASSISTANT CHIEF CD serves as coordinator of the Standard Operations Division and has administrative responsibility over this division.

2. The INVESTIGATIONS SECTION is responsible for determining whether the C/ME has jurisdiction over any reported deaths, and if so, then this section is responsible for removing these bodies to the C/ME's Office.

> a. Staffing for this section includes:
>> 1.)   1 senior deputy CD serves as section chief.
>> 2.)   3 deputy CD.
>
> b. Additional staff may be called in, as appropriate for the situation.

3. The AUTOPSY SECTION is responsible for performing the pathological examination and determining identity for bodies brought to the C/ME facility by the Investigations Division.

> a. Staffing for this section includes:
>> 1.) 1 associate pathologist serves as section chief.

2.) 2 autopsy technicians.

b. Additional staff may be called in, as appropriate for the situation.

4. The MEDICAL RECORDS SECTION is responsible for maintaining files on all standard cases coming through the C/ME's Office, including autopsy protocols and death certificates.

a. Staffing for this section includes:

1.) The assistant CD serves as section chief.

2.) 2 medical secretaries.

b. Additional staff may be called in, as appropriate and necessary for the situation.

Section II. NOTIFICATION AND RESPONSE PROCEDURES

A. Contacting C/ME Office during a disaster.

1. During disasters with eleven (11) or more fatalities, it is anticipated that the C/ME will be notified via the standard telephone or radio methods and by an authorized law enforcement or emergency management agency.

2. Agencies contacting the C/ME will give the following preliminary information to the C/ME deputy who will complete the DISASTER NOTIFICATION INFORMATION (DNI) FORM:

a. Name, agency and phone number of caller.

b. Nature of incident.

c. Estimated number of fatalities.

d. Location of incident (including emergency map grid number for aviation disasters).

e. Time incident occurred.

f. Contact person at scene.

g. Best route of entry to scene.

h. Any special hazards at the disaster scene or in the handling of bodies.

B. Notification Sequence

The following procedure is applicable after a disaster incident with 10 or more fatalities is reported to the C/ME.

1. After completion of the DNI form, the deputy receiving notification will inform the Senior CD on duty of the situation.

2. If necessary, the Senior Deputy will call back the reporting agency or individual to determine the scope of the situation, and obtain any additional specific details.

3. The Senior Deputy will then contact the Chief CD for instructions on response.

4. The Chief Deputy will send a C/ME ambulance and 2 deputies to the scene to advise the Chief Deputy of the situation, and to ensure that evidence

preserving guidelines concerning deceased individuals are being followed.

5. The Chief Deputy will notify the C/ME and determine the appropriate level of response.

6. At the direction of the C/ME or CD, the Senior Deputy on duty will contact specific C/ME personnel to report for duty, as the need dictates.

  a. These should include:

    1.) All senior deputies and supervisors.

    2.) All forensic pathologists.

    3.) The Forensic Odontologist.

    4.) The Forensic Anthropologist.

    5.) Off-duty deputies and other personnel, as needed.

7. C/ME personnel requested to report for emergency service will report directly to the C/ME's Office, unless instructed otherwise.

  a. Do not park in the drive-ways of the building. Alternate parking will be arranged for all personnel.

  b. All personnel should carry their C/ME Office Identification Card and badge.

8. At the direction of the C/ME or CD, the following INTERAGENCY NOTIFICATIONS will be made as the need dictates:

  a. County Sheriff's Office. For building/scene security, vehicles and two-way walkie-talkie radios for C/ME Office personnel.

  b. County Department of Forensic Labs.

  c. County Emergency Management Office. For any supplies, equipment, facilities and information needed.

  d. County Funeral Directors Association. For establishing funeral director policies implemented by the C/ME during a disaster.

  e. American Red Cross. For emergency Social Service Disaster Workers to assist with interviewing possible victim's families, and providing them psychological support.

  f. County Mental Health/Mental Retardation Unit. For mental health counselors to assist with interviewing possible victim's families, and providing psychological support.

  g. County Police. For additional two-way walkie-talkie radios.

  h. County Department of Aviation. For aviation disasters or at the request of military search and rescue personnel.

  i. Federal Bureau of Investigation (FBI). For activation of the FBI Fingerprint Disaster Squad.

  j. County Critical Incident Stress Debriefing (CISD) Team. For worker counseling during and after the disaster incident.

k. National Disaster Medical System (NDMS). For regionalized disaster medical evacuation. Program administered by Veteran's Administration, with Pittsburgh as a regional evacuation site.

C. Response Sequence

1. After the appropriate notifications are made, appropriate C/ME personnel will be shuttled to the scene in Sheriff's Office vehicles.

2. All responding C/ME personnel will be briefed on any special scene hazards, or hazards in the handling of bodies.

3. Non-uniformed C/ME personnel responding to a GPIA incident in other than marked Coroner or Sheriff's vehicles will be issued the "Broken Wing" Emergency Pass (one per vehicle).

4. One Senior Deputy will report to the County Emergency Operations Center and stand by.

5. When responding to an airport incident, C/ME personnel will report to the Airport Field Maintenance Building from which they will be escorted to the scene.

Section III. DISASTER PROCEDURES/PROTOCOLS

A. Chief Deputy (CD)

1. Will take charge of C/ME operations at the disaster scene.

2. If more than 50 fatalities, he/she will establish the location for a temporary forensics area, with the proper equipment and supplies.

3. The Chief Deputy will coordinate obtaining a list of possible victims, which is necessary for identification purposes.

B. Disaster Operations Division

Scene C/ME operations will commence after the scene is secured and all EMS rescue efforts have concluded.

1. Body Recovery Section

a. Body recovery will not be conducted at night unless extenuating circumstances exist.

b. Incident sites and perimeters will be guarded by both police and dog patrols to prevent both potential looting and any wild animals from disturbing evidence. Sites will also be fully lighted at night.

c. Police or sheriff's personnel will be assigned to guard the triage staging morgue to prevent looting.

d. Caution, as appropriate for the situation, will be taken at the scene and in the handling of all remains.

e. The forensic pathologist or forensic anthropologist in charge of this section will assemble the Recovery Teams.

f. The anthropologist will obtain a blueprint or map of the incident site and establish an appropriate gridding system.

g. Overall scene photographs will be taken prior to body recovery.

h. When remains are discovered, the area will be searched for all body parts and personal effects, a BODY RECOVERY FORM will be completed, the location will be marked with a flag (or other appropriate device), as well as on the site map, the body will be PHOTOGRAPHED and then placed in a pre-numbered disaster bag.

i. Bodies will then be removed to the staging morgue by fire and/or military personnel, with 4 or 6 man carries to minimize fatigue.

j. Commingled remains will be sorted as much as possible by the recovery team prior to removal.

k. If there are more than 15 fatalities, then a refrigerated truck will be obtained for body storage and transport to the morgue facility.

2. Security Section

a. Initially, must provide security to the incident site and staging morgue, as described above.

b. Deputy Sheriffs will seal access to the C/ME Office and the temporary morgue to authorized personnel only.

c. A deputy will be assigned to both the temporary morgue and the C/ME Office to assist the deputy sheriffs in credentialing all those individuals who desire entrance.

3. Examination and Identification Section (MORGUE PROCESSING)

a. For incidents with less than 51 fatalities, all bodies will be examined and released from the morgue building. Otherwise, all examinations will occur at the designated temporary forensic area established in proximity to the disaster site.

b. Each body, as it is removed from the storage area, will be assigned a TRACKER, who will remain with the body through all aspects of the processing. The Tracker will also maintain possession of the case file for the body from each exam station, with the BODY TRACKING FORM.

c. Bodies brought to the disaster morgue will be PHOTOGRAPHED upon arrival with the following views:

    1.) Full body - Polaroid.

    3.) Full body - Color Slide.

d. Co-mingled remains will be further sorted, if necessary, by the anthropologist. Additionally, the ANTHROPOLOGY TEAM will examine all bodies and body parts to obtain preliminary identification information (e.g., age, race and sex).

e. A postmortem case file will be created for each body or body fragment.

f. All bodies will then be completely PHOTOGRAPHED with the following views:

　　1.) Identification.

　　2.) Full body with personal effects displayed on chest.

　　3.) Any other views deemed appropriate by the pathologist.

　　Note: These photographs should be color slides with at least 1 Polaroid "back-up" for each view.

g. PERSONAL EFFECTS will be inventoried, documented and then stored in the guarded, established location.

h. The next station is FULL-BODY X-RAY FILMS for all bodies.

　　1.) The X-ray area will be separated by a 20 foot perimeter for all other morgue activities.

　　2.) The radiation health specialist will monitor exposure levels for all individuals in this station.

i. The bodies will next be FINGERPRINTED. Footprints may also be taken if deemed appropriate.

j. The bodies then go to the FORENSIC DENTISTRY STATION, where they undergo the following procedures:

　　1.) Access to the dentition.

　　2.) X-ray films and photographs of the teeth and supporting structures.

　　3.) Dental examination and charting.

k. Bodies are then autopsied by the FORENSIC PATHOLOGY TEAM following standard C/ME Office procedures.

　　1.) At the discretion of the C/ME and/or the Senior Pathologist, a decision will be made as to which bodies necessitate full autopsies.

　　2.) The LABORATORY "RUNNERS" will pick up lab samples after they are obtained during the autopsy.

　　3.) NOTE: In transportation accidents, the National Transportation Safety Board requires specific laboratory tests and thorough autopsy protocols on all crew members. Consult the NTSB Human factors Chairman for specific information.

　　4.) All bodies will then be EMBALMED and CASKETED prior to release.

　　　　a.) See the Funeral Director Relations Section.

4. Records and Computer Services Section

　　a. Members of this section will first work with Red Cross and County MH/MR personnel to obtain antemortem identification information

from families of possible victims using the DISASTER VICTIM IDEN-
TIFICATION INFORMATION form.

b. Section members will then work to obtain these records.

    1.) Local records will be obtained by deputy sheriffs using C/ME
subpoenas.

    2.) Non-local records will be obtained by faxed subpoena followed
up by mailed original. These records will be forwarded via special
disaster account, established with an overnight express mail service.
Note: The Solicitor will assist in obtaining all required records not
covered by a C/ME Subpoena.

c. An antemortem case file will be created for each possible victim.

d. There will be 7 files established as follows:

    1.) Male antemortem records (filed alphabetically by last name).

    2.) Female antemortem records (filed alphabetically by last name).

    3.) Male postmortem records (filed numerically by case number).

    4.) Female postmortem records (filed numerically by case num-
ber).

    5.) Fragmented postmortem remains records (filed numerically by
case number).

    6.) Male positive identification (filed alphabetically by last name
and cross-referenced by case number).

    7.) Female positive identification (filed alphabetically by last name
and cross referenced by case number).

e. HAND SORTED IDENTIFICATION (FOR LESS THAN 50 VIC-
TIMS)

    1.) After 50% of the composite records are completed, the ante-
mortem records will be placed on long tables, grouped by sex and
fragmented remains.

    2.) Postmortem records will then be checked for matches in identi-
fication information.

f. COMPUTER ASSISTED IDENTIFICATION (FOR MORE THAN
50 VICTIMS)

    1.) CAPMI (or Match-Pics/Tooth-Pics) will be used in incidents
where there are more than 50 victims, OR where there are many
fragmented remains with less than 50 victims.

    2.) Optical mark reader (OMR) forms will be read into the CAPMI
database in groups of 10 or more. Antemortem and postmortem
forms must be entered separately.

    3.) When 75% of the records are entered into the database, a search
will be made for the top 3 matches for each record to commence
identification.

4.) The suggested matches will then be checked by hand to determine whether a positive match exists.

g. There will be a log book which contains a column for date, time, type of record and person who signed out the record. An entry should be made each time a record is signed out and again on the same line when the record is returned.

1.) An effort should be made to limit the number of personnel who have access to the records.

h. Whenever records are returned, all file contents will be verified by the list on the outside of the envelope.

i. VICTIM IDENTIFICATION

1.) Once positive identifications are made, through as many methods as possible, an IDENTIFICATION SUMMARY FORM will be completed.

2.) Then a State Death Certificate will be completed per standard C/ME's Office procedure.

3.) The identification information will then be relayed to the C/ME and the Public Information Spokesperson for next-of-kin notification and media release.

j. All AUTOPSY REPORTS will be prepared by the Standard Operations Division Medical Records Section (see below).

k. After the completion of the identification and examination, all original records and X-ray films will be duplicated and returned to their sources with a statement regarding whether a positive identification was obtained.

5. Funeral Director Relations Section

a. In conjunction with the Examination and Identification Section and the County Funeral Directors Association, arrangements will be made to EMBALM and CASKET all bodies at the morgue facility.

b. In cooperation with the C/ME, funeral director representatives will work with next-of-kin to make shipping and/or burial arrangements.

c. If necessary, a request will be made to the State Office of Vital Statistics to supply a representative for expediting out-of-state body shipping requests.

6. In the interest of health, efficiency and accuracy, all Division personnel should take a half-hour break every 3 hours plus meal breaks, and they should not work more than 14 to 16 hours in a 24 hour period.

C. Standard Operations Division

1. The Assistant Chief Deputy will organize all sections in this division to examine and release the bodies currently at the C/ME's Office, as quickly as possible.

2. Investigations Section

    a. The protocol for this section is the same as for standard C/ME's Office procedure.

    b. Efforts will be made, when appropriate, to release bodies directly from the scene.

    c. Efforts will also be made to minimize time involved with body pick-up efforts by grouping trips.

3. Autopsy Section

    a. The protocol for this section is the same as for standard C/ME's Office procedure.

    b. Examinations will be completed as quickly as possible, so that personnel will be available to back-up the disaster operations personnel.

    c. In cooperation with the funeral directors, bodies at the morgue will be released as quickly as possible so that a maximum amount of storage space will be available.

4. Medical Records Section

    a. The protocol for this section is the same as for standard C/ME's Office procedure.

    b. Autopsy reports will be prepared with the following priority:

        1.) Disaster victim crew members (if disaster results from a transportation accident).

        2.) Homicide cases.

        3.) Remainder of disaster victims.

        4.) All other C/ME Office cases.

5. All questions regarding the disaster will be referred to the C/ME or Public Information Spokesperson.

6. In the interest of health, efficiency and accuracy, all Division personnel should take a half-hour break every 3 hours plus meal breaks, and they should not work more than 14 to 16 hours in a 24 hour period.

D. Fiscal/Administrative Assistant

1. Will maintain a detailed log of all expenditures associated with the disaster response. This includes additional standard operations expenses.

2. Will maintain the hourly work records of every C/ME employee during the disaster response.

3. In cooperation with the Chief Forensic Photographer, arrangements will be made to document the C/ME's Office response with both photographs and videotape.

E. Public Information Spokesperson (or C/ME)

1. At the beginning of the disaster response, all the news media will be informed of the C/ME contact person for information. This will be the only person whom the press will deal with throughout the disaster response.

2. Be honest and correct misinformation (e.g., number of fatalities) with what is currently known. This honesty will go a long way to achieving the desired cooperation.

3. Make sure that the press understands that identification information will not be released until the notification of next-of-kin.

4. Make no speculations as to the cause of the incident. That is someone else's job, and such questions should be referred to that individual.

Section IV. EQUIPMENT AND SUPPLIES

A. Pre-incident equipment preparation and storage.

    1. Equipment and supplies from standard C/ME storage will be diverted for disaster response.

        a. The equipment and supplies used must be thoroughly documented for reimbursement purposes.

        b. "Rescue 12" at the local International Airport has some limited C/ME's Office supplies including:

            1.) Body bags.

            2.) Body parts bags.

            3.) Body location flags.

        Note: These supplies are located on the back right and left shelves on Rescue 12.

    2. Additional equipment, supplies and refrigerated trucks will be arranged through the County Emergency Management Office. Such a request will be coordinated through the Senior Deputy liaison at the Emergency Operations Center.

B. Uniforms

    1. All C/ME personnel will wear their standard uniform.

Note: Those individuals working with the disaster operations should dress appropriately for the weather, as much time will be spent outside.

    2. It is advised that disaster operations personnel wear boots to protect feet from injury due to moving gurneys.

    3. All members of the Imaging Team will wear radiation monitoring badges at all times.

    4. Supervisory personnel from C/ME will wear some indicator to rapidly distinguish them in a crowd (e.g., arm band).

Note: Arm bands can also be used to distinguish different teams of C/ME personnel at the disaster scene.

    5. All C/ME personnel will carry their office identification card and badge for credentialing both at the disaster scene and at the morgue building.

Section V. POST-INCIDENT PROTOCOLS

A. Psychological Debriefing

It is recognized that mass disaster work is quite stressful and that this stress has different effects on various individuals.

1. The County Critical Incident Stress Debriefing Team or a clinical psychologist and/or psychiatrist should be available both during and after an incident, to speak individually with C/ME personnel who would like to discuss any concerns or difficulties which they have.

NOTE: Debriefing will not occur until after the disaster response.

2. Individuals assigned to the disaster response will receive a pre-incident briefing prior to their scene assignment.

3. Within 72 hours after completion of a C/ME disaster response, all personnel will attend either a group or individual debriefing session to ensure that appropriate coping strategies are being utilized.

4. Any individual with longer-term needs will be referred to the appropriate follow-up professional.

5. Any person with a stress response during the disaster will be reassigned to the Standard Operations Division, as is deemed appropriate by the C/ME or Chief Deputy.

B. Operational Debriefing

1. After an ACCO disaster response, all personnel who worked in the response will participate in a preliminary operational debriefing meeting.

a. This meeting will consider at least the following:

1.) Office activation and response procedures.

2.) Office disaster operations.

3.) Office standard operations.

4.) Communication.

5.) Body recovery, identification and examination procedures.

6.) Recommendations to improve future responses.

2. After the preliminary debriefing, the C/ME administrative personnel will have a detailed debriefing meeting.

a. This debriefing will consider at least the following:

1.) Results from preliminary debriefing

2.) Financial costs for entire response (see below).

Section VI. TRAINING PROTOCOLS

A. New C/ME Personnel

1. New Personnel starting at C/ME will receive as part of their general orientation, information on the C/ME's Office disaster preparedness and response procedures including:

a. An overview of C/ME disaster organization.

.b. A copy of the written C/ME disaster policies for review.

c. Orientation on the use of the airport emergency grid maps.

NOTE: These maps are located in each ambulance, in the deputies' room, and in the senior deputies' office.

d. Viewing the office's disaster training videotapes.

B. On-going Training

1. C/ME will have an office-wide disaster drill at least once a year. These can be either table-top or actual drills.

NOTE: The scenarios can vary as can the scope of each drill (e.g., autopsy procedures, body recovery procedures with a plane crash, dealing with special scene and body hazards, etc.).

2. Special consideration will be given to incorporating the outside agencies with which the C/ME has standing arrangements for assistance during disasters.

Section VII. APPENDICES

A. C/ME Disaster Organizational Diagram

B. Activation Diagram

C. Body Flow Diagram

D. Disaster Morgue Diagram

E. Identification Processing Diagram

Appendix A

C/ME's Office
Disaster Operations Organizational Diagram

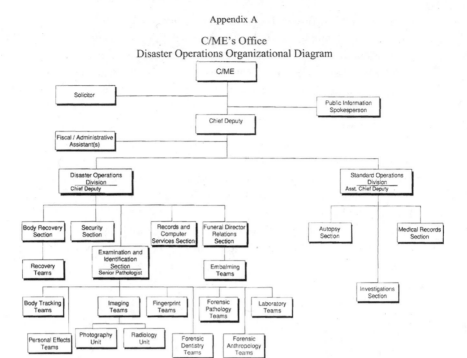

Appendix B
C/ME
Activation Diagram

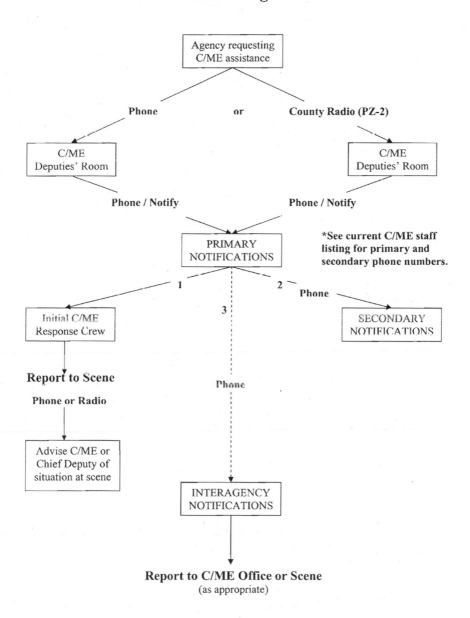

Appendix C
Body Flow for the Mass Disaster Morgue

1. Log-In Remains
2. Personal Effects Inventory
3. General Body Photography
4. Preliminary Anthropology Examination
5. Full Body X-Ray Films
6. Fingerprint Examination
7. Oral Access
8. Dental X-Ray Films and Dental Photography
9. Dental Examination
10. Pathology Examination (Including Anthropology Exam and Laboratory Analysis)
11. Issue Death Certificate
12. Embalm & Casket Body for Release to Funeral Director

Appendix D

Typical Disaster Morgue Layout
(example for aircraft hangar set-up)

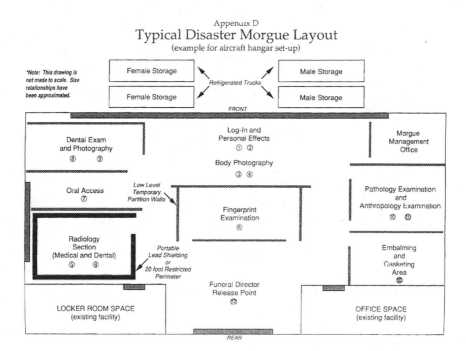

*Note: This drawing is not made to scale. Size relationships have been approximated.

Female Storage

Female Storage

Refrigerated Trucks

Male Storage

Male Storage

FRONT

Dental Exam and Photography
⑧   ⑨

Log-In and Personal Effects
① ②

Body Photography
③ ④

Morgue Management Office

Oral Access
⑦

Low Level Temporary Partition Walls

Fingerprint Examination
⑥

Pathology Examination and Anthropology Examination
⑩   ⑪

Radiology Section (Medical and Dental)
⑤   ⑧

Portable Lead Shielding or 20 foot Restricted Perimeter

Embalming and Casketing Area
⑫

Funeral Director Release Point
⑬

LOCKER ROOM SPACE (existing facility)

OFFICE SPACE (existing facility)

REAR

Appendix E
Disaster Victim Identification Processing

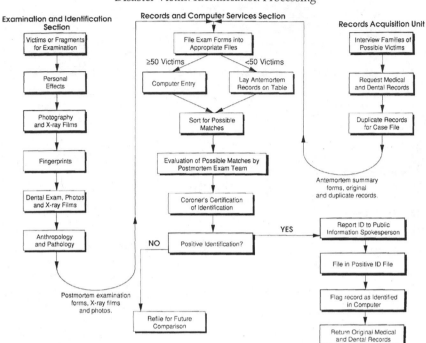

Chapter 7

Medical Examiners, Coroners, and Biological Terrorism: A Guidebook for Surveillance and Case Management

Kurt B. Nolte, M.D.,[1-2*] Randy L. Hanzlick, M.D.,[2-3†] Daniel C. Payne, Ph.D.,[4] Andrew T. Kroger, M.D.[5] William R. Oliver, M.D.,[6*] Andrew M. Baker, M.D.,[7*] Dennis E. McGowan,[3*] Joyce L. DeJong, D.O.,[8*] Michael R. Bell, M.D.,[7] Jeannette Guarner, M.D.,[9] Wun-Ju Shieh, M.D., Ph.D.,[9] and Sherif R. Zaki, M.D., Ph.D.[9]

The material in this report originated in the Epidemiology Program Office, Stephen B. Thacker, M.D., M.Sc., Director; the Division of Public Health Surveillance and Informatics, Richard Hopkins, M.D., M.S.P.H., Acting Director; the National Center for Infectious Diseases, James M. Hughes, M.D., Director; and the Division of Viral and Rickettsial Diseases, James LeDuc, Ph.D., Sc.D., Director.

Summary

Medical examiners and coroners (ME/Cs) are essential public health partners for terrorism preparedness and response. These medicolegal investigators support both public health and public safety functions and investigate deaths that are sudden, suspicious, violent, unattended, and unexplained. Medicolegal autopsies are essential for making organism-specific diagnoses in deaths caused by biologic terrorism. This report has been created to (1) help public health officials understand the role of ME/Cs in biologic terrorism surveillance and response efforts and (2) provide ME/Cs with the detailed information required to build capacity for biologic terrorism preparedness in a public health context. This report provides background information regarding biologic terrorism, possible biologic agents, and the consequent clinicopathologic diseases, autopsy procedures, and diagnostic tests as well as a description of biosafety risks and standards for autopsy precautions. ME/Cs' vital role in terrorism surveillance requires consistent standards for collecting, analyzing, and disseminating data. Familiarity with the operational, jurisdictional, and evidentiary concerns involving biologic terrorism-related death investigation is critical to both ME/Cs and public health authorities. Managing terrorism-associated fatalities can be expensive and can overwhelm the existing capacity of ME/Cs. This report describes federal resources for funding and reimbursement for ME/C preparedness and response activities and the limited support capacity of the federal Disaster Mortuary Operational Response Team. Standards for communication are critical in responding to any emergency situation. This report, which is a joint collaboration between CDC and the National Association of Medical Examiners (NAME), describes the relationship between ME/Cs and public health departments, emergency management agencies, emergency operations centers, and the Incident Command System.

Introduction

Terrorist events in recent years have heightened awareness of the risk of terrorist acts involving unconventional agents, including biologic and chemical weapons. The need for terrorism preparedness and planning for response at multiple levels is now recognized, including planning and response by medical examiners, coroners (ME/Cs), and the medicolegal death-investigation system.

Federal, state, and local agencies have developed plans to detect and respond to terrorism by using a multidisciplinary approach that requires active participation of health-care providers, law enforcement, and public health and safety staff. Because ME/Cs have expertise in disease surveillance, diagnosis, deceased body handling, and evidence collection, they serve a vital role in terrorism preparedness and response. ME/Cs should ensure that their role in surveillance for unusual deaths—and response to known terrorist events—is a critical part of the multidisciplinary response team. Terrorism-related drills and practical exercises conducted by public health, law enforcement, and public safety agencies should include training on postmortem operations and services.

This report, prepared as a joint effort between the National Association of Medical Examiners (NAME) and CDC, is a first step in providing specific guidance to ME/C death investigators and public health officials. This report can help bridge gaps that exist in local terrorism preparedness and response planning. By discussing the substantial contributions of ME/Cs, this report can also serve as a foundation for identifying the needs of medicolegal death-investigation systems and for addressing those needs through adequate training and funding.

This report provides guidance, identifies support services and resources, and discusses the roles and responsibilities of ME/Cs and affiliated personnel in recognizing and responding to potential biologic terrorism events. Certain questions being asked by ME/Cs and their public health partners are answered in this report, including the following:

- What are the likely biologic agents to be encountered?
- What are the expected case fatality rates and time courses for the different agents?
- What types of ongoing surveillance are needed to detect potential biologic terrorism-associated incidents?
- What protective equipment and procedures are needed to ensure the safety of death investigation and forensic pathology personnel?
- What are the appropriate facilities in which to perform postmortem examinations in cases of suspected biologic terrorism?
- What are the best methods for ensuring biosafety during the mortuary process?
- How will hospitals, emergency personnel, health departments, and ME/Cs effectively communicate during a suspected or known incident?
- How will local ME/C systems interact with the Federal Bureau of Investigation (FBI) and other investigative agencies?
- What is the minimum extent of examination that will be required? For example, will a complete autopsy be required in every suspected case to support the criminal justice process?
- What pathology-specific tests are available; which ones are the best to use to make an accurate diagnosis; and which ones are the best for making a rapid diagnosis?
- Which laboratories are best suited to perform the necessary postmortem testing?
- What role does public health law play in determining disposition of bodies?
- What legal authority do public health agencies have in making decisions during potential biologic terrorism events?
- What federal resources are available to assist ME/Cs?

Background
Medicolegal death investigators

CDC has identified medicolegal death investigators (i.e., ME/Cs) as essential partners in terrorism preparedness and response.[1] This report is designed to assist ME/Cs and their public health partners in developing appropriate capacity for recognizing and responding to deaths that are potentially a consequence of biologic terrorism.

The organization of medicolegal death investigative systems within the United States varies by state.[2] As ME/Cs and public health and public safety departments prepare to respond to terrorism-associated events, each state should consider how its medicolegal death investigation system is organized. These systems can be medical examiner-based (twenty-one states and the District of Columbia), coroner-based (ten states), or both (nineteen states) (Figure 7.1). Typically, coroners are elected lay persons who use medical personnel to assist in death investigation and autopsy performance. Medical examiners are usually appointed physicians and pathologists who have received special training in death investigation and forensic pathology.

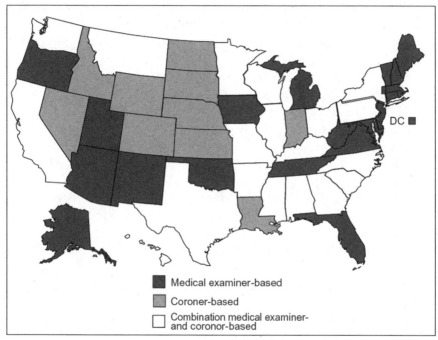

Figure 7.1 *Medicolegal death investigative systems in the United States*

Medicolegal death investigation systems can be either centralized (i.e., investigations emanate from one state-level office) or decentralized (i.e., investigations are conducted in more than one regional-, county-, or city-based office). A total of twenty-three states plus the District of Columbia have centralized systems; twenty-seven states are decentralized. States with medical examiner systems might have a state-based medical examiner office, and also have county-level autonomous medical examiner offices that perform their own autopsies and manage their own data and administrative systems.

ME/C offices can also vary in their organizational position within the government. ME/C offices might be a component of the public health department or the public safety department, or be independent of other government agencies.

All types of medicolegal death investigation systems should be considered when determining the roles, responsibilities, and participation of ME/Cs in a jurisdiction's terrorism preparedness and response plans.

Biologic terrorism

Biologic terrorism is defined as "the use or threatened use of biologic agents against a person, group, or larger population to create fear or illnesses for purposes of intimidation, gaining an advantage, interruption of normal activities, or ideologic activities. The resultant reaction is dependent on the actual event and the population involved and can vary from a minimal effect to disruption of ongoing activities and emotional reaction, illness, or death."[3] In the United States in 1984, an outbreak of terrorism-related Salmonella dysentery caused 715 persons to become ill, but no fatalities resulted.[4] In 2001, the intentional distribution of anthrax spores through the U.S. Postal Service resulted in five deaths from inhalational anthrax.[5-8] MEs were critical members of the response team during the anthrax outbreak, performing autopsies on each fatality to confirm the cause of death as anthrax and to identify the manner of death as homicide.

ME/Cs have state statutory authority to investigate deaths that are sudden, suspicious, violent, unattended, or unexplained;[9] therefore, these investigators have a role in recognizing and reporting fatal outbreaks, including those that are possibly terrorism-related, and a role in responding to a known terrorist event.[10-12] Deaths of persons at home or away from health-care facilities fall under the jurisdiction and surveillance of medicolegal death investigators,[13] who often identify infectious diseases that are not terrorism-related. For example, in 1993, MEs recognized an outbreak of hantavirus pulmonary syndrome, a disease with symptoms that can mimic terrorism-related illnesses.[14] Deaths of patients in hospitals can also fall under medicolegal jurisdiction if the patient dies precipitously before an accurate diagnosis is made or if a public health concern exists.[10] Fatalities caused by known terrorist events are homicides and therefore fall under the statutory jurisdiction of ME/Cs.

Risk assessment for potential biologic terrorism is an uncertain process. Hypothetical terrorism scenarios can involve a limited number of cases or millions of cases, with proportionate numbers of fatalities. For example, in 2002, the Dark Winter smallpox exercise included in the scenario 3 million fourth-generation cases of smallpox and approximately 1 million deaths.[15] In 2000, the TOPOFF (Top Officials) plague exercise included in the scenario 2,000 fatalities in a one-week period.[16] Given such possibilities if a biologic terrorist event occurred, ME/Cs should proactively identify appropriate resources and links to the public health, emergency response, healthcare, and law enforcement communities. With appropriate resources and links, ME/Cs can assist with surveillance for infectious disease deaths possibly caused by terrorism and provide confirmatory diagnoses and evidence in deaths clearly linked to terrorism. Conversely, public health agencies should recognize ME/Cs as a vital part of the public health system and keep them informed of infectious disease outbreaks occurring in their jurisdictions so that they are better able to recognize related fatalities. Additionally, public health agencies should provide ME/Cs with appropriate resources to enhance their surveillance and response capacities for terrorism.

An ME/C's principal diagnostic tool is the autopsy. This procedure enables pathologists to identify the dead, observe the condition of the body, and reach conclusions regarding the cause and manner of death. Autopsies are valuable in diagnosing unrecognized infections, evaluating therapy, understanding the pathogenesis and route of infection for uncommon or emerging infections, and developing evidence for subsequent legal proceedings.[10,17] In 1979, an anthrax outbreak occurred that was associated with an unintentional release of spores from a bioweapons factory in the Soviet city of Sverdlovsk; pathologists used autopsies to identify the cause of death as anthrax and the route of infection as inhalation.[18] In a 1945 smallpox outbreak, autopsy pathologists, rather than clinicians, were the physicians who recognized the sentinel case.[19]

Probable Biologic Terrorism Agents, Diseases, and Diagnostic Tests
Agent categories
In this report, the list of potential biologic terrorism agents has been prioritized on the basis of the risk to national security (Box 7.1).[1] Biologic agents are classified as high-risk, or Category A, because they can (1) be easily disseminated or transmitted person to person; (2) cause high mortality, with potential for major public health impact; (3) might cause public panic and social disruption; or (4) require special action for public health preparedness. The second highest priority, or Category B, agents include those that (1) are moderately easy to disseminate; (2) cause moderate morbidity and low mortality; or (3) require enhanced disease surveillance. The third highest priority, or Category C, agents include emerging pathogens that can be engineered for future mass dissemination because of (1) availability; (2) ease of production and dissemination; or (3) potential for high morbidity and mortality and major health impact.

Recognizing pathologic features of different biologic agents is important, as demonstrated by the inhalational and cutaneous anthrax cases that occurred in the United States during 2001.[5,8,20–23] The autopsy of the index patient was performed to determine how the person had acquired anthrax (cutaneous, gastrointestinal, or inhalational). After inhalational anthrax was diagnosed, public health officials were able to better define potential sources of the airborne *Bacillus anthracis* spores.

Box 7.1
Classification of Biologic Terrorism Agents

Category A Agents
- Variola major (smallpox)
- *Bacillus anthracis* (anthrax)
- *Yersinia pestis* (plague)
- *Clostridium botulinum* toxin (botulism)
- *Francisella tularensis* (tularemia)
- Hemorrhagic fever viruses, including
     - Filoviruses including Ebola and Marburg hemorrhagic fever
     - Arenaviruses, including Lassa (Lassa fever) and Junin (Argentine hemorrhagic fever) and related viruses

Category B Agents
- *Coxiella burnetii* (Q fever)
- *Brucella* species (brucellosis)
- *Burkholderia mallei* (glanders)
- Alphaviruses including Venezuelan encephalomyelitis and eastern and western equine encephalomyelitis viruses
- Ricin toxin from *Ricinus communis* (castor beans)
- Epsilon toxin of *Clostridium perfringens*
- *Staphylococcus* enterotoxin B
- Food- and waterborne pathogens
     - *Salmonella* species
     - *Shigella dysenteriae*
     - *Escherichia coli* O157:H7
     - *Vibrio cholerae*
     - *Cryptosporidium parvum*

Category C Agents
- Nipah virus
- Hantaviruses
- Tickborne hemorrhagic fever viruses
- Tickborne encephalitis viruses
- Yellow fever virus
- Multidrug-resistant *Mycobacterium tuberculosis*

Diagnostic tests

If possible, given the constraints of case volume and biosafety concerns, complete autopsies with histologic sampling of multiple organs should be performed in deaths potentially caused by infections with biologic terrorism agents. Autopsy diagnostic procedures for the Category A agents include microscopic examination, combined with the collection of specimens for additional tests that will aid in determining a definitive organism-specific diagnosis. Blood, cerebrospinal fluid, and tissue samples or swabs should be placed in transport media that will allow bacterial and viral isolation. Serum should be collected for serologic and biologic assays. Tissue samples should be frozen for polymerase chain reaction (PCR). Tissue samples should also be placed in electron microscopy fixative (glutaraldehyde). Microscopic examination of formalin-fixed, paraffin-embedded tissues stained with hematoxylin and eosin (H&E) is essential to characterizing the patterns of tissue damage defining a syndrome and establishes a list of possible microorganisms in the differential diagnosis. To enhance surveillance for these conditions, a matrix of potential pathology-based syndromes has been developed to guide autopsy pathologists in recognizing potential cases.[24] Special stains (e.g., tissue Gram and silver impregnation stains [Steiner's or Warthin-Starry]), can be helpful in identifying bacterial agents. Additionally, specific immunohistochemical (IHC) and direct fluorescent assays (DFA) for the Category A terrorism agents have been developed and are available at CDC.† These tests can be performed on formalin-fixed tissues. Clinical and pathologic characteristics of the Category A agents and corresponding diagnostic methods are summarized in this report (Tables 7.1 and 7.2).

Table 7.1
Selected Epidemiologic Characteristics of Illnesses
Caused by Category A Biologic Agents*

Disease	Incubation period	Duration of illness	Case fatality rates
Inhalational anthrax	1–6 days	3–5 days	Untreated, 100% Treated, 45%
Botulism	6 hours– 10 days	24–72 hours	Outbreak-associated, first patient, 25% Subsequent patients, 4% Overall, 5%–10%
Tularemia	1–21 days	2 weeks	Untreated, 33% Treated, <4%
Pneumonic plague	2–3 days	1–6 days	Untreated, 40%–70% Treated, 5%
Smallpox	7–17 days	4 weeks	Overall, 20%–50%
Viral hemorrhagic fevers	4–21 days	7–16 days	Overall, 53%–88%

* Source: CDC. Bioterrorism: Agent Summary. Atlanta, GA: US Department of Health and Human Services, CDC, 2001.

Table 7.2
Primary Pathologic Features and Differential Diagnoses of Illnesses Caused by Category A Biologic Agents

Agent/disease	Primary pathologic features	Differential diagnosis
Smallpox virus (variola major)	Multiloculated vesicles, ballooning degeneration of epithelial cells, intracytoplasmic inclusions (Guarnieri bodies)	Chicken pox, monkeypox, parapox, tanapox, herpes simplex, secondary syphilis
Bacillus anthracis (anthrax)	Inhalational anthrax—hemorrhagic mediastinitis, hemorrhagic lymphadenitis, hemorrhagic pleural effusion	Inhalational anthrax—community acquired pneumonia, pneumonic tularemia or plague, hantavirus pulmonary syndrome, bacterial/fungal/tuberculous mediastinitis or meningitis, fulminate mediastinal tumors, aortic dissection
	Cutaneous anthrax—hemorrhage, edema, necrosis, perivascular infiltrate, vasculitis	Cutaneous anthrax—rickettsialpox, spider bite, ecthyma gangrenosum, ulceroglandular tularemia
	Gastrointestinal anthrax—hemorrhagic enteritis, hemorrhagic lymphadenitis, mucosal ulcers with necrosis in the terminal ileum and cecum, peritonitis	
	CNS involvement—hemorrhagic meningitis	
	Bubonic plague—acute lymphadenitis with surrounding edema	Bubonic plague—tularemia, other bacterial adenitis
	Pneumonic plague—severe, confluent, hemorrhagic, and necrotizing bronchopneumonia, often with fibrinous pleuritis	Pneumonic plague—inhalational anthrax, community acquired pneumonia, pneumonic tularemia, hantavirus pulmonary syndrome

continued on next page

Table 7.2
Primary Pathologic Features and Differential Diagnoses of Illnesses Caused by Category A Biologic Agents (continued)

	Septicemic plague—generalized lymphadenitis, foci of necrosis in lymph nodes and other reticuloendothelial organs, disseminated intravascular coagulation (DIC) with widespread hemorrhages and thrombi	Septicemic plague—other bacterial sepsis
	CNS involvement—meningitis	Plague meningitis—other bacterial or fungal meningitis
Yersinia pestis (plague)	Ulceroglandular tularemia—skin ulcer with associated suppurative necrotizing lymphadenitis	Ulceroglandular tularemia—cutaneous anthrax, rickettsialpox, spider bite, ecthyma gangrenosum
	Glandular tularemia—suppurative necrotizing lymphadenitis without associated skin ulcer	Glandular tularemia—pyogenic bacterial infections, cat-scratch disease, syphilis, chancroid, lymphogranuloma venereum, tuberculosis, nontuberculous mycobacterial infection, toxoplasmosis, sporotrichosis, rat-bite fever, anthrax, plague
Francisella tularensis (tularemia)	Oculoglandular tularemia—eyelid edema, acute conjunctivitis and edema, small conjunctival ulcers, regional lymphadenitis	Oculoglandular tularemia—pyogenic bacterial infections, adenoviral infection, syphilis, cat-scratch, disease, herpes simplex virus infection
	Pharyngeal tularemia—exudative pharyngitis or tonsillitis with ulceration, pharyngeal membrane formation, regional lymphadenitis	Pharyngeal tularemia—streptococcal pharyngitis, infectious mononucleosis, adenoviral infection, diphtheria
	Typhoidal tularemia—systemic involvement, DIC, focal necrosis of major organs	Typhoidal tularemia—typhoid fever, brucellosis, Q fever, disseminated bacterial, mycobacterial or fungal infection, rickettsioses, malaria
	Pneumonic tularemia—acute inflammation, diffuse alveolar damage	Pneumonic tularemia—community-acquired pneumonia, pneumonic plague, hantavirus pulmonary syndrome
Viral hemorrhagic fevers	Filoviruses (Ebola and Marburg)—massive hepatocellular necrosis, filamentous inclusions in hepatocytes, extensive necrosis in other major organs, diffuse alveolar damage	Other systemic infections caused by viral, bacterial, or rickettsial agents
	Arenaviruses (Lassa, Junin, Machupo, Guanarito)—massive hepatic necrosis, diffuse alveolar damage	

Anthrax
Agent: Bacillus anthracis

Pathologic findings. Anthrax has three pathologic forms. **Cutaneous anthrax** is characterized by an eschar that forms where the bacteria entered the skin (Figure 7.2). Microscopically, the epidermis has necrosis and crusts, whereas the dermis demonstrates necrosis, edema, hemorrhage, perivascular inflammation, and vasculitis. The lymph nodes that drain the skin site eventually become enlarged, necrotic, and hemorrhagic. **Gastrointestinal anthrax** is distinguishable by hemorrhagic ulcers in the terminal ileum and caecum accompanied by mesenteric hemorrhagic lymphadenitis and peritonitis. **Inhalational anthrax** is characterized by hemorrhagic mediastinal lymphadenitis (Figure 7.3) accompanied by pleural effusions. Histologically, lymph nodes have abundant edema, hemorrhage, and necrosis with limited inflammatory infiltrate (Figure 7.4).[18,25–29] As any of the three anthrax forms progresses, the bacteria can spread to abdominal organs, producing petechial hemorrhages, and to the central nervous system, producing hemorrhagic meningitis (i.e., cardinal's cap) (Figure 7.5).

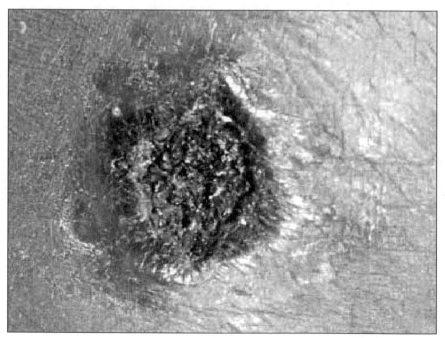

Figure 7.2 *Cutaneous anthrax—eschar lesion. Public Health Image Library, CDC*

Figure 7.3 Inhalational anthrax—hemorrhagic mediastinal lymphadenitis surrounding trachea; inset, cross-section of trachea surrounded
by hemorrhagic soft tissue and lymph nodes. Reprinted courtesy of
New York City Office of the Chief Medical Examiner.

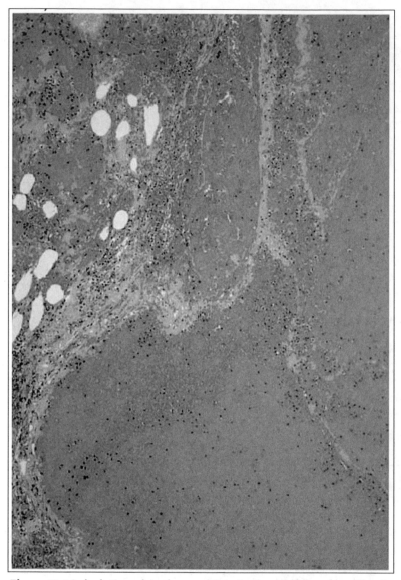

Figure 7.4 *Inhalational anthrax — histologic section of mediastinal lymph node with hemorrhage, necrosis, and sparse inflammatory cell infiltrate (hematoxylin and eosin stain). Infectious Disease Pathology Activity, CDC*

Figure 7.5 Anthrax—hemorrhagic meningitis. *Public Health Image Library, CDC*

Diagnostic specimens. Performing a complete autopsy with histologic sampling of multiple organs will help determine the distribution of bacilli and the portal of entry. The specimens that harbor the highest number of *B. anthracis* organisms vary by the pathologic form of anthrax. For example, diagnosis of cutaneous anthrax requires skin samples from the center and periphery of the eschar, whereas for inhalational anthrax, pleural fluid cell blocks, pleura tissue, and mediastinal lymph nodes have the highest amounts of bacilli and antigens.

Diagnostic tests. If the patient has not received antibiotics, bacilli can be observed in tissues with H&E, Gram, and silver impregnation stains and IHC assays (Figures 7.6 and 7.7). However, after antibiotic treatment has been instituted, only silver stains and IHC assays will highlight the bacilli. IHC assays for *B. anthracis* can demonstrate bacilli, bacillary fragments, and granular bacterial fragments in formalin-fixed tissues, even after ten days of antibiotic treatment. Although a DFA test is available for *B. anthracis,* it is not used on formalin-fixed tissues.

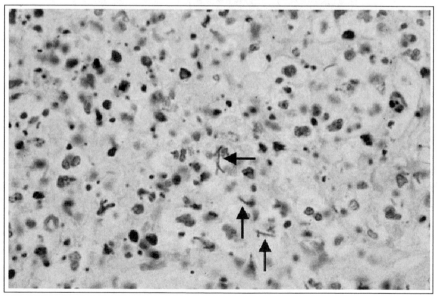

Figure 7.6 Anthrax — *Bacillus anthracis rods in mediastinal lymph node (Gram stain). Infectious Disease Pathology Activity, CDC*

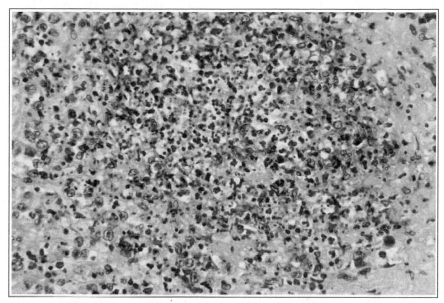

Figure 7.7 Anthrax—*Bacillus anthracis rods, bacillary fragments and granular bacterial fragments in spleen (immunohistochemistry). Infectious Disease Pathology Activity, CDC*

Plague
Agent: *Yersinia pestis*

Pathologic findings. Similar to anthrax, the clinicopathologic manifestations of plague are classified on the basis of the portal of entry of *Y. pestis*. Bubonic plague refers to an acute lymphadenitis that occurs after the bacteria have penetrated the skin (Figure 7.8). Usually, skin lesions are inconspicuous or have a small vesicle or pustule that might not be evident at the time the infected lymph node (bubo) appears. Histologically, the bubo exhibits edema, hemorrhage, necrosis, and a ground-glass amphophilic material that represents masses of bacilli. Primary pneumonic plague refers to the infection caused by inhalation of airborne bacteria, producing intra-alveolar edema accompanied by varying amounts of acute inflammatory infiltrate and abundant bacteria. Primary septicemic plague occurs when *Y. pestis* enters through the oropharyngeal route. In septicemic plague, the cervical lymph nodes draining the infected region will display the previously described pathologic features. As the disease progresses, bacteria are distributed widely throughout the body, and findings consistent with shock and disseminated intravascular coagulation are observed. Septicemic plague with bacterial seeding of the lungs results in secondary pneumonic plague (Figure 7.9A, left).[30–35]

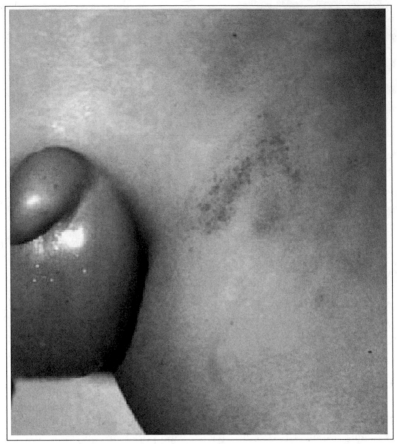

Figure 7.8 Bubonic plague—lymphadenitis. New Mexico Office of the Medical Investigator

Diagnostic specimens. Performing a complete autopsy with histologic sampling of multiple organs will help determine the distribution of bacteria and the portal of entry. Enlarged, soft, hemorrhagic lymph nodes should be sampled and tested for *Y. pestis*. The lungs should be sampled to determine whether a primary or secondary infection existed.[30]

Diagnostic tests. *Y. pestis* can be visualized in formalin-fixed tissues by using H&E, Gram, silver impregnation, and Giemsa stains; however, specific identification of the bacilli in tissues can only be performed by using IHC or DFA (Figure 7.9B, right).

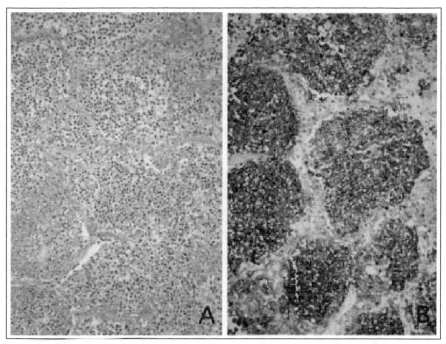

Figure 7.9 Secondary pneumonic plague—Histologic sections of lung
with (A, left) neutrophilic infiltrate in space (hematoxylin and eosin
stain) and (B, right) pestis bacteria (immunohistochemistry). Infectious Disease Pathology Activity, CDC

Tularemia
Agent: *Francisella tularensis*

Pathologic findings. Tularemia can also have multiple clinicopathologic
forms, depending on the portal of entry, including ulceroglandular, oculoglandular,
glandular, pharyngeal, typhoidal, and pneumonic. In all forms, the primary draining
lymph nodes demonstrate necrotizing lymphadenitis surrounded by a neutrophilic
and granulomatous inflammatory infiltrate. In the ulceroglandular form, a skin ulcer
or eschar with corresponding lymph node involvement is present, but skin lesions
are absent in the glandular form. In the oculoglandular form, the eye exhibits con-
junctivitis with ulcers and soft-tissue edema. The pharyngeal form is characterized
by pharyngitis or tonsillitis with ulceration. The lungs in pneumonic tularemia exhibit abundant fibrinous necrosis accompanied by varying amounts of mixed inflammatory infiltrate (Figure 7.10A, left). Typhoidal tularemia refers to systemic
involvement with focal areas of necrosis in the major organs and disseminated intravascular coagulation, but lacks a group of primary draining lymph nodes.[36-40] In
cases of tularemia sepsis, organisms can be seen with blood smears (Figure 7.11).

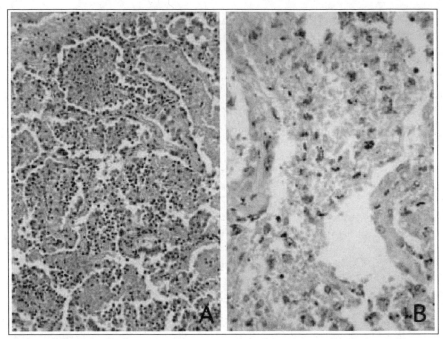

Figure 7.10 *Primary pneumonic tularemia—histologic sections of lung with (A, left) neutrophilic infiltrate in alveolar space (hematoxylin and eosin stain) and (B, right) Francisella tularensis bacteria (immunohistochemistry). Infectious Disease Pathology Activity, CDC.*

Diagnostic specimens. Performing a complete autopsy with histologic sampling of multiple organs will help determine the distribution of bacteria and the portal of entry. Enlarged, necrotic lymph nodes should be sampled and tested for *F. tularensis*. Culture swabs from the potential portals of entry (e.g., skin, conjunctiva, or throat) can be useful.

Diagnostic tests. The microorganisms are difficult to demonstrate with special stains; however, IHC and DFA have been successfully used in formalin-fixed tissues to demonstrate the bacteria (Figure 7.10B, right).

Botulism
Agent: Absorption of Clostridium botulinum toxin

Pathologic findings. *C. botulinum* elaborates a potent, preformed neurotoxin. The most important diagnostic feature of botulism is the clinical history because the histopathologic changes are nonspecific (e.g., central nervous system hyperemia and microthrombosis of small vessels).[41]

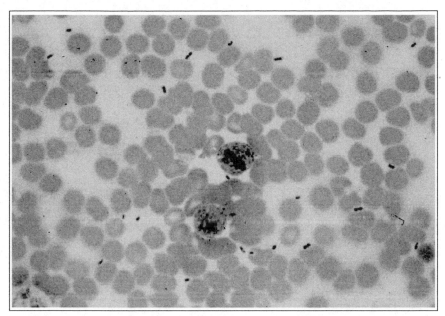

Figure 7.11 *Tularemia—blood smear demonstrating Francisella tularensis bacteria (Giemsa stain). Infectious Disease Pathology Activity, CDC.*

Diagnostic specimens. When botulism is suspected because of a symmetrical, descending pattern of weakness and paralysis of cranial nerves, limbs, and trunk, the pathologist should obtain tissue for anaerobic cultures from the suspect entry sites (i e , wound, gastrointestinal tract, or respiratory tract) and serum for botulinum toxin mouse bioassay.

Diagnostic tests. Microbiologic culture and botulinum toxin mouse bioassay with serum are necessary.

Smallpox
Agent: Variola virus (Orthopoxvirus)

Pathologic findings. Smallpox is an acute, highly contagious illness caused by a member of the *Poxviridae* family. *Variola major* refers to the form with a higher mortality rate, and variola minor or alastrim is a milder form. The lesions develop at approximately the same time and rate, starting in the palms and soles and spreading centrally; they first appear as macules and papules, and then progress to vesicles and umbilicated pustules (Figure 7.12), followed by scabs and crusts, and end as pitted scars. Occasionally, a hemorrhagic and uniformly fatal form occurs. This form has extensive bleeding into the skin and gastrointestinal tract and can be grossly taken for meningococcemia, acute leukemia, or a drug reaction.[42] Microscopically, the skin exhibits multiloculated, intraepidermal vesicles; ballooning degeneration of epithelial cells; intracytoplasmic, paranuclear, and eosinophilic viral inclusions (i.e., Guarnieri bodies) (Figure 7.13); and occasionally intranuclear viral changes. Secondary infections (e.g., bronchitis, pneumonia, and encephalitis) can complicate the clinical appearance.[43–48]

Diagnostic specimens. Cutaneous lesions are the most important sample for smallpox. Samples should include fluid from vesicles to be studied by electron microscopy, and skin samples fixed in formalin for histopathology and immunohistochemistry. Performing a complete autopsy with histologic sampling of multiple organs will help determine the extent and distribution of the virus, as well as the occurrence of secondary infections.

Diagnostic tests. Electron microscopic studies of vesicle fluid or skin samples can identify characteristic viral particles (Figure 7.14). IHC studies have demonstrated the virus in the epithelial cells and in the subjacent fibroconnective tissue.

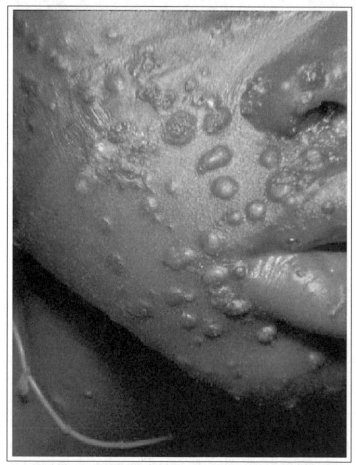

Figure 7.12
Smallpox—
cutaneous
papules and
vesicles.
Public
Health Im-
age Library,
CDC.

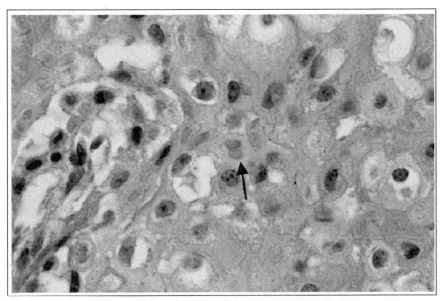

Figure 7.13 Smallpox—histologic section of skin with intraepidermal vesicles and ballooning degeneration of epithelial cells with viral inclusions (Guarnieri bodies [arrow]) (hematoxylin and eosin stain). Infectious Disease Pathology Activity, CDC.

Viral Hemorrhagic Fevers
Agents: Multiple

Viruses that can cause hemorrhagic fevers belong to different families, including Filoviridae (Ebola, Marburg viruses), Flaviviridae (yellow fever, dengue viruses), Bunyaviridae (Rift Valley fever, Crimean Congo, Hantaan, Sin Nombre viruses), and Arenaviridae (Junin, Machupo, Guanarito, Lassa viruses).

Pathologic findings. The term viral hemorrhagic fever is reserved for febrile illnesses associated with abnormal vascular regulation and vascular damage. Common pathologic findings at autopsy include petechial hemorrhages and ecchymoses of skin, mucous membranes, and internal organs. Although systemic hemorrhages occur in the majority of viral hemorrhagic fevers, certain agents infect specific cells and thus histopathologic features can differ among agents. Necrosis of liver and lymphoid tissues, as well as diffuse alveolar damage, occur in the majority of viral hemorrhagic fevers, but can be more prominent for certain infections (e.g., midzonal hepatocellular necrosis is prominent in yellow fever, but not in dengue). Viral inclusions can be visualized in hepatocytes with Ebola or Marburg infections by using light and electron microscopy (Figure 7.15).[49–54]

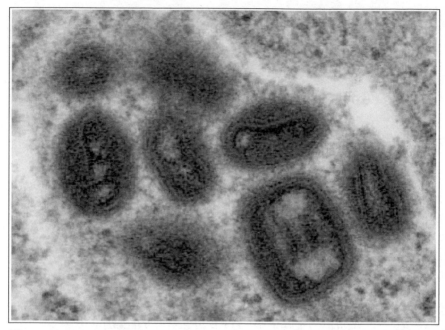

Figure 7.14 Intracellular mature variola virus particles grown in cell culture. Note: The barbell-shaped inner core and two lateral bodies are surrounded by an outer membrane. One brick-shaped particle is also illustrated (thin section electron microscopy). Infectious Disease Pathology Activity, CDC.

Diagnostic specimens. Performing a complete autopsy with histologic sampling of multiple organs can determine the extent of the disease and help identify the specific virus. After a specific etiologic agent has been isolated or identified from an index case, targeted sampling of additional cases with similar symptoms can decrease the exposure of autopsy personnel to these hazardous agents and still yield diagnostic material. For example, during outbreaks of Ebola hemorrhagic fever in Africa, using IHC on skin punch biopsy samples was sufficient to provide a diagnosis in a substantial number of fatalities and minimized the risk to the medical personnel who obtained the specimens.[49]

Diagnostic tests. Serum and skin samples can be tested by using PCR, immunohistochemistry, and electron microscopy (Figure 7.16). Additionally, serum can be inoculated into experimental animals or culture cells for viral isolation.

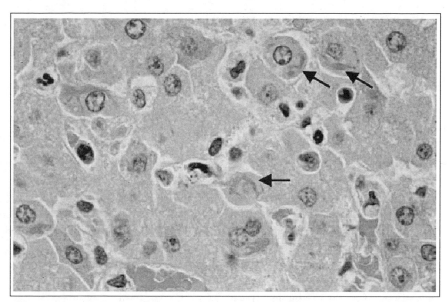

Figure 7.15 Ebola hemorrhagic fever—necrotic hepatocytes with filamentous intracytoplasmic inclusions (arrows) (hematoxylin and eosin stain). Infectious Disease Pathology Activity, CDC.

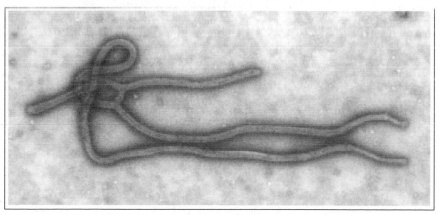

Figure 7.16 Ultrastructural appearance of Ebola virus (electron microscopy negative stain). Infectious Disease Pathology Activity, CDC.

Laboratory Response Network

CDC, in collaboration with the Association of Public Health Laboratories (APHL), the FBI, and other federal agencies, has developed the Laboratory Response Network (LRN) as a multilevel system of linked local, state, and federal public health laboratories as well as veterinary, food, and environmental laboratory partners.[55-57] The primary components of LRN are the state public health laboratories representing each of the fifty states. Within certain states, laboratories are located in different counties and more populated cities. In addition, federal laboratories within LRN include CDC, the Food and Drug Administration (FDA), the Environmental Protection Agency (EPA), the U.S. Army Medical Research Institute of Infectious Diseases (USAMRIID), and other Department of Defense laboratories.

Each laboratory has been assigned a designation (Table 7.3), predicated on their diagnostic capability, ranging from sentinel status (i.e., Level A for presumptive-level screening) through national laboratory status (i.e., Level D for genetic subtyping and confirmatory testing).[55-57] Hospital clinical laboratories are designated as sentinel laboratories (Level A); they have a rapid rule out and forward mission when handling presumptive clinical cases. County, city, and state public health laboratories are designated as confirmatory reference facilities (Level B, core, or Level C, advanced), depending on their degree of containment capacity and technical proficiency in performing agent-specific confirmatory analyses and rapid presumptive testing by PCR for nucleic acid amplification and time-resolved fluorescence for antigen detection. The Level D designation is reserved for CDC and USAMRIID laboratories. No regional laboratories exist; the network functions by channeling the specimens through the designated levels to a pathogen-specific conclusion.

ME/Cs should submit specimens from suspected biologic terrorism-related cases to the state public health laboratory through the local or county laboratory that serves their jurisdiction, unless their standard reporting protocol makes them a direct client of the state laboratory. These primary laboratories conduct the tests that fall within the scope of their ability and refer specimens to the state laboratory for more advanced tests. The state laboratory processes and refers specimens in a similar manner to other state laboratories or CDC (Figure 7.17). Contact information for all state diagnostic laboratories is included in this report (Appendix A). The point of contact for ME/Cs should remain the laboratory where the specimens were first submitted, unless they are directed to contact a reference laboratory (e.g., a state laboratory) to track the progress of the testing. Before the need for LRN services arises, ME/Cs should establish contact with the public health laboratory serving their jurisdiction and determine how the laboratory services can be best accessed when needed. Such a relationship might require a memorandum-of-understanding, which should be prepared and agreed to in advance.

Table 7.3
Selected Characteristics and Capabilities by Functional Level of the Laboratory Response Network for Terrorism

Laboratory Level	Biosafety Level (BSL)	Capabilities	Testing Resource
D	BSL-4	• Probe for universal agents • Perform all Level A– C tests • Validate new assays • Detect genetic recombinants • Provide specialized reagents • Bank isolates • Molecular typing • Negative stain electron microscopy for smallpox virus	CDC; U.S. Army Medical Research Institute of Infectious Diseases
C	BSL-3	• Nucleic acid amplification assays • Molecular typing • Toxicity testing • Provide surge capacity	Selected state public health laboratories
B	BSL-3 Recommended or BSL-2 facilities with BSL-3 practices	• Rule in specific agents • Isolate and identify • Forward specimens to higher level laboratories • Process environmental samples • Perform confirmatory testing • Antimicrobial susceptibility testing	Selected state and county public health laboratories and other veterinary, environmental, and food testing laboratories
A	BSL 2	• Antimicrobial susceptibility testing • Rule out specific agents • Early detection of presumptive cases • Forward specimens to higher level laboratories	Clinical and other sentinel laboratories

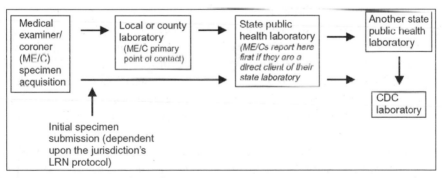

Figure 7.17 *Process for submitting specimens containing suspected Category A, B, or C* biologic agents (except smallpox virus) for testing within the Laboratory Response Network (LRN) * Note: Dependent upon the LRN-designated capacity (Level A, sentinel; Level B, core; Level C, advanced), laboratory confirmation might occur on-site or require referral to the next higher-level laboratory for confirmatory testing or correct biocontainment.*

All specimens that are to be tested for potential biologic terrorism pathogens are handled through the same reporting and submission process except specimens potentially containing smallpox virus. Because smallpox virus should only be handled in a Biosafety Level 4 facility, the specimen should be transported to CDC.[57] If ME/Cs suspect this agent, they should notify their state public health department, which can test for other agents that cause a vesiculopustular rash (i.e., varicella zoster, vaccinia, and monkeypox viruses) and either further test or refer the specimen for rapid presumptive screening for smallpox virus by PCR. The same laboratories will be able to coordinate submission of the specimen to CDC as needed for pathogen confirmation. In advance, ME/Cs should establish contact with the state health department representative who would coordinate smallpox specimen submission. In their surveillance capacity and concurrent with specimen submission, ME/Cs should notify the epidemiologic investigation unit in their local or state health department of the suspected smallpox-infected decedent.

Biosafety Concerns
Autopsy risks

Biosafety is critical for autopsy personnel who might handle human remains contaminated with biologic terrorism agents. Tularemia, viral hemorrhagic fevers, smallpox, glanders, and Q fever have been transmitted to persons performing autopsies (i.e., prosectors); certain infections have been fatal.[49,58-70] Infections can be transmitted at autopsies by percutaneous inoculation (i.e., injury), splashes to unprotected mucosa, and inhalation of infectious aerosols.[71] All of the Category A pathogens are potentially transmissible to autopsy personnel, although the degree of risk varies considerably among these organisms.

Additionally, autopsies of persons who die as the result of terrorism-related infections might expose autopsy personnel to residual surface contamination with infectious material. For example, botulinum toxin has the potential to be inhaled by autopsy personnel if it is present on the body surface at the time of examination.[72] Heavy surface contamination of the body is unlikely because of the incubation period for the majority of infectious agents and the likelihood that a victim will have bathed and changed clothes after exposure and before becoming symptomatic and dying.[73] However, if such residual material (e.g., powder) is present, examination and specimen collection should be undertaken by using appropriate biosafety procedures to protect autopsy and analytic laboratory personnel from possible exposure to more concentrated infectious material.

Because human remains infected with unidentified biologic terrorism pathogens might arrive at autopsy without warning, basic protective measures described in this report should be maintained for all contact with potentially infectious materials.[74,75] In addition to these measures, certain high-risk activities (e.g., use of oscillating saw) are known to increase the potential for worker exposure and should be performed with added safety precautions.

Autopsy precautions

Existing guidelines for biosafety and infection control for patient care are designed to prevent transmission of infections from living patients to care providers, or from laboratory specimens to laboratory technicians.[76,77] Although certain biosafety and infection-control guidelines are applicable to the handling of human remains, inherent differences exist in transmission mechanisms and intensity of potential exposures during autopsies that require specific consideration.[71]

As with any contact involving broken skin or body fluids when caring for live patients, certain precautions must be applied to all contact with human remains, regardless of known or suspected infectivity. Even if a pathogen of concern has been ruled out, other unsuspected agents might be present. Thus, all human autopsies must be performed in an appropriate autopsy room with adequate air exchange by personnel wearing appropriate personal protective equipment (PPE).[71] All autopsy facilities should have written biosafety policies and procedures; autopsy personnel should receive training in these policies and procedures, and the annual occurrence of training should be documented.

Standard Precautions are the combination of PPE and procedures used to reduce transmission of all pathogens from moist body substances to personnel or patients.[77] These precautions are driven by the nature of an interaction (e.g., possibility of splashing or potential of soiling garments) rather than the nature of a pathogen. In addition, transmission based precautions are applied for known or suspected pathogens. Precautions include the following:

- airborne precautions. Used for pathogens that remain suspended in the air in the form of droplet nuclei and that can transmit infection if inhaled;
- droplet precautions. Used for pathogens that are transmitted by large droplets traveling 3–6 feet (e.g., from sneezes or coughs) and are no longer transmitted after they fall to the ground; and
- contact precautions. Used for pathogens that might be transmitted by contamination of environmental surfaces and equipment.

All autopsies involve exposure to blood, a risk of being splashed or splattered, and a risk of percutaneous injury.[71] The propensity of postmortem procedures to cause gross soiling of the immediate environment also requires use of effective containment strategies. All autopsies generate aerosols; furthermore, postmortem procedures that require using devices (e.g., oscillating saws) that generate fine aerosols can create airborne particles that contain infectious pathogens not normally transmitted by the airborne route.[71,78–81]

PPE

For autopsies, standard precautions can be summarized as using a surgical scrub suit, surgical cap, impervious gown or apron with full sleeve coverage, a form of eye protection (e.g., goggles or face shield), shoe covers, and double surgical gloves with an interposed layer of cut-proof synthetic mesh.[71] Surgical masks protect the nose and mouth from splashes of body fluids (i.e., droplets > 5 μm); they do not provide protection from airborne pathogens.[82,83] Because of the fine aerosols generated at autopsy, prosectors should at a minimum wear N-95 respirators for all autopsies, regardless of suspected or known pathogens.[84] However, because of the efficient generation of high concentration aerosols by mechanical devices in the autopsy setting, powered air-purifying respirators (PAPRs) equipped with N-95 or high-efficiency particulate air (HEPA) filters should be considered.[85–87] Autopsy personnel who cannot wear N-95 respirators because of facial hair or other fit limitations should wear PAPRs.

Autopsy procedures

Standard safety practices to prevent injury from sharp items should be followed at all times.[77] These include never recapping, bending, or cutting needles, and ensuring that appropriate puncture-resistant sharps disposal containers are available. These containers should be placed as close as possible to where sharp items are used to minimize the distance a sharp item is carried. Filled sharps disposal containers should be discarded and replaced regularly and never overfilled.[77]

Protective outer garments should be removed when leaving the immediate autopsy area and discarded in appropriate laundry or waste receptacles, either in an antechamber to the autopsy suite or immediately inside the entrance if an antechamber is unavailable. Handwashing is requisite upon glove removal.[77]

Engineering strategies and facility design concerns

Air-handling systems for autopsy suites should ensure both adequate air exchanges per hour and correct directionality and exhaust of airflow. Autopsy suites should have a minimum of twelve air exchanges/hour and should be at a negative pressure relative to adjacent passageways and office spaces.[84] Air should never be returned to the building interior, but should be exhausted outdoors, away from areas of human traffic or gathering spaces (e.g., air should be directed off the roof) and away from other air intake systems.[88,89] For autopsies, local airflow control (i.e., laminar flow systems) can be used to direct aerosols away from personnel; however, this safety feature does not eliminate the need for appropriate PPE.

Clean sinks and safety equipment should be positioned so that they do not require unnecessary travel to reach during routine work and are readily available in the event of an emergency. Work surfaces should have integral waste-containment and drainage features that minimize spills of body fluids and wastewater.

Biosafety cabinets should be available for handling and examination of smaller infectious specimens; however, the majority of available cabinets are not designed to contain a whole body.[76,90] Oscillating saws are available with vacuum shrouds to reduce the amount of particulate and droplet aerosols generated.[80] These devices should be used whenever possible to decrease the risk of dispersing aerosols that might lead to occupationally acquired infection.

Vaccination and postexposure prophylaxis

Vaccines are available that convey protection against certain diseases considered to be potentially terrorism-associated, including anthrax, plague, and tularemia.[76] However, these vaccines are not recommended for unexposed autopsy workers at low risk. Consistent application of standard safety practices should obviate the need for vaccination for *B. anthracis* and *Y. pestis*. In 2003, the U.S. Department of Health and Human Services (DHHS) initiated a program to administer vaccinia (smallpox) vaccine to first responders and medical personnel. In this context, persons who might be called on to assess remains or specimens from patients with smallpox should be included among this group (Box 7.2).[91]

Box 7.2
Smallpox Immunization Considerations for
Medicolegal Death Investigators*

Because the distribution of the smallpox vaccine to the civilian U.S. population was discontinued in 1983,° essentially all U.S. residents having contact with a smallpox case are at increased risk for infection. Although probably susceptible to smallpox, with appropriate precautions, medicolegal death investigators can reduce their risk of smallpox infection if they must examine or autopsy a decedent suspected to be infected with smallpox. Three risk-reduction activities during the postmortem period might be considered, (1) voluntary vaccination after the occurrence of smallpox has been confirmed in the community; (2) modification of autopsy procedures to limit the possible aerosolization of smallpox virus; and (3) exclusion of embalming procedures (see text). In the event of mass fatalities resulting from a smallpox outbreak, CDC

continued on next page

recommends that health departments consider planning for vaccinating mortuary personnel and their families.◊ This recommendation is relevant for medical examiners, coroners, and other forensic death investigators who have a high likelihood of handling smallpox-infected decedents during a mass fatality event.

In considering vaccination plans, attention should be given to the risk of adverse effects from smallpox vaccination as well as to its potential benefits. During a smallpox-associated mass fatality event, the federal government might propose that vaccinia inoculations be offered on a voluntary basis to appropriate personnel. Vaccinia inoculations have been effective in preventing smallpox infection but also pose certain risks for causing adverse reactions in the vaccinee and, less frequently, for spreading the vaccinia virus to other close contacts. Because of the increased risk of adverse effects, the Advisory Committee on Immunization Practices (ACIP) recommends that the following persons not receive vaccinia inoculation:

- persons with immunosuppressive conditions;
- those receiving immunosuppressive medical treatments or pharmaceutical regimens;
- those with eczema or who have a close contact having eczema;
- anyone who is allergic to the vaccine or any of its components;
- women who are breastfeeding;
- anyone aged < 12 months; and
- pregnant women or women expecting to become pregnant within four weeks.[1]

ACIP recommends that persons be excluded from the pre-event smallpox vaccination program who have known underlying heart disease, with or without symptoms, or who have more than three known major cardiac risk factors (i.e., hypertension, diabetes, hypercholesterolemia, heart disease at age fifty years in a first-degree relative, and smoking).** Persons at increased risk for adverse reactions to the vaccine should be counseled regarding the potential risks before being vaccinated.

continued on next page

* Source: Adapted from Payne DC. Smallpox considerations for forensic professionals. *National Association of Medical Examiners (NAME) News* 2003;11(1):2.

° Source: CDC. Smallpox vaccine no longer available for civilians in the United States. *MMWR* 1983;32:387.

◊ Source: CDC. Smallpox response plan, smallpox vaccination clinic guide. Annex 3–38. Atlanta, GA: U.S. Department of Health and Human Services, CDC, 2002. Available at http://www.bt.cdc.gov/ agent/smallpox/response-plan/files/annex-3.pdf.

ɪ Source: CDC. Recommendations for using smallpox vaccine in a preevent vaccination program: supplemental recommendations of the Advisory Committee on Immunization Practices (ACIP) and the Healthcare Infection Control Practices Advisory Committee (HICPAC). *MMWR* 2003;52(No. RR-7):1–16. Available at http:// www.cdc.gov/mmwr/preview/mmwrhtml/rr5207a1.htm.

**Source: CDC. Supplemental recommendations on adverse events following smallpox vaccine in the pre-event vaccination program: recommendations of the Advisory Committee on Immunization Practices [Notice to readers]. *MMWR* 2003;52:282–4. Available at http://www.cdc.gov/mmwr/preview/mmwrhtml/mm5213a5.htm.

The administration of prophylactic antibiotics to autopsy workers exposed to potentially lethal bacterial pathogens is sometimes appropriate. For example, autopsy personnel exposed to *Y. pestis* aerosols should consider receiving such treatment regardless of vaccination status.[92] Similarly, because tularemia can result from infection with a limited number of organisms, an exposure to *F. tularensis* should also prompt consideration of antimicrobial prophylaxis. However, decisions to use antimicrobial postexposure prophylaxis should be made in consultation with infectious disease and occupational health specialists, with consideration made of vaccination status, nature of exposure, and safety and efficacy of prophylaxis.

Decontamination of body-surface contaminants

If human remains with heavy, residual surface contamination (i.e., visible) must be assessed, they should be cleansed before being brought to the autopsy facility and after appropriate samples have been collected in the field. Surface cleaning should be performed with an appropriate cleaning solution (e.g., 0.5 percent hypochlorite solution or phenolic disinfectant) used according to manufacturer's instructions. If the number of remains requiring autopsy is limited (i.e., one or two), cleaning of heavily contaminated remains can be undertaken in an autopsy facility that has the infrastructure, capacity, and hazardous materials (HAZMAT)-trained personnel to perform the cleaning safely. Heavily contaminated remains should not be brought to facilities where patient care is performed. Both personnel carrying contaminated remains and personnel occupying areas through which remains are being carried should wear PPE. HAZMAT personnel should perform large-scale decontamination outdoors in a controlled setting. To ensure mutual understanding of the roles and responsibilities of HAZMAT and death-investigation personnel in situations with contaminated remains, ME/ Cs should develop response protocols with HAZMAT personnel before such an event occurs.

Waste handling

Liquid waste (e.g., body fluids) can be flushed or washed down ordinary sanitary drains without special procedures. Pretreatment of liquid waste is not required and might damage sewage treatment systems. If substantial volumes are expected, the local wastewater treatment personnel should be consulted in advance. Solid waste should be appropriately contained in biohazard or sharps containers and incinerated in a medical waste incinerator.[73,75]

Storage and disposition of corpses

The majority of potential biologic terrorism agents (*B. anthracis*, *Y. pestis*, or botulinum toxin) are unlikely to be transmitted to personnel engaged in the nonautopsy handling of a contaminated cadaver. However, such agents as the hemorrhagic fever viruses and smallpox virus can be transmitted in this manner. Therefore, standard precautions[77] should be followed while handling all cadavers before and after autopsy.

When bodies are bagged at the scene of death, surface decontamination of the corpse-containing body bags is required before transport. Bodies can be transported and stored (refrigerated) in impermeable bags (double-bagging is preferable), after wiping visible soiling on outer bag surfaces with 0.5 percent hypochlorite solution. Storage areas should be negatively pressured with 9–12 air exchanges/hour.

The risks of occupational exposure to biologic terrorism agents while embalming outweigh its advantages; therefore, bodies infected with these agents should not be embalmed. Bodies infected with such agents as *Y. pestis* or *F. tularensis* can be directly buried without embalming. However, such agents as *B. anthracis* produce spores that can be long-lasting and, in such cases, cremation is the preferred disposition method. Similarly, bodies contaminated with highly infectious agents (e.g., smallpox and hemorrhagic fever viruses) should be cremated without embalming. If cremation is not an option, the body should be properly secured in a sealed container (e.g., a Zigler case or other hermetically sealed casket) to reduce the potential risk of pathogen transmission. However, sealed containers still have the potential to leak or lose integrity, especially if they are dropped or are transported to a different altitude.[93]

ME/Cs should work with local emergency management agencies, funeral directors, and the state and local health departments to determine, in advance, the local capacity (bodies per day) of existing crematoriums, and soil and water table characteristics that might affect interment. For planning purposes, a thorough cremation produces approximately 3–6 pounds of ash and fragments. ME/Cs should also work with local emergency management agencies to identify sources and costs of special equipment (e.g., air curtain incinerators, which are capable of high-volume cremation) and the newer plasma incinerators, which are faster and more efficient than previous incineration methods. The costs of such equipment and the time required to obtain them on request should be included in state and local terrorism preparedness plans.

ME/C's Role in Biologic Terrorism Surveillance

ME/Cs should be a key component of population-based surveillance for biologic terrorism. They see fatalities among persons who have not been examined initially by other physicians, emergency departments, or hospitals. In addition, persons who have been seen first by other healthcare providers might die precipitously, without a confirmed diagnosis, and therefore fall under medicolegal jurisdiction. Autopsies are a critical component of surveillance for fatal infectious diseases, because they provide organism-specific diagnoses and clarify the route of exposure.[94] With biologic terrorism-related fatalities, organisms identified in autopsy tissues can be characterized by strain to assist in the process of criminal attribution.

Models for ME surveillance for biologic terrorism mortality include sharing of daily case dockets with public health authorities (e.g., King County, Washington, and an active symptom-driven case acquisition and pathology syndrome-based public health reporting system developed in New Mexico[24]). Different areas of responsibility exist for ME/Cs regarding their role in effective surveillance for possible terrorism events. The following steps should be taken in local jurisdictions to enable ME/Cs to implement biologic terrorism surveillance:

- Death-investigation laws should be changed to enable ME/Cs to assume jurisdiction and investigate deaths that might constitute a public health threat, including those threats that are probably communicable.
- Any unexplained deaths possibly involving an infectious cause or biologic agent should be investigated to make etiology (organism)-specific diagnoses.[94]

- Uniform standards for surveillance should be used. For example, the Med-X system developed in New Mexico[24] uses a set of antemortem symptoms to determine autopsy performance. The system's syndromic approach to post-mortem diagnosis allows alerting of public health authorities to specific con-stellations of autopsy findings that could represent infectious agents before the specific agent is identified. Diseases caused by biologic terrorism agents are rare. To enhance surveillance for these conditions, a matrix of potential pathology-based syndromes (Table 7.1) has been developed to guide au-topsy pathologists in recognizing potential cases.[24]

- Electronic information and data systems should be designed to allow rapid recognition of excess mortality—incorporating the ability to assess possible commonalities among cases—and rapid communication/notification of such information to public health authorities who can use the information for ef-fective response.

- Close working relationships should be developed between ME/Cs and local or state health departments to facilitate two-way communication that includes alerts to ME/Cs of possible outbreaks or clusters of nonfatal infectious diseases, which might have unrecognized fatal cases, and appropriate reporting by ME/Cs to public health authorities of notifiable disease conditions. Additionally, public health authorities should notify ME/Cs of the epidemiology of biologic terror-ism-associated and other emerging infectious diseases in their community.

ME/C's Role in Data Collection, Analysis, and Dissemination

For public health surveillance, criminal justice, and administrative purposes, ME/Cs should promptly, accurately, and thoroughly collect, document, electronically store, and have available for analysis and reporting, case-specific death-investi-gation information. Initially, depending upon local resources and legal restric-tions, all aspects of data management and use might not need to occur in-house. Recognizing that numerous entities use medicolegal death-investigation data, ME/Cs should establish collaborations with public health and law enforcement professionals to achieve the goal of complete, accurate, and timely case-specific death-investigation data. Advance planning and policy development should also clarify to whom such data may be released and under which circumstances. To facilitate this process, the following steps should be taken:

- Death-investigation information should be documented on standard forms that are consistent in content, at a minimum, with the Investigator's Death Investigation Report Form (IDIRF) and Certifier's Death Investigation Re-port Form (CDIRF).[95]

- Death-investigation data should be stored in an electronic database consistent with, at a minimum, the content outlined in the Medical Examiner/Coroner Death Investigation Data Set (MCDIDS).[96] These data elements should be updated periodically.
- Electronic death-investigation data sets should include the results of laboratory tests that are performed in the case in question.
- Entry of data into an electronic database should be prompt so that the database is current.
- Electronic databases should allow searching for and grouping of cases by disease or injury and circumstances of death.
- Electronic death-investigation data should be stored in open, nonproprietary formats so that it can be shared as needed.
- Death-investigation records should be stored in accordance with state or local regulations. Ideally, these records should be stored in perpetuity in a format that ensures future retrieval. The format or media of electronic records might require periodic updating.
- Mechanisms should be in place to ensure that electronic death investigation data can be shared with public health authorities, law enforcement agencies, and other death-investigation agencies while providing for appropriate confidentiality and control of the release of information to authorized personnel or organizations only.
- ME/Cs should have specific policies that outline the organizations and agencies that are authorized to receive death-investigation information and the conditions in which such information may be released.
- Policies and mechanisms should be in place to avoid releasing death investigation information inappropriately and to avoid withholding information that should be available to the public.
- ME/C offices should consider establishing links with state or local public health agencies, academic institutions, or other health organizations to promote epidemiologic analysis and use of their medicolegal death-investigation data in an ongoing manner. Certain ME/C offices have determined that employing a staff epidemiologist is beneficial.

Jurisdictional, Evidentiary, and Operational Concerns
Federal role

On February 28, 2003, Homeland Security Presidential Directive 5 (HSPD-5) modified federal response policy.[97] Under the new directive, the Secretary of Homeland Security is the principal federal official for domestic incident management. Pursuant to the Homeland Security Act of 2002 (Public Law 107-296), the Secretary of the U.S. Department of Homeland Security (DHS) is responsible for coordinating federal operations within the United States to prepare for, respond to, and recover from terrorist attacks, major disasters, and other emergencies. The Secretary will coordinate the federal government's resources used in response to or recovery from terrorist attacks, major disasters, or other emergencies if and when any one of the following four conditions applies: (1) a federal department or agency acting under its own authority has requested the assistance of the secretary; (2) the resources of state and local authorities are overwhelmed and federal assistance has been requested by the appropriate state and local authorities; (3) more than one federal department or agency has become substantially involved in responding to the incident; or (4) the Secretary has been directed to assume responsibility for managing the domestic incident by the president.

HSPD-5 further stipulates that the U.S. Attorney General, through the FBI, has lead federal responsibility for criminal investigations of terrorist acts or terrorist threats by persons or groups inside the United States, or directed at U.S. citizens or institutions abroad, where such acts are within the federal criminal jurisdiction of the United States. The FBI, in cooperation with other federal departments and agencies engaged in activities to protect national security, will also coordinate the activities of the other members of the law enforcement community to detect, prevent, preempt, and disrupt terrorist attacks against the United States. In the event of a weapons of mass destruction (WMD) threat or incident, the local FBI field office special agent in charge (SAC) will be responsible for leading the federal criminal investigation and law enforcement actions, acting in concert with the principal federal officer (PFO) appointed by the U.S. Department of Homeland Security and state and local officials.

The FBI has a WMD coordinator in each of the agency's fifty-six field offices (Appendix B). These persons are responsible for pre-event planning and preparedness, as well as responding to WMD threats or incidents. ME/Cs are encouraged to contact their local FBI WMD coordinator before an incident to clarify roles and responsibilities, and ME/Cs should contact the coordinator in any case where concerns or suspicions exist of a potential WMD-related death.

The FBI assertion of jurisdiction at the scene of a terrorist event would not necessarily usurp (or relieve) ME/Cs from their statutory authority and responsibility to identify decedents and determine cause and manner of death. Such an arrangement is consistent with the performance of medicolegal death investigation where other federal crimes are involved. ME/Cs who conduct terrorism-associated death investigations should be prepared to present their medicolegal death investigation findings in federal court.

Public health agency authority

State public health laws might establish the health department's specific authority to control certain aspects of operations, personnel, or corpses in a public health emergency. For example, the Center for Law and the Public's Health at Georgetown and Johns Hopkins Universities, at the request of CDC, has created a model state emergency health powers act for adoption by states.[98] Different states have either enacted versions of this act or are in the process of introducing similar legislative bills.[99] ME/Cs should know specifically how existing state laws might provide for the health department to take control and dictate the disposition of human remains (burial or cremation). A state's emergency health powers act might also provide for

- mandatory medical examinations for ME/C personnel;
- isolation and quarantine of the public or ME/C personnel;
- vaccination against and treatment for illnesses among ME/Cs; and
- control, use, and destruction of facilities.

ME/Cs and health departments should work together as part of the emergency planning process to determine which emergency health powers might be established by the health department and under what circumstances these might be invoked for each potential biologic terrorism agent. Determining how health departments and ME/C operations can best interact, including documenting concerns regarding the availability of death-investigation personnel and the control and disposition of human remains, should be emphasized. ME/Cs should take part in community exercises to clarify and practice their role in the emergency response process.

General operations

In the majority of terrorism-associated scenarios, ME/Cs are responsible for identifying remains and determining the cause and manner of death. To that end, ME/Cs might need to enlist additional local, state, or federal assistance while maintaining primary responsibility for death investigation. ME/Cs should request this assistance from the local or state emergency operations center (EOC), as appropriate. The probable source of federal assistance is the Disaster Mortuary Operational Response Team (DMORT). However, DMORT has not yet developed capacity to respond to events precipitated by the release of biologic agents (further details regarding DMORT and other federal agencies are discussed in following sections).

Where possible, postmortem examinations for identifying remains and determining cause and manner of death should occur within the local or state jurisdiction where victims have died. Local resources dictate whether the statutory ME/C system can accomplish this with existing personnel and within existing facilities, or whether additional local, state, or federal assistance is necessary. Moving substantial numbers of human remains, particularly those contaminated by a biologic agent (known or unknown) to locations considerably distant from the scenes of death is neither feasible nor safe. Two potential strategies can be used to augment the biosafety capacity of local agencies having limited resources. One strategy would be to develop a mobile Biosafety Level 3 autopsy laboratory. Another strategy would be to develop regional Biosafety Level 3 autopsy centers that can handle cases from surrounding jurisdictions or states. A combination of the two approaches will probably achieve the best coverage of national needs.

Postmortem examinations and evidence collection

A large-scale biologic event might create more fatalities than combined local, state, and federal agencies can store and examine.[15] Small or rural jurisdictions might be overwhelmed by a relatively limited number of fatalities, whereas larger state or city ME/C offices could conceivably process greater numbers of human remains. No formulas exist that can be used to determine in advance the autopsy rate and the extent of autopsy that might be needed. In the event of a biologic event, ME/Cs should perform complete autopsies on as many cases as feasible on the basis of case volume and biosafety risks. These autopsies should meet the standards that forensic pathologists usually meet for homicide cases. Conferring with the FBI and appropriate prosecutorial authorities early in the process will ensure that appropriate documentary and diagnostic maneuvers are employed that will support the criminal justice process. Similarly, interacting with public health authorities early in the death-investigation process should ensure that appropriate diagnostic evaluations are conducted to support the public health investigation and response.

After the etiologic agent has been determined, certain (or all) other potentially related fatalities can be selectively sampled to confirm the presence of the organism in question. ME/Cs should coordinate the decision to transition from complete autopsies to more limited examinations with law enforcement and public health professionals. Selective sampling could include skin swabs and needle aspiration of blood or other body fluids, tissues for culture, or biopsies of a particular tissue or organ for histologic diagnostic tests (e.g., immunohistochemical procedures and electron microscopy). The required specimens from a limited autopsy and the diagnostic procedures employed will be dictated by the nature of the biologic agent. Guidelines for targeted organs or tissues for culture or analysis were discussed previously. As with all homicides, chain-of-custody for specimens should be maintained at all times.

Whenever a complete autopsy is performed, the goals should be to (1) establish the disease process and the etiologic agent; (2) determine that the agent or disease is indeed the cause of death; and (3) reasonably rule out competing causes of death. When limited autopsies or external examinations are performed, ME/C personnel should

- identify the deceased;
- document the appearance of the body;
- establish that the presenting clinical symptoms and signs are consistent with the alleged etiologic agent;
- confirm the presence of the etiologic agent in the body;
- state with reasonable probability that the alleged agent was the underlying cause of death (e.g., inhalational anthrax infection); and
- state with reasonable probability the likely immediate cause of death (e.g., pneumonia, meningitis, or mediastinitis).

Forming a reasonably sound medical opinion regarding cause and manner of death can be accomplished with knowledge of the presenting syndrome and circumstantial events, external examination of the body, and testing of appropriate specimens to document the etiologic agent. For example, in a confirmed smallpox outbreak, identifying the deceased, externally examining the body and photographing the lesions, and obtaining samples from the lesions for culture or electron microscopy might be adequate.

Biologic evidence obtained at autopsy can be sent to local or state health department laboratories, and other physical evidence can be sent to the usual crime laboratory, unless otherwise instructed by the FBI. Laboratories within LRN, as described previously, are responsible for coordinating the transfer of evidence or results to the FBI, U.S. Attorney General, or local and state legal authorities, as appropriate. Consistent with routine practice, ME/Cs should document all evidence transfers adequately.

Cause and Manner of Death Statements

Death certificates are not withheld from the public record, even when the cause of death is terrorism-related. The cause of death section should be used to fully explain the sequence of the cause of death (e.g., "hemorrhagic mediastinitis due to inhalational anthrax"). If death resulted from a terrorism event, the manner of death should be classified as homicide. The "how injury occurred" section on the death certificate should be completed, and it should reflect how the infectious agent was delivered to the victim (e.g., "victim of terrorism; inhaled anthrax spores delivered in mail envelope"). The place of injury should be the statement of where (i.e., geographic location) the agent was received.

Reimbursement for Expenses and Potential Funding Sources

Additional funding for ME/Cs might be needed for either preparedness or use during an actual biologic terrorism event. ME/Cs should prepare financially for potential future terrorist events that might be similar to the anthrax attacks of October–November 2001. In crisis situations, funding is retroactive but no less a concern.

Preparedness funding can support multiple activities, including training of ME/Cs for large-scale terrorism events. Certain activities involving training of ME/Cs have occurred through DMORT, a program authorized by the DHHS Office of Emergency Preparedness to rapidly mobilize ME/Cs to respond to incidents of mass fatality. Preparedness funding can also support surveillance activities in ME/C offices. As part of the Bioterrorism Preparedness and Response cooperative agreements with state health departments, CDC has provided funding to New Mexico and other states that are pursuing ME/C surveillance systems as an enhancement to their traditional surveillance systems. The New Mexico Office of the Medical Investigator has been a recipient of this funding through the New Mexico Department of Health since the inception of the cooperative agreement program. This funding has supported development of specialized surveillance techniques for deaths caused by potential agents of biologic terrorism[24] and recognition of ME/Cs as a key resource for all phases—early detection, case characterization, incident response and recovery—of a public health emergency response. CDC encourages pursuit of this enhanced (ME/C) surveillance capacity through cooperative agreements with states, if the state has made adequate progress with other critical capacity goals.

ME/Cs might obtain preparedness funding by integrating their response activities into the existing EOCs that have been established at selected state and county levels (integration of ME/C offices into this framework is discussed in Communications and the Incident Command System). When ME/C offices are integrated into the emergency response system, ME/Cs have an opportunity to make emergency management officials aware of ME/C emergency responsibilities and resource needs.

The sources of funding for consequence management, including medicolegal death investigation, will depend on the scope of the terrorism event. In events with a limited number of deaths, funding for activities related to the detection and diagnosis might remain at the office level. Because terrorism deaths are homicides, these deaths will contribute to an office's jurisdictional workload, and future planning for preparedness funding should be considered. Certain ME/C offices are already a part of the local or state public health department or are already affiliated with an EOC. ME/C offices, health departments, and EOCs are strongly encouraged to forge links for effective preparedness and response and to participate in joint training exercises to maximize preparedness funding.

In events with multiple deaths, a federal emergency might be declared. As long as ME/Cs' offices are officially working through the state or local EOC, certain expenses associated with the response (e.g., cost of diagnostic testing) can be submitted to the Federal Emergency Management Agency (FEMA) for reimbursement. In the majority of localities, these requests for resources required for appropriate response during an event should be submitted through local emergency management agencies that are part of state and local EOCs. Costs will probably be covered by the agency that has jurisdiction over the disaster (e.g., FEMA). In cases where a presidential disaster declaration is made, testing costs, victim identification, mortuary services, and those services that are covered by the National Disaster Medical System (a mutual aid network that includes DHHS, the Department of Defense, and FEMA)[100] are reimbursable under Emergency Support Function 8 (Health and Medical) of the Federal Response Plan (FRP).

Under FRP, FEMA covers 75 percent of reimbursement costs; the remaining 25 percent are covered by the state through emergency funds or in-kind reimbursement. FEMA also supports state emergency funds through the DHHS electronic payments management system. In an emergency, all requests for reimbursement flow from their point of origin, in this case from an ME/C, through the state EOC/emergency management agency, to FEMA.§ Before an event, ME/C's should clarify the procedures to follow to ensure that they will be reimbursed for expenses incurred as part of their emergency response.

DMORT

DMORT is a national program that includes volunteers, divided into ten regional teams responsible for supporting death investigation and mortuary services in federal emergency response situations involving natural disasters and mass fatalities associated with transportation accidents or terrorism. Team members are specialists from multiple forensic disciplines, funeral directors, law enforcement agents, and administrative support personnel. Each team represents a FEMA region. DMORT members are activated through DHS after mass fatalities or events involving multiple displaced human remains (e.g., a cemetery washout after a flood).

The primary functions of DMORT include the identification of human remains, evidence recovery from the bodies, recovery of human remains from the scene, and assisting with operation of a family assistance center. Whenever possible, identification of the bodies is made by using commonly accepted scientific methods (e.g., fingerprint, dental, radiograph, or DNA comparisons).

Upon activation, DMORT members are federal government employees. When DMORT is activated, representatives from DHS are also sent to manage the logistics of deployment. The FBI most commonly staffs the fingerprint section of the morgue. The Armed Forces DNA Identification Laboratory in Rockville, Maryland, has traditionally performed DNA analyses; the arrangements for this testing are negotiated separately with the local ME/C.

After a request for DMORT assistance has been made, one of two Disaster Portable Morgue Units (DPMUs) and DMORT staff are sent to the disaster site. DPMUs contain specialized equipment and supplies, prestaged for deployment within hours to a disaster site. DPMUs include all of the equipment required for a functional basic morgue with designated workstations and prepackaged equipment and supplies. DPMUs can operate at Biosafety Level 2, but do not have the ventilatory capacity necessary to protect prosectors and other nearby persons from airborne pathogens. DPMUs also contain equipment for site search and recovery, pathology, anthropology, radiology, photography, and information resources, as well as office equipment, wheeled examination tables, water heaters, plumbing equipment, electrical distribution equipment, personal protective gear, and temporary partitions and supports. DPMUs do not have the materials required to support microbiologic sampling. When a DPMU is deployed, members of the DPMU team (i.e., a subset of DMORT) are sent to the destination to unload the DPMU equipment and establish and maintain the temporary morgue. Additional equipment is required locally after DMORT activation. At a minimum, this equipment includes a facility in which to house the morgue equipment, a forklift to move the DPMU equipment into the temporary morgue facility, and refrigerated trucks to hold human remains.

ME/Cs can request DMORT response after a mass fatality or after an incident resulting in the displacement of a substantial number of human remains. ME/Cs should follow state protocols for DMORT requests. Typically, ME/Cs contact the state governor's office, which then requests DMORT from DHS. The request should include an estimate of how many deaths occurred (if known), the condition of the bodies (if known), and the location of the incident. When deployed, DMORT supports ME/Cs in the jurisdiction where the incident occurred. All medicolegal death investigation records created by DMORT are given to ME/Cs at the end of the deployment, and ME/Cs are ultimately responsible for all of the identifications made and the documents created pertaining to the incident.

DMORT-WMD Team

The DMORT-WMD team is composed of national rather than regional volunteers. The primary focus of DMORT-WMD is decontamination of bodies when death results from exposure to chemicals or radiation. DMORT-WMD is developing resources to respond to a mass disaster resulting from biologic agents. However, this team might have difficulty in responding to such an event if the deaths occur in multiple locations.

The major forensic disciplines (i.e., forensic dentistry, forensic anthropology, and forensic pathology) as well as funeral directors, law enforcement, criminalists, and administrative support persons are represented on the DMORT-WMD team. Members of DMORT WMD undergo specialized training that focuses on chemical and radiologic decontamination of human remains. The DMORT-WMD unit has separate equipment, stored separately from the DPMU, including PPE (up to and including level A suits), decontamination tents, and equipment to gather contaminated water. DMORT-WMD teams are requested and deployed in the same manner as general DMORTs.

Communications and the incident command system

ME/Cs are key members of the biologic terrorism detection and management response team in any community and should be integrated into the comprehensive communication plan during any terrorism-associated event. Routine and consistent communication among ME/Cs and local and state laboratories, public health departments, EOCs, communication centers, DMORT, and other agencies, is critical to the success of efficient and effective biologic terrorism surveillance, fatality management, and public health and criminal investigations. Planning for different emergency scenarios and participation in disaster response exercises are necessary to ensure effective response to a terrorism event.

Each state and certain counties have some type of emergency operation center that has been organized to provide a coordinated response during a terrorism event. ME/Cs should verify their jurisdiction's EOC contact point and work with them periodically regarding concerns related to preparedness and response.

All EOCs follow the Incident Command System (ICS),[100] an internationally recognized emergency management system that provides a coordinated response across organizations and jurisdictions. The ICS structure allows for individual EOC decision making and different information flow in each state. ME/Cs should determine how the EOC functions in their jurisdiction.

Each ICS is composed of a managing authority that directs the response of health department, law enforcement, and emergency management officials during a planning exercise, emergency, or major disaster. In addition to assessing the incident and serving as the interagency contact, ICS also coordinates the response to information inquiries and the safety monitoring of assigned response personnel. The ICS organizational framework, includes planning, operations, logistics, and finance/administration sections.[101] ME/Cs are most likely to participate in the operations team, which makes tactical decisions regarding the incident response and implements those activities defined in action plans. This team might also include public health, emergency communications, fire, law enforcement, EMS, and state emergency management agency staff.

During a suspected terrorism event, ME/Cs should be responsible for the following actions to facilitate communication:

- Promptly inform laboratory, public health, and law enforcement personnel of findings of investigations of suspected biologic terrorism-related deaths as well as personnel needs and new developments. To expedite information exchange, ME/Cs should familiarize themselves with the appropriate contact persons and agencies for response in their jurisdictions.
- Answer the EOCs' requests to collect and report data in a timely manner.
- Coordinate communication of their activities with the state emergency management agency and EOCs for their jurisdiction to avoid release of confidential or speculative information directly to the public or media.[102]

Conclusion

ME/Cs are essential public health partners for terrorism preparedness and response. Despite state and local differences in medicolegal death-investigation systems, these investigators have the statutory authority to investigate deaths that are sudden, suspicious, violent, and unattended, and consequently play a vital role in terrorism surveillance and response. Public health officials should work with ME/Cs to ensure that these investigators can assist with surveillance for infectious disease deaths possibly caused by terrorism and provide confirmatory diagnoses and evidence in deaths linked to terrorism. This process should involve an assessment of local ME/C standards for accepting jurisdiction of potential infectious disease deaths and performing autopsies, laboratory capacity for making organism-specific diagnoses, and autopsy biosafety capacity. Ideally, ME/Cs should

- perform complete autopsies with histologic sampling of multiple organs in deaths potentially caused by biologic terrorism agents, given the constraints of case volume and biosafety concerns;
- have access to routine microbiologic testing for organism-specific diagnoses in potential infectious disease deaths;
- ensure protection from both airborne and bloodborne pathogens for all occupants of the autopsy facility (Biosafety Level 3);

- participate in a standardized ME/C surveillance model for infectious disease mortality (e.g., Med-X); and
- document death investigative information on standard forms that are stored in an searchable electronic format and that can be shared with public health authorities.

If biologic terrorism-related fatalities occur, ME/Cs are responsible for identifying remains and determining the cause and manner of death. Routine and consistent communication among ME/Cs and local and state laboratories, public health departments, EOCs, law enforcement, and other agencies is critical to the success of efficient and effective biologic terrorism surveillance, fatality management, and public health and criminal investigations. To prepare for this possibility, ME/Cs should

- contact their local FBI WMD coordinator to clarify roles and responsibilities;
- understand how local public health laws might impact ME/C function;
- become familiar with the capacity of local or state EOCs, ICS, and the process for submitting response-associated expenses for federal reimbursement;
- be aware of the process for submitting biologic and physical evidence in potential biologic terrorism-related fatalities,
- understand the procedure for writing cause and manner of death statements in terrorism-related fatalities; and
- identify appropriate health department officials for the reporting of notifiable or suspicious infectious diseases or potential biologic terrorism-related deaths.

The majority of ME/C facilities do not have the capacity to perform autopsies at Biosafety Level 3 as a consequence of facility design features that are expensive to fix. In addition, DMORT does not have the capacity to respond to events precipitated by the release of biologic agents. These limitations might affect local, state, and national surveillance for infectious disease deaths of public health importance, including those deaths potentially caused by terrorism. Two potential strategies might be used in the future to augment the biosafety capacity of local agencies having limited resources. One strategy would be to develop a mobile Biosafety Level 3 autopsy laboratory. Another strategy might be to develop regional Biosafety Level 3 autopsy centers that can handle cases from surrounding jurisdictions or states. A combination of the two approaches will probably achieve the best coverage of national needs.

Acknowledgements

This report was prepared with the assistance and support of the members of NAME, Michael A. Graham, M.D., President. The concept for this report originated with Lynda Biedrzycki, M.D. (member of NAME), of the Waukesha County, Wisconsin, Medical Examiner's Office. The preparers of this report appreciate the early organizational efforts of John Teggatz, M.D., of the Milwaukee County, Wisconsin, Medical Examiner's Office, and the editorial comments of Victor Weedn, M.D., J.D., Carnegie Mellon University; Mary Ann Sens, M.D., Ph.D., University of North Dakota School of Medicine and Health Sciences; Samuel L. Groseclose, D.V.M., CDC. The preparers also thank Aldo Fusaro, M.D., of the Cook County, Illinois, Medical Examiner's Office for compiling Appendix B.

† Additional information is available by contacting CDC by telephone (404-639-3133) or by fax (404-639-3043).

§ Robert T. Stafford Disaster Relief and Emergency Assistance Act, as amended by Public Law 106-390, October 30, 2000, United States Code, Title 42, The Public Health and Welfare, Chapter 68, Disaster Relief.

¶ State requests should be directed to the Department of Homeland Security, National Disaster Medical System Section, by telephone at 301-443-1167 (or 800-USA-NDMS) or by fax at 301-443-5146 (or 800-USA-KWIK)

The Authors

1. University of New Mexico School of Medicine, Albuquerque, New Mexico; 2. Division of Public Health Surveillance and Informatics, Epidemiology Program Office, CDC; 3. Fulton County Medical Examiner's Office, Atlanta, Georgia; 4. Epidemiology and Surveillance Division, National Immunization Program, CDC; 5. Immunization Services Division, National Immunization Program, CDC; 6. Georgia Bureau of Investigation, Trion, Georgia; 7. Hennepin County Medical Examiner's Office, Minneapolis, Minnesota; 8. Sparrow Hospital, Lansing, Michigan; and 9. Division of Viral and Rickettsial Diseases, National Center for Infectious Diseases, CDC. *Member of the National Association of Medical Examiners (NAME).

Disclaimer. All MMWR HTML versions of articles are electronic conversions from ASCII text into HTML. This conversion may have resulted in character translation or format errors in the HTML version. Users should not rely on this HTML document, but are referred to the electronic PDF version and/or the original MMWR paper copy for the official text, figures, and tables. An original paper copy of this issue can be obtained from the Superintendent of Documents, U.S. Government Printing Office (GPO), Washington, DC 20402-9371; telephone: (202) 512-1800. Contact GPO for current prices.

**Questions or messages regarding errors in formatting should be addressed to mmwrq@cdc.gov.

Page converted: 6/9/2004

References

1. CDC. Biological and chemical terrorism: strategic plan for preparedness and response; recommendations of the CDC Strategic Planning Workgroup. *MMWR* 2000;49(No. RR-4):1–14.

2. Hanzlick R, Combs DL. Medical examiner and coroner systems: history and trends. *JAMA* 1998;279:870–4.

3. Brachman P. S. Bioterrorism: An update with a focus on anthrax. *Am I Epidemiol.* 2002;155:981–7.

4. Török TJ et al. A large community outbreak of salmonellosis caused by intentional contamination of restaurant salad bars. *JAMA* 1997;278:389–95.

5. Jernigan JA et al. Bioterrorism-related inhalational anthrax: the first 10 cases reported in the United States. *Emerg. Infect. Dis.* 2001;7:933–44.

6. Borio L et al. Death due to bioterrorism-related inhalational anthrax. *JAMA* 2001;286:2554–9.

7. Bush LM et al. Index case of fatal inhalational anthrax due to bioterrorism in the United States. *N. Engl. J. Med.* 2001;345:1607–10.

8. CDC. Update: Investigation of bioterrorism-related inhalational anthrax: Connecticut, 2001. *MMWR* 2001;50:1049–51.

9. Combs DL, Parrish RG, Ing R. *Death Investigation in the United States and Canada, 1995.* Atlanta, GA: U.S. Department of Health and Human Services, CDC, 1995.

10. Nolte KB, Yoon SS, Pertowski C. Medical examiners, coroners, and bioterrorism. *Emerg. Infect. Dis.* 2000;6:559–60.

11. Nolte KB. Medical examiners and bioterrorism. *Am. J. Forensic Med. Pathol.* 2000;21:419–20.

12. Nolte KB. Evaluation of inhalational anthrax. *JAMA* 2002;287: 984–5.

13. Luke JL, Halpern M. Sudden unexpected death from natural causes in young adults. *Arch. Pathol.* 1968;85:10–7.

14. Nolte KB, Simpson GL, Parrish RG. Emerging infectious agents and the forensic pathologist: The New Mexico model. *Arch. Pathol. Lab. Med.* 1996;120:125–8.

15. O'Toole T, Mair M, Inglesby TV. Shining light on "Dark Winter." *Clin. Infect. Dis.* 2002;34:972–83.

16. Inglesby T, Grossman R, O'Toole T. A plague on your city: Observations from TOPOFF. *Clin. Infect. Dis.* 2001:32:436–45.

17. Schwartz DA, Bryan RT, Hughes JM. Pathology and emerging infections–quo vadimus? *Am. J. Pathol.* 1995;147:1525–33.

18. Walker DH, Yampolska O, Grinberg LM. Death at Sverdlovsk: What have we learned? *Am. J. Pathol.* 1994;144:1135–41.

19. Dworetzky M. Smallpox, October 1945. *New Engl. J. Med.* 2002;346:1329.

20. CDC. Update: investigation of anthrax associated with intentional exposure and interim public health guidelines, October 2001. *MMWR* 2001;50:889–93.

21. CDC. Update: Investigation of bioterrorism-related anthrax and interim guidelines for exposure management and antimicrobial therapy, October 2001. *MMWR* 2001;50:909–19.

22. CDC. Update: Investigation of bioterrorism-related anthrax and interim guidelines for clinical evaluation of persons with possible anthrax. *MMWR* 2001;50:941–8.

23. CDC. Update: Investigation of bioterrorism-related anthrax and adverse events from antimicrobial prophylaxis. *MMWR* 2001;50: 973–6.

24. Nolte KB et al. Medical examiner surveillance for bioterrorism mortality [Abstract]. Presented at the National Association of Medical Examiners Annual Meeting, October 2001, Richmond, Virginia; 39–40.

25. Grinberg LM et al. Quantitative pathology of inhalational anthrax, I: Quantitative microscopic findings. *Mod. Pathol.* 2001;14:482 95.

26. Abramova FA et al. Pathology of inhalational anthrax in 42 cases from the Sverdlovsk outbreak of 1979. *Proc. Natl. Acad. Sci. U.S.A.* 1993;90:2291–4.

27. Albrink WS et al. Human inhalation anthrax: A report of three fatal cases. *Am. J. Pathol.* 1960;36:457–71.

28. Jaax NK, Fritz DL. "Anthrax" [Chapter 41]. In Conner DH et al., eds. *Pathology of Infectious Diseases*, Vol 1. Hong Kong, Appleton and Lange Co, 1997;397 406.

29. Perl D. P. and Dooley J. R. Anthrax [Section 5, Chapter 1]. In: Binford CH, Conner DH, eds. *Pathology of Tropical and Extraordinary Diseases*, Vol. 1 Washington, DC: Armed Forces Institute of Pathology, 1976;118–23.

30. Guarner J et al. Immunohistochemical detection of Yersinia pestis in formalin-fixed, paraffin-embedded tissue. *Am. J. Clin. Pathol.* 2002;117:205–9.

31. Jones AM, Mann J, Braziel R. Human plague cases in New Mexico: Report of three autopsied cases. *J. Forensic. Sci.* 1979;24:26–38.

32. Finegold MJ. Pneumonic plague in monkeys: An electron microscopic study. *Am. J. Pathol.* 1969;54:167–85.

33. Finegold MJ et al. Studies on the pathogenesis of plague: Blood coagulation and tissue responses of Macaca mulatta following exposure to aerosols of Pasteurella pestis. *Am. J. Pathol.* 1968;53:99–114.

34. Smith JH, Reisner BS. Plague [Chapter 79]. In: Conner DH. et al., eds. *Pathology of Infectious Diseases,* Vol 1. Hong Kong: Appleton and Lange Co., 1997;729–38.

35. Smith JH. Plague [Section 5, Chapter 3]. In: Binford CH, Conner DH, eds. *Pathology of Tropical and Extraordinary Diseases,* Vol 1. Washington, DC: Armed Forces Institute of Pathology, 1976:130–4.

36. Guarner J et al. Immunohistochemical detection of Francisella tularensis in formalin-fixed paraffin-embedded tissue. *App. Immunohistol. Molec. Morphol.* 1999;7:122–6.

37. Evans MA et al. Tularemia: A 30-year experience with 88 cases. *Medicine* 1985;64:251–69.

38. Schmid GP et al. Clinically mild tularemia associated with tick-borne Francisella tularensis. *J. Infect. Dis.* 1983;148:63–7.

39. Gallivan MV et al. Fatal-cat transmitted tularemia: Demonstration of the organism in tissue. *South. Med. J.* 1980;73:240–42.

40. Geyer SJ, Burkey A, Chandler FW. Tularemia [Chapter 92]. In Conner, DH et al., eds. *Pathology of Infectious Diseases,* Vol 1. Hong Kong: Appleton and Lange Co., 1997;869–73.

41. Schwartz DA, Geyer SJ. Clostridial infections [Chapter 54]. In: Conner DH et al., eds. *Pathology of Infectious Diseases,* Vol 1. Hong Kong: Appleton and Lange Co., 1997;517–32.

42. Henderson DA. Smallpox and monkeypox [Chapter 103]. In: Guerrant RL, Walker DH, Weller PF, eds. *Tropical Infectious Diseases: Principles, Pathogens, and Practice.* Philadelphia, PA: Churchill Livingstone, 1999;1095–108.

43. Cruickshank JG, Bedson HS, Watson DH. Electron microscopy in the rapid diagnosis of smallpox. *Lancet* 1966;2:527–30.

44. Murray HGS. Diagnosis of smallpox by immunofluorescence. *Lancet* 1963;1:847–8.

45. Bras G. Morbid anatomy of smallpox. *Doc. Med. Geog. Trop.* 1952;4:303–51.

46. Councilman WT, Magrath GB, Brinckerhoff WR. Pathological anatomy and histology of variola. *J. Med. Research* 1904;11:12–134.

47. Cockerell CJ. Poxvirus infections [Chapter 29]. In: Conner DH et al., eds. *Pathology of Infectious Diseases,* Vol 1. Hong Kong: Appleton and Lange Co., 1997;273–9.

48. Strano AJ. Smallpox [Section 1, Chapter 14]. In: Binford CH, Conner DH, eds. *Pathology of Tropical and Extraordinary Diseases,* Vol 1. Washington DC: Armed Forces Institute of Pathology, 1976;65–7.

49. Zaki SR, Shieh WJ, Greer PW et al. Novel immunohistochemical assay for the detection of Ebola virus in skin: implications for diagnosis, spread, and surveillance of Ebola hemorrhagic fever. *J. Infect. Dis.* 1999;179(Suppl 1): S36–47.

50. Zaki SR, Kilmarx PH. Ebola virus hemorrhagic fever [Chapter 17]. In: Horsburgh CR, Nelson AM, eds. *Pathology of Emerging Infections.* Washington, DC: American Society for Microbiology, 1997;299–312.

51. Zaki SR, Goldsmith CS. Pathologic features of filovirus infections in humans. In: Klenk H. D., ed. *Marburg and Ebola Viruses.* Berlin, Germany: Springer-Verlag, 1998;97–116.

52. Gubler DJ, Zaki SR. Dengue and other viral hemorrhagic fevers [Chapter 3]. In: Nelson AM, Horsburgh CR, eds. *Pathology of Emerging Infections 2.* Washington, DC: American Society for Microbiology, 1998;43–72.

53. Zaki SR, Peters CJ. Viral hemorrhagic fevers [Chapter 37]. In: Conner DH et al., eds. *Pathology of Infectious Diseases,* Vol 1. Hong Kong: Appleton and Lange Co., 1997;347–64.

54. Child PL. Viral hemorrhagic fevers [Chapter 2]. In: Binford CH, Conner DH, eds. *Pathology of Tropical and Extraordinary Diseases,* Vol. 1. Washington DC: Armed Forces Institute of Pathology, 1976;5–11.

55. CDC. *Summary on the Laboratory Response Network.* Atlanta, GA: US Department of Health and Human Services, CDC, 2002. Available at http://www.cdc.gov/cic/functions-specs/function4Docs/nLRNvision-summary.doc.

56. CDC. *Laboratory Response to Biological Terrorism.* Atlanta, GA: US Department of Health and Human Services, CDC, 2002. Available at http://www.cdc.gov/programs/bio.htm.

57. Robinson-Dunn B. Microbiology laboratory's role in response to bioter-rorism. *Arch. Pathol. Lab. Med.* 2002;126:291–4.

58. Weilbaecher Jr JO, Moss ES. Tularemia following injury while performing post-mortem examination on human case. *J. Lab. Clin. Med.* 1938;24:34–8.

59. Alibek K, Handelman S. *Biohazard: The Chilling True Story of the Largest Covert Biological Weapons Program in the World—Told from the Inside by the Man Who Ran It.* NY: Random House, Inc., 1999.

60. White HA. Lassa fever: A study of 23 hospital cases. *Trans. R. Soc. Trop. Med. Hyg.* 1972;66:390–401.

61. Heymann DL et al. Ebola hemorrhagic fever: Tandala, Zaire, 1977–1978. *J. Infect. Dis.* 1980;142:372–6.

62. Culley AR. Smallpox outbreak in South Wales in 1962. *Proc. R. Soc. Med.* 1963;56:339–43.

63. Benn EC. Smallpox in Bradford 1962: A clinical review. *Proc. R. Soc. Med.* 1963;56:345.

64. Pospisil L. Contribution to the history of glanders in the Czech Republic. *Veterinarni Medicina* 2000;45:273–6.

65. Pike RM. Laboratory-associated infections: Incidence, fatalities, causes, and prevention. *Annu. Rev. Microbiol.* 1979;33:41–66.

66. MacCallum FO, Marmion BP, Stoker MGP. Q fever in Great Britain: Isolation of Rickettsia burneti from an indigenous case. *Lancet* 1949;2:1026–7.

67. Harman JB. Q fever in Great Britain: Clinical account of eight cases. *Lancet* 1949;2:1028–30.

68. Robbins FC, Rustigian R. Q fever in the Mediterranean area: Report of its occurrence in allied troops. IV. A laboratory outbreak. *Am. J. Hyg.* 1946;44:64–71.

69. Commission on Acute Respiratory Diseases. Laboratory outbreak of Q fever caused by the Balkan grippe strain of Rickettsia burneti. *Am. J. Hyg.* 1946;44:123–57.

70. Beck MD et al. Q fever studies in southern California, II: An epidemiological study of 300 cases. *Public Health Rep.* 1949;64:41–56.

71. Nolte KB, Taylor DG, Richmond JY. Biosafety considerations for autopsy. *Am. J. Forensic. Med. Pathol.* 2002;23:107–22.

72. Holzer VE. Botulismus durch inhalation [German]. *Med. Klin.* 1962; 41:1735–40.

73. CDC, Association for Professionals in Infection Control. *Bioterrorism readiness plan: A template for healthcare facilities.* Atlanta, GA: U.S. Department of Health and Human Services, CDC, 1999. Available at http://www.cdc.gov/ncidod/hip/Bio/13apr99APIC-CDCBioterrorism.PDF.

74. Sewell DL et al. *Protection of laboratory workers from occupationally acquired infections; approved guideline,* 2d ed., Vol 1, No. 23. Wayne, PA: National Committee for Clinical Laboratory Standards (NCCLS), 2001. Publication no. M29-A2.

75. Garner JS. Guideline for isolation precautions in hospitals. Hospital Infection Control Practices Advisory Committee. *Infect. Control Hosp. Epidemiol.* 1996;17:53–80

76. CDC, National Institutes of Health. Biosafety in Microbiological and Biomedical Laboratories, 4th ed. Washington, DC: U.S. Department of Health and Human Services, U.S. Government Printing Office, 1999. Available at http://www.cdc.gov/od/ohs/biosfty/bmbl4/bmbl4toc.htm.

77. Garner JS. Guideline for isolation precautions in hospitals, Part I: Evolution of isolation practices. Hospital Infection Control Practices Advisory Committee. *Am. J. Infect. Control* 1996;24:24–31.

78. Jewett DL et al. Blood-containing aerosols generated by surgical technique: A possible infectious hazard. *American Industrial Hygiene Association Journal* 1992;53: 228–31.

79. Green FHY, Yoshida K. Characteristics of aerosols generated during autopsy procedures and their potential role as carriers of infectious agents. *Appl. Occup. Environ. Hyg.* 1990;5:853–8.

80. Kembach-Wighton G, Kuhlencord A, Saternus KS. Knochenstaube bei der autopsie: Entstehung, ausbreitung, kontamination (Sawdust in autopsies: Production, spreading, and contamination) [Article in German]. *Der Pathologe* 1998;19:355–60.

81. Johnson GK, Robinson WS. Human immunodeficiency virus-1 (HIV-1) in the vapors of surgical power instruments. *J. Med. Virol.* 1991;33:47–50.

82. Pippin DJ, Verderame RA, Weber KK. Efficacy of face masks in preventing inhalation of airborne contaminants. *J. Oral Maxillofac. Surg.* 1987;45:319–23.

83. National Institute of Occupational Health and Safety. *Final rule: Respiratory protective devices.* 42 CFR Part 84. Federal Register 1995;60:3035–98.

84. CDC. Guidelines for preventing the transmission of Mycobacterium tuberculosis in healthcare facilities, 1994. *MMWR* 1994;43(No. RR-13):1–132.

85. Shieh W-J et al. High risk autopsy of fatal Lassa fever cases in Sierra Leone [Abstract 857]. *Lab. Invest.* 78,147A. 1998.

86. Nolte KB, Foucar K, Richmond JY. Hantavirus biosafety issues in the autopsy room and laboratory: Concerns and recommendations. *Hum. Pathol.* 1996;27:1253–4.

87. Inglesby TV et al. Plague as a biological weapon: Medical and public health management. *JAMA* 2000;283:2281–90.

88. Peters HJ. Morgue and autopsy room design [Chapter 9]. In: Hutchins GM, ed. *Autopsy Performance and Reporting.* Skokie, IL: College of American Pathologists, 1990; 51–4.

89. American Institute of Architects. Guidelines for Design and Construction of Hospital and Healthcare Facilities. Washington, DC: American Institute of Architects Press, 2001.

90. CDC, *National Institutes of Health. Primary Containment for Biohazards: Selection, Installation and Use of Biological Safety Cabinets,* 2nd ed. Washington, DC: U.S. Government Printing Office, 2000.

91. CDC. Recommendations for using smallpox vaccine in a pre-event vaccination program: supplemental recommendations of the Advisory Committee on Immunization Practices (ACIP) and the Healthcare Infection Control Practices Advisory Committee (HICPAC). *MMWR* 2003;52(No. RR-7):6.

92. CDC. Prevention of plague: Recommendations of the Advisory Committee on Immunization Practices (ACIP). *MMWR* 1996;45(No. RR-14):1–15.

93. Mallak CT, Ritchie EC. *Investigation, Identification, and repatriation of contaminated fatalities [Abstract G46].* Presented at the American Academy of Forensic Sciences annual meeting, February 16–21, 2004, Dallas, Texas.

94. Nolte KB. Emerging infectious agents and the forensic pathologist: making organism specific diagnoses. *N.A.M.E. News* 1997;5(6):4.

95. Hanzlick R, Parrish RG. Death investigation report forms (DIRFs): generic forms for investigators (IDIRFs) and certifiers (CDIRFs). *J. Forensic Sci.* 1994;39:629–36.

96. CDC. Medical Examiner/Coroner Death Investigation Data Set (MCDIDS), January 1995. Atlanta, GA: US Department of Health and Human Services, CDC, 1995. Available at http://www.cdc.gov/epo/dphsi/mecisp/forms/MC-DIDS95A.doc.

97. Bush GW. Homeland security Presidential directive/HSPD 5: Management of domestic incidents. Washington, DC: the White House, 2003. Available at http://www.fas.org/irp/offdocs/nspd/hspd-5.html.

98. Center for Law and the Public's Health at Georgetown and Johns Hopkins Universities. Model State Emergency Health Powers Act, as of December 21, 2001. Washington, DC: Center for Law and the Public's Health, 2002. Available at http://www.publichealthlaw.net/MSEHPA/MSEHPA2.pdf.

99. Gostin LO et al. Model State Emergency Health Powers Act: Planning for and response to bioterrorism and naturally occurring infectious diseases. *JAMA* 2002;288:622–8.

100. Federal Emergency Management Agency. Basic Incident Command System (ICS). Emmitsburg, MD: Federal Emergency Management Agency, 2003. Available at http://training.fema.gov.

101. Dekalb County Board of Health Center for Public Health Preparedness. Dekalb and Fulton counties bioterrorism response plan. Atlanta, GA: Dekalb County Board of Health, 2001. Available at http://www.dekalbhealth.net.

102. CDC. Smallpox Response Plan and Guidelines (version 3.0). Atlanta, GA: US Department of Health and Human Services, CDC, 2002. Available at http://www.bt.cdc.gov/agent/smallpox/response-plan/index.asp.

Chapter 8

The Role of Funeral Directors and Mortuary Personnel within the DMORT Operations in Mass Disasters

Mark Roper

The unique qualifications of the funeral director in her or his normal workplace qualifies the DMORT mortuary officer to work in a wide range of roles within a mass fatality disaster operation. These roles include embalming, casketing, transporting decedents, death notification and death certificate compilation, morgue setup, Family Assistance Center, body escorts, photography of the remains, search and recovery, and holding and refrigeration of the decedents. Many of these roles are within the normal function of the funeral director in his daily discipline.

The task of working with dead human bodies and grieving family members can be psychologically and physically demanding. The funeral director is trained in those demands and his or her experience associated with handling dead human remains is beneficial to the mass fatality disaster operation. The funeral director must understand that a disaster operation does magnify the physical and psychological stress demands, and therefore is open to professional counseling or Critical Incident Stress Debriefing.

Embalming

This section will ensure that thorough disinfection, preparation, and restoration are accomplished on each body or part of a body when appropriate authorization is given by the next-of-kin. Next-of-kin may contract with a funeral home to perform this function, and may authorize cremation as the final means of disposition.

- Appropriate DMORT embalming case reports shall be completed and inserted into the DVP.
- Disaster specific guidelines for embalming should be established following the DMORT SOP as closely as possible.

- Embalmers shall use embalming and minor reconstructive surgery techniques that will enhance the possibility of viewability of the deceased.

The Embalming Unit Leader or a designee will be responsible for assigning licensed embalmers who possess knowledge of postmortem reconstructive surgery to the task of classifying each human remains on the type of embalming, preservation techniques, and postmortem surgery to be used.

Refrigerated Storage

This section will number trailers or other storage facilities and keep an accurate log of human remains and the locations in which they are stored and restored. Staffing and equipment will vary according to disaster specific needs.

Recommended Staffing:
Unit Leader
Three personnel for inside trailer and moving decedents
Two personnel on ground for maintenance and logging

Recommended Equipment:
Clipboard and log, gloves, flashlight, jackets for inside personnel, body gurneys, padlocks.

- The log shall reflect the reference number and destination of remains when taken out of storage.
- There should be three personnel assigned to enter the storage area to remove bodies as needed. There should be two ground personnel who will transfer the body to the admitting area of the morgue.
- The unit leader will monitor the refrigeration units and assure that they are properly serviced. The recommended temperature is 35–38 degrees Farenheit.
- Company name and logo on all trailers should be covered.
- If trailers are used, approximate space requirements is 20 adult whole bodies per 40-foot trailer. At no time shall bodies be stacked upon each other.

Remains of decedents must be handled with the utmost respect and care. DMORT team members will ensure that all human remains (identified, unidentified, common tissue, or any other types of remains) are stored with dignity, prepared with professionalism, and transported with consideration.

Post-Identification Holding in the Incident Morgue
Once remains have been identified, they are securely stored in an environment
that retards decomposition and maintains the chain of custody.

Procedure:
- Following identification, remains should be stored in a designated refrigerator trailer or similar container. This container should be designated only for identified remains.
- Supervisor receives from driver the trailer lock key, if any
- Sufficient personnel should be used to carry the litter or move the gurney so that remains are not harmed and so that lifting injuries are reduced.
- A movement log sheet will indicate the following:
  ◊ Number(s) of the body bag(s) comprising the decedents remains
  ◊ Date and time in or out of storage
  ◊ Name and signature of tracker
  ◊ Name and signature of storage worker releasing or accepting body bag
  ◊ If more than one refrigerator is used, record which unit the body bag is going in or coming out

Death Notification
The documentation of the identification, the cause and manner of death, and final
disposition are required by law and used for vital statistics and the initiation of probate. The death certificate is the legal instrument for this documentation. The Medical Examiner/Coroner (ME/C) is responsible for all legal documentation pertaining
to death certification.

- The medical examiner/coroner is expected to complete her portion of the certificate and transmit the document concurrent with the release of the decedent.
- When no human remains are recovered, or scientific efforts for identification prove insufficient, a court-ordered certification of death may be sought.

The nature of the victim identification process demands that the next-of-kin
(NOK) be involved in certain decisions regarding the remains of the decedent.
Their decision on these matters must be documented and followed.

NOK will be notified by the ME/C when identification is made. In the case
of complete remains, this notification should be followed fairly quickly by release to the designated funeral home.

Where appropriate, as in cases of fragmentation or commingling, the ME/C will explain to the families the available options for disposition of any subsequently identified remains and assist them with that process. These options include:

- Notification each time additional remains are identified.
- Notification at the end of the identification process.
- Return the currently identified remains to the family for final disposition.
- Return of all remains at end of the identification process.
- Other requirements the family may have will be considered if they do not impact overall identification efforts.

Funeral Home Contact Information
To coordinate the shipping of remains and any NOK considerations, the receiving funeral home will be contacted and information exchanged.

- The required information should be gathered at the time the medical examiner/coroner makes the positive ID notification to the NOK.
- The information required from the NOK:
  ◊ Name of funeral home
  ◊ Contact person at funeral home
  ◊ Location (city, state, zip code)
  ◊ Telephone and fax number
  ◊ If the exact address, fax number, email address, and contact person is known, this can be recorded.
  ◊ Obtain from the funeral home the best airport or train station to which to ship the decedent.

Inform the funeral home of the schedule once the transportation arrangements have been confirmed.

Reassociation of Remains

In situations where remains are fragmented and commingled, identified remains may be reassociated so that remains belonging to individuals are returned together to the next-of-kin. Often, because DNA analysis is the method used to conduct these identifications, the physical reassociation of remains can take place several weeks or months after an accident.

- Remains will be reassociated one decedent at a time.

- Remains related to a particular decedent will be removed from the storage container (refrigerator trailer) and moved into an area designated for reassociation.
- The appropriate documentation will be used to select the appropriately numbered remains for that decedent.
- Remains will be examined to ensure that the physical characteristics are identical to those on the associated documentation.
- After review, all remains associated with the decedent will be placed in the appropriate container, such as a casket, transfer case, body bag, etc.
- Remains will then be returned back to storage or sent to embalming if being conducted in the incident morgue.
- If remains are to be released, they should be sent to Final Identification Review before release.

Transportation

Transportation of Remains to Incident Morgue

Transportation of remains from the crash site, or temporary morgue, to the morgue site will be professional and dignified. Care should be taken to ensure all remains are properly bagged, tagged, inventoried and placed in a refrigeration trailer or other appropriate vehicle for transportation to the morgue.

A log sheet will be maintained indicating the following:

- Assigned body number for each remain being transported
- Number of remains being transported in the vehicle
- The license number of the transporting vehicle
- The name of the driver of the vehicle
- Signature of driver accepting responsibility for remains
- Date and time vehicle leaves crash site for morgue
- Enclosed professional funeral vehicles or refrigerated trailers should be used.
- Remains will not be stacked.
- Determine the number of refrigerated trailers needed for transport (approximately 20 adult whole bodies per 40-foot trailer).
- Place vehicles in a secure area near accident site with easy access to load remains.
- Once bagged, tagged and placed on a litter, the remains will be carried to the vehicle and loaded.
- Use sufficient personnel to carry each litter to reduce lifting injuries.

- Trailer doors will be locked and remain locked while human remains are inside.
- Vehicle driver will deliver the door key to morgue refrigerator storage supervisor.
- Vehicle driver will be provided the route and will proceed directly to the morgue with no deviations.
- Police escort may be arranged with the local or state law enforcement.

Transportation of Decedents from Morgue

This section coordinates the transport of released human remains from the morgue to a designated location, such as an airport for transport to the receiving funeral home.

- A minimum of two licensed funeral directors should staff this section
- The burial-transit-cremation permit and other documentation required by the receiving funeral home will be secured from the Information Resources Section.
- The burial-transit-cremation permit and other documentation will be placed in the "Head" envelope.
- The completed "Head" envelope will be securely affixed to the head end of the outside container.
- Hearses or other appropriate vehicles normally used to transport decedents will be used.
- The Unit Leader shall be responsible for assuring that all necessary release and transfer documentation is in order and shall maintain a log reflecting the date, time, transfer vehicle identification, transfer personnel identification, and destination.
- Transfer personnel shall wear professional attire during the transfer.
- Movement of the hearses may be coordinated in "procession" style if appropriate. Police escorts may be used when necessary.
- An adequate number of casket bearers (team members, volunteer funeral directors, etc.) should be present for loading and off-loading so as to mitigate bearer injury or chances of mishandling the remains.
- Drivers should be instructed to travel directly to the destination and directly back to the morgue without any stops except at a designated staging area or to refuel.

Photography

Photography of remains is an essential and standard process for forensic examination. Each body or numbered fragment will be photographed. DMORT typically relies on the local jurisdiction medicolegal or law enforcement personnel to take photographs. DMORT personnel can take photographs if required.

Procedure
- For complete bodies, standard autopsy-type photographs will be taken (anatomical position).
- Where possible, full-face photographs will be taken.
- All photographs will contain the morgue reference number as well as a reference scale where applicable.
- The entire remain will be present in the photograph.
- Photography station personnel will maintain a photo log.
- Photographs of personal effects will be taken prior to removal.
- Digital cameras are preferable to film cameras.
- Digital image files will be provided to the IR section for inclusion into VIP.
- Hard copies of digital photographs will be placed in the DVP when available.

Casketing

This section is charged with placing human remains in a casket and the disposition of the remains to a designated site.

Recommended Staffing:
- Three licensed funeral directors (one designated as Unit Leader)
- Three assistants

Recommended Equipment:
- Casket trucks
- Tags, markers
- Desk, chairs
- Refer to DPMU Listing

Points of Consideration:
- Place bodies in caskets as necessary. The outside of the casket shall bear the name of the deceased.
- Maintain a log reflecting the disposition of the body. The log shall identify the date, time, and to whom the body was released.

- The Unit Leader shall assure that the appropriate DMORT form is signed by the person to whom the body is released. The form shall be inserted into the DVP.
- If any personal effects are released with the body, the appropriate DMORT form must be signed by the person to whom the body is released. The form shall be inserted into the DVP.

Search and Recovery

- The DMORT Search and Recovery Unit Leader will survey and assess the situation making note of necessary information about the disaster at hand, including: number of bodies, security issues, worker safety issues, and special requests by investigating agencies. The Search and Recovery Unit Leader will develop a search plan for the area and identify the number of personnel, equipment, and special resources, such as cadaver search canine needed to accomplish the mission. This information will be passed on to the Operations Section Chief through the Disaster Site Division Supervisor.
- The Search and Recovery Unit Leader will conduct a briefing of the Search and Recovery Unit members prior to commencing activities. In addition to pertinent information regarding the mission at hand, the Search and Recovery Unit Leader will identify and alert search team members of specific safety issues known at the time.
- The Search and Recovery Unit will conduct its operation in the most efficient manner possible. However, it must focus on standard practices of evidence preservation.
- Careful scene documentation will be carried out in the form of sketches, video, and/or photos.
- When applicable, the site will be divided into sectors and then grids.
- Suitable stakes or marking will be placed at the location of each body part. Numbers will be assigned to each body and each body part and records kept, identifying the location of the body within the disaster site.
- The Search and Recovery Unit will be divided into smaller units as needed.
- Extensive efforts will be implemented to achieve recovery of all human tissue, which will be collected and transferred to the morgue.

- Wallets and jewelry or other items attached to a body will not be removed. They will be transferred to the morgue with the body.

When the situation dictates, the Search and Recovery Unit may be required to remove the remains from the immediate site and transfer them to an evacuation area. In the event an evacuation area is not necessary the remains will be transferred to the morgue utilizing the best method available.

Temporary Morgue

Principle: In some transportation disasters, an area will be designated as the temporary or holding morgue. This morgue is where remains are held until transport to the incident morgue. Some initial examination and documentation of remains may take place in this morgue.

Procedure: The temporary morgue should be a permanent or semi-permanent structure nearby the accident site. In some cases, a tent or vehicle will be used, particularly in rural areas. When the remains are removed from the accident site, they will be placed in body bags or a similar appropriate container/bag. This container/bag will be marked with the site recovery number pertaining to the remains. The container/bag will be placed in the temporary morgue and will be logged into the inventory system in the morgue. Once removed from the morgue, the remains will again be logged as such.

Body Escorts

- It shall be the duty of the Unit Leader to ensure that all escorts have been thoroughly briefed as to their duties and shall maintain a log of their names, and date and time of duty.
- Volunteers from a state funeral director and embalmers disaster team work well as escorts. Escorts will be carefully evaluated regarding their personal medical fitness taking into account conditions such as heart problems, high blood pressure, pregnancy, special impairments, etc. and for their experience associated with handling dead human remains. Stress factors will also be monitored carefully on all personnel serving as escorts.
- If using volunteers, the Body Escort Unit Leader should verify at the end of each operational period, the number of volunteers that will return for their next assigned operational period and ensure proper staffing is available.

- The Body Escort Unit Leader shall assign at least one body escort to each container, pouch or evidence bag containing human remains before it begins processing through the morgue system. When the human remains have been processed though all appropriate morgue sections the body escort shall return the DVP to the Unit Leader. The Body Escort Unit Leader shall assure that all forms in the DVP have been accurately completed before releasing or reassigning the escort.
- It is the responsibility of the escort to transfer a body through the various sections of the morgue for processing and remain with the body until all processing aspects are completed.
- It is the responsibility of the escort to ensure section personnel complete, sign, and insert completed forms in the DVP.
- The Body Escort Unit Leader is responsible for returning all DVPs to the Admitting/Processing Group Supervisor.
- The escorts shall be staged in the escort section of the morgue, which shall be near or next to the admitting section.

Family Assistance Center

The DMORT FAC team supports the local medicolegal authority in the collection of antemortem data collection, including the collection of DNA samples. Working with the FAC, the DMORT FAC team interviews the next-of-kin, collects antemortem information, and transfers this information to the Information Resource Center. If requested, the team will also provide information to the next-of-kin and assist the medicolegal authority with death notifications.

Chapter 9

Forensic Engineering in Mass Disasters: Analysis, Prevention, and Mitigation

Steven C. Batterman, Ph.D.[1]

Introduction

When many people, including professionals, hear the words "mass disaster" they typically think in terms of response, rescue, recovery, remains, reaction, retaliation, etc. However, all of the aforementioned connote a retrospective view, i.e., the mass disaster has already occurred and the central problem is one of managing and coordinating the appropriate response to the mass disaster. As critical as management and coordination of the response to a mass disaster obviously are, they are simply not good enough for engineers and are only one part of the process of managing the mass disaster. The portion which is often overlooked by the media, and which does not get the up-front attention it deserves, is the concept of preventing or mitigating the effect of a potential mass disaster in the first place by proper engineering design and preparedness.

A major goal of engineering is to design systems in order to avoid failures by acting prospectively, not retroactively, when it comes to design. Engineering design relies on sophisticated analyses and techniques to account, in advance, for severe inputs in order to minimize the probability of potential failures and resulting casualties. Another, of course, is to analyze engineering failures which may have occurred in order to learn the lessons of the failure to prevent future recurrences. It must be emphasized that major engineering design failures are relatively rare when compared to the overwhelming majority of successful engineering systems and designs that operate without failure for the lifetime of the design, when properly maintained. However, a major distinction of an engineering failure, regardless of the cause and which uniquely distinguishes engineering from other professions, is that thousands of casualties can occur from a single failure event. Compare this, for example, to the typical medical malpractice situation where only one victim may result. Engineers are ever mindful of their obligation and mandate to design safely and, in fact, the first fundamental canon of the Code of Ethics of Engineers states "Engineers shall hold paramount the safety, health and welfare of the public in the performance of their professional duties."

The main purpose of this chapter is to focus attention on engineering aspects of the prevention and mitigation of mass disasters, although of course properly managing a mass disaster is critical once it has occurred. Remarks shall also be made concerning the forensic analysis of failures. It is noted at this juncture that the lay person's view of an engineering failure is one that gets wide media publicity such as the recent collapse of the I-35W bridge in Minneapolis on August 1, 2007, or the massive explosion of the space shuttle Challenger on January 28, 1986 (which was witnessed by millions of people on worldwide television), or the sinking of the submarine USS Thresher. To an engineer, however, failure has a connotation depending on the use and purpose of an engineering system, which may involve only a loss of function and does not necessarily involve the loss of life. Since the subject of this chapter is mass disasters, further attention shall be devoted to failures which have the potential for massive loss of life along with the means for preventing or mitigating such disasters. However, it is emphasized that regardless of the precise type of failure that a system may undergo, it is an engineering design maxim, or fundamental principle, that SUCCESS IN DESIGN IS FORESEEING FAILURE. This means that during the design process engineers postulate or assume various failure modes and then design the system to prevent or mitigate the failure. As shall be seen, the assumed failure modes may involve extreme inputs.

We shall briefly consider the origin of mass disasters which can arise from several causes, and shall include examples. It is noted that the lines between the areas listed below can become blurred since, for example, an aircraft can crash into a building by accident, as has happened several times, or an aircraft can be used as a terrorist weapon and purposely crashed into a building, i.e., September 11, 2001. We shall make remarks herein on the following five areas:

1. Terrorism (attacks on buildings, aircraft, etc.)
2. Design Errors (Failure resulting from a design error, e.g., Hyatt Regency Skywalk Collapse.)
3. Catastrophic Natural Events (such as earthquakes, hurricanes, tornadoes, tsunamis, etc.)
4. Engineering Design (meaning the type of design to accomplish a given task, recognizing that design is not unique. For example, Chernobyl v. Three Mile Island.)
5. Accident or Malfunction (Catastrophic results due to accidents or due to poor operational management, e.g., Bhopal, India)

Terrorism

Unfortunately, we live in a world where international and domestic terrorism is a fact of life for now and the foreseeable future, and must be factored into engineering designs. As we are all aware, terrorist attacks on buildings and aircraft have caused mass disasters, apart from suicide bombers indiscriminately targeting large gatherings of people. Although the United States is not immune from mass disasters caused by natural catastrophes, such as hurricanes and earthquakes, it is likely that a significant number of Americans consider terrorism as the primary source of future mass disasters. Consider the following:

Pan Am 103

On 21 December 1988, a small terrorist bomb, or IED (Improvised Explosive Device), consisting of only 0.34 to 0.40 kg of Semtex-H which was strategically located in a piece of luggage immediately adjacent to the fuselage of a Boeing 747, destroyed the aircraft known as Pan Am 103 over Lockerbie, Scotland. The IED was hidden in a Toshiba radio-cassette player and contained a detonator consisting of a barometric device plus a timer. The aircraft broke up in flight due to crack propagation around the fuselage originating at the blast site, there was no on-board fire, and no passengers were killed by the blast itself. 270 fatalities occurred, which included all on board (243 passengers + 16 crew members) and 11 residents of Lockerbie, when large sections of the aircraft crashed into the town. In the decades of the 1970's, 1980's and 1990's, electronic devices were the favorite hiding places for terrorist bombs. Since electronic devices were and are getting smaller, IED's hidden in such devices necessarily have to get smaller. Effective engineering means exist for preventing or mitigating the structural damage of this threat in at least two ways. First, blast resistant luggage containers can be used by the airlines which will effectively contain the blast without aircraft structural damage. Blast resistant (not blast proof) containers have been tested and do resist the explosion of IED's which are the size of the Pan Am 103 IED. Second, the fuselage can be redesigned such that blow-out regions exist in the cargo sections of the aircraft, along with hardened cargo bay floors and roofs. When an IED detonates in such sections only that section will blow out without cracks propagating around the entire fuselage causing aircraft break-up.

September 11, 2001

The collapse of the two World Trade Center (WTC) towers is an example where terrorists used essentially fully fueled airliners as effective weapons. However, it is not commonly appreciated that the WTC towers withstood the direct impact forces extremely well, and would have remained standing but for the subsequent fires. The outer perimeter columns obviously sustained structural damage in the immediate impact areas but there was sufficient redundancy and strength in the remaining perimeter and core columns to allow load redistribution and to support the building loads. However, the impacts dislodged fireproofing and the fires caused thermal weakening of the perimeter and core columns in the impact areas. Eventually the thermally weakened columns buckled and could not support the weight of the towers above the impact areas. The columns below the impact areas could not support the dynamic loading caused by the collapse of the floors above and the towers collapsed in a sequential fashion. The collapse of the WTC towers is known as progressive collapse where the floors pancaked into one another as each floor was sequentially subjected to increasing loading from above, beyond the capacity of the structure below to sustain the loads.

A controversy exists concerning the design of the WTC since the collapses of the towers appears disproportionate to the initial structural damage caused by the initial aircraft impacts. The controversy revolves around the framed tube concept utilized for the design of the WTC, i.e., perimeter columns, load bearing external walls and internal load bearing core structure, used for very tall buildings although foreseeable aircraft impacts into tall buildings occurred long before the advent of 9/11 terrorism. To name a few, it is noted that a B-25 bomber crashed into the Empire State Building on July 28, 1945 and an Army C-45 Beechcraft crashed into the Bank of Manhattan Building in NYC on May 20, 1946. Each building sustained major damage at the impact sites, but neither building underwent a progressive collapse. The initial engineering and architectural structural choice of the WTC framed tube concept, along with the fireproofing used and lack of other fire protection features, may thus be open to criticism and allegations of defective design in view of the fact that plane crashes into tall buildings were reasonably foreseeable at the time the WTC was designed. This is also an example where the type of design can influence the outcome of whether or not a mass disaster will occur as a function of the input loadings.

Murrah Federal Building, Oklahoma City, July 19, 1985
The truck bomb which destroyed the reinforced concrete Murrah Federal Building (built in 1976) is also an example of progressive collapse, where the collapse was disproportionate to the initiating cause. The

blast caused damage to the columns on the lower level of the building. However, due to the lack of reinforcing steel in critical areas the upper floors underwent a progressive, sequential collapse after the failure of the lower columns. It has been estimated that if the building had been built or retrofitted to the seismic standards of the 1990's, as much as 50-80% of the damage, and perhaps some of the resulting injuries and 168 fatalities could have been prevented.

Design Errors

On July 17, 1981 a suspended skywalk in the Hyatt Regency Hotel in Kansas City, MO collapsed during a TGIF dance party, leading to 114 deaths and more than 200 people injured. The structural collapse was the most deadly in American history due to a design error. Forensic investigation and analysis after the collapse indicated that a design detail change made during construction caused the collapse when the walkway suspension rods for the fourth floor walkway pulled out of their connection to the walkway box beam supports. The fourth floor walkway then fell onto the second floor walkway causing it to collapse as well. This failure is an example of where a small but critical change in a design detail, which was made simply to facilitate construction of the walkway, was either not checked or was mistakenly found to be not deficient. Fortunately, bona fide design errors are relatively rare but the nature of an engineering system, such as a building that directly interacts with the public, is that even one error can cause a multitude of fatalities and injuries.

Catastrophic Natural Events

There is no practical and feasible way to completely eliminate damage and casualties that can be caused by natural events such as earthquakes, hurricanes, tsunamis, tornadoes, etc. However, the loss of life and property damage can be considerably reduced by the implementation of improved construction techniques and building codes, which are enforced by local authorities. Of course, cultural considerations and socio-economic constraints in given regions cannot be ignored. This is particularly true in developing countries which may make the population vulnerable to a natural catastrophe when it does occur.

Earthquakes are worthy of special mention since building codes and construction techniques in earthquake zones of the United States do offer reasonable protection against the type of mass disaster following the 1906 San Francisco earthquake. It should be noted that casualties and property damage depend on several factors which include, but are not limited to, the magnitude and duration of the earthquake, population density, distance of buildings/structures from the quake epicenter, type of buildings/structures and their construction, and the time of day (people may be asleep at home, or at work, or traveling to work - all of which will have different casualty outcomes for the same earthquake). Furthermore, the intention of building codes is to prevent complete or total collapse of structures in earthquake zones, and no building code will ever state that structures should not suffer any damage in quakes of all magnitudes.

Engineers have been very successful in preventing and/or mitigating mass disasters in earthquake zones where seismic building codes have been implemented and strictly enforced. The State of California is a case in point where engineers who design structures have to be specifically qualified in earthquake resistant design. It is also worth noting that adherence to seismic building codes also offers structures blast protection since the probability of progressive collapse will be minimized.

Type of Engineering Design

When the collapses of the WTC towers was discussed it was noted that the type of engineering design can influence the eventual failure outcome. Another significant example in the annals of engineering is a comparison of the nuclear reactors which failed at Three Mile Island (TMI), Dauphin County, PA on March 28, 1979, and at Chernobyl in the Ukraine on April 26, 1986.

Unit 2 at TMI was a pressurized water reactor that experienced a valve failure on the secondary side. The reactor automatically shut down when the valve failure occurred, as it was supposed to by design, and could never have gone super-critical. However, due to ensuing operator errors, radioactive steam was released into the containment structure which houses the reactor (which itself is also contained within a reactor pressure vessel) and a partial core meltdown did occur before the operators realized a loss of coolant accident (LOCA) had occurred. The containment structure is a reinforced concrete structure with 12 foot thick walls, and was designed to withstand aircraft impacts as well as enormous internal pressures. No explosion occurred, the containment structure was not breached, all the radiation was contained within the containment structure, and even the reactor pressure vessel itself retained its structural integrity even though about one-third of the fuel melted. Significantly, there were no injuries to TMI workers or to members of nearby communities.

There is no doubt that TMI was a serious accident and there were indeed operational blunders, along with some valve design issues. However, overall TMI was an engineering success not an engineering failure, and the media hype and spin surrounding the accident essentially doomed the nuclear industry in the United States for decades.

Compare the situation at TMI to that which occurred at Chernobyl when Unit #4 exploded, which was one of four reactors. The reactors at Chernobyl were graphite-moderated water cooled reactors which have never been built outside the Soviet Union. Very significantly, however, unlike TMI the reactors were not housed within a robust containment structure.

The explosion occurred during a reactor experiment when safety systems, along with safety regulations, were bypassed. Ironically, the purpose of the experiment was to test one of the safety systems while the reactor was running on low power. Thirty-one people died in the immediate aftermath of the explosion, mostly fighting graphite fires, and a large radioactive cloud blanketed a major portion of Europe. In order to contain the radiation the remains of the reactor were sealed in a concrete sarcophagus. Several workers died from radiation exposure during the building of the sarcophagus. The sarcophagus itself is now failing and has large holes and cracks which allows radioactive dust to escape. Estimates of delayed health effects from radiation vary widely with the WHO estimating that as many as 9,000 of the 6.6 million most highly exposed people may die from cancer.

The Chernobyl accident was the worst accident in the history of nuclear power. Initially the accident was blamed solely on operator error but was later revised to include design defects. The major design defect in the Chernobyl design was the lack of a strong containment structure housing the reactor, similar to the TMI containment structure which averted a tragedy in the United States.

Accidents and Malfunctions

Proper engineering design can minimize the probability of mass disasters occurring from accidents or malfunctions. Consider the following two examples:

Nuclear Cask Design

Nuclear casks are large cylindrical structures, constructed of either steel (8 feet in diameter by 18 feet long) or reinforced concrete (11 feet in diameter by 20 feet long), which are used to used to transport spent nuclear fuel from reactors to permanent storage locations. The casks are transported on railroad flatbed cars which pass through population centers. Hence, in order to avoid a mass disaster, the casks are designed to survive, without leakage, in the event of a railroad accident or an impact from a fighter type jet aircraft or an engine falling off a large jetliner, such as a 767. The aircraft impacts can be accidental, although the probability of an accidental impact is very low, or it can be from an intentional terrorist attack, again using aircraft as weapons.

Bhopal, India

It is likely that the greatest industrial accident in history occurred in Bhopal, India in the early morning hours of December 3, 1984 at the site of a Union Carbide chemical plant. That night deadly methyl isocyanate (MIC) gas leaked from storage tanks and a dense cloud of gas spread over the city as people slept. At least 3000 people died immediately and, to date, it is estimated that more than 20,000 have died with up to 120,000 more still suffering from the effects of the gas.

The initiating cause of the gas leak was due to a malfunction when water inadvertently entered the MIC storage tanks and caused a runaway chemical reaction, followed by a rapid rise in temperature and pressure leading to the escape of the gas. Investigation revealed that none of the plant's safety systems were operational on the night of the accident, and the plant was inadequately staffed. In addition to poor plant maintenance, and allowing operation without safety systems in place, Union Carbide was severely criticized for locating the pesticide plant so close to a heavily populated area for purely economic reasons. Unfortunately, this disaster is an example where human error was the substantial causal factor although proper safety system design could have prevented the tragedy.

Concluding Remarks

The major purpose of this chapter is to indicate that by acting prospectively, i.e., in advance by considering potential failures resulting from extreme inputs, proper engineering design can prevent or mitigate conditions that could lead to mass disasters. In addition to that mentioned herein, it should be noted that engineering techniques, including digital forensics, are also very significant in counter-terrorism and counterintelligence activities which are obvious preventive measures against mass disasters arising from terrorist acts.

Endnote

1. Forensic Engineering Consultant, Batterman Engineering, LLC, Cherry Hill, New Jersey. Professor Emeritus, School of Engineering and Applied Science, School of Medicine, University of Pennsylvania, Philadelphia. Adjunct Professor, College of Medicine, Drexel University, Philadelphia.

Chapter 10

Psychopathy, Media and the Psychology at the Root of Terrorism and Mass Disasters

Michael Welner, M.D.

10.1 Introduction and Definitions

What is terrorism? Is it defined differently today? Should it be? Engaging the psychology of terrorism requires a clear acceptance and understanding of what terrorism actually is.

The challenge of understanding terror confronts decision makers and thought-leaders who sometimes enjoy the comfort of remoteness from terror acts. The news media's abandonment of focus on fact for the sympathies of its reporters[1] has nurtured ambiguity into contemporary understanding of the definition of terrorism. The by-product of this whitewashing has included attaching moral equivalence between terror and the actions of terrorists' targets;[2] or, validating such terror as an acceptable stimulus to change.[3]

The visceral impact of terror ensures that targets of terrorism will never need to be educated as to the meaning of the word "terrorism." Furthermore, as the very goals of terror include chaos and confusion, it behooves all of us to revisit what terror is, and its aims, in order not to be indeed victimized by terror's less vivid objectives.

This chapter is written with the objective of maintaining purity in use of the word "terrorism," for it is the flip exploitation of "terrorism" that cleverly handicaps efforts to expose terror. To appreciate the meaning of terror is to recognize the urgency to eliminate it as one of the lowest, most disgusting forms of human expression. But emotion must be dispensed within the belly of the beast—for it is emotion of the victim that terror seeks to manipulate as well. Discipline and resolve is needed for the study of anything incendiary, lest we mishandle something explosive and cause untimely and unwanted damage.

Terrorism, as defined for the application of this chapter, is a strategy of action through which, in target, timing, significance, or substance, aims at a broader unknown civilian society by design in such a way as to inspire fear and anxiety, and to intentionally affect a population to cause them to avoid conventional actions of their daily life. The intended targets of violence are not only the physical targets; rather, the broader society.

A common distinction, however erroneous, is that terrorism does not occur as part of a military action or war.[4] That distinction, however, ignores the goals of war and those organizations that employ terrorism as a strategy. War is designed to a strategic end, of capturing land, strategic targets, and resources, or defending the same. The endpoint of war is not a primary targeting of civilians in order to inspire a traumatic, terrorized effect on them. Terrorism may be part of war—it is a strategy of war declared by terrorists.

Small organizations with no sovereignty haven't the luxury of formally declaring war. Without clarification, virtually anything violent that such non-sovereign organizations do might then be considered terror. And likewise, if some special allowance is made for the context of war, governments in wartime would therefore have moral allowance to exploit the conditions of war to carry out genuine terrorism. However, the human condition transcends issues of statehood with standing armies as opposed to ragtag guerillas. Terrorism is as terrorism does.

For these reasons, parsing out the setting of "war" from consideration of terror serves only the convenience of avoiding suggesting allegiances that inspire charges of bias of one's view of a particular conflict. But what good is academic consideration of terrorism if it cowers to fear of unjustified criticism, and ignores the trauma of so many affected by what should genuinely be considered terrorism? This chapter aims to preserve a consistency in defining terror so that it may be held accountable long after the covers of this book are closed.

The term "terror" is occasionally used interchangeably with "revolutionary." This, too, is inexact—for revolution is radical change, and can be brought about by a variety of means, nonviolent or violent. Even violent means need not necessarily inspire fear and disruption in the lives of uninvolved civilians. "Revolution" is, in actuality, a term of respectability, as change has been the engine of progress for many societies. Terrorism euphemizes itself by ascribing its motives as revolutionary; there is nothing reformatory about terror for the sake of destruction or personal aggrandizement. And terror has proven to fall far short of revolution. History reflects that revolution has followed the will of the masses, not the savaging of those masses through terrorist acts.

The forensic psychiatric perspective on terror borrows from evaluations of criminal responsibility. Defendants who present for psychiatric assessment in the American justice system have acknowledged involvement in a crime, and seek to mitigate responsibility in presenting themselves and their rationale to psychiatrists. As such, articulate rationale and poignant explanations are native to virtually all criminal defendants, regardless of education. All criminals — whether sane or insane — are people who can, when pressed, provide some digestible explanation for their actions if not driven from frank intoxication. The importance of psychology to terrorism, in leadership, ideology, recruitment, training, targeting, and methods of action, demands investigative verification of motives and behaviors as integral components of what distinguishes terrorism from other controversial policies or crimes.

Science lends itself to the study of terrorism by diving underneath canned advocacy to untangle the forces driving an organization, its adherents, its helpers, its targets, its timing, its actions, and its outcomes. Evidence and collateral information-gathering is a necessary part of this exercise, just as it is in every credible investigation. What falls short of this diligence perpetuates terror by misidentifying it and negating the impact that defines it.

Terrorism pursues the goal of power: real, perceived, and financial. Its *modus operandi* for achieving these ends has features common across cultures and conflicts. The success of that terror, however, depends very much on the leadership of a specific terror organization, its financing, how the terror group goes about achieving its impact, and the complex relationship terrorists have with the media that observes and frames that impact for the public that terrorists wish to reach.

10.2 Media as a *Modus Operandi*

Terror creates fear and confusion in the community of the target, making routine activity difficult or avoided. This tumult causes a broader society to focus on the terrorism and to consider the legitimacy of the terrorists' agenda. To maximize the likelihood of such an end, terror must be exceptionally media-sensitive, targeting symbols, dates, images, and influencing perceptions directly and subtly.

Like the most cynically devised political campaigns, terror specifically focuses on attention-seeking, bringing the terrorists notoriety, perceived omnipotence, and through that, validity to the terrorist group. Terror creates an exaggerated perception of a gang's influence in broader society and then, generates momentum among sympathetic observers to more actively enlist in that gang.

Terrorism is sometimes chosen to achieve sociopolitical end by militant groups who haven't the resources, diplomatic credentials, or might to confront an enemy militarily. Attention-seeking acts of seemingly spectacular or symbolic scope therefore counterbalance the realities that a given terror group may have only a small number of hard-core adherents.

Mass media is therefore the oxygen and an essential ingredient of terror. Free press, and the antiestablishment spirit that drives acknowledgment in news organizations today, is readily manipulated by terror organizations that cloak themselves in rhetoric that claims to speak for the dispossessed masses.

Why, in fact, has there been so little terrorism germinating in Communist China, and North Korea, two of the most repressive societies on earth? Because the press in those countries is so repudiating to disorder and nonconformity that any successfully destructive terrorist initiative would gain no traction, glamorization, or consideration from the press beyond the act itself.

For this reason, terror goes where the press is, goes where the press goes. Charles Manson targeted Hollywood, and his Manson family became legend for it. Colombia's FARC and the Phillipines' Abu Sayyaf kidnapped and executed Americans on several occasions. President Akhmad Kadyrov of Chechnya was blown up during an official 2004 state celebration that was being covered by world media.

Before the media age, and in particular before communications linked the world with such immediacy, the potential for spectacular destruction to inspire anxiety in a surviving community was far more limited. Thus, small organizations with little substance or sincerity could not gain a foothold in any society without a clear ideology behind them, and a more deliberate method of attracting followers. That was an age of poets and writers, of orators and intellectuals who inspired through ideas. Now, fireballs and blood-soaked images are used to recruit[5] and inspire consideration of ideas, whose power carries an endorsement of the capacity to end life, or the security of a way of life.

Terrorism, for this reason, has become far more widespread with the increasing appreciation of mass media and public information as the real instruments of power. American political campaigns raise money and orchestrate appearances to maximize exposure to the voting public and citizenry. A media magnate is the Prime Minister of Italy. Public relations companies that engage news organizations are essential arms of foreign policy.[6]

It should therefore not be surprising that terrorists measure their achievement by their ability to gain widespread attention for themselves. Terrorists would live in a cave for months to years to hide from police, but can always be found by the Associated Press for an interview. Al-Manar, the official television station of Hizbullah, reaches 10 million homes and is one of the five most-watched television stations in the entire Arab World.[7]

Terrorism is "spin" in its most destructive form. You will not see, for example, exclamations of pain from Spanish victims of the 2004 Madrid train bombings in the mosques of Morocco, where the terror was planned. However, impact of Spain's national fear of Islamic power is celebrated as a victory.

Terror has a psychological underpinning—but there is no sensitivity to those suffering terror. The notion that terrorists seek to have their enemies experience their helplessness, inferiority, humiliation, and terror is spurious; for the planned actions depersonalize victims and do not embrace their feelings. Rather, terror focuses on the media and mass response to the event. Bombing is a sensational crime: Explosions, along with dramatic assassinations, have been used to dramatic effectiveness by the IRA in Northern Ireland and Great Britain, the Liberation Tigers of Tamil Eelam (LTTE) in Sri Lanka, and elsewhere.

Moslem terrorists, Arab Moslem terrorists in particular, have made suicide bombing unique to their contemporary honored culture. The inspiration for suicide bombing, however, and the impact of its terror spectacle, cannot ignore the impact of the LTTE (also known as the Tamil Tigers) and the perversity of their *modus operandi*.

The Tamil Tigers had a penchant for recording, through videos and photography, their political assassinations. The Tamil's filming of the 1991 assassination of India's Prime Minister Rajiv Gandhi enabled the solving of that case, as the photographer perished in the suicide bomb attack but his film somehow survived.[8]

Terror targets communities in such a way as to maximize horror, shock, dismay, and grief. Numbers tell part of the story; attacks may be selected to defile religious holidays and worship, target charity or rescue workers, or students and children.[9] The impact extends and amplifies anxiety in the surviving community, and may also communicate a message within the terror organization or the community of its supporters.[10]

Impact enables the terror organization to extend far beyond its sheer numbers. For example, Peru's Senderoso Luminoso (Shining Path) never claimed more than several thousand adherents in its heyday. Yet, in the 1980s, rebels of the Shining Path took over larger sections of the Peruvian countryside by killing villagers en masse, often hacking them with machetes. The most formidable terror movement of its time, Shining Path inspired fears of shaking the very foundation of the government of Peru, and was responsible for an estimated 30,000 deaths.[11]

There is no need to identify with terrorism and the stated missions of its leaders in order to understand them. For much of the rationalization and philosophy attached to terrorism originates from sympathetic writers and thinkers who seek to make sense of the unthinkable after it happens. Goetzel termed these individuals "radical theorists."[12] Some of these radical theorists are even showcased in respectable texts as experts in terrorist theory, and use such platforms to heap historical revisionism into near-delusional reconsideration of whom terrorists actually are. By instilling confusion in the otherwise well-armed potential targets of terrorism, these radical theorists and their benefactors in academia[13] and the media[14] are facilitators, providing air cover to future terror cells who exploit passivity in interdiction efforts. Resolve weakens, and the cooperative relationship between law enforcement and the community that is so needed to ferret out criminals in hiding becomes sorely undermined.

The terror-leaders themselves are more concerned with attention-seeking, and reaping the rewards of a successful terror operation. As such, the academic discourse of terrorism has in certain circles done much to encourage and foster terror, by creating an intellectual foundation for seemingly antiestablishment causes that those thinkers may identify with. With no theory or ideology well-articulated, terror is more readily appreciated for its true essence—violent crime.

Sometimes, the leaders of such terror movements have hardly advanced their own theories beyond street philosophy. The press and academia then add the agenda for them. Prabhakaran even recruited a journalist to write an ideological manifesto, long after establishing his Tamil Tigers.[15] This backward development of ideology illustrates the fundamental dishonesty of the purported link between terrorism and problem resolution that radical theorists advance to negate appreciation of terrorism as unacceptably subhuman.

One example where terror advocacy has gathered little traction because it has not inspired support among the antiestablishment press is the American white supremacist movement. Author William Pierce published novels which have been gobbled, manifesto-like, by adherents.[16] Rather than looking for "root causes" of his agenda, the leftist press has appropriately dismissed Pierce, whatever his education and ability to compose a coherent tome, as an annihilationist who simply exploited the disaffected contemporary white male to promote overt race and religious war. Far more oxygen of rationalization and justification is given, by comparison, to rationalizations for the nihilism of Palestinian nationalism.

10.3 Terrorist Leaders

The most successful leaders of terrorism organizations are often examples of psychopathy. The psychopath, on a personal scale, has the exquisite sensitivity to tap into the soft spots of the person and soul he wishes to seduce. On a smaller scale, the psychopath's target is money, sex, or drugs—essentially, the ingredients of hedonism. More sophisticated tastes drive some psychopaths to seek power as an aphrodisiac.

The essence of psychopathy is disruptive. Cold, remorseless, exploitative, impulsive, and grandiose in scope, often violent, lawless, diversely criminal, and relating to others as objects rather than people, the psychopath is a fundamentally destructive, callous temperament. The West German terrorist, Michael Baumann, recalled reacting to Charles Manson as "quite funny."[17] Given the tool for a functional or constructive path, the terror leader-psychopath cannot help but to create chaos, and to be functionally disruptive. A psychopath leader's core dysfunction is often the reason why terror movements do not endure.

Some have invoked malignant narcissism as a model for terrorist leaders, particularly when their brutality is also accompanied by signs of competent leadership.[18] When the grandiosity of psychopathy and malignant narcissism attaches (1) purpose to (2) sizeable scope of destruction, and (3) gains control of others, terror movements are born. In such circumstances, terror leaders effortlessly exploit sensitive religious and political issues to enlist devotees.

Nihilism is at the core of malignant narcissism. For the grandiosity and exploitation organizes around a hatred and an exaggerated paranoia for a target enemy. Malignant narcissists are more functionally capable of leading than psychopaths, even if their agenda so involves terror. Many leaders from even recent history, with legacies of inspiring terror among their own peoples and others, were malignant narcissists who could successfully negotiate a number of aspects of leadership. The apparent gains of Germany, for example, were testament to Adolf Hitler's capabilities long before the dominant influence of his nihilism became universally appreciated.

Malignant narcissism grows from a youth of subjugation, repression, and powerlessness. Ascribing the origins of psychopathic terror leaders to their own experience of trauma and oppression is, however, disingenuous. Vellupilai Prabhakaran, founder of the Tamil Tigers of Sri Lanka, was educated, doted on, and experienced his parents as loving, if strict. Osama bin Laden emerged from a privileged family to cofound al-Qa'eda with Mahmoud Salim, an engineer; Ayman al-Zawahiri, a pediatrician, led the virulent strain of Egyptian Jihad Islami that later folded into bin Laden's network. Likewise, the disingenuousness of the "disenfranchised" characterization extends to non-Moslem terror as well. Abimael Guzman, son of a prosperous businessman and top student in a Catholic school, grew up to found Shining Path in Peru.

Prabhakaran, whatever his healthy example, cultivated a fascination with death which initially limited itself to killing animals. But he became king of the hill when he hunted human game, murdered a moderate mayor, and drew others who fell under the spell of his shocking violent brazenness into the Tamil Tigers liberation movement.

As a matter of political predation, Prabhakaran had no peer; he was responsible for killing many political figures, including India's Prime Minister Rajiv Gandhi (1991), Sri Lankan President Ranasinghe Premadasa (1993), and numerous elected members of the Sri Lankan Parliament. Prabhakaran readily acknowledged in his earlier days, however, that he had no ideological underpinning, and was more motivated by action and excitement.[19] Asked at one time to name his heroes, he cited Clint Eastwood's personification. No one has doubted Prabhakaran's operational savvy; yet victims of the Tamil Tigers included Tamils who were inclined to more peaceful means of achieving Tamil autonomy in Sri Lanka.

How is a nihilistic terror leader able to advance such a malignant agenda beyond being isolated as a homicidal crackpot? Because no matter how unusual that terror leader is, he is distinguished by his ability to hold others under his sway, with the charisma of his personal appeal, the power of his communication, and his exquisite capacity to manipulate. Prabhakaran has, for example, inspired highly dedicated and disciplined cadres of followers, austere and conserving of resources.

How, then, are psychopath terrorist leaders different from successful politicians, or even malignant narcissists? After all, successful political movements routinely exploit populist sentiments in order to ascend. Politicians guided by the aim of public service, however, do serve the needs of public when given the opportunity. The psychopath terrorist leader, even when improbably given authority and autonomy, will not successfully transition into a servant of his community, but rather a more elaborated terrorist leader, or simply a person who profits and exploits what he has been given for material aggrandizement.

Psychopaths satisfy a penchant for destruction as antisocial personalities by proxy. Antisocial personality by proxy refers to the capacity of one person to satisfy criminally destructive aims by inspiring others to cultivate destructiveness within themselves.[20]

Yasser Arafat is a stunningly vivid study in psychopathy, and the life cycle of the psychopath as terrorist leader. An Egyptian bourgeois turned into a devoted Marxist by KGB foreign intelligence, he committed his first murder at age twenty. The KGB had trained him at its Balashikha special-ops school east of Moscow and in the mid-1960s decided to groom him as the future PLO leader.[21]

Ion Pacepa, former head of Romanian Intelligence, and the highest ranking former Soviet bloc intelligence officer to ever defect to the West, chillingly wrote of the creation of Arafat,

> In 1972, the Kremlin put Arafat and his terror networks high on all Soviet bloc intelligence services' priority list, including mine. Bucharest's role was to ingratiate him with the White House. We were the bloc experts at this . . . KGB chairman Yuri Andropov in February 1972 laughed to me about the Yankee gullibility for celebrities. We'd out-

grown Stalinist cults of personality, but those crazy Americans were still naïve enough to revere national leaders. We would make Arafat into just such a figurehead and gradually move the PLO closer to power and statehood. Andropov thought that Vietnam-weary Americans would snatch at the smallest sign of conciliation to promote Arafat from terrorist to statesman in their hopes for peace.[22]

The KGB attached Arafat to the grievances of Arabs displaced by lost wars attempting to destroy the nascent state of Israel. Since pan-Arab pride successfully suffused with vehement anti-Zionism passions, Arafat emerged in 1968 as a solitary alternative to Arab armies that had been repeatedly proven impotent to achieve the mission of an oil-wealthy region.

Financed by the deep pockets of the Soviet bloc and Arab governments, and successful at employing the necessary brutality to eliminate political alternatives, Arafat eventually assumed leadership of a people, who came to be known as Palestinians, to ascribe to his methods for achieving their political self-determination.

After being expelled from Syria in 1968, he based himself in Jordan, where he and his Fatah faction soon began terrorizing the local people, running extortion rackets against businesses, and undermining the Jordanian regime. Black September followed in 1970: Jordan's King Hussein launched a huge and bloody war against the Palestinians, killing thousands and leading to the expulsion of Arafat and his army in 1971. In Lebanon a decade later, with Palestinian thugs looting banks and destroying the local government,[23] Arafat was later expelled to Tunisia.[24]

Ultimately, Arafat masterminded the biggest hijacking (four aircraft at once), the largest number of hostages (3,000 at one time), the largest ransom extorted ($5 million from Lufthansa) and the greatest number and variety of terrorist targets (forty civilian aircraft, five passenger ships, thirty embassies or diplomatic missions and schools).[25]

Recalled Pacepa,

We Romanians were directed to help Arafat improve his extraordinary talent for deceiving. The KGB chief of foreign intelligence, General Aleksandr Sakharovsky, ordered us to provide cover for Arafat's terror operations, while at the same time building up his international image. 'Arafat is a brilliant stage manager,' his letter concluded, 'and we should put him to good use.' In March 1978 I secretly brought Arafat to Bucharest for final instructions on how to behave in Washington. You simply have to keep on pretending that you'll break with terrorism and that you'll recognize Israel—over, and over, and over.[26]

Facing elimination by Israel in Beirut, Arafat succeeded in gaining American protection for his transfer to Tunisia—only months before 243 Marines were killed in a suicide bomb attack by Hizbullah. And in 1993, Arafat was bestowed political leadership of the Palestinian Authority under an Oslo peace treaty that eventually won him a Nobel Peace Prize.

His consolidation of legitimized power, from 1993, enabled Arafat to leverage and to successfully embezzle those monies showered upon his people by Israel, the United States and the international community, perpetuate the poverty of many of his people,[27] while manipulating additionally extending and deepening the enmity of the Palestinians toward Israel. By maintaining poverty and creating an identity of disempowerment of internal repression, invoking religious symbols and objectives such as the spurious deification of Jerusalem, and finally, the attachment of empowerment to "martyrdom," Arafat exploited his control to trick the Arabs under his control to buy into terror and nihilism on an unprecedented scale. He constructed, within his media and education systems, a foundation of fundamental demonization of Israel, from which Arafat could create symbols of Palestinian empowerment through self-destruction—notwithstanding that his ascent to legitimacy through the 1993 Oslo Accords, was predicated upon his fostering a sense of peaceful coexistence among his people.

Arafat transformed the identity of "Palestinians" into a cause that transcended any semblance of reality or proportion, and thus Arafat brilliantly seduced the international community into showering him with unprecedented largesse and protection. Specifically, from the Oslo Accords until the end of 2001, more than $5.5 billion was given to the PA in aid. This translates to $1,330 a Palestinian. In comparison, the Marshall Plan to rebuild Europe after World War II provided each European with $272 in today's dollars.[28] All this while terror continued unabated.

However, like any psychopath, Arafat had no constitutional wherewithal for leadership of a country. He was not programmed, after all, as a leader of men, but rather an exploiter of men.

In the twenty years before the Oslo Accords, gave Yasser Arafat sovereign authority, the number of Israelis killed by Palestinian terrorists was approximately 400. In the ten years that followed, that number was approximately 1,600, nearly 1,000 of which came during the war initiated by Arafat in 2000 and dubbed the "intifada."[29] Arafat's preparation, financing, coordination, and launching[30] of the offensive in 2000 has, as of this writing, accounted for almost 4,000 deaths (approximately 75 percent of which are Palestinian),[31] including the deaths of Palestinians who blew themselves up in 113 separate incidents.[32] Nothing compares in scale. In so doing, despite being a beneficiary of financial support of the billions of the Arab world, Arafat successfully cultivated—even among Israelis—the perception that the people in his control, the nominal Palestinians, were a "David" fighting an asymmetrical war against a Goliath, Israel.

According to *Forbes* magazine, Yasser Arafat is today the sixth wealthiest among the world's "kings, queens and despots," with more than $300 million stashed in Swiss bank accounts.[33] Others actually estimate that figure to be much higher.[34] Yet unlike despots who also appeared on that list, such as Saddam Hussein, Arafat had no oil reserves to exploit; rather, the only asset he has is a media-created cause from which he draws hundreds of millions from Europe,[35] Asia, the Arab world,[36] the U.S.,[37] Israel, and the U.N.[38] The IMF disclosed that its own audit uncovered the fact that Arafat, between 1995 and 2000, diverted fully $591 million from the PA budget into a special bank account under his personal control.[39]

As such, Yasser Arafat represents, at this writing, the most successful psychopath terrorist leader in history. Any aspiring terrorist leader would do well to study his life as a how-to guide for achieving any and all aims of terrorism, including astonishing longevity. Remembering that Arafat was shaped by intelligence agencies, students of terrorism must recognize that intelligence agencies may create weapons of mass destruction that actually have a heartbeat.

Terrorist leaders may successfully gain sanctuary from posing as symbolic martyrs. Such psychopaths successfully manipulate with baseless rhetoric that they should not be killed, lest they inspire others in multiple.[40] Yet these terror leaders—simply because they lead terrorism but nothing more, contribute so little materially to the lives of those they ostensibly advocate for that they are rendered irrelevant by the placid history that follows their passing.

Extortionists that promise protection of organized crime, for example, are not replaced by crime waves. Charles Manson was not replaced by multiples of his antiestablishment cause. Neither was Sheikh Ahmed Yassin, obliterated former founder of Hamas. Once Yassin's successor, Ahmed-Abdel Rantisi, was blown up by the Israeli military three weeks later, there followed no great rush to assume the throne of Hamas. Although Shining Path's Abimael Guzman was replaced by Oscar Ramirez Durand, the latter could never inspire more than a few hundred followers in an underground movement, before eventually being captured.[41]

Old as terrorism is, there is no prevailing legacy of a terrorist whose "martyred" legacy has inspired future generations to terror. Rather, terror leaders do their inspiring while they have the living identity and the validation of attention to inspire those to whom they are exposed.

Now dead, the psychopath terrorist leader can no longer employ the techniques of manipulation that emotionally and materially enslave his followers. Free from such haze, and finding tranquility in the aftermath of their leader's demise, followers discover that there is nothing inspiring about the nihilistic life of yesteryear.

Cinque, of the Symbionese Liberation Army, was such an example. Years after he captured national attention with the kidnapping of newspaper heiress Patty Hearst, and was later killed, Cinque inspired no one. William Harris, one of his devotees who survived the crime spree that inspired intervention by law enforcement and ended in a Waco-style conflagration, later observed, "I wish everyone would forget us."[42]

10.4 Terrorist Followers and Soldiers

Terrorist soldiers are obviously not born terrorists, nor made terrorists by their eventual targets. Their hatred and depersonalization of their victims, and their sacrifice for an agenda is shaped by the terror leaders they answer to.

Some terror followers may originate from poverty, and from powerlessness. Their anger and disenfranchisement is sharpened into an experience of feeling attacked. Then, the terror follower is focused by manipulative terror-leaders into viewing violence as the only remaining solution.[43]

Other terror-followers are spiritually driven souls who are cause-driven and eschew the material world that is nevertheless available to them. John Walker Lindh may have ended up in an Afghan rat hole, but he certainly did not grow up in one. These pathways are best dissected on an individual-by-individual basis.

It is easier to recruit terror followers from angry, alienated or marginalized populations, for these folks exist in identities that offer them little. Civil disobedience in disenfranchised workers proved to be a fertile soil for the later seeds of leftist terror organizations from Kurdistan to Colombia. Likewise, for this reason, Muslim terror recruitment from American prisons is so successful.[44]

It is not necessarily because they are broken that the disaffected opt for terror. Rather, the acceptance of their lot, within a radicalized if "righteous" life path, fosters their identification with the terror leader, their openness to his ultimate agenda, and channels their well-credentialed anger. The seduction is never the terror itself; rather, a legal, often pious purpose becomes the foundation for acquainting with the terror follower. But the terror leaders cannot help but view people with a violent past as ripe and especially desirable recruiting targets.

Do terror followers really differ, substantially, from other violent criminals? After all, prisons are littered with disaffected, violent, powerless, alienated men and women. A Northern Ireland study that compared politically-driven murderers compared to other murderers found that the former were of average intelligence and educational background, more psychologically stable, with less likelihood of substance abuse.[45] Of course, these conclusions reflect that as a group, terrorists are noticeably less damaged than common criminals, and therefore warrant even less sympathy than common murderers. Such data also distinguishes the more pronounced overall wretchedness of the common murderers' earlier life experiences.

Nevertheless, individuals who are not yet violent or criminal may be sensation-seeking, yearning to be part of something befitting their education and privileged upbringing, gnawing at the opportunity to buck convention, or to confront authority. The terror leader need only manipulate the raw ingredients, once he realizes they are there. The deeper that the terror group member sinks into activities of the group, the more alienated from the enemy—be it the government, organized society, even his or her former self—that the terror group member becomes. At that point, identification with the terror leader becomes that much more cemented, even as the repressiveness or brutality of the terror leader manifests itself.

The extant literature has provided little understanding on the significance of life events on inspiring terrorists to violence. The poignant stories we imagine of powerless folk who are terribly abused, who rise up to engage in terrorism to avenge, do exist. However, those stories are far more associated with members of terror groups who join in order to engage in paramilitary activities, such as Northern Ireland residents might join the IRA to fight British troops or loyalists.

Those terror followers who attack civilian targets, however, killing strangers in spectacular numbers or ghoulishly desecrating them, such as Shining Path was known to do, were never tormented by those innocent villagers they terrorized and slaughtered. What, then, inspired them to such carnage?

The same dynamic, in fact, that inspires members of the IRA or Chechens or Basques, who have not experienced death or direct aggression at the hands of their victims. When terror leaders exploit symbolism, demonize and dehumanize the enemy, value destruction in accordance with its magnitude, manipulate a sense of urgency, and isolate terror members from the outside world, including their peripheral sympathizers, even families, focus enables the mission to divest itself of conscience. Suicide bombers are even able to relinquish the fundamental human instinct of survival, having bought into the fraud of receiving seventy-two virgins and heaven as a reward for blowing one's self up.

Successful con artistry is why terror movements cannot be inspired without psychopaths; for terror followers are much more than mere property-destroying political advocates, more violent than assaultive paramilitaries. They are terrorists carrying out terror, carrying out unconscionable acts of depravity that they were never born to do, nor were reared by parents and spouses who loved them, to do. What Tamil woman is reared to hack a baby to death with a machete? Only a sinister guiding infrastructure can groom the terrorist and shape and train him or her for the mission.

Thus, there is no terror follower without terror leaders; for no matter what the follower has witnessed, no matter how banal killing has come, no matter the abuse, the billions of people who live these daily realities do not submit themselves as soldiers in the War on Terror. Namibia is not a hub of suicide bombing, nor is Cambodia. Raped women the world over have not mobilized to armed attack on facilities housing sex offenders. Israelis who have watched their children blown to bits do not themselves hijack Saudi Air planes and fly them into a Mecca Hilton during the Hajj. But if each of these peoples' traumas and grievances were exploited, and they inspired by messianic, charismatic psychopathic leaders, they would embrace a terror agenda. (Charisma, however, has its limits; even Prabhakaran of Sri Lanka has swelled his ranks by the forced recruitment of scores of children as young as ten years old.[46])

Such exploitation of the zealotry of followers is on full display in the Palestinian Authority, where terror leaders rarely, if ever, submit themselves or their children to suicide bomb. In a letter to the editor of the London Arabic-language daily *Al-Hayat*, Abu Saber M.G., the father of a young Palestinian who carried out a suicide bombing in an Israeli city, wrote:

> Four months ago, I lost my eldest son when his friends tempted him, praising the path of death. They persuaded him to blow himself up in one of Israel's cities. When the pure body of my son was scattered all over, my last signs of life also dispersed, along with hope and my will to exist. Since that day, I am like [an] apparition walking the earth, not to mention that I, my wife, and my other sons and daughters have become displaced since the razing of the home in which we lived. But the last straw was when I was informed that the friends of my eldest son the martyr were starting to wrap themselves like snakes around my other son, not yet seventeen, to direct him to the same path towards which they had guided his brother, so that he would blow himself up too to avenge his brother, claiming "he had nothing to lose."
>
> Do the children's lives have a price? Has death become the only way to restore the rights and liberate the land? And if this be the case, why doesn't a single one of all the sheikhs who compete amongst themselves in issuing fiery religious rulings, send his son? Why doesn't a single one of the leaders who cannot restrain himself in expressing his joy and ecstasy on the satellite channels every time a young Palestinian man or woman sets out to blow himself or herself up send his son?[47]

This lament is the essence of the aforementioned antisocial personality by proxy, the mechanism by which a terror leader is able to manipulate followers to do his or her destructive bidding.[48] Similar dynamics occur in criminal enterprises, when a predatory instigator may inspire an explosive follower to effect the destruction he could not do, or do alone. Or, the leader inspires the actor so that he or she may evade direct responsibility for the crime.

Both qualities manifest themselves in terrorism. Psychopathic leaders like Charles Manson whipped up violent inspiration his followers, enabling carnage far more dramatic than anything the diminutive Manson could have ever accomplished on his own. Moreover, by remaining physically removed from a number of the crime scenes of the terrorism he inspired, Manson was able to assert that he was not involved and could not be held responsible.

Studies of terrorist followers show them, like their leaders, to be preoccupied with power, absolute in their thinking, and to externalize the causes of their personal problems, as well as potential solutions for those difficulties.[49] Terror enables them to transfer from a meaningless sense of identity to an omnipotent one.[50]

Terror followers gain strength from believing that what they are doing is right; the illegality of their actions may be known to them, but they reach a point in their indoctrination that they no longer care. In the case of the Tamil Tigers, their intensity may be such that they are prepared to die for the sake of the group. Each regular member of the LTTE carries a cyanide pill and is pledged to committing suicide rather than being captured by the enemy.[51]

Adherence is cultivated by a variety of means. A leader who establishes a brutal control over adherents mutes internal discourse and potential derailment of objectives.[52] The PKK's Abdullah Ocalan was quoted as saying, "I establish a thousand relationships every day and destroy a thousand political, organizational, emotional and ideological relationships. No one is indispensable for me. Especially if there is anyone who eyes the chairmanship of the PKK. I will not hesitate to eradicate them. I will not hesitate in doing away with people."[53]

The terror leader answers to no one, in order to maintain control. It is a delicate dance for the terror leader to maintain an identity of piety and righteousness among his following in the face of what might be obviously destructive actions.

That terror recruits are more educated, from more cultivated backgrounds, is understandable. After all, in order to carry out terror intimate to the enemy and at times, in an international setting, a recruit has to have the constitution and skills to blend into a strange environment.[54]

Why are followers young men? Men because males are more given to destruction as an expression of masculine identity. Young because idealism in the more naive outpaces the capacity for skepticism of life experience. Young because the older and more personally entangled haven't the freedom to cast aside other responsibilities unless the cause has sufficient real urgency, and terror movements do not. Not surprisingly, when asked of his earlier experiences in the Weathermen, former activist Bill Ayers observed, "We were young with an edge of certainty and arrogance that I would be hard-pressed to recreate or even fully understand again."[55]

The Sri Lankan experience, however, uniquely demonstrates how women have been incorporated into terror. The practical needs of assembling enough able bodies to overcome an organizational mandate that LTTE members kill themselves upon capture overcomes gender bias. In so doing, the LTTE demonstrates that women may not be naturally given to banal killing, but indoctrination overcomes all.[56] Not surprisingly, LTTE propaganda rails at the oppression of women in Sri Lankan society, hailing female recruitment to terror as an alternative to caste oppression.[57]

Unfortunately, radical theorists and those intellectuals who parrot them are not so willing to dismiss such destructiveness as the product of foolhardy youth or exploited certitude until many years and many wasted lives later. And the attention these academics give, in its platitudes and substance, becomes a sustaining nutrient for the otherwise nonviable integrity of terror.

10.5 Ideology

Terror followers show a willingness to submit to the governing ideology. Faith-based and capable of strong conviction, they have the qualities that make for successful soldiers being dispatched to battle. It is the service of the greater ideology that allows for their willingness to break the laws of the state or to even risk their lives. Terrorist leaders create the perception of urgency. Perception of urgency will capture the idealistic; urgency will capture all. For this reason, themes of existential threats are frequently manipulated by terror leaders.

Ideologies underlying terror have traditionally been political. While religious themes are readily invoked by the Islamofascist global terror initiative, their objective of a global theocracy is clearly political. The use of violence to terrorize, therefore, is best understood by discerning the power goals of those who plot and instigate it.

Italian terrorism in the 1970s was dominated from the right by the (*Ordine Nuovo*) New Order, which sought to mobilize an authoritarian identity in Italy modeled on German Nazism. To do so required creating chaos, and a yearning among the people to restore order, by any means necessary. New Order and (*Avanguardia Nazionale*) National Vanguard, rather than seek attention for their crimes, blamed far-left groups in order to foment tension.[58]

This *modus operandi* actually reflects the blueprint actually developed by Carlos Marighella for organizing, funding, and carrying out terror operations to the end of leftist revolution.[59] Marighella proposed that terror attacks would inspire a repressive response from forces in power, brutal to the point of aligning the population with the leftists seeking to overthrow the government.

Sometimes ideology attaches closely to the attention-seeking agenda. The leftist Red Brigades, operating in Italy in the 1970s and 1980s, kidnapped and murdered rightist and centrist political figures it deemed symbolic to worsening the plight of the working class. While the Red Brigades avoided bombings and other mass casualty attacks so frequently employed by terrorists, the group's high profile killings—the most stunning of which was former Italian Prime Minister Aldo Moro in 1978—attempted to instigate wider political impact. The media's repudiation for the spectacle of their criminality, however, thwarted any hopes that sensationalism would inspire a following, and the Red Brigades dwindled to irrelevance.

Contemporary attention to terror focuses on Islamofascism because its tentacles have extended across oceans and continents. Islamofascist terror, most notoriously embodied by al-Qa'eda, is the most internationalized, most well-financed, most-ambitious (in political objectives and in weapons acquisition) such effort in history. Consequently, Islamofascist terror has inspired unprecedented international cooperation in law enforcement and transaction monitoring.

Islamofascism, sponsored financially by legitimate[60] and illegitimate businesses[61,62] and through direct financial or logistical support from countries such as Iran, Syria,[63] and Saudi Arabia,[64] characteristically aims at a Muslim fundamentalist dominance to the host government. That agenda is reflected in attacks directed at the state—or targeting Western or non-Moslem (particularly Jewish) influences.

Suicide terror has been optimized by Islamofascism (Dar es-Salaam, Iraq, Istanbul, Beirut, Buenos Aires, Casablanca, Nairobi, Russia, Chechnya, Bali) through truck and vehicle bombs. In 2002 in Bali, nightclubs were bombed.[65] In Tanzania and Kenya in 1998, it was U.S. embassies that were attacked,[66] in Istanbul and Tunisia, synagogues,[67] in Nairobi, an Israeli-owned hotel,[68] and in Casablanca, a Jewish club.[69]

Even in Moslem countries, Islamofascists have used terror to overthrow influences that were more moderate in their orientation. Anwar el-Sadat of Egypt was killed by the Muslim Brotherhood.[70] Even though that crime was vigorously prosecuted, and Egypt remains essentially a non-fundamentalist dictatorship, Islamofascist terror organizations have persisted in Egypt over the past two decades, just as they has in other prominent Arab countries such as Saudi Arabia.

In Northern Iraq, Ansar al-Islam, seeded by al-Qa'eda and comprised of Moslems from around the Arab world, has fomented jihad in autonomous Iraqi Kurdistan since just before the 9/11 attacks.[71] More recently, Ansar al-Islam has been implicated in attacks against those countries in Iraq who support the U.S. presence there.

In Pakistan, General Pervez Musharraf has survived several assassination attempts by Islamofascist terrorists from Harkat ul-Mujaheddin al-Almi. Also in

Pakistan, over seventy Shiite physicians have been killed by terrorists in recent years,[72] and numerous attacks have targeted Christians, including charity workers.[73]

In Indonesia, Islamists terrorist initiatives to impose Islamic Law, or Sharia, have contributed to over 19,000 deaths since 1999. Christians have been targeted for forced circumcision and conversion, and otherwise isolated and intimidated. A similar agenda in Bangladesh has also targeted Buddhists and Hindus, subjecting them to amputations, rapes in front of family, and religious institutions torched and destroyed.[74]

Abu Sayyaf, operating in the south of the Phillipines, seeks an independent Islamic state in the Mindanao province. That group has garnered international notoriety for kidnapping foreigners, including American nationals, despite a membership of no more than a thousand fighters. Abu Sayyaf operates independently from the much more numerous Moro National Liberation Front (MNLF), though their common advocacy for Moslem autonomy, and financial support from al-Qa'eda, solidify the Abu Sayyaf presence in spite of vigorous Phillipine government efforts to stamp them out.[75]

While Chechnya attracts little attention relative to other terror stages, Chechen Islamofascists have been responsible for some of the most deadly terror attacks of recent years. Only this year, Chechens carried out a suicide bombing on a Moscow subway,[76] and more recently, assassinated the country's President Kadyrov, a Moslem who rejected the fundamentalist direction of the terror movements.[77] Acting in concert with Arab Islamofascists, the Chechens have a long track record for spectacular terror, including a hostage takeover of a Moscow theater in 2002 that ended in the deaths of nearly 100 hostages at the hands of Russian police.

The very fatal resolution to that hostage takeover, which involved the use of a ventilated gas, was endorsed by Russian President Vladimir Putin, who warned of Islamofascist efforts to create a "worldwide caliphate."[78] Said Putin to a reporter from *Le Monde*, "If you want to become an Islamic radical and have yourself circumcised, I invite you to come to Moscow. I would recommend that he who does the surgery does it so you'll have nothing growing back afterward."[79] In that regard, President Putin reflected the exasperated, perhaps desperate reaction of a society already subjected to its share of terrorist attacks. That is the very point of terror—to create anxiety and unease through spectacular civilian destruction.

Terror failed to generate supportive traction for leftist organizations like Germany's Baader-Meinhoff gang and Italy's Red Brigades, and nationalist groups like the ETA. Yet terror has been quite successful for many of the Islamofascist movements, certainly for the Palestinian nationalist terrorists. The difference appears to be that the Islamofascists have intimidated the media into silence, rather than a response of repudiation as the press demonstrated in Europe and South America, and the United States in earlier years. Palestinian terrorists have succeeded in actually cultivating support in the media by a remarkably successful creation of false history and fabrications[80] on which to cast themselves as victims, and to generate external support.

It is easy to understand why the tools of inspiration for terror are often religious, especially given research findings that terror followers are generally more intelligent, more educated, and less psychiatrically impaired than other violent criminals. Scripture is hard to find dispute with, and traditionally more viscerally affecting than nationalism.

Some political terror employs philosophical reference, enough that the leader creates a perception of his brilliance for the mastery of such inscrutable writings. Likewise, it is difficult to argue—at least successfully—with a zealous and charismatic leader who displays an unusual command of subject matter, which others normally equate with great intellect and wisdom. The terror leaders, insights overidealized, pull the strings of the vulnerabilities of their followers, be they a background of poverty, social alienation, romantic rejection, or class disenfranchisement.

It may be more difficult, however, to fathom why the educated would work themselves up to the end of self-destruction simply because a government is not religious enough, or a Western presence competes against the local religious influence. For this, leaders pulling the intellectual strings of Islamofascist terror have borrowed from the writings of such well-credentialed professors as Edward Said, late of Columbia University. Said, in his well-read book *Orientalism*, blamed the very progress of the West for the shortcomings and developmental retardation of the Arab world.[81] As such, the book provided vigorous intellectual argumentation for the now widely adopted idea of Arabs being a victimized people. In Arabic academia, scores of externalizing scholars provide readily available theological and philosophical sophistry to fuel the nihilistic barbarism that has metastasized around the world. As such, one can understand why the very existence of the West is reason enough for the nuclear-minded Islamofascists to eliminate the advanced world as we know it.

Blaming the successful, empowered establishment is a familiar canard of terrorists, be their agenda religious or political. The inspiration for IRA terror was the exclusion of Catholics from opportunity and representation in Protestant-run Northern Ireland, as well as ongoing violent confrontation with Protestant militants. The Marxist Shining Path gained adherents among the indigenous peoples of Peru who felt the ruling government perpetuated their poverty.

Timothy McVeigh, for example, can readily be accepted at his representation—or, by the assertions of those who share his ideology: a person driven to his Oklahoma City destruction by the U.S. government's handling of the Waco incident. Yet, McVeigh was neither personally affected by the Waco inferno, nor an adherent of David Koresh's Branch Davidian church.[82] McVeigh was a disenfranchised military veteran which closer scrutiny exposes as simply a person who found the notion of spectacular destruction enticing. Attached to an expedient grievance, he transitioned from a dead-end military vet into a trained killer who, rejected for the Green Berets, did find expression of his skills in a sufficiently empowering manner. But does that say he was powerless? And rendered powerless by the U.S. government? Or only that McVeigh perceived himself to be powerless unless he could act out his homicidal fantasies?

It is easier to dismiss the sincerity of McVeigh's rejoinder than it is the Islamofascists' assertions only because the latter have the luxury of many miles of distance from the accountability of honest scrutiny. Still, closer consideration exposes the fact that the insatiable Western appetite for oil empowers a society that has contributed little technology, humanities, or science to the rest of the world, nor itself. Just as Western medicine and agriculture provides improved quality of life, and indeed, life, to the Arab and Moslem world.

Suicide bombing utilized by groups like Hamas, Islamic Jihad, and Arafat's Al-Aksa Brigades and Fatah in the conflict between Israelis and Palestinians, reflects dynamics unique to its participants. Citizens of the Palestinian Authority are indoctrinated to the degree that killing themselves in the furtherance of the elimination of Israel is the highest honor one can achieve;[83] there are those who seek death for spiritual and material rewards (from heaven to seventy-two virgins to monies for their families).

Those allowed proximity to the process of brainwashing suicide bombers observed just how important it is for the best and brightest to be brainwashed into self-destruction. In a London *Times* article, Hala Jaber wrote of what he learned of the selection of bombers during his visit to the Gaza hideout of an al-Aksa Brigades cell.

> Those who excel militarily and show steely composure in stressful situations are most likely to be chosen. The young men must be reasonably religious, convinced of the meaning of "martyrdom and jihad (holy war)" . . . The commander observes candidates over several days as they go about their routine business in public and at home. If the assessment is positive, he informs them of their selection.
>
> An intense twenty-day period of religious study and discussion ensues between the commander and each candidate. Verses from the Koran about a martyr's attainment of paradise are recited constantly.

The candidate is reminded of the good fortune that awaits him in the presence of prophets and saints, of the unimaginable beauty of the houri, or beautiful young woman, who will welcome him and of the chance he will have to intercede on behalf of seventy loved ones on doomsday. Not least, he is told of the service he will perform for his fellow countrymen with his sacrifice.

"Of course I am deeply saddened when I have to use a suicide attacker. I am very emotional and at times I cry when I say good-bye to them," the commander said softly. "These men were not found on the streets. These are educated men who under normal circumstances would have the potential of being constructive members of society. If they did not have to carry out such a mission, they could have become a doctor, a lawyer or a teacher."

Once the bomber's preparations are complete, he is collected by another member of the unit who accompanies him on the final journey to his target. It is only just before the assault that he is told the details of his operation, whether he will be a bomber or will attack with grenades and guns until he is shot dead. Ten to fifteen minutes before being dropped at the target, the bomber straps on a hand-tailored vest filled with about ten kilos of explosive and five kilos of nails and metal. He is then given his final instructions about the precise point at which he should detonate himself.

The later he knows the better for the martyr, since he will not have much time to think of the target nor to experience doubts," the commander said.[04]

Other terror followers adopt the notion that death is inevitable, so best to die in a manner that is most advantageous, and most damaging to the Israeli enemy. Not surprisingly, Palestinian terror masters have also recruited those with terminal illnesses[85] and others with emotional crises.[86] Exploitation by psychopathy, of course, means that the end justifies the means. Exhorting[87] and deploying children[88] to kill themselves as they do, therefore, without regard to their capacity to consent to such a mission, reflects such *modus operandi*.

It is a fairly popular short-sightedness for some to engage terrorism by suggesting that it can be eliminated by addressing "root causes" of terror. That exercise serves the end of the psychopath terror leader, for placing the onus on the victim drives attention to an agenda, hereby legitimizing the terror leader in the eyes of previously skeptical; furthermore, it diverts attention from the enormity of a terrorist group's decision to victimize innocents who had no connection to their grievance; distracts the target of terrorism from the resolve to eradicate it;

and completes the mission of the psychopath leader to provide him justification for the exercise of his fundamentally apocalyptic personality.

Indeed, disaffection has legitimate roots for some. For those who experience ongoing fear and direct oppression, it is easier to develop a sense that violence, even homicidal violence, is a necessary survival skill.[89] They are the ones who require less manipulation, less indoctrination with political theory. But any study of those who opt for political violence has never controlled for an underlying rageful personality that may have been driven by internal family dynamics, alcoholism, or an assortment of factors. Violence as an expression that the actor believes in still reflects a reservoir of anger, unique to that individual, that a "cause" provides a justifiable outlet for. Not surprisingly, research does show a higher incidence of nonpolitical criminality among paramilitary prisoners in Northern Ireland.[90]

Yet of those orphaned, nearly killed, or injured in American military actions that did not surgically avoid civilian casualties, none were among the nineteen air hijackers who perpetrated 9/11. Was it indeed the grievance, and only that? Would there have been a 9/11 if there were no madrassas and Afghanistan training camps to indoctrinate followers with an absolute approach to the world?

If grievances make terror, where are the Japanese terrorists who originated from Hiroshima-destroyed families? Perhaps if the Japanese media had the vehement externalization and manipulative nihilism seen in the Arab media, America would have seen far more dumped on its shores than cheap steel. Disaffection may have merit, but the disaffected may seek alienation as an end, as an identity. Terror-leaders, psychopathically attuned to such vulnerability, all too easily tap into such dead-end spirit to channel it into the history-altering destruction of their agenda of personal grandiosity.

Basque separatist terror gained initiative under the Spanish dictatorship of Generalissimo Francisco Franco. Basques had long struggled to resolve a wish for autonomy versus outright independence from Spain and France, with roots in preserving a Basque language and culture that Basques felt was threatened by immigrants' dilution and diminution. Franco traditionally responded violently to dissent, and violent response to Spain was thus more acceptable among Basques. This contributed to the popularity, in the 1960s, of the ETA (Euzkadi Ta Azkata-suna—Basque Nation and Liberty).

In the years following Franco's death, however, a far less repressive Spain and various aspects of autonomy and cultural preservation diminished the urgency for many to support violent terror against Spain. Yet even in recent years, in spite of a more conciliatory Spanish government affording Basques a number of areas of autonomy, incidents of terror continue as ETA has carried out a number of high profile political assassinations. The media has been clearly unsympathetic to the ETA in the wake of the assassinations, and their repudiation has interfered with the group's ability to translate high visibility and impact death into successful recruitment of new adherents.[91] The ETA example demonstrates that even as one addresses sensitive root causes, terror leaders with a destructive and nihilistic bent would prefer to retain the prerogative to remain apocalyptic.

The Tamil situation in Sri Lanka has some similarities to the Basque separatist movement. But so fierce and authoritarian was the LTTE that India harbored great concern about acceding to what may have been otherwise legitimate nationalistic aspirations of a disenfranchised people. Sometimes terror is so effective, therefore, that others are afraid to address its grievance for fear of further empowering what shows to be an unquenchable thirst for death.

Is poverty inspiring Islamofascist terror? Facts demonstrate otherwise. Economic downturns in Indonesia and Malaysia, for example, were not accompanied by upsurges in terror, and militant Islam is powered by the prosperous and educated of the more prosperous and educated Moslem nations.[92] On the other hand, economic downturn in Nigeria[93] has witnessed a turn to Islamic fundamentalism—albeit through changes in state laws, rather than enlistment in terror organizations.

A study of Hizbullah terrorists in Lebanon and Palestinian terrorists in Israel and the Palestinian Authority noted that no correlation was found between participation in violence and economic depression; violence increased when local economic conditions and optimism were getting better, and after a period during which education levels among young Palestinians had risen remarkably.[94]

Manipulating symbolism is a key component of successful development of a terror agenda. One example of the distortion of symbolism is seen in the exploitation of the concept of "humiliation" by those who explain contemporary Islamofascist terror. The United States is particularly flagellated for victimizing those soldiers of terror, for "humiliating" them. Yet, is there any more humiliated person in the Arab world than the Arab woman? Or the non-Moslem prevented from practicing his faith? Why, then, did we not see Buddhist terrorists driven by the humiliation of the destruction of the Bamiyan Buddhas by the Taliban Islamofascists?[95]

Because the realities of "humiliation" are exaggerated—the terror leaders exploit this word, however, to smartly manipulate people who are under their absolute or media control. "Eyewitness accounts" maximize the emotions of powerlessness and humiliation in viewers of such pan-Arab media as *al-Jazeera*, for example.[96]

Yet, historically oppressed peoples like American Indians, displaced, exterminated, disenfranchised, have not embraced terror as a vehicle for resolving their grievances. Why? Because there has not yet been a psychopath to emerge and exploit American Indian grievances to foment terror in White America.

Kuwait was liberated by the United States only recently, in 1991, from an occupying Iraq that pillaged the country. Yet only one decade later, Kuwaiti endorsement for the September 11th terror attacks on America as morally justifiable was by far more frequent than six other countries in the Arab world, and almost three times as frequent as among Iranians.[97] These astonishing figures were supplemented with Kuwaiti's greatest expressed resentment as U.S. policy toward the Palestinians. And yet, it was the Kuwaitis themselves who summarily evicted 300,000 Palestinians from their country at the end of Gulf War I. There had not been any Palestinian suicide bombings in Kuwait City; the Palestinians were thrown out simply because of their allegiance with Saddam Hussein.

Closer examination of the "root causes" then reveals the simpler truth that Kuwaiti power increasingly rests in the hands of fundamentalists who ideologically support the ambitions of the Islamofascists, yet are too disingenuous to explain their siding with terrorism any other way than to dream up a way to bring tiny Israel into their domestic affairs, from thousands of miles away. Such is the fraud of those who prefer simple homilies to more textured understandings of what drives alliances on a country-by-country, relationship-by-relationship basis.

Not all ideologies are such to outshine the attention created by the criminal activities of a given terror group. The Marxist Fuerzas Armadas Revolucionarios de Colombia (FARC) is known for its drug trafficking, kidnapping and extortion, operating in Colombia, Ecuador, Venezuela, and Panama. Its success as a profit-engineering rural-based crime operation eclipses its political substance. Terror as a *modus operandi* works for organized crime; visible attacks that send messages to the rest of the community are readily adaptable to terrorists who have an ostensible political agenda as well.

Terrorism exploits grievances of its adherents—or their inherent tendencies toward sensation-seeking behavior—in order to legitimize violence, to achieve more sinister or selfish motives. Those grievances may escalate to hatred for those responsible for the perceived injustice. When organized terrorism is at work, the grievance is manipulated to inspire an emotion of hatred. Why, then, do the adherents of some terrorist organizations hate the United States, for example? Because their leaders cleverly attach emotional pitch to grievances that may be legitimate, or features of the target that excite the solders-in-training.

Clearly, those from repressed, backward societies such as the Arab world generally have far more basis for growing up alienated and identifying with causes espousing chaos. But personal experiences of those growing up in developed nations, such as Europe, rendered the future followers of the Red Brigades, Manson Family, and Baader Meinhof every bit as vulnerable to the ministrations of a psychopath terror leader—whatever their political interest.

Manipulated hatred of terror becomes a rationalized expression that, viewed impassively, is entirely purposeless. For all his brilliance as the accomplished college professor, for example, what did Abimael Guzman's Shining Path accomplish by targeting the Peace Corps, social workers, priests, and leftist activists for public displays of grotesque brutality?

The value of exploring the stated "root causes" rests only, therefore, in confronting terror soldiers over time with the reality that their concerns are being co-opted and manipulated for a psychopathic leaders' aims, and that their needs are better met through nonterrorist means. Dr. William Pierce of the National Alliance suggested that whites in America face racial extinction because of forced ethnic diversification and imposed multiculturalism. What, then, does attention to solving the root cause of white supremacist terror do? Elimination of the Columbia School of Journalism for its ethnically diverse composition? Obviously not. But those same journalists have the power, viewing truth under stark light, to pour a bucket of cold water over the heads of the manipulated, whether they mistakenly envision the end of white America or the end of Islamic-dominated Saudi Arabia.

The psychopath terror leader thus exposed loses adherents, attention, and financial backing, and proceeds to self-destruction (as in the case of the Symbionese Liberation Army), prison (as in the case of the Manson family), or relative irrelevance (Shining Path).

It is for this reason that the resolute, even emphatic rejection of terror is a necessity. For such repudiation robs terror of the counterfeit romanticism its psychopathic leaders shroud it with. Such interdiction is not retaliation; rather it is crime prevention. In Israel, for example, eighty three Israelis were killed by Palestinian suicide bombers between 1996 and 1997.[98] After Israel Prime Minister Benjamin Netanyahu let it be known to Palestinian Authority chairman Yasser Arafat that Israel was prepared to respond to terror with military might, only one Israeli died from a suicide bombing in the three years that followed—notwithstanding that Arafat's Palestinian Authority continued its policy of indoctrinating its own people to kill as many Israeli Jews as they could.[99]

Crime prevention can be carried out without sadism, just as law enforcement routinely respectfully apprehends even the most vicious killers and notorious killers. Psychopaths may operate with completely insensitive viciousness, but when confronted with firm limits, they respond with restraint borne of instinctual survivalism. Thus, terror ends when it becomes clear to the psychopath leader that his own survival, or his own symbolic notoriety, is no longer in his control and at the whim of those his terror organization victimizes.

As long as there will be religion, and the devotion to higher spiritual callings; as long as there will be haves and have-nots of any variety, there will always be an agenda that a terror leader can exploit, in order to foment the gaudy destruction of his fantasy. Eliminating the psychopaths who exploit agendas and ideologies, or isolating terror masters so that they no longer can draw attention—oxygen, eliminates terror. For psychopathy is the root of terrorism, not ideology.

Furthermore, terror's success advances with the paralysis of society. Therefore, it is necessary for a resolute response demonstrating that terrorist actions have not at all inspired fear and avoidance in the target society or community. Terror's end will result from the community that rejects the illusion of its paralysis that terrorists strive to orchestrate.

Endnotes

1. K. Lopez. "The media elite: Behind the ego." *New York Post,* November 2, 2003.

2. V. Hanson. "Why the Muslims misjudged us." *City Journal* 12(1) (2002).

3. V. Hanson. "The abuse of history." *National Review Online,* May 24, 2002.

4. W. Reid. "Controlling political terrorism: Practicality, not psychology." In *The Psychology of Terrorism: A Public Understanding,* C. Stout, ed. (Westport, CT: Praeger, 2002) p. 2.

5. "Terror, lies and videotape." *CBSNews.com,* May 15, 2002.

6. E. Kintisch. "Top D.C. lobbyists facing heat over Saudi ads." *Forward,* May 31, 2002.

7. A. Jorisch. "Al Manar: Hizbullah TV, 24/7." *Middle East Quarterly,* winter 2004.

8. "How LTTE murderers killed Rajiv Gandhi." *India Today,* July 7, 1996.

9. L. Beres. "The unique cowardice of Palestinian terrorism." Dept. Political Science, Purdue University, March 6, 2003.

10. R. Dowling. "Terrorism and the media: A rhetorical genre." *J. of Communication* 36(1):12–24 (1986).

11. *Patterns of Global Terrorism 2001*. U.S. Department of State, April 2002.

12. T. Goetzel. "Terrorist beliefs and terrorist lives." In *The Psychology of Terrorism: A Public Understanding,* C. Stout, ed. (Praeger Westport, CT: Praeger, 2002), p. 100.

13. T. Dalrymple. "A terrorist returns." *City Journal,* May 31, 2002.

14. M. Shaviv. "When terrorism is the story." *Jerusalem Post,* June 27, 2002.

15. A.S. Balasingham. *Liberation Tigers and the Tamil Eelam Freedom Struggle* (Madras, India: Liberation Tigers of Tamil Eelam, 1983).

16. Law Enforcement Agency Resource Network, ©2004 Anti-Defamation League.

17. M. Baumann. *Terror or Love? Bommi Baumann's Own Story of His Life as a West German Urban Guerilla* (NY: Grove Press, 1979).

18. R. Robins and J. Post. *Political Paranoia: The Psychopolitics of Hatred* (New Haven: Yale Press, 1997).

19. N. Swamy. *Tigers of Lanka, from Boys to Guerillas* (1994 Delhi: Konark, 1994).

20. T. Stawar. "Antisocial personality by proxy." *Journal of Psychology* 131(1) (1997).

21. I. Pacepa. "The KGB's man." *Wall Street Journal,* September 22, 2003.

22. Ibid.

23. D. Brooks. "A brief history of Yasir Arafat." *Atlantic Monthly,* July-August 2002.

24. D. Bossie. "Yasser Arafat: Nazi trained." *Washington Times,* August 9, 2002.

25. S. Lunev. "Just who are Arafat and the Palestinians?" *Newsmax.com,* June 27, 2002.

26. I. Pacepa. "The KGB's man." *Wall Street Journal,* September 22, 2003.

27. M. Charen. "The suffering Palestinians." *Townhall.com,* May 20, 2003.

28. R. Ehrenfeld. "Arafat's wrong turn." *New York Sun,* March 5, 2003.

29. E. Karsch. "Arafat's War." *Address to Middle East Forum,* Philadephia, PA December 2, 2003.

30. D. Warren. "Arafat's Cover is Now Truly Blown." *Ottawa Citizen,* April 2, 2002.

31. Palestine Red Crescent Society, May 29, 2004.

32. Israel Foreign Ministry, May 29, 2004.

33. N. Vardi. "Auditing Arafat." *Forbes,* March 17, 2003.

34. Ibid.

35. "Swallow the Money." *Wall Street Journal Europe,* July 16, 2002.

36. R. Ehrenfeld. "U.S. vs. Arafat." *National Review Online,* September 19, 2003.

37. R. Ehrenfeld. "Arafat's purse." *National Review,* September 13, 2002.

38. D. Fischer. "What exactly is the U.N. doing in its refugee camps (with our money)?" *Weekly Standard,* May 13, 2002.

39. "Arafat's investments." *New York Post,* October 2, 2003.

40. A. Tamimi. "Advice for the U.S.: Don't make al-Qaeda's leader a martyr." *Time,* March 10, 2003.

41. "Shining Path leader taken without a shot." *CNN.com,* July 14, 1999.

42. Sterngold, J. "Four former radicals are charged in 1975 killing in bank robbery." *New York Times,* Jan 17, 2002. pp. 1, 26.

43. Bell, S. "The unseen hand behind suicide bombers," *National Post,* May 20, 2002.

44. Thomas, C. "Radical recruiting in America's prisons," *Tribune Media Services,* June 20, 2002.

45. Lyons, H. and Harbison, H. "A comparison of political and non-political murderers in Northern Ireland 1974–1984." *Journal of Medicine, Science, and the Law* 26:193–197 (1986).

46. Gunaratna, R. "LTTE child combatants." *Jane's,* July, 1998.

47. Abu Saber, M.G. "Let Hamas and Jihad leaders send their own son," *Al-Hayat,* October 1, 2002.

48. Stawar, T. "Antisocial personality by proxy," *Journal of Psychology* 131(1) (1997).

49. Post, J. "Terrorist organization and motivation." *Testimony before the Senate Armed Services Committee,* November 2001.

50. Kfir, N. "Understanding suicidal terror through humanistic and existential psychology." In *The Psychology of Terrorism: A Public Understanding,* C. Stout, ed. (Praeger Westport, CT: Praeger, 2002).

51. Dixit, I N *Assignment Colombo* (Delhi, India: Konarak, 1998).

52. Volkan, V. *Bloodlines: From Ethnic Pride to Ethnic Terrorism* (NY: Farrar, Straus, and Giroux, 1997).

53. Witschi, B. "Who is Abdullah Ocalan?" *CNN Interactive.*

54. Kreuger, A. and Maleckova, J. "The Economics and the education of suicide bombers." *New Republic,* June 24, 2002.

55. Ayers, B. *Fugitive Days: A Memoir* (Boston: Beacon, 2001).

56. Harrison, F. "Up close with the Tamil Tigers." *BBC* January 29, 2002.

57. A. Ann. "Freedom birds of Tamil Eelam." http://www.eelamweb.com/women/.

58. M. von Tangen Page. *Prisons, Peace, and Terrorism: Penal Policy in the Reduction of Political Violence in Northern Ireland, Italy and the Spanish Basque Country,* 1968–97 (London: MacMilllan, 1998) 90–118.

59. C. Marighella. *Minimanual of the Urban Guerilla* (Abraham Guillen Press, 1969).

60. D. McGrory. "Al-Qaeda bought $20M diamonds to hide finances." *(London) Times,* December 30, 2002.

61. "Islamic insurgency groups financed by drugs." *Middle East News Line,* . March 14, 2002.

62. G. Wright. "Hizbullah suspects plead guilty: Six of ten accept U.S. Attorney deal on money laundering." *Charlotte Observer,* March 12, 2002.

63. "Syria number two terror sponsor, Gilmore Commission finds." *World Tribune.com,* January 8, 2003.

64. R. Ehrenfeld. "Trail of funds." *National Review Online,* September 16, 2003.

65. R. Peters. "The Bali attack is a sign of the terrorists' desperation." *Wall Street Journal,* October 15, 2002.

66. "Bombings in Nairobi, Kenya and Dar es-Salaam, Tanzania." August 7, 1998 www.state.gov, updated January 20, 2001.

67. "Tunisia synagogue blast kills 5." *CNN.com,* April 12, 2002.

68. "Al-Qaeda blamed for Kenya attacks." *CNN.com,* November 28, 2002.

69. "Car bombs explode in Casablanca." *MSNBC.com,* May 17, 2003.

70. "The swastika and the crescent." Southern Poverty Law Center Intelligence Report, http://www.splcenter.org/intel/intelreport/article.jsp?pid=242.

71. J. Schanzer. "Ansar al-Islam: Back in Iraq." *Middle East Quarterly,* winter 2004.

72. S. Inskeep. "Killing of doctors in Karachi, Pakistan." *National Public Radio,* March 19, 2002.

73. K. Khan. "7 Christians executed at charity in Pakistan." *Washington Post,* September 25, 2002.

74. D. Pipes and J. Schanzer. "Militant Islam's new strongholds." *New York Post,* October 22, 2002.

75. S. Rogers. "Beyond the Abu Sayyaf." *Foreign Affairs,* February, 2004.

76. J. Dougherty. "Moscow Metro blast kills 39." *CNN.com,* February 6, 2004.

77. "Chechen president killed by bomb." *BBC News,* May 9, 2004.

78. A. Evans-Pritchard and J. Strauss. "West in mortal danger from Islam, says Putin." *Daily Telegraph,* November 12, 2002.

79. "C'mon Vlad: Tell us how you really feel." *Wall Street Journal,* November 13, 2002.

80. J. Farah. "The Jews took no one's land." *World Net Daily,* November 19, 2002.

81. E. Said. *Orientalism* (NY: Vintage, 1979).

82. L. Michel and D. Herbeck. *American Terrorist: Timothy McVeigh and the Oklahoma City Bombing* (NY. Regan Books, 2001).

83. J. Kay. "The terrorist and Palestinian society feed off one another." *National Post,* September 11, 2003.

84. H. Jaber. "Inside the world of the Palestinian suicide bomber." *(London) Times,* March 24, 2002.

85. D. Rudge. "Report: Bomber was AIDS carrier." *Jerusalem Post,* June 18, 2002.

86. A. Fischman. "How Hamas turned adulteress into suicide bomber." *Yediot Ahronot,* January 18, 2004.

87. A. Lerner. "Arafat tells kids to die on Int'l Children's Day." *Jerusalem Post,* June 1, 2003.

88. T. Harnden. "I did it because people don't like me." *Daily Telegraph,* March 26 2004.

89. von Tangen Page, note 58, pp. 12–16.

90. Ibid.

91. "Violence marks 5th day of protests in Spain." *CNN.com,* July 15, 1997.

92. D. Pipes. "God and Mammon: Does poverty cause militant Islam?" *National Interest,* winter 2001–2002.

93. P. Lyman. "The U.S. can't allow 50 million Muslims to descend into extremism." *Wall Street Journal,* November 27, 2002.

94. D. Walker. "Education may be key to extremist actions." *Guardian,* July 29, 2002.

95. J. Mapes. "Explosions tear at Afghan statues." *National Geographic,* March 9, 2001.

96. R. Alt. "The al-Jazeera effect." *Weekly Standard,* April 21, 2004.

97. Gallup Organization. "Poll of the Islamic World." Washington D.C., March, 2002.

98. Israeli Ministry of Foreign Affairs.

99. C. Krauthammer. "How Arafat raised an entire generation to murder." *Washington Post,* March 29, 2002.

Chapter 11

Current Trends in Forensic Investigations of Human Rights Abuse: Human Identification of Mass Graves

Erin H. Kimmerle, Ph.D.

Introduction

As nations transition from war and armed conflict to peace, forensic science is increasingly an essential tool for documenting and illustrating crimes through physical evidence. It is through this lens that historical events will be judged, peace building established, and murdered remains returned to grieving families. Investigations into International Humanitarian Law (IHL) rely on the forensic sciences and anthropology in particular for critical evidence that establishes the nature and pattern of crimes committed and provides a means for human identification. Forensic scientists, lawyers, and judges are challenged to break new ground due to the unique and changing circumstances of societies transitioning to new forms of judicial systems. From international tribunals to local truth commissions, international protocols provide a guide through which the processes of fact-finding missions and criminal prosecution may be navigated. Yet the unique social, cultural, and biological variables of diverse situations from Bosnia to Darfur require investigators to apply scientifically accepted and proven methods, and at the same time remain adaptable in their framework to ensure the applicability of methods to changing contexts.

Anthropologists contribute ethnographic interviews, the collection of antemortem data, biological profiles to establish the initial parameters of identification, body search and recovery, exhumation, death investigations, trauma reconstructions, and expert testimony to investigations of IHL. Investigations into HHRR violations must consider complex issues of population variation, cultural relevance, and rules of evidence for a multitude of judicial frameworks to ensure the admissibility of evidence in court. International protocols and scientific methods are discussed for human identification from the creation of biological profiles to the use of DNA. The purpose of this chapter is to discuss current issues and trends in the application of forensic science and anthropology to investigations of human rights abuses and IHL, through examples spanning from domestic truth commissions to international *ad hoc* criminal tribunals. Finally, recommendations for best practice standards towards international research, training, and investigative services are outlined.

What is the human rights (HHRR) context?

The Universal Declaration of Human Rights (adopted by the United Nations General Assembly on December 10, 1948) states:

> Whereas disregard and contempt for human rights have resulted in barbarous acts which have outraged the conscience of mankind, and the advent of a world in which human beings shall enjoy freedom of speech and belief and freedom from fear and want has been proclaimed as the highest aspiration of the common people,
>
> Whereas it is essential, if man is not to be compelled to have recourse, as a last resort, to rebellion against tyranny and oppression, that human rights should be protected by the rule of law...

Increasingly human rights enforcement is upheld through criminal and forensic investigations into violations against International Humanitarian and Human Rights Laws. In the wake of genocide occurring in the former Yugoslavia and Rwanda, international criminal courts were established. The United Nations Security Council established the International Criminal Tribunal for Rwanda[1] (ICTR); and the International Tribunal for the Prosecution of Persons Responsible for Serious Violations of International Humanitarian Law Committed in the Territory of the Former Yugoslavia since 1992 (ICTY). Throughout many nations, domestic courts and truth commissions have also investigated human rights violations, acts of terrorism, armed conflicts and extra-judicial executions. The forensic sciences are critical to these missions as they provide a foundation for judicial reform based on physical evidence. Often these cases are investigated years after the events occurred which is why anthropology plays such a central role. Anthropologists provide expertise on grave detection and exhumation, as well as laboratory analysis for human identification and trauma analysis derived from skeletal remains.

Forensic investigations into HHRR abuses and war crimes are generally characterized by a high number of victims, an even higher number of missing persons, conflicts that occurred over long periods of time (sometimes many years) and over large geographical areas such as the entire country or region of the world (Figure 11.1). In contrast to many mass disasters falling under the purview of natural events, in HHRR cases the context is criminal. Investigations may also be conducted over many years and under changing legal authority; therefore the crime scenes are complex, the cultural and biological parameters are highly variable, and the entire judicial process may be in transition (Table 11.1). In spite of this complexity and the significant challenges it imposes, perpetrators of war crimes, crimes against humanity, genocide, and violations to the Geneva Conventions are successfully prosecuted (Skinner 1987, Snow et al. 1984, Kirschner and Hannibal 1994, Scott and Conner 1997, Burns 1998, Ferllini 1999, Campobasso et al. 2000, Haglund 2001, Cordner and McKelvie 2002, Fondebrider 2002, Okoye et al. 2006). Forensic and anthropological evidence has been critical to many cases of prosecution for these crimes. For example, cases prosecuted by the ICTR (*The Prosecutor v. Kayishema ICTR-95-1* and *The Prosecutor v. Rutaganda ICTR-96-3*) and the ICTY (*The Prosecutor v. Jelisic IT-95-10, The Prosecutor v. Cesic IT-95-10-1/a, The Prosecutor v. Krsti_ IT-98-33, The Prosecutor v. Limaj et. al. IT-03-66*, and *The Prosecutor v. Popovic et. al. IT-05-88*) have relied on anthropological and other forensic evidence.

Figure 11.1 *Kosovan women wait for the bus. Without sanitation pick-up, the potential for disease is more likely. The absence of basic infrastructure following armed conflict highlights the threat to basic human security (Image by EH. Kimmerle, 2000).*

Table 11.1
Characteristics of Investigations into Human Rights Abuse, War Crimes, Genocide, and Acts of Terrorism and Armed Conflict

- They tend to occur on a massive scale, over a wide geographical area, and over long periods of time.
- They tend to result in a high number of fatalities.
- There is typically a high number of internally displaced persons or refugees.
- There may be more injured persons than fatalities.
- Criminal acts tend to be investigated years after the incident.
- Records and evidence may be altered or destroyed to cover-up crimes.
- Continued conflict may result in prolonged humanitarian crises and basic human security threats that further delay judicial process.
- Entire families or cities may be destroyed, along with antemortem information about the deceased.
- Many atrocities occur with the authority, or assumed authority of the police, military or government and in such cases, evidence may be hidden, altered or destroyed.
- Individual skeletal remains often exhibit multiple injuries possibly even resulting from multiple mechanisms of injury (i.e., gunfire and explosions).

Towards Human Identification: The Biological Profile

The biological profile is a set of descriptive characteristics about an individual based on *postmortem* data estimated from the skeleton (Table 11.2). This profile provides critical information and the first step in the identification process. The more complete and accurate the profile, the narrower the pool of missing persons will become, which should eventually lead to an identification. Estimating descriptive information about an individual based on biological features offers a specific type of information about the deceased (Figures 11.2–4). These initial parameters are critical to excluding cases and narrowing the pool of possible matches. Once a short list is established of possible identities, other methods for *positive identification* may be tested, such as comparisons of dental records (Brannon and Morlang 2002) or DNA analysis (Cowell and Mostad 2003). Victims may be *presumptively identified* based on multiple lines of evidence, building from the biological profile, and include evidence such as the identification of clothing or personal artifacts, as well as exclusionary methods that eliminate cases (Table 11.3).

Table 11.2
Methods for Biological Profiling Based on Skeletal Data

Method	Skeletal Traits
Sex estimation	Pelvic Morphology
	Pelvic Metric Analysis
	Cranial Metric Analysis
	Cranial Morphology
	Long Bone Metric Analysis
Age at Death Estimation	Pubic symphysis morphology
	Sternal rib morphology
	Dental metrics
	Osteoarthritis and Degenerative Joint Changes
	Dental ware
	Cranial sutures
Stature Estimation	Long Bone Metric Analysis
Ancestry or Ethnicity Estimation	Cranial Metric Analysis
	Cranial Morphology
	Post cranial metric analysis
	Post-cranial morphology

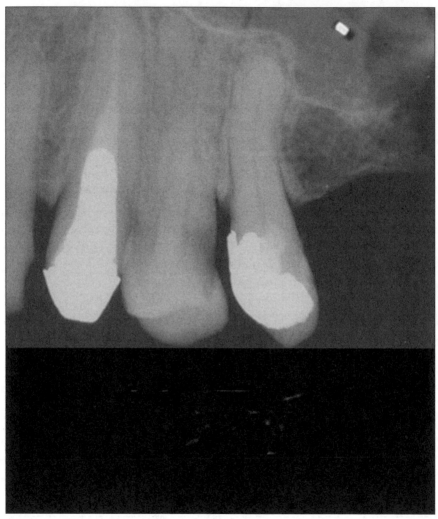

Figure 11.2 *Postmortem dental radiograph. Images such as this are collected through postmortem examination so that there is a record to compare antemortem dental radiographs, charts, or information provided by surviving family members. The presence of dental modification means there may be an antemortem record with which to compare. Such a comparison is only possible late in the identification process, once there is a tentative idea of victim identity (Printed with the permission of the United Nations, ICTY).*

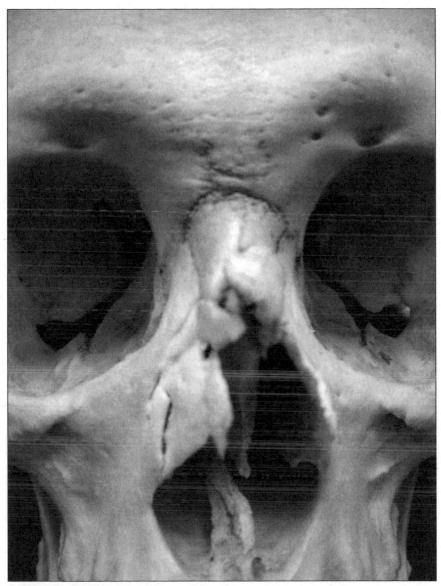

Figure 11.3 Close-up frontal view of the skull of an adult male, exhibiting a healed antemortem nasal fractures. Healed trauma such as this may be one contributing factor to limiting the pool of possible matches between decedents and missing persons (Image by EH. Kimmerle, USF Osteology Collection).

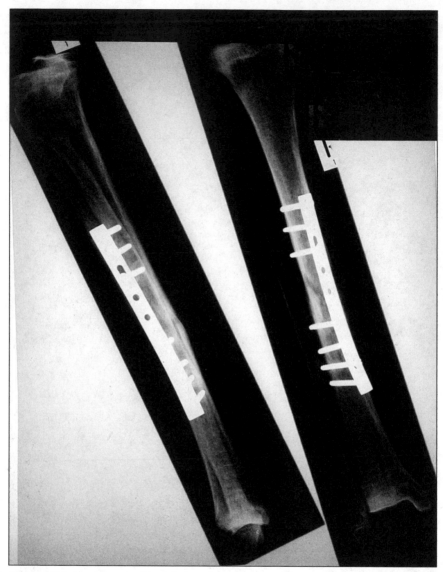

Figure 11.4 *Radiograph of right tibia (from multiple views), exhibiting antemortem surgical plates resulting from fracture. As with any trait unique to an individual, this may be one limiting factor in the identification process (Printed with the permission of the United Nations, ICTY).*

Table 11.3
Types of Identification

Identification	Description
Presumptive Identification	Identification based on characteristics or variables that most likely associated the decedent with the missing person, but is based on data that could be subject to change (i.e., clothing, identification papers found in a wallet).
Positive Identification	Known antemortem information is matched with postmortem data, the variables are based on non-changing data (i.e., DNA, fingerprints, visual identification of a face, radiographic images of bony structures).
Collective Identity	Identification of an individual to a particular group or population (i.e., age, sex, ethnicity).

One of the major challenges to victim identification, particularly in cases of *multiple or mass graves*, is recovery (Haglund 2001). Victims recovered from mass graves or in other human rights contexts may only partially be recovered (Figures 11.5a–c). Incomplete recovery results from the commingling of remains due to the multitude of victims buried together as well, efforts to hide graves by repeatedly digging them up to rebury in different locations (*secondary burials*). Consequently, body parts become *commingled*, separated into different graves or locations, and damaged from shovels or heavy equipment (Figures 11.6–7). Bone tissue may degrade or become contaminated, thereby limiting the use of DNA testing for identification. Associating disarticulated body parts is also compromised as recovery occurs in stages from multiple geographical sites. Due to time and financial constraints it is not feasible to test every bone for DNA. Therefore in regions where mass graves have been uncovered (i.e., Bosnia), the number of unidentified remains is much higher than in contexts where single grave interments were primarily used (i.e., Kosovo).

Figure 11.5a *Three stages of the excavation process of a mass grave are illustrated. Note in (5a) the outline of the parameters of a grave are clear due to color differences in the soil. The color of the soil that is disturbed, verses undisturbed, varies. (These images are printed with the permission of the United Nations, ICTY.)*

Figure 11.5b *Three stages of the excavation process of a mass grave are illustrated. In (5b), archaeologists are working to expose the first layer of bodies. Heavy equipment is used when possible however, excavation close to the surface of the remains requires careful, meticulous hand troweling. (These images are printed with the permission of the United Nations, ICTY.)*

Figure 11.5c *Three stages of the excavation process of a mass grave are illustrated. The first layer of human remains is exposed in Figure 11.5c. This grave was a secondary site therefore, the bodies are severely commingled. (These images are printed with the permission of the United Nations, ICTY.)*

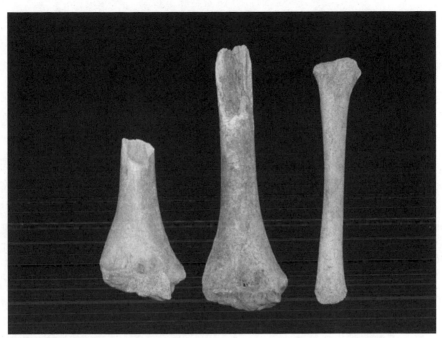

Figure 11.6 *Frontal view of two right humeri and one left tibia, representing three individuals. The minimum number of individuals is estimated based on duplicated skeletal elements (i.e., two right arms) and one left tibia (leg). It is known that left tibia comes from a different individual than the other two bones because of the size. The tibia is from a younger aged juvenile. Therefore, the remains of three juveniles are present (Image by FH. Kimmerle, USF Osteology Collection).*

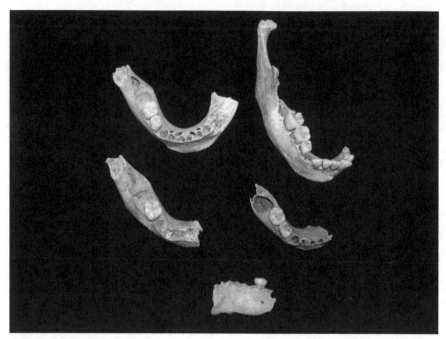

Figure 11.7 Five manibublar fragments are present, representing the fragmented skeletal remains of five juveniles. The fragments are duplicated (based on anatomy) and differ in age (based on dentition and the eruption of teeth), therefore the minimum number of individuals is five (Image by EH. Kimmerle, USF Osteology Collection).

Trauma Analysis: Estimating the Cause of Death

Broken bones are reconstructed to estimate the cause and manner of death resulting from trauma. The mechanisms of injury, such as gunfire, sharp force trauma, blunt force trauma, penetrating shrapnel or blasting injuries create skeletal defects and fracture patterns that are clearly interpreted from skeletal remains. Such injuries must be clearly distinguished from *postmortem* modification resulting from taphonomic or burial factors, scavenging animals, or environmental degradation. The evidence of injury is essential for establishing the manner and cause of death. Overall the pattern and distribution of injuries also provides clear evidence as to the nature of crimes committed over time and place (Figures 11.8–9).

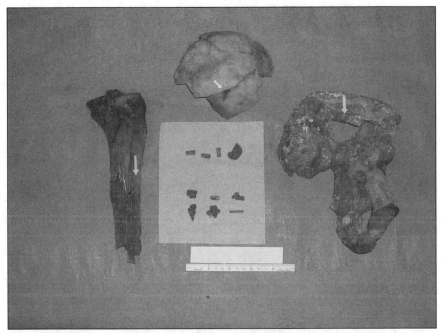

Figure 11.8 *Shrapnel and fractured skeletal remains (a cranial fragment, left ilium, and right tibia), with a large defect from penetrating injury (ilium) are pictured. These injuries resulted from a blast injury (Printed with the permission of the United Nations, ICTY).*

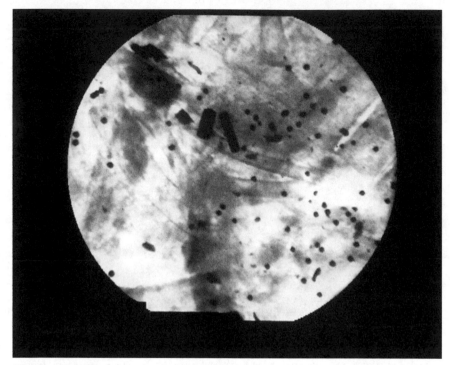

Figure 11.9 *Fluoroscope image of fragmented skeletal remains and shrapnel fragments. Shrapnel results from the materials used to construct an explosive ordinance, whether it is military issued or impoverished (for example, a pipe bomb). The fluoroscope is very useful for providing a radiographic image of the remains, prior to postmortem analysis. The detection of shrapnel is useful for identifying small ballistic evidence (Printed with the permission of the United Nations, ICTY).*

Interpreting trauma in an epidemiological framework (Coupland 2001, Reza et. al. 2001, Taback and Coupland 2005), considers many factors about the individual, weapon, and environment where the incident occurred, such as the age and sex of the individual, their health at the time of the incident, the location (i.e., in a bus, building, or outside), the ability of victims to defend themselves, the type of weapon, size of ammunition, and distance of fire. These are just some of the variables that affect wound morphology and fracture patterns but provide essential information in the interpretation of trauma and reconstructions of circumstances surrounding the fatal event.

Conclusion and Recommendations

Prosecuting war crimes and genocide is different from the domestic homicide investigations under which most forensic and anthropological methods for human identification, demography, trauma analysis, cause of death estimation, and expert testimony has originated. For example, there is a great need for calibration of biological methods based on local population data from various regions throughout the world. The accuracy and applicability of biological methods developed on American samples has been shown to vary when applied across populations. Both the Defense and the Prosecution have a stake in how the demographic data of murdered victims are interpreted, particularly in cases of suspected genocide since the *nature of who the victims were* speaks to the intention of the crime, i.e., *The Prosecutor v. Georges Anderson Nderubumwe Rutaganda (ICTR-96-3), The Prosecutor v. Radislav Krstic (IT-98-33-A),* and *The Prosecutor v. Popovic et al. (IT-05-88-PT).* Similarly, the applicability of *antemortem* data for establishing presumptive, positive, and collective identifications fluctuates in a multi-cultural setting. For example, the applicability of dental and medical records in post-conflict societies is not only a matter of access to such records, but a question of changing health during conflict, when human securities are compromised through repression or war. In such cases the *antemortem* and *postmortem* records may become incompatible. Increasingly, the identification of victims is itself viewed as a human rights issue and in combination with medico-legal death investigations, can provide a means through which transitional justice initiatives are sought.

Acknowledgements

I would like to thank Dr. Matthias Okoye for inviting me to contribute to this book, for his leadership in forensic science education, and his mentorship through the years.

Endnotes

1. ICTR was established by the Security Council, acting under Chapter VII of the Charter of the United Nations, UN Security Resolution 1994/995, provides a mandate to investigate crimes committed in Rwanda in 1994.

2. The ICTY was established by the Security Council, UN Security Council Resolution 1993/827.

Bibliography

Brannon RB, Morlang WM. Jonestown tragedy revisited: the role of dentistry. J For Sci 2002;47(1):3-7.

Burns K. 1998. Forensic anthropology and human rights issues. In: Reichs K (Ed.). *Forensic osteology: Advances in the identification of human remains.* Second edition. Springfield, IL: Charles C. Thomas, pp. 63-85.

Campobasso CP, Falamingo R, Vinci F. 2003. Investigation of Italy's deadliest building collapse: Forensic aspects of a mass disaster. *J of Forensic Sci* 48(3):635-39.

Cordner S, McKelvie H. 2002. Developing standards in international forensic work to identify missing persons. *IRRC* 848(84):867-884.

Coupland RM. 2005. 2001. Armed Violence. *Medicine and Global Survival* 7:33-37.

Cowell RG, Mostad P. A clustering algorithm using DNA marker information for sub-pedigree reconstructions. *J For Sci* 2003;48(6):1239-48.

Ferllini R. 1999. The role of forensic anthropology in Human Rights issues. In: Fairgrieve S (Ed). *Forensic osteologic analysis: A book of case studies.* Springfield, IL: Charles C. Thomas, pp. 287-301.

Fondebrider L. 2002. Reflections on the scientific documentation of human rights violations. *IRRC* 84:885-891.

Haglund WD. 2001. Recent mass graves, an introduction. In: Haglund WD, Sorg MH, (Eds.). *Advances in forensic taphonomy: method, theory and archaeological perspectives.* Boca Raton, FL: CRC Press, pp. 234-262.

Kirschner RH, Hannibal KE. 1994. The application of the forensic sciences to Human Rights investigations. *Medicine and Law* 13(5-6):451-60.

Okoye, MI, Kimmerle EH, Baraybar JP. 2006. Forensic Investigations of Human Rights Violations, Abuse, Mass Graves, and War Crimes. In *Forensic Sciences*, C. H. Wecht (Ed.). Volume 2: LexisNexis Matthew Bender.

Reza A, Mercy JA, Krug E. 2001. Epidemiology of violent deaths in the word. *Injury Prevention.* 7:104-111.

Scott DD, Conner M 1997. Context delicti: archaeological context in forensic work. In Haglund WD, Sorg MH (Eds). *Forensic taphonomy: The postmortem fate of human remains.* Boca Raton, FL: CRC Press, pp. 27-38.

Skinner MF. 1987. Planning the archaeological recovery of evidence from recent mass graves. *Forensic Sci Int.* 34:267-87.

Snow CC, Levine L, Lukash L, Tedeschi LG, Orrego C, Stover E. 1984. The investigation of human remains of the "Disappeared" in Argentina. *American Journal of Physical Anthropology* 5(4):297-99.

Taback N, Coupland R. 2005. Towards collation and modeling of the global cost of Armed violence on civilians. *Medicine, Conflict and Survival.* 21(1):19-27.

The Prosecutor v. Kayishema and Ruxindana, Case No ICTR-95-1; International Criminal Tribunal for Rwanda. In: www.un.org/ictr

The Prosecutor v. Rutaganda, Case No ICTR-96-3; International Criminal Tribunal for Rwanda. In: www.un.org/ictr

The Prosecutor v. Goran Jelisic, Case No. IT-95-10; Trial and Appeals Chamber Judgments, December 14, 1999 and July 5, 2001. International Criminal Tribunal for the former Yugoslavia. In: http://www.un.org/icty/jelisic/trialc1/judgement/index.htm

The Prosecutor v. Ranko Cesic "Brcko", Case No IT-95-10/1; Trial Chamber Judgment, March 11, 2004. International Criminal Tribunal for the former Yugoslavia. In: http://www.un.org/icty/cesic/trialc/judgement/ces-tj040311e.pdf

The Prosecutor v. Radislav Krstic, Case No. IT-98-33-T; Judgment. 2001. International Criminal Tribunal for the former Yugoslavia. In: http://www.un.org/icty/krstic/TrialC1/judgement/krs-tj010802e.pdf, Appeals Chamber judgment of 19 April 2004, www.un.org/icty/Supplement/supp49-e/krstic.htm, Trial transcript, www.un.org/icty/transe33/000530it.htm, Trial Chamber judgment, www.un.org/icty/krstic/TrialC1/judgement/index.htm

The Prosecutor v. Fatmir Limaj, Haradin Bala and Isak Musliu, Case No. IT-03-66-PT; Decision on Prosecution's Motion to Amend the Amended Indictment, ("Second Amended Indictment" attached to the "Prosecution's Motion to Amend the Amended Indictment" filed on 6 November 2003). 2004. International Criminal Tribunal for the former Yugoslavia. In: http://www.un.org/icty/limaj/trialc/decision-e/040212.pdf

The Prosecutor v. Zdravko Tolimir, Radivoje Miletic, Milan Gvero, Vinko Pan-durevic, Ljubisa Beara, Vujadin Popovic, Drago Nikolic, Milorad Trbic and Ljubomir Borovcanin, Case No IT-05-88-PT; Transcripts February 20-21, March 13-15, International Criminal Tribunal for the former Yugoslavia. In: http://www.un.org/icty/transe88/070220ED.htm

Chapter 12

The Role of Forensic Anthropologists in Mass Disasters and the Issues and Challenges in the Anthropological Identification of Mass Disaster Victims

Erin H. Kimmerle, Ph.D. and Annette Doying, B.A.

Introduction

Hurricanes, tornadoes, earthquakes, floods, airplane crashes, train derailments, bridge collapses, explosions, fires, bombs, and terrorism have one thing in common—these events create disasters on a scale that shatters communities, levels cities, and results in high numbers of casualties with an even higher number of wounded and displaced persons (Table 12.1). Terms such as *mass disaster, critical incident* or *mass fatality incident* have been used to describe the context in which unexpected, large-scale destruction and death have resulted. The context of critical incidents is highly variable but typically these events are isolated in time and place. They tend to be single incidents. They are public and generally the situation is known immediately. Woven throughout the framework of disaster response in the United States, collaboration and cooperation act to ensure that victims are served by a network of diverse talents. From search and rescue to the distribution of basic commodities, teams composed of multi-agency members contribute their particular area of expertise. At the most extreme end of the response effort, teams of responders are involved in managing the deceased. Pathologists, anthropologists, dentists, detectives, and grief counselors all take their place alongside firefighters, law enforcement officers, and National Guardsmen in the multi-agency response environment involving fatalities. The role of anthropology in these situations is focused on recovering human remains, sorting commingled bodies and body parts, estimating the number of victims, and human identification.

Table 12.1
Characteristics of Mass Disasters with Regard to Human Remains

- Context of incident highly variable, including natural and man-made disasters.
- Event may or may not involve a crime scene.
- Tendency to be a single incident.
- Limited in time and geographical location.
- The pool of missing persons generally known, at least in the United States.
- Tendency to be highly destructive.
- Generally poor recovery of human remains.
- Highly public events.
- There may be more people wounded and displaced than killed, depending on the cause of the incident.

In this chapter, the increasingly prevalent role of forensic anthropology in mass disasters is reviewed. The challenges to human identification in situations with high numbers of casualties are outlined such as sorting through fragmented and commingled human remains to estimate the *minimum number of individuals*; access to *antemortem* information about missing persons, the different types of identification processes, the challenges that occur with massive destruction to tissues by fire or explosive forces, and the role of anthropological evidence for human identification. Finally, the issues and challenges facing investigators in mass disasters in the United States and internationally are discussed.

What is forensic anthropology?

Anthropologists are trained in biology, cultural studies, and archaeology. Forensic anthropology is a subfield of Biological Anthropology whose experts are broadly trained in human biology, anatomy, variation, and evolution (Table 12.2). As a result, anthropologists bring many areas of expertise to forensic investigations that aid with body or grave detection and exhumation and the *postmortem* analysis of burned, fragmented, decomposing or skeletonized remains. Anthropologists create *skeletal biographies* from human remains that estimate the age at death, sex, stature, ancestry, skeletal pathology, and unique individual characteristics of the individual. This biological description of an individual provides the first parameters in the identification process. In addition, forensic anthropologists provide expertise that differentiates skeletal trauma occurring *perimortem*—that is, at or around the time of death—and which likely contributed to the cause of death. *Postmortem* artifacts resulting from decomposition or modification to the body from natural forces (i.e., the effects of environmental variables like fire or flooding) can be differentiated from human modification (i.e., intentional dismemberment by a person attempting to conceal a body, an explosive force, or an artifact from burial). Forensic anthropologists provide expert scientific opinion in medicolegal death investigations. They may be called to a scene, work in a morgue or provide expert testimony in court. Traditionally, they inventoried teeth and documented dental structures and modifications for comparison with dental records that could be used for identification. Increasingly, forensic dentists are contributing to that area of expertise.

Table 12.2
Forensic Anthropology

- Anthropology → Biological Anthropology → Forensic Anthropology
- Advanced training in osteology, anatomy, human variation and evolution, skeletal pathology, and archaeology.
- Provide scientific expertise as to skeletal parameters of age-at-death, sex, stature, ancestry, unique traits, skeletal pathology, healed trauma, trauma related to the cause of death, and the time since death.
- Aid with body search and recovery.
- Provide expert witness testimony.

Anthropologists are in the position to contribute: 1) a biological profile as the first step in the identification process, 2) a biological profile that contextualizes the victims within a social framework (more victims of disasters are elderly, underrepresented minorities, or in poor health) which provides a greater understanding of social-level vulnerabilities to disaster, and 3) skills specific to cemetery re-interment operations (i.e., flood events, landslides, earthquakes or other natural disasters often result in physical disruption of cemetery sites).

Global Examples of Anthropology in Mass Disasters

Forensic anthropologists and dentists have assisted most often in cases of aircraft accidents (i.e., Muhlemann et al. 1979, Randall 1991, Saul and Saul 2003), military casualties from large-scale accidents (i.e., Brannon and Morlang 2004), mass atrocities such as the Jonestown deaths of 923 people (Brannon and Morlang 2002) or the Branch Davidian Compound (Ubelaker et al. 1995), terrorist bombings (i.e., Kahana et al. 1997), natural disasters such as volcanoes (Wagner et al. 1988) or hurricanes (i.e., Lew and Wetli 1996), and building or structural accidents (i.e., Campobasso et al. 2003). In the context of the United States, state and federal systems have organized to respond to the immediate challenge of managing such disasters by providing mobile morgue operations, death investigations, and systems for human identification for the government, such as the national DMORT (Disaster Mortuary Operational Response Team) or Florida FEMORS (Florida Emergency Mortuary Operations Response System) systems. Part of the FEMORS (FEMORS 2007) mission is:

> The rapid and accurate identification of mass fatality victims is of critical importance to any disaster mitigation operation. Issues of probate cannot be resolved until a death certificate has been issued by the Medical Examiner. FEMORS was created to serve the needs of Medical Examiners in their mission to bring dignity and professionalism to caring for the deceased.

The tsunami that affected South Asia in 2004 directly affected twelve countries with more than 230,000 deaths and well over 100,000 people still missing, many of whom were travelers from foreign countries outside of the affected area (UN News Room 2006). With so many fatalities and an infrastructure destroyed, many bodies were not recovered, not buried, or were burned without documentation. In some cases, bodies were photographed and fingerprinted prior to being buried in mass graves. In such an event, investigators are challenged to manage critical incidents and respond to the humanitarian and legal necessity of human identification. UN envoy, former President Bill Clinton wrote (UN News Room 2006): "As we have learned in other parts of the world in the wake of massive disasters—from Kobe to New Orleans, Tangshan to Bam—rebuilding the physical, social, and human capital of shattered communities takes years." Providing assistance through medicolegal death investigations for human identification is critical for families who are searching for the missing. The issues and challenges facing investigators in the United States and internationally are similar, though the mechanisms in place, access to resources, and trained personal may vary greatly. Warren wrote (1978;388):

> Personal identification of human remains, as a science and as an art, occurs in a variety of sociocultural contexts. Unknown remains resulting from accidents and homicides occupy the attention of identification specialists in criminalistics, and unknowns resulting from military engagements and mass disasters are the focus of identification specialists in both military and civilian agencies. Each group of specialists has, within its respective identification agency, its own techniques and methods for establishing identity, and each group has its own criteria with which to verify identification.

Warren (1978) pointed out that the process of identification depends on the group of victims being investigated and who is conducting the investigation, as processes and techniques may vary substantially. Consequently, there is a need for research and education and professional training to share experience and ensure accuracy in the identification methods used.

Another area of involvement for forensic anthropologists serving on the DMORT teams in New Orleans following Hurricane Katrina (2005) was the recovery of a different kind of storm victim. In addition to the identification of those who died as a result of the storm, obtaining antemortem information on the victims, and locating missing persons, DMORT was also involved with the recovery of disturbed grave sites. Storm surges from Hurricanes Katrina and Rita disinterred or damaged caskets, vaults and tombs at many cemeteries and DMORT conducted operations, which included the recovery, identification, casketing and return of these disturbed remains to the appropriate local jurisdictions. The Cemetery Affairs section of the Louisiana Family Assistance Center (LFAC) surveyed 82 cemeteries in nine Louisiana parishes. This area covered 7,727 square miles (an area larger than the State of New Jersey). Sixty-eight of the surveyed cemeteries revealed damage to 924 tombs and 598 vaults (State of Louisiana 2006).

Issues and Challenges in Identification

Human identification is based on a variety of methods to estimate parameters about an individual and consists of a process that gathers information, interprets data to estimate information about a person, and excludes cases, thereby limiting the pool of potential matches throughout the process (Table 12.3). In disasters, a variety of resources are utilized to develop an understanding of the identity of the decedent. In transportation accidents, the passenger manifest is relied upon; in natural disasters, public records of residency and familial relationships prove useful; in acts of terrorism or technological disasters, eyewitness accounts are often an initial resource for documenting the possible identity of those impacted. There are different types of human identification, such as:

- Presumptive Identification—Establishes the likely identity of the person based on information or from methods that is not exclusive to only the deceased, such as a physical description matching a missing persons report, clothing, identification papers in a wallet.
- Collective Identification—The general descriptive characteristics of the individual that place them within a particular cultural, demographic, religious or ethic group.

- Positive Identification—The identity of the individual is established through information that is exclusive to the individual, and is derived from a comparison of ante- and postmortem information, unique to that individual.

In cases where identity cannot be established, identification remains *indeterminate* or *unknown*.

Table 12.3
Challenges to Human Identification in Mass Disasters

- The high number of fatalities means there are many victims.
- Access to *antemortem* data.
- The destructive nature of critical incidents.
- Damage to tissues due to explosions or fire.
- Counting the number of victims may be based on small body fragments and may represent the minimum number, not the total number of fatalities.
- The high amount of structural collateral intermixed with fragmented human remains.
- Tracking data and remains throughout the recovery process, as associated materials may be recovered at different times or in different locations.

Access to Antemortem Data

Determining who is missing, obtaining access to *antemortem* records, and managing large amounts of data are primary tasks for operating identification processes on any scale. Data that comes from family members or someone who knew the deceased is critical for the process to work; therefore such information must be attainable and accurate. Further, as the process and recovery effort continues, new information is made available and therefore decedent data banks are evolving throughout the process. Lorton and Langley (1986) warned about biological traits used in the identification process that may change over time such as weight, hair color or style, and clothing. This raises a very important point about data reliability, and also about how a person's biological description may be viewed by the witness giving the description. Statements such as "he was tall" may be misleading, if the witness and the interviewer have a different perspective about what is "tall."

In the days, weeks, and months following Hurricane Katrina's August 2005 landfall in the U.S. Gulf Coast region, human remains of the storm's victims continued to be discovered. In New Orleans, the DMORT teams worked with the Louisiana Family Assistance Center (LFAC) whose mission was to: 1) reunify loved ones with the victims of Hurricanes Katrina and Rita, 2) assist in the identification of the missing, and 3) support the re-interment of the displaced victims from public cemeteries. Five months after the storm came ashore, 3,200 people remained missing. Finding information to match physical traits present on the human remains was extremely difficult as most dental and doctor offices were flooded or severely wind damaged and therefore most patient records were destroyed. Katrina's unique challenges were also a condition of the unprecedented and massive population displacement in the United States that occurred as a result of the event. The movement of this large population of displaced people resulted in additional difficulties for identification, as possible sources of antemortem records were missing. Further, it acted as a barrier in obtaining the next of kin's authority to release federally protected *antemortem* medical records.

Conditions resulting from Hurricane Katrina made the identification of human remains complex. Decomposition reduced many of those not discovered in the earliest days of the event to skeletons. As a result, forensic anthropologists became a critical component in the identification process. An Associated Press (2006) article illustrates the time that elapsed before some of the deceased were found:

> The state medical examiner said Thursday that about 400 addresses will be turned over to New Orleans police and fire officials to be checked again for people reported missing after Hurricane Katrina. The addresses were culled from the list of 3,200 people still officially unaccounted for nearly five months after Hurricane Katrina hit the Gulf Coast and broken flood walls allowed water to spew into most of the city.
>
> Doctor Louis Cataldie, the state's medical examiner, asked local police and fire officials to recheck the addresses because authorities have consistent information about people missing from those locations. Most are in heavily flooded areas of the New Orleans area, including east New Orleans and Saint Bernard Parish.
>
> New Orleans police and fire officials said addresses throughout the city have been checked for the deceased. But, after some of the most severely damaged neighborhoods were reopened to residents, several families returned to wrecked homes to find a missing relative deceased inside.

The LFAC Final Report (State of Louisiana 2006) provides information on victim demography. More than half of all victims were classified by LFAC as African American, a fact that holds significant social meaning. The age distribution demonstrates that older adults were the primary victims of Hurricane Katrina. The demographic distribution highlights the social vulnerability of a specific segment of the New Orleans population. Many older adults live on fixed incomes and have age-related constraints placed on their ability to self-transport. Additionally, older adults may exhibit greater reluctance to leave their place of residence.

Explosions and Body Parts

One of the largest obstacles to identification is incomplete recovery. Commonly, mass disasters consist of highly destructive forces that create fragmented tissues such as high-speed crashes and may include burning from fire or explosions. Trauma to the body results from primary causative agents, and secondarily to flying debris. Moreover, human remains may be mixed with structural debris, fuel, or other hazardous chemicals. For these reasons, recovery is generally incomplete for any given body and typically not all of the victims are recovered. Therefore, unique features about a person may never be known if only fragments or incomplete body tissues are recovered. Events that are explosive or involve intensive fires often result in victims being reduced to the most absolute of elements— bones and teeth. Prolonged and intense fire, particularly resulting from explosions or aircraft accidents, fragment, discolor and alter the morphology of bone. Despite this, it is often possible to identify trauma, unique physical characteristics, or dental work for burned remains for human identification (Fairgrieve 1994).

Counting the Dead

Given the high number of victims and structural damage involved in cases of mass disasters, managing human remains may be challenging. Complex sites involve cases where body parts from an individual may be located in different areas, or recovered at different times. Often, the scene of a disaster is handled much like a crime scene, because some disasters *are* crime scenes. Both disaster sites and crime scenes contain clues which will lead investigators to better understand the nature of the event with the bodies of the dead and the objects around them often providing critical information. As more tissues are recovered, they may associate with materials already processed. The challenge is to sort human tissue to calculate the most likely number of individuals and associate remains when possible. Therefore, keeping track of materials as they are processed through the *postmortem* system is critical for later matching of associated pieces of evidence.

Skeletal Biographies and the Process of Identification

Methods for estimating each aspect of the skeletal biography utilize different areas of the skeleton (Table 12.4). The more complete the recovery, the more options there are to use a range of methods. Alternatively, when only small body fragments are present, it may be that the features needed are absent, thereby limiting the ability for individual estimation. Estimating skeletal parameters about the decedent from biological information provides the critical first step in establishing individual identity.

Table 12.4
Variables Estimated from the Skeleton for Identification

- Age at death
- Sex
- Stature
- Ancestry
- Unique Skeletal Markers or Congenital Anomalies
- Skeletal Pathology
- Trabecular bone or skeletal morphology for radiographic comparisons
- Dental inventory, pathology, modification, or anamaly

Anthropologists assist with identification in cases where methods of visual recognition or fingerprinting are not options. According to Larsen (1997), the skeleton is a voice of the past—the last remaining evidence of a person's identity. Composed of minerals, collagen, dentin and enamel, bone and teeth respond to individually unique inherited and environmental conditions including physical and nutritional stressors experienced throughout life. Since bone and teeth are generally responsive to these stressors their shape, size, and condition reveal life history at both the individual and the population level. The study of the skeleton provides an understanding of the individual as a functioning, living human being and member of a population.

Estimating the biological parameters about a victim through anthropological methods is the first step in the exclusion process (Figures 12.1–6). *Is the victim male or female; young or old; tall or short?* The ever-present challenge is to avoid false exclusions. In other words, the objective is to narrow the pool of possible matches between decedents and missing persons, yet keep the list long enough so as to not falsely exclude the victim. Additionally, dentition (Figure 12.7), unique individualizing traits about a person, such as congenital (non-pathological) skeletal anomalies (Figure 12.8), healed trauma (Figure 12.9), or skeletal disease may provide parameters as to a victim's possible identity.

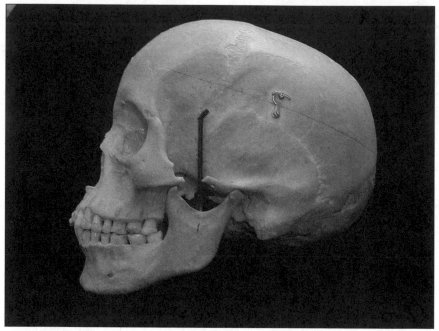

Figure 12.1a *Adult, female skull, left side. Note the gracile features: small browridge and overall size, gracile mandible, small mastoid process and nuchal area on the base of the skull. Overall, the morphology of the skull is gracile, small, and indicative of female traits (Image by EH. Kimmerle, USF Osteology Collection).*

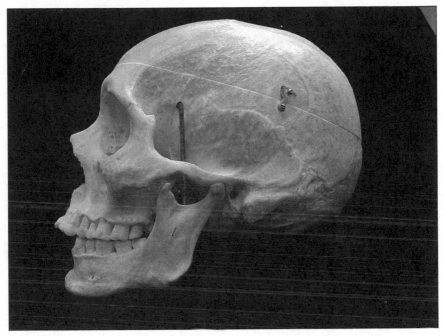

Figure 12.1b *Adult, male skull, left side. Note the robust features: a large browridge, projecting mandible, retreating forehead, large mastoid process, large occipital protuberance. Overall, the morphology of the skull is well developed, large, robust and Indicative of male traits (Image by FH. Kimmerle, USF Osteology Collection).*

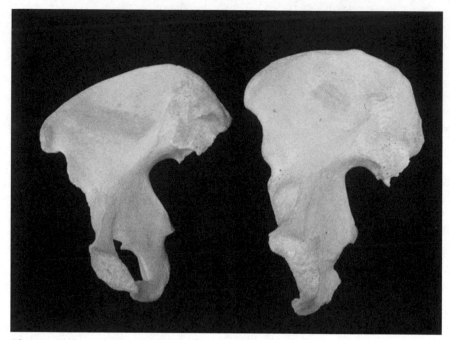

Figure 12.2a *Adult, anterior view of right pelvis. A female (left) and a male (right) are compared. The size and shape of the pelvis provide reliable data for sex estimation (Image by EH. Kimmerle, USF Osteology Collection).*

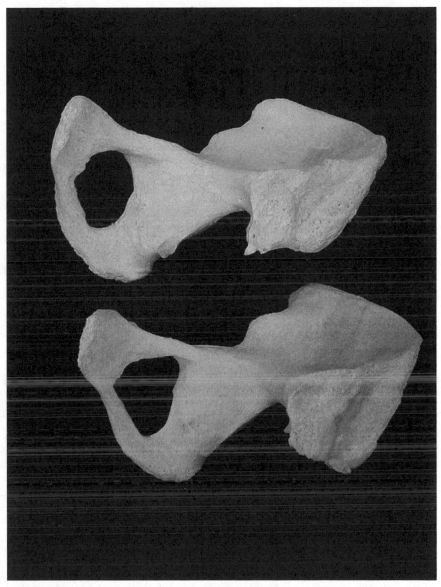

Figure 12.2b *Adult, lateral view of right pelvis. A male (top) and a female (bottom) are compared, illustrating morphological differences between them (Image by EH. Kimmerle, USF Osteology Collection).*

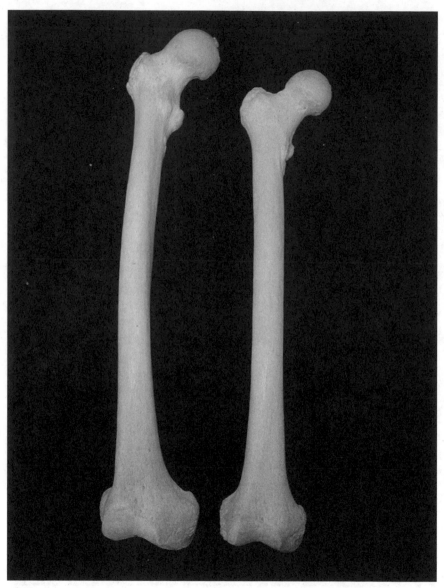

Figure 12.3 Comparison of two right femora, from a male and female. Note the apparent size difference. Post-cranial metric analysis provides and accurate means for estimating the sex of a skeleton. This is particularly useful for contexts where human remains are fragmented (Image by EH. Kimmerle, USF Osteology Collection).

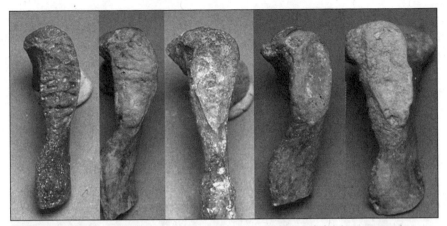

Figure 12.4 The pubic symphysis (a trait on the pelvis) is routinely used to estimate the age of adults. Pictured here are the right symphyseal faces from five individuals, whose ages at death were a) 20 years, b) 27 years, c) 40 years, d) 65 years, and e) 81 years (these images were printed with the permission of the United Nations, ICTY).

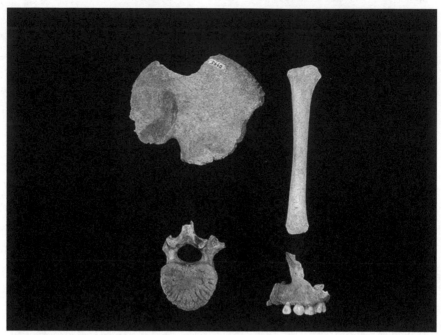

Figure 12.5 *Bones from four different individuals are pictured here. The ilium is unfused to the rest of the pelvis. The tibial shaft is small and none of the epiphyses have yet fused. The vertebral arch is fused to the centrum, but the ephyseal ring is not yet fused to the body. The maxilla is unfused and deciduous teeth are present. Based on age these remains come from four different individuals (Image by EH. Kimmerle, USF Osteology Collection).*

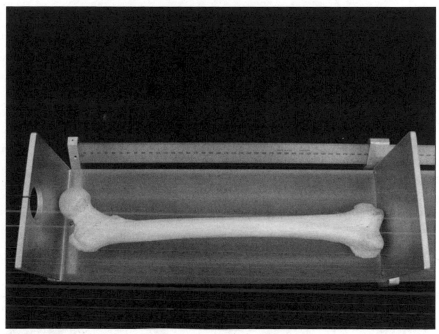

Figure 12.6 *The right femur is being measured in the osteometric board for stature. Any long bone or long bone fragment can be used for stature, however the bones of the legs provide the more accurate estimate for a decedent's height (Image by EH. Kimmerle, USF Osteology Collection).*

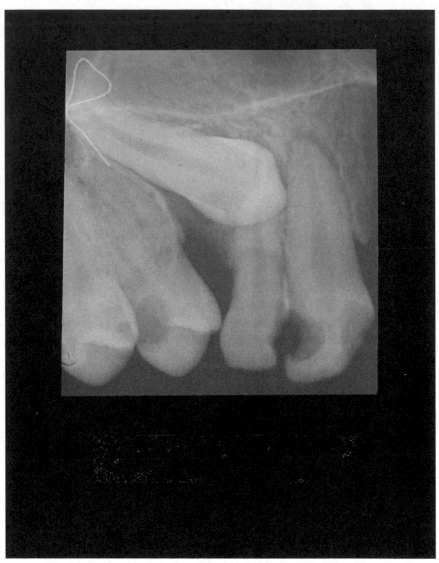

Figure 12.7 Radiograph of the right maxilla from an adult. Note the impacted canine. This feature would be very useful for identification, if antemortem records of some form can be established related to dental parameters (image printed with the permission of the United Nations, ICTY).

Figure 12.8 Lower vertebrae of an adult individual who suffered scoliosis and osteoarthritis. Both conditions could be useful for identification if family members or medical records indicated such conditions were present. While these conditions are not rare among the population, they serve as variables that help to limit the pool for identification and are used in combination with many other lines of evidence (image printed with the permission of the United Nations, ICTY).

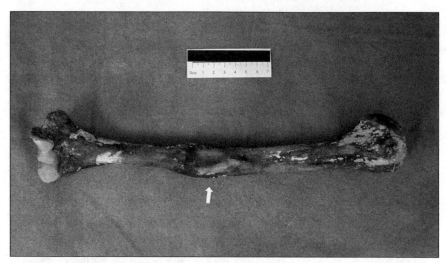

Figure 12.9 *Left humerus (upper arm bone) from an adult individual. The arrow is pointing out a healed fracture to the midshaft of the bone. Healed trauma may be another useful variable to aid in the identification process (image printed with the permission of the United Nations, ICTY).*

The radiographic comparison of unique physical traits, healed trauma, or skeletal morphology is a valuable tool in cases where *antemortem* radiographs of missing persons are available (Rouge et al. 1993, Warren et al. 2000). Commonly, chest X-rays (Kuehn et al. 2002), cranial anomalies (Rouge et al. 1993) and trabecular bone (Kahana et al. 1998) have been used. Radiography can be useful as an exclusion technique or to confirm positive identifications. Successful positive identification has been used for frontal sinuses (Christensen 2005), mastoid sinuses (Smith et al. 2002), and healed trauma or other unique skeletal features (Kahana et al. 2002). Clothing and personal effects is an important limiting factor in reducing the pool and method of exclusion (Primorac et al. 1996). Material evidence may also have evidentiary value about the decedent's identity or cause of death. Unique dental parameters or comparisons between *antemortem* and postmortem dental records offers a variety of very reliable and fast methods for positive identification (Brannon and Kessler 1999). This is particularly useful in cases of mass disasters since dental structures often survive the more destructive forces. Finally, innovative methods for DNA analysis are proving helpful, particularly in cases where there is a strong presumptive identification (Olaisen et al. 1997, Cowell and Mostad 2003).

Conclusion and Recommendations

Anthropology has many areas of expertise that aid humanitarian and criminal efforts following mass disasters. Increasingly, the methods used to estimate biological profiles are applied across populations. There is a great need for research that investigates more skeletal traits to estimate biological parameters than traditionally have been used such as the use of the calcaneus for sex estimation (Introna et al. 1997) and applied among different populations (Bidmos and Asala 2004). There is also a need for research that estimates biological parameters for different populations taking into account biological variation and secular change. As American responders and forensic investigators continue to refine disaster response protocols and readiness, they are in the position to offer assistance internationally, both in terms of investigative services as well as education.

Acknowledgements

We thank Dr. Matthias Okoye for inviting us to submit this chapter.

Bibliography

Aceh B. 2004. Tsunami death toll tops 56,000 Officials just reaching hardest hit areas in Indonesia. CNN News report, Tuesday, December 28, 2004. http://www.cnn.com/2004/WORLD/asiapcf/12/28/asia.quake/index.html

Associated Press. 2006. Targeted List of 400 Homes to Be Rechecked. January 23, 2006. Retrieved March 5, 2007. In: http://www.wafb.com/Global/story.asp?S=4384702

Bidmos, M. A. and S. A. Asala. 2004. Sexual dimorphism of the calcaneus of South African blacks. *Journal of Forensic Sciences* 49(3):446–50.

Brannon, R. B. and H. P. Kessler. 1999. Problems in Mass-Disaster Dental Identification: A Retrospective Review. *Journal of Forensic Sciences* 44(1):123–127.

Brannon, R. B. and W. M. Morlang. 2004. The USS Iowa disaster: success of the forensic dental team. *Journal of Forensic Sciences* 49(5):1067–68.

Campobasso, C. P., R. Falamingo, and F. Vinci. 2003. Investigation of Italy's deadliest building collapse: Forensic aspects of a mass disaster. *Journal of Forensic Sciences* 48(3):635–39.

Christensen, A. M. 2005. Testing the Reliability of Frontal Sinuses in Positive Identification. *Journal of Forensic Sciences* 50(1):145–149.

CNN News Report. 2005. Tsunami death toll. CNN, Tuesday, February 22, 2005. In: http://cnnstudentnews.cnn.com/2004/WORLD/asiapcf/12/28/tsunami.deaths.

Cowell, R.G. and P. Mostad. 2003. A clustering algorithm using DNA marker information for sub-pedigree reconstruction. *Journal of Forensic Sciences* 48(6):486–495.

Fairgrieve, S. I. 1994. SEM analysis of incinerated teeth as an aid to positive identification. *Journal of Forensic Sciences* 39(2):557–65.

FEMORS. 2007. Mission Statement, In: http://www.femors.org/about.asp.

Introna, Jr., F., G. Di Vella, C. P. Campobasso and M. Dragone. 1997. Sex determination by discriminant analysis of calcanei measurements. *Journal of Forensic Sciences* 42(4):725–28.

Kahana, T., L. Goldin, and J. Hiss. 2002. Personal Identification Based on Radiographic Vertebral Features. *American Journal of Forensic Medicine and Pathology* 23(1):36–41.

Kahana, T., J. Hiss, and P. Smith. 1998. Quantitative Assessment of Trabecular Bone Pattern identification. *Journal of Forensic Sciences* 43(6):1144–47.

Kahana, T., J. A. Ravioli, C. L. Urroz, and J. Hiss. 1997. Radiographic identification of fragmentary human remains from a mass disaster. *American Journal of Forensic Medical Pathology* 18(1):40–44.

Kuehn, C. M., K. M. Taylor, F. A. Mann, A. J. Wilson, and Harruff. 2002. Validation of chest x-ray comparisons for unknown decedent identification. *Journal of forensic sciences* 47(4):725–29.

Larsen, C. S. 2000. *Skeletons in Our Closet: revealing our past through bioarchaeology*. Princeton, NJ: Princeton University Press.

UN News Room. 21 December 2006. Lessons from Asia tsunami recovery effort must be passed on, UN envoy Clinton. In: http://www.un.org/apps/news/story.asp?NewsID=21077&Cr=tsunami&Cr1.

Lew, E. O. and C. V. Wetli. 1996. Mortality from Hurricane Andrew. *Journal of Forensic Sciences* 41(3):449–52.

Lorton, L. and W. H. Langley. 1986. Decision-making concepts in postmortem identification. *Journal of Forensic Sciences* 31(1):190–96.

Muhlemann, H. R., E. Steiner, and M. Brandestini. 1979. Identification of mass disaster victims: The Swiss Identification System. *Journal of Forensic Sciences* 24(1):173–81.

Olaisen, B., M. Stenersen, and B. Mevaag. 1997. Identification by DNA analysis of the victims of the August 1996 Spitsbergen civil aircraft disaster. *Nature Genetics* 15(4):402–5.

Primorac, D., S. Andelinovic, M. Definis-Gojanovic, I. Drmic, B. Rezic, M. M. Baden, M. A. Kennedy, M. S. Schanfield, S. B. Skakel, and H. C. Lee. 1996. Identification of War Victims from Mass Graves in Croatia, Bosnia, and Herzegovina by the Use of Standard Forensic Methods and DNA Typing. *Journal of Forensic Sciences* 41(5):891–94.

Randall, B. 1991. Body retrieval and morgue operation at the crash of United Flight 232. *Journal of Forensic Sciences* 36(2):403–9.

Rouge, D., N. Telmon, P. Arrue, G. Larrouy, and L. Arbus. 1993/ Radiographic identification of human remains through deformities and anomalies cranial bones: A report of two cases. *Journal of Forensic Sciences* 38(4):997–1007.

Saul, F. P., and J. M. Saul. 2003. Planes, trains, and fireworks: The evolving role of the forensic anthropologist in mass fatality incidents. In *Hard Evidence: Case studies in forensic anthropology*, ed. D. W. Steadman, 266–77. Upper Saddle River, NJ: Prentice Hall.

Smith, D. R., K. G. Limbird, and J. M. Hoffman. 2002. Identification of Human Skeletal Remains by Comparison of Bony Details of the Cranium Using Computerized Tomographic (CT) Scans. *Journal of Forensic Sciences* 47(5):937–39.

State of Louisiana: Louisiana Family Assistance. 2006. Reuniting the Families of Katrina and Rita: Final Report of the Louisiana Family Assistance Center. Retrieved March 5, 2007, from http://www.dhh.louisiana.gov/offices/reports.asp?ID=303&Detail=396.

Ubelaker, D. H., D. W. Owsley, M. M. Houck, E. Craig, and W. Grant. 1995. The role of forensic anthropology in the recovery and analysis of Branch Davidian Compound victims: recovery procedures and characteristics of the victims. *Journal of Forensic Sciences* 40(3):335–40.

Wagner, G. N., M. A. Clark, E. J. Koenigsberg, and S. J. Decata. 1988. Medical evaluation of the victims of the 1986 Lake Nyos Disaster. *Journal of Forensic Sciences* 33(4):31–44.

Warren, C. P. 1978. Personal identification of human remains: An overview. *Journal of Forensic Sciences* 23(2).

Warren M.W., K. R. Smith, P. R. Stubblefield, S. S. Martin, and Walsh-Haney. 2000. Use of radiographic atlases in a mass fatality. *Journal of Forensic Sciences* 45(2):467–70.

Chapter 13

The Application of Forensic Entomology to Mass Disasters

Timothy E. Huntington, M.S.

Introduction

During a mass disaster incident the loss of human life overwhelms the local resources and rescue and recovery efforts may be prolonged by the scope of the incident, both in terms of size of the area affected and the dangers and obstacles facing the responding agencies. Because of this potential delay in the recovery of human remains, the likelihood that necrophilous (carrion-feeding) insects will be associated with some or all of the bodies following a mass disaster incident is high. During periods of warm weather, blow flies will arrive on fresh remains within minutes after death, and egg laying will commence shortly thereafter. Due to this rapid colonization and potentially delayed recovery of human remains, it is important for responders to mass disaster scenes to understand and appreciate how these insects can affect the scene, and what information about the disaster or its victims they can provide.

Background and Application of Forensic Entomology

Insects make up the dominant life form on the planet (Triplehorn and Johnson 2005), so it is little wonder that they may be found during the course of a variety of types of forensic investigations. Forensic entomology, the use of insects as evidence, has a long and rich history stemming back to ancient China (McKnight 1981). For a historical perspective, see Benecke (2001).

Medicocriminal entomology, the branch of forensic entomology dealing with human death, is an established science which has been used to estimate the time, location, cause, and manner of death in cases of homicide, suicide, and accidental deaths throughout the world. Medicocriminal entomology has gained in acceptance and is applied in the investigations of hundreds of human fatalities every year (Catts and Goff 1992).

When applied to forensic investigations, the primary use of entomology is to estimate the time since death, or postmortem interval (PMI), during death investigations. Although questions related to the location or manner of death may also be addressed using entomological evidence, the vast majority of forensic entomology cases continue to focus on PMI estimates (Haskell 2007). After a period of 24–48 hours, forensic entomology is one of the few methods for accurately estimating the PMI (Greenberg and Kunich 2002), though entomological analysis has been successful for estimating the PMI after many years have passed (Haskell et al. 1997). Flies, particularly blow flies (Diptera: Calliphoridae), are the first to locate and colonize a dead animal, often within seconds or minutes after death when conditions are favorable. The adult flies deposit eggs on the body, which then hatch into maggots, the stage that is responsible for removing much of the soft tissue on terrestrial bodies. After feeding, maggots migrate from the body to pupate, from which the adult will emerge. Because insects are cold-blooded, their rate of development varies with the environmental temperatures; that is, generally speaking, the warmer it is the faster the insects will develop and the cooler it is the slower they will develop. Therefore, by knowing the species of fly, the stage of development, and the temperatures that the insect experienced during development, a forensic entomologist may accurately estimate the age of a particular insect found on a body. Because the delay between death and colonization are often minimal, this knowledge may be applied to the PMI of a body and an estimate of PMI may be made. By knowing the ecological habits of the insects, inferences related to the specifics of a case may be made, such as the effects on insect colonization of a body found indoors (Goff 1991).

Several texts on the subject of forensic entomology are available (Smith 1986, Catts and Haskell 1990, Byrd and Castner 2001, Greenberg and Kunich 2002) and it has been featured as a special topic in several forensic science and pathology books (Hall and Haskell 1995, Haskell et al. 1997, Haskell 2006, Anderson and Cervenka 2002).

Forensic Entomology and Mass Disasters

Following any mass disaster incident, there are four key needs with which the use of forensic entomology may assist: investigation of the incident, complete recovery of victims, disease control, and identification of victims.

Investigation of the incident

While natural disasters focus the investigation on recovery and identification of victims, man-made disasters (terrorism, accidents, structural failures, mass homicides/suicides, etc.) require that investigations determine factors causing or contributing to the disaster (Wagner and Froede 2006).

The true forte of forensic entomology has always been in the estimation of the time since death (Johnston and Villeneuve 1897, Catts and Goff 1992, Amendt et al. 2004). Although most mass disasters occur at a time and place that is nearly immediately acknowledged, some incidents may go unrecognized for some time. For example, the mass suicide in Jonestown, Guyana, in 1978 left over 900 corpses in a tropical environment, with examination of the remains not taking place until after six days postmortem. This allowed for rapid decomposition, including insect colonization, prior to examination (Thompson et al. 1987). Were a similar event to take place, without the aid of suicide notes or the like, investigations as to the timing of the event would be necessary, and in cases of advanced decomposition entomological analysis would be necessary to determine the PMI (Haskell 2006). At times, it may be necessary to determine if death may have occurred prior to a mass disaster incident, and entomological analysis could prove to be extremely useful to investigators in such an instance.

Other questions related to investigations of mass disasters may also be answered through entomological analysis. For example, defects on a body ranging from small abrasions to massive tissue loss and perforated skin are all caused by insects, and may be confused with a variety of perimortem wounds (Byrd and Castner 2001; Saukko and Knight 2004). Postmortem movement of a corpse, either through natural (floods, high winds, etc.) or mechanical transportation may be proven through entomological means (Haskell et al. 1997). The presence of a number of different illicit and legal drugs may be confirmed by analyzing maggots where sufficient tissue is absent (Goff and Lord 1994, 2001; Campobasso et al. 2004).

Complete recovery of victims

The goal of every recovery effort following a mass disaster incident should be the complete recovery of every victim, due to legal, ethical, and investigative standards. In disasters such as airline crashes, where high velocity impact causes fragmentation and scattering of human remains, complete recovery may be a difficult and prolonged venture. Complete fragmentation of the body is possible at high g-force levels, and small portions of a single body may be scattered over a wide area (Sledzik and Rodriguez 2002). Fragmentation of the cranium, for example, not only scatters the skull fragments but also the brain, resulting in many small pieces of jelly-like material scattered over the site (Hill 1989).

This bone fragmentation and tissue destruction often leads to remains that are virtually indistinguishable from the surrounding substrate. Although the distinction between tissue and non-tissue would be easily made in a laboratory setting, this is often not practical. Recovery efforts following a mass disaster are by definition massive undertakings, and the manpower and resources required to sift through every inch of debris and soil looking for tissue fragments is extensive, and may not even yield a complete recovery. For example, two days of searching following the crash of a Pan Am jet in Maryland in 1963 yielded an estimated 33 percent of the total weight of the passengers on board. Likewise, the total recovery of human remains following the crash of a ValuJet plane in Florida in 1996 was estimated at 26 percent of the total passenger weight (Mittleman 2000).

Insects offer a rapid means of locating fragmented remains and distinguishing between tissue and non-tissue in the field following such an occurrence. Because of their keen sense of smell, insects such as blow flies will rapidly find and alight on even small pieces of tissues. Following the 1994 crash of American Eagle Flight 4184 near Roselawn, Indiana, a forensic entomologist was brought to the crash site to aid in finding fragmented tissue by following where the blow flies would land (N.H. Haskell, personal communication). Investigators with little or no training in entomology may still use this aid in locating these remains, as noting the presence of flies congregated in a small area takes very little if any practice. It would also be possible to contact a forensic entomologist for the purposes of releasing large numbers of captive-bred blow flies at the site with the goal of following the flies to additional remains. It should be noted that this method of detection is hindered by cool temperatures, inclement weather, and low-light conditions, or if the remains are located in an aquatic environment.

Even in mass disaster situations where victims have not been fragmented, insects may prove useful for the purpose of locating hidden remains. Because blow flies are readily attracted to corpses that are hidden from view, those involved in search and recovery missions at the scenes of structural collapse or other rapid burials should watch for the presence of blow flies and other insects that may give clues as to the whereabouts of victims. Adult flies can negotiate very small openings to reach a body, and may be the only indication of a body's being under a pile of rubble.

Disease control

Arthropod-vectored diseases are a major concern following many types of natural disasters due to the increase in population and density of disease-carrying flies and mosquitoes (Ligon 2006). Many publications have addressed the control of medically important insects following this type of disaster (e.g., Wisner and Adams 2002), and these concerns would fall under the category of medical, rather than forensic, entomology.

However, there are examples of mass disaster scenarios that could involve the spread of disease by forensically important blow flies. For example, the potential threat of a bioterrorism attack using aerosolized anthrax (*Bacillus anthracis*) has been brought to the forefront of the media and disaster preparedness organizations in recent years in the wake of the current "War on Terror." Projected human mortality from such an attack is approximately 85 percent for infected individuals, and death would likely occur within three days after the onset of symptoms (Inglesby et al. 1999). One topic scarcely detailed by so called "preparedness plans" for such an attack is the proper disposal of victims.

Because of the rapid rate of colonization of human corpses by insects such as blow flies, one could easily understand how such a mass fatality incident would result in many decomposing corpses infested with maggots. Included in that number would be the many animals affected by such an attack, wild and domestic, which would almost certainly receive less attention to proper disposal than those human corpses. This issue is of concern because in the early 1900's, experiments were performed that proved that blow fly maggots that feed on the corpse of an animal that had been infected with anthrax carry the spores of the bacterium through pupation, and after they have emerged as adult flies (Graham-Smith 1914). This means that each fly that had fed upon a single infected animal or human corpse following such a bioterrorism attack would be capable of spreading the pathogen over a much wider area than the original attack. In the case of blow flies, several species have been known to travel over 60 km from their point of origin (Braack 1981, MacLeod and Donnelly 1963). This fact, combined with the ability for flies to mechanically transmit pathogens to whatever they may come into contact (Graham-Smith 1914, Greenberg 1971) makes these flies incredibly dangerous, especially when several thousand flies may result from a single small animal corpse. Blow flies feeding on infected corpses have also been shown to carry other potential bioterrorism agents, such as plague and tuberculosis (Hall 1948).

Further research is needed to know if this secondary transmission by blow flies of other potential bioterrorism agents is possible, but it would seem prudent to ensure proper and immediate disposal of all infected human and animal corpses following a mass disaster incident of bioterrorism.

Identification of victims

The critical need for the rapid positive identification of victims following mass disaster incidents typically relies on dental, anthropological, radiological, and/or criminalistic studies of the remains (Wagner and Froede 2006). Entomological analysis of insects collected from victims typically does little to facilitate identification, though such instances may exist. In scenarios where response to the scene is delayed, and maggot infestations are extensive, the maggots themselves may be tested for the presence of human DNA to identify the person that they have fed upon (Wells et al. 2001, Zehner et al. 2004). In situations where there are maggots present, but no obvious remains, these maggots could serve as a viable means of identification.

Techniques for extracting human DNA from maggots are described by Wells et al. (2001), Linville and Wells (2002), Linville et al. (2004), and Zehner et al. (2004).

Of special consideration to the identification of victims is the ability for maggots to continue to feed even after an infested body has been placed in a morgue cooler. Considerable destruction of identifying characters is possible in a short period of time, so rapid processing of even slightly decomposed remains is critical to avoid the loss of key features (Huntington et al. 2007).

Collecting and Preserving Entomological Evidence

Like most forms of forensic evidence, entomological evidence must be collected and preserved in an appropriate manner to prevent damage to the sample. Many of the typical forensic evidence collection skills required by any other forensic discipline are relevant when collecting entomological samples, so little additional training may be required for the investigator prior to recovering insect evidence.

Procedures for collecting and preserving entomological evidence have been described by several excellent texts, and readers are encouraged to consult these for detailed descriptions of collection procedures (see Catts and Haskell 1990, Byrd and Castner 2001, Haskell 2006).

Choosing a Forensic Entomologist

Although virtually anyone with a minimum of preparation and training can collect entomological evidence, only experts in forensic entomology are qualified to analyze this evidence. Entomology is a widely practiced field of expertise, and entomologists abound at colleges and universities across the country, as well as in the private sector; but the vast majority of these are not trained in the field of forensic entomology and would be under-qualified to aid in a forensic investigation, even though they may hold several advanced degrees in a non-forensic area of entomology.

A forensic entomologist should hold an advanced degree in entomology (Ph. D. preferred, though a master of science degree may suffice) in the areas of insect ecology, medical entomology, insect behavior, or insect taxonomy, specializing in carrion ecology and/or forensically important insects. Publication in peer-reviewed journals (either entomology or forensic science) demonstrates competency in their research, and membership in the American Academy of Forensic Sciences (AAFS), the Entomological Society of America (ESA), and the North American Forensic Entomology Association (NAFEA) show a level of dedication to the profession. Currently the sole certifying organization for forensic entomology is the American Board of Entomology (ABFE), which marks the highest standard when choosing a consulting entomologist. Members and diplomates that have been certified by the ABFE must have demonstrated knowledge in all areas of forensic entomology, including identification of forensically important insects and analysis of case reports, and must have published in peer-reviewed journals on the subject of forensic entomology and have case experience. A current list of ABFE members, along with their contact information, can be found on the internet.

Conclusion

One of the challenges in dealing with and investigating mass disasters is recognizing each of the opportunities for new sources of information that present themselves. Insects can be an important source of evidence in many instances, and could become threats to public health in others. By recognizing the many aspects of forensically important insects, investigators will be better prepared to manage mass disasters in the unfortunate event that they find themselves faced with one.

References

Amendt, J., R. Krettek, and R. Zehner. 2004. Forensic entomology. *Naturwissenschaften* 91:51–65.

Anderson, G. S. and V. J. Cervenka. 2002. Insects associated with the body: their use and analyses, In *Advances in Forensic Taphonomy: Method, Theory, and Archaeological Perspectives*, ed. W. D. Haglund and M. H. Sorg. Boca Raton, FL: CRC Press LLC.

Benecke, M. 2001. A brief history of forensic entomology. *Forensic Sci Int* 120: 2–14.

Braack, L. E. O. 1981. Visitation patterns of principal species of the insect complex at carcasses in the Kruger National Park. *Koedoe* 24:33–49.

Byrd, J. H. and J. L. Castner, Eds. 2001. *Forensic Entomology: The Utility of Arthropods in Legal Investigations*. Boca Raton, FL: CRC Press LLC.

Campobasso, C. P., M. Gherardi, M. Caligara, L. Sironi, and F. Introna. 2004. Drug analysis in blowfly larvae and in human tissues: a comparative study. *Int J Legal Med* 118(4):210–14.

Catts, E. P. and M. L. Goff. 1992. Forensic entomology in criminal investigations. *Ann Rev Entomol* 37:253–72.

Catts, E. P. and N. H. Haskell, Eds. 1990. *Entomology and Death: A Procedural Guide*. Clemson, SC: Joyce's Print Shop.

Goff, M. L. 1991. Comparison of insect species associated with decomposing remains recovered inside dwellings and outdoors on the island of Oahu, Hawaii. *J Forensic Sci* 36(3):748–53.

Goff, M. L. and W. D. Lord. 1994. Entomotoxicology: a new area for forensic investigation. *Am J Forensic Med Pathol* 15:51–57.

Goff, M. L. and W. D. Lord. 2001. Entomotoxicology: insects as toxicological indicators and the impact of drugs and toxins on insect development, In *Forensic Entomology: The Utility of Arthropods in Legal Investigations*, ed. J. H. Byrd and J. L. Castner. Boca Raton, FL: CRC Press LLC.

Graham-Smith, G. S. 1914. *Flies in Relation to Disease; Non Blood-Sucking Flies*. Cambridge, U.K.: The University Press.

Greenberg, B. 1971. *Flies and Disease (Vol. 2)*. Princeton, NJ: Princeton University Press.

Greenberg, B. and J. C. Kunich. 2002. *Entomology and the Law: Flies as Forensic Indicators*. Cambridge, U.K.: Cambridge University Press.

Hall, D. G. 1948. *The Blowflies of North America*. Washington, D.C.: The Thomas Say Foundation.

Hall, R. D. and N. H. Haskell. 1995. Forensic entomology—applications in medicolegal investigations, In *Forensic Sciences*, ed. C. Wecht. New York: Matthew Bender.

Haskell, N. H. 2006. Time of death and changes after death: Forensic entomology, In *Spitz and Fisher's Medicolegal Investigation of Death: Guidelines for the Application of Pathology to Crime Investigation, 4th ed.*, W. U. Spitz and D. J. Spitz. Springfield, IL: Charles C. Thomas.

Haskell, N. H. 2007. Insect evidence distribution: tabulation of primary indicator species, the life stage, and the season of year used in final analysis from 100 North American cases. American Academy of Forensic Sciences Proceedings. Vol 13:220.

Haskell, N. H., R. D. Hall, V. J. Cervenka, and M. A. Clark. 1997. On the body: insects' life stage presence and their postmortem artifacts, In *Forensic Taphonomy: The Postmortem Fate of Human Remains,* ed. W. D. Haglund and M. H. Sorg. Boca Raton, FL: CRC Press LLC.

Hill, I. R. 1989. Mechanism of injury in aircraft accidents- a theoretical approach. *Aviation, Space, and Environmental Medicine* 60(7, suppl.):A18–25.

Huntington, T. E., L. G. Higley, and F. P. Baxendale. 2007. Maggot development during morgue storage and the effects on the estimation of the postmortem interval. *J Forensic Sci* 52(2):453–58.

Inglesby, T. V., D. A. Henderson, J. G. Bartlett, M. S. Ascher, E. Eitzen, A. M. Friedlander, J. Hauer, J. McDade, M. T. Osterholm, T. O'Toole, G. Parker, T. M. Perl, P. K. Russell, and K. Tonat. 1999. Anthrax as a biological weapon: medical and public health management. *JAMA* 281:1735–45.

Johnston, W. and G. Villeneuve. 1897. On the medico legal application of entomology. *Montreal Med J* 26(2):6-90.

Ligon, B. L. 2006. Infectious diseases that pose specific challenges after natural disasters: a review. *Seminars in Pediatric Infectious Diseases* 17(1): 36–45.

Linville, J. G. and J. D. Wells. 2002. Surface sterilization of a maggot using bleach does not interfere with mitochondrial DNA analysis of crop contents. *J Forensic Sci* 47(5):685–87.

Linville, J. G., J. Hayes, and J. D. Wells. 2004. Mitochondrial DNA and STR analyses of maggot crop contents: effects of specimen preservation technique. *J Forensic Sci* 49(2):341–44.

MacLeod, J. and J. Donnelly. 1963. Dispersal and interspersal of blowfly populations. *J Animal Ecol* 32:1–32.

McKnight, B. E. 1981. *The Washing away of Wrongs: Forensic Medicine in Thirteenth-Century China.* Ph.D. dissertation. Ann Arbor, MI: University of Michigan.

Mettleman, R. E. 2000. *The crash of ValuJet Flight 592: a forensic approach to severe body fragmentation.* Miami, FL: Miami-Dade County Medical Examiner Department.

Saukko, P. and B. Knight. 2004. *Knights Forensic Pathology, 3rd ed.* London: Arnold.

Sledzik, P. S. and W. C. Rodriguez. 2002. Damnum fatale: the taphonomic fate of human remains in mass disasters, In *Advances in Forensic Taphonomy: Method, Theory, and Archaeological Perspectives*, ed. W. D. Haglund and M. H. Sorg. Boca Raton, FL: CRC Press LLC.

Smith, K. G. V. 1986. *A Manual of Forensic Entomology.* Ithaca, NY: Cornell University Press.

Thompson, R. L., W. W. Manders, and W. R. Cowan. 1987. Postmortem findings of the victims of the Jonestown tragedy. *J Forensic Sci* 32:433–43.

Triplehorn, C. A. and N. F. Johnson. 2005. *Borror and DeLong's Introduction to the Study of Insects, 7th ed.* Belmont, CA: Thomson Brooks/Cole.

Wagner, G. N. and R. C. Froede. 2006. Medicolegal investigation of mass disasters, In *Spitz and Fisher's Medicolegal Investigation of Death: Guidelines for the Application of Pathology to Crime Investigation, 4th ed.,* ed. W. U. Spitz and D. J. Spitz. Springfield, IL: Charles C. Thomas.

Wisner, B. and J. Adams. 2002. *Environmental Health in Emergencies and Disasters.* Geneva, Switzerland: WHO.

Wells, J. D., F. Introna, G. Di Vella, C. P. Campobasso, J. Hayes, and F. P. Sperling. 2001. Human and insect mitochondrial DNA analysis from maggots. *J Forensic Sci* 46(3):685–87.

Zehner, R., J. Amendt, and R. Krettek. 2004. STR typing of human DNA from fly larvae fed on decomposing bodies. *J Forensic Sci* 49(2):337–40.

Chapter 14

Developing Core Competencies in Disaster Medicine

David McCann, M.D.

Where is the Life we have lost in living?
Where is the wisdom we have lost in knowledge?
Where is the knowledge we have lost in information?
  — *TS Eliot, Choruses from "The Rock", 1934*

Introduction

The emerging specialty of Disaster Medicine requires the development of a set of core competencies for physicians. Some initial efforts in this direction have occurred[1] but have been geared toward general healthcare training as opposed to physician specialty training. Throughout the last four years, the American Board of Disaster Medicine has convened recognized medical experts in disaster medical preparedness and response from around the United States. These physician leaders have defined the key attributes which a consultant in Disaster Medicine should master to optimally practice in the nascent discipline. In this chapter, these core competencies will be delineated and the implementation of physician board certification in Disaster Medicine will be discussed.

The History of the American Board of Disaster Medicine

The overwhelming events of the terrorist attacks of 9/11 generated a significant increase in interest in Disaster Medicine within the medical community. It became clear that terrorism could be visited upon the United States at any time. Beginning in 2003, the American Board of Physician Specialties (ABPS) started calling together recognized experts in Disaster Medicine. As the group germinated and grew, so did the idea of creating a physician board certification process for recognition of expertise in Disaster Medicine. Thus was born the American Board of Disaster Medicine (ABODM). Its purpose was to delineate core competencies in the emerging specialty of Disaster Medicine and then develop a psychometrically defensible, rigorous examination process through which physicians could demonstrate their expertise in the field.

In 2004, Florida was hit by 4 strong hurricanes within 3 months—Charley, Frances, Ivan and Jeanne. A number of the ABODM founding members were active in the Disaster Medical Assistance Teams (DMATs) which responded to the devastation wrought throughout the Sunshine State (which was jokingly called the Plywood State by the middle of hurricane season). The hurricanes of 2004 caused a redoubling of efforts by the ABODM to define the core competencies of Disaster Medicine while simultaneously designing a unique examination process for board certification.

Then came 2005 and the cataclysmic damage to the US Gulf Coast caused by Hurricanes Katrina and Rita. Once again, a number of our ABODM founders were deployed, a few for many weeks, trying to help the worst hit areas—coastal Mississippi and Louisiana with New Orleans being a story unto itself. The prolonged deployments caused an understandable but temporary diminution of ABODM development activities. Fortunately, the year 2006 was relatively quiet from a disaster point of view, and we were able to finish up the written examination development in time for rollout in June 2007. We will discuss more about this later in this chapter.

In early 2007, the ABODM was joined by her sister organization—the American Academy of Disaster Medicine (AADM). The Academy will act as the research, policy-making and political arm of Disaster Medicine so that ABODM can deal solely with its mission to continually improve and disseminate the board certification exam process we developed.

What Is Disaster Medicine?

The ABODM subscribes to the following definition of Disaster Medicine: the medical specialty that cares for patients and communities throughout the disaster life cycle. However, to really understand Disaster Medicine as a specialty, one must look beyond the prevailing reductionism prevalent in modern medical thought. In the last hundred years, generalist medical practitioners have given way to ever more highly specialized physicians who know a great deal about one system of the body. So, we have pulmonologists who study the lungs and cardiologists who study the heart, etc. These are classic examples of reductionism in medicine—"knowing more and more about less and less until one knows everything about nothing" as the old adage says.

While the age of specialization has brought tremendous advances in our understanding of disease mechanisms and treatment, it has also caused a significant, unintended downside—there is now a significant shortage of generalists who understand the patient as a whole, or can see the overall medical situation in perspective. Thus, while reductionism has benefited medicine by promoting significant research advances, it has also hurt medicine by decreasing the role of the generalist who sees the patient as more than a "sum of all systems".

Disaster Medicine, similarly, is a nascent specialty which is antithetical to reductionist thinking. Instead, it springs from the nexus of many other specialties as illustrated in the diagram below—what we like to call **'The Disaster Medicine Blastocyst'** (see Figure 14.1). It is clear from the Venn diagram that Disaster Medicine draws its subject matter and expertise from many other medical specialties such as Psychiatry, Emergency Medicine, Surgery, Pediatrics, etc. What should be made equally clear and is a foundational premise of the ABODM is this: Disaster Medicine is *not* merely a sub-specialty of Emergency Medicine as many in the Emergency Medicine field would purport. Rather, it is a unitive, creative way of thinking which springs from the best of all the major medical disciplines as well as Emergency Management. In a disaster situation, we believe all medical specialties can have a role to play in response and recovery. All the medical specialties can offer unique perspectives that can be helpful. Similarly, Disaster Medicine specialists can come from any medical discipline provided they have operational knowledge of the core competencies unique to our discipline.

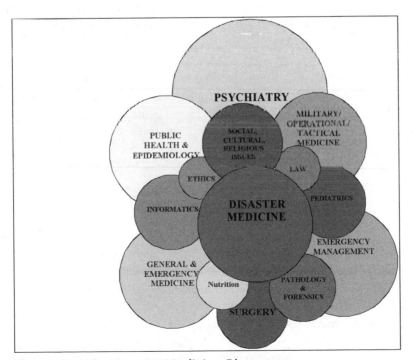

Figure 14.1 *The Disaster Medicine Blastocyst*

Maturing the Blastocyst

Now that we have seen the embryonic 'Disaster Medicine Blastocyst', this begs the question—how do we help mature the embryonic blastocyst to its full potential?

In our opinion at ABODM, several things are required for Disaster Medicine to progress as a specialty:

- Core competencies delineation
- Disaster research methodologies and funding
- Teaching centers of excellence
- Board certification for physician experts in Disaster Medicine
- The will to do it

Note that these elements are not in any particular order. While it is true that a hierarchical, logical approach to discipline development is traditional, a more chaotic, organic approach is becoming normative in the Information Age. The latter approach will serve Disaster Medicine well.

Using core competencies as an approach to discipline development is considered by some to be "reductionist, component driven and inappropriate in professional education programs."[2] There may be some truth to this opinion but it need not dissuade the use of such an approach as long as the shortcomings are recognized and compensated for.

Core Competency

What exactly is a core competency? The original definition arose from business theory. Specifically, CK Prahalad and Gary Hamel coined the term in the *Harvard Business Review* in 1990. Basically, a core competency is:

- A unique bundle of skills and technologies that enables a company to provide particular benefits to customers
- Something that is fundamental and defining for the organization
- Something that forms the content of the business

Given the above definition, what are some characteristics of a core competency?

- It must significantly contribute to customer-perceived value.
- It must be unique compared with competitors.
- It should create opportunities for entry into new product markets.

While the idea of a core competency came from the business world, it is certainly applicable in the medical world as well. Adapting the idea to a medical core competency, one derives the following definition of a medical core competency:

- It should be a characteristic that defines and distinguishes one medical discipline from others
- It should be a sentinel characteristic of the medical discipline that requires mastery by all competent practitioners in that discipline
- It should be verifiable and testable (if possible) through psychometrically valid methodologies

Hsu and coworkers[1] suggested core competencies in disaster preparedness and response for all healthcare professionals (as opposed to what ABODM has developed which is specifically geared to Disaster Medicine physician specialists) which include the following:

- Recognize a potential critical event and implement appropriate initial actions
- Apply principles of critical event management
- Demonstrate critical event safety principles
- Understand the institutional emergency operations plan
- Demonstrate critical event communications
- Understand the Incident Command System and the worker's particular role in it
- Demonstrate the knowledge and skills needed to fulfill a given role during a critical event

We at ABODM agree with Hsu and colleagues that these are essential competencies for healthcare workers responding to a disaster. We would add numerous others to the list for physician specialists in Disaster Medicine. Before we discuss these additions, however, first we must define the difference between a competency and a capability.

Core Knowledge Competency versus Core Performance Capability

Although there is an intuitive link between a competency and a capability, the two terms are not interchangeable. According to Verna Allee,[3] a core knowledge competency includes those domains of expertise, knowledge and technical acumen that are unique to a particular discipline. On the other hand, a core performance capability refers to those processes and functions that enable delivery of discipline-related services with speed, efficiency and professional excellence. Based on an understanding of these definitional differences, we at the ABODM have defined the following Core Knowledge Competencies for a Disaster Medicine physician specialist to master in order to be considered competent.

In general, the Disaster Medicine Specialist:

- Understands and applies an "all hazards approach" to disaster situations
- Realizes that while every disaster is unique, they share common characteristics which render the "all hazards approach" as an ideal disaster paradigm

So what is the "all hazards approach"? The phrase was popularized by the National Disaster Life Support Educational Foundation and basically means that one must be "ready for anything". Rather than learning what to do in a hurricane versus what to do in an earthquake versus what to do in a nuclear explosion, the all hazards approach allows disaster works to respond to any disaster, manmade or natural, using certain basic principles.

Moving along, we will now consider the specific core knowledge competencies recommended by the ABODM over an above the two general competencies noted above. The Disaster Medicine Specialist:

- 01.00   Incident Command System (ICS)
    a.   Has knowledge and skills needed to perform as a disaster team member under the ICS (NB—ICS is a command and control system developed in California in the 1970s for wildfire fighting—it is a flexible, military-like system which brings a unity of command out of the chaos of a disaster)
    b.   Understands the structure and functions of ICS including span of control, etc
    c.   Understands how to set up a command post and establish site safety
    d.   Understands how to set up hot, warm and cold zones in a potential HAZMAT situation
    e.   Understands stockpile issues including contracting and resupply

- 02.00   Preparation and Mitigation
    a.   Participates in planning for disaster preparation and mitigation
    b.   Understands and can fill major planning role in Public Health
    c.   Able to design, facilitate and critique all levels of disaster drills from table top exercises to community-wide, multidisciplinary disaster scenarios
    d.   Can set up a shelter
    e.   Understands credentialing, grants & funding, interagency agreements, emergency management assistance compacts (EMACs), transportation issues (EMS vs. airlift vs. other)

- 03.00   Triage
  a. Understands and can implement a triage system in any disaster situation
  b. Has operational knowledge of major triage systems and can appropriately tag and track patients:
     1. START/RPM
     2. JumpSTART (peds)
     3. MASS

- 03.05   Decontamination & Personal Protective Equipment (PPE)
  ◊ Can follow appropriate decon principles and procedures
  ◊ Understands various PPE levels (A, B, C, D)
  ◊ Can don & doff at least Level C PPE

- 04.00   Public Health and Safety
  ◊ Advises on and coordinates aspects of public health and safety throughout the disaster life cycle
    » Environmental—sanitation, water, nutrition, immunizations, evacuation, scene control, weather monitoring/modeling, shelters, dispersion monitoring & modeling
    » Disease surveillance and epidemiology, prophylaxis, emerging disease modeling (e.g. SARS), vector control
    » Complex humanitarian disasters—pharmacy services, refugees, physical recovery, morgue services, special populations

- 05.00   Psychosocial Considerations
  ◊ Provides psychosocial support throughout disaster life cycle:
    » Recognize, assess and treat incident-related stress in first responders and their families (force protection) as well as community members/victims
    » Understands role of clergy, NGOs, volunteers, grief counselors (e.g. CISM)
    » Understands unique psychosocial needs of special populations—especially children

- 06.00   Support Assistance
  ◊ Works with various groups and organizations to optimize disaster planning, mitigation, response and recovery
    » NDMS, Community police/fire/EMS/Public Works, military personnel, FBI, Community Emergency Response Teams (CERTs), CDC and US Public Health Service

»   Understands issues related to use of volunteers (training, handling, liability and responsibility.

- 07.00   Communication and Documentation
  ◊   Maintains appropriate communication and documentation
    »   Understands chain of communication
    »   Understands role of public information officer (PIO)
    »   Understands basics of medical record keeping especially toe tags
    »   Understands basics of evidentiary documentation
    »   Understand basic types of communication equipment, encryption and frequencies

- 08.00   Regulatory, Legal and Ethical Principles
  ◊   Complies with regulatory, legal, ethical and moral principles
    »   Understands HIPAA, EMTALA, COBRA, Stafford Act, JCAHO, NIMS, NRP, OSHA, NIOSH, ADA, Sovereign Immunity, Good Samaritan Act, Federal Tort Claims Act
    »   Understands confidentiality, consent, withdrawal of care, profiling, professionalism

- 09.00   Assessment and Treatment
  ◊   Assesses and treats injuries and illnesses resulting from all hazards in any environment
  ◊   Has specific knowledge & skills to treat:
    »   Electrocution
    »   Infection
    »   Toxins (chem/bio)
    »   Blast trauma
    »   Radiation
    »   Penetrating and ballistic trauma
    »   Blunt trauma
    »   Crush Syndrome
    »   Near Drowning/Submersion injury
    »   Exposure
    »   Dehydration
    »   Starvation
    »   Psych Needs

- 10.00   Pathology and Forensics
  - ◊   ID remains (DNA, forensic anthropology, forensic odontology
  - ◊   Visual observation of trauma/infections of all categories listed in 09.00
  - ◊   Autopsy and clinicopathologic correlations
  - ◊   Collection and testing of biological materials for future medicolegal inquiries

Now that we have delineated the Core Knowledge Competencies for Disaster Medicine, we shall proceed to the Core Performance Capabilities

In general, the Disaster Medicine Specialist shall first and foremost be a competent, caring, well-trained physician who can perform appropriate medical care in any environment from a first class, first world hospital to the most austere third world conditions while maintaining a positive, creative, problem-solving attitude. As well, the Disaster Medicine Specialist:

- Understands and functions well within the ICS and the Hospital Incident Command System (HICS)
- Has operational knowledge of major triage systems and can perform efficient triage in mass casualty situations
- Has the resilience and psychological skill set to maintain calm composure while "all hell breaks loose"
- Can lead and manage complex multidisciplinary disaster training, education, preparedness and disaster response programs
- Can be dropped into any part of the disaster life cycle anywhere and still function appropriately as a disaster consultant
- Can design, facilitate, and critique disaster drills from table top exercises to community-wide, multiagency disaster simulations
- Can perform disaster planning and mitigation functions at the local, state or federal level as needed
- Can coordinate and perform successful decontamination procedures in CBRNE (chem, bio, radiological, nuclear and explosive events) incidents including set up of zones
- Can don & doff at least Level C PPE and can perform duties while dressed out in PPE
- Can quickly recognize potentially hazardous situations and acts to prevent harm to self and teammates
- Has political and social skills to liaise among various populations, all levels of government and the military, both nationally and internationally—i.e., PLAYS WELL WITH OTHERS

- Has the skills to prepare for and respond to complex humanitarian disasters including refugee crises
- Maintains the highest professional ethics at all times, in every situation
- Has ability to perform psychological first aid for adults and children and to recognize when higher level psychiatric care is needed.

The Road Forward

The written examination bank of questions for the ABODM board certification in Disaster Medicine is now compiled. Candidates successful in passing the written exam will subsequently be taking an oral examination the form of which is nearly complete.

Our plan after the ABODM exam is fully implemented is to then develop a board certification process for allied health professionals who wish to be disaster specialists. There has been significant interest in such an allied board from nurses, paramedics, physician assistants, nurse practitioners, respiratory therapists etc.

We are hoping to forge alliances with various other disaster medical groups such as the World Association for Disaster and Emergency Medicine (WADEM) and other, similar groups throughout the world. Further, through our sister organization, the American Academy of Disaster Medicine, we are already reaching out to residency and fellowship training sites for Disaster Medicine. Over the next few years, we intend on developing and supporting postgraduate programs in Disaster Medicine for medical residents so inclined.

Those of us who have been involved since the beginning of the ABODM are gratified at the explosion of interest in Disaster Medicine. It is our fervent hope that we can help lead this new specialty to the great heights we foresee for it. It should be a wonderful adventure!

References

1. Hsu, EB et al. (2006). Healthcare worker competencies for disaster training. *BMC Med Ed* 6:19.

2. Education Committee Working Group of the World Association of Disaster and Emergency Medicine. (2004). International standards and guidelines on education and training for the multi-disciplinary response to major events that threaten the health status of. a community. *Prehospital and Disaster Medicine* 19 (2): Supplement 2.

3. Allee, V. (1997). *The Knowledge Evolution: Expanding Organizational Intelligence*. Buttersworth-Heinemann, Boston. Pg 21.

Chapter 15

Mass Disaster Litigation in the United States

Bassel F. El-Kasaby, Esq.

Background

The common law tort system in the United States has three main policy objectives: deterrence, spreading losses, and remedial justice (Dobbs and Hayden 1997). Despite these underlying objectives, tort jurisprudence did not evolve uniformly in each state or jurisdiction where it is followed. Some states have even enacted specific tort reforms and liability limits. Today, several trends and jurisdictional rifts have emerged as they relate to certain common law doctrines involving tort liability. To add another layer of complexity, certain federally mandated reforms and regulations pre-empt both state court and legislative decisions that operate within their scope. It is important to note, however, that the extent of federal pre-emption regarding tort liability has been generally limited.

Common law tort liability is based on fault. This includes liability for carriers, owners, operators, and maintenance personnel. The liability of manufacturers, however, can be established without proving fault under the American products liability regime. Even though fault-based liability is prevalent, some states have adopted no-fault tort systems, mostly in the area of automobile insurance. A small number of states impose statutory limits on liability for insurance purposes in automobile accidents and even general aviation.

The threshold of fault required to establish liability is based on the common law standard of negligence. Broadly speaking, negligence is an act or omission that breaches a duty owed by a person to others. A person's duty has traditionally been measured according to the "reasonable person" standard. By comparing the act or omission in question to that of a "reasonable person," juries are charged to make a finding as to fault. A jury must also find that the act or omission in question were the proximate cause of the damages or injury. Juries also usually determine the amount of damages owed, taking into account any possible contributory negligence on the part of the plaintiff. Finally, juries in some cases award punitive damages if the degree of fault exceeds the negligence standard (Dobbs and Hayden 1958; *Mamalis v. Atlas Van Lines*, 1989; *Palsgraf v. Long Island Railroad*, 1928).

Although generally falling within the purview of the common law of contracts, an insurance contract is different from ordinary contracts in at least two ways. First, the insurance contract cannot be strictly a gamble. This means that the insured must have a actual interest in the property subject to the contract. Any monetary interest in an aircraft, such as ownership or lease, will generally be sufficient for this purpose. Second, the insurer and the insured are held to the standard of utmost faith in dealing with each other under the insurance contract (*Stripcich v. Metropolitan Life Ins. Co,* 1928). As such, the insured is under an obligation to disclose all known risks and material facts to the insurer. The insurer uses this information in assessing the risk and deciding whether or not to accept the risk at a given price. Although the insurer is held to a similar standard, any ambiguity in the insurance contract will usually be resolved in favor of the insured (*Mutual of ENUMCLAW Insurance CO v. WISCOMB*, 1982; Margo 1996).

The insurer's specific duties depend on the promises exchanged in the insurance contract. Most contracts create two main obligations on the insurer. First, the insurer is required to shield the insured from liability by paying out judgments and settlements according to the specific risks and exclusions of the policy. Second, the insurer has an obligation to defend the insured in litigation. The insurer also has the prerogative of investigating, negotiating, and settling claims. In a sense, the insurer steps in the insured's shoes for the purpose of any liability covered in the contract. Note, however, that in most states, insurance companies cannot be named in a lawsuit along with the insured. Most states have also adopted rules against admitting evidence of insurance to juries (Dobbs and Hayden 1997, p. 705; Margo 1996).

While most states operate under the tort system, there is nothing to prevent a party from purchasing insurance outside of the traditional tort scheme. For example, a party may elect to purchase insurance that covers losses regardless of fault. Though not widely available, such insurance could supplement or replace a party's liability coverage under the fault liability system. In addition, a few states have adopted variations of the Keeton-O'Connell plan for no-fault automobile insurance. Similarly, most states have also enacted no-fault workers' compensation and unemployment statutes. No fault schemes usually abolish the tort system for claims up to a certain limit and impose losses on insurers regardless of fault. This type of insurance system also typically abolishes pain and suffering damages and imposes mandatory deductibles on the insured (Dobbs and Hayden 1997, p. 894).

Owners, operators of aircraft, along with other "Deep Pockets," are frequent targets for litigation. Their liability is based mostly on common law negligence, vicarious liability, and/or the contractual relationship between the injured party and the insured. Common carriers in particular are held to a heightened standard of care in transporting passengers (*Griffith v. United Airlines*, 1964; Margo 1996). Note that while a plaintiff must show fault in order to prevail in a negligence claim, the cost of defending or settling nuisance claims can still be substantial.

In addition to liability under the common law of negligence, manufacturers can also be held strictly liable for defects in their products. The doctrine of strict products liability holds the manufacturer, wholesaler, and retailer jointly and severally liable for injuries resulting from a manufacturing or design defect in their products. Plaintiffs in such cases can choose to sue all or any defendants, and are given some legal protection in cases of bankruptcy, mergers, and even some corporate brand strategies. Any entity in the resale chain of the product can be liable, so long as the product was not substantially modified before they acquired it. Moreover, a plaintiff is not required to show fault in such cases. This doctrine of strict liability originated in the English common law governing ownership of wild animals. It was subsequently developed and applied in the United States to decide negligence claims where the defendants participated in ultra-hazardous activities, including early aviation. While courts in the United States gradually abandoned this strict standard in the case of aviation negligence, the concept has been simultaneously expanded to cover products of various kinds, including airplanes and related products. Courts have long insisted that this product liability system, imposing liability without requiring a finding of fault, encourages innovation while maximizing safety to the consumers (Restatement 2d. of Torts, 1965; Dobbs and Hayden 1997).

Liability of individual operators and maintenance personnel is a less important issue in mass tort litigation. Liability in such cases can be imputed, however, to the entities they work for under the doctrine of respondeat superior, or vicarious liability. Air carriers and maintenance companies are attractive targets for litigants because they usually have the financial ability to pay large damage awards. Such companies can also incur liability as owners of the aircraft under some states' statutes. Similarly, aircraft financiers and investors do not usually operate the aircraft they are financing. Therefore, their conduct is less likely to give rise to a cause of action in the case of loss resulting from the negligence of a carrier. However, they may be drawn into litigation for supplying defective aircraft or parts (Margo 1996).

Aviation as an Example

For many decades, aviation was considered by state courts to be an ultra-hazardous activity (Restatement 2d of Torts, 1977, § 520). Such activities also included pyrotechnics, explosives, and chemical manufacturing. Persons and entities engaged in such dangerous activities were traditionally held to a heightened standard of care by common law courts, amounting in many cases to strict liability. Due to safety improvements in the last few decades, however, aviation is no longer considered an unreasonably dangerous activity.

Even though ground damage and injury to passengers is no longer subject to strict liability claims, air carriers must still maintain a very high degree of care as providers of public transportation. Carriers are held liable for the slightest negligence if it is the proximate cause of damage to persons or property. In addition, the doctrine of res ipsa loquitur (the thing speaks for itself) has been widely applied to airline accidents. This makes it easier for plaintiffs to prevail in such cases. Lastly, courts have held violations of federal regulations, such as the FARs, to be negligence per se, with consequences similar to strict liability (*Gatenby v. Altoona Aviation Corp.,* 1968).

In addition to liability issues, many insurance contracts explicitly exclude coverage for incidents where administrative rules are violated. Some courts have held that exclusions of this sort can apply to violations such as failure to observe certification requirements, maintenance, and safety issues. Coverage may be denied under the contract in these cases even where no causal connection is established between the violation and the damage or loss (Boone 1983).

In terms of negligence, liability for losses is subject to the common law developments in the jurisdiction whose substantive law governs each individual claim. Typically, the law of the jurisdiction where the accident occurred governs liability claims arising from that accident. However, other factors might also affect the jurisdiction, venue, and choice of law governing the claim. Although federal pre-emption is yet to have a broad impact on state tort liability, state courts will often give weight to federal regulations on many issues relating to fault (Tepley and Whitten 1999).

Notwithstanding the above, federal regulations have an impact on state court findings of liability insofar as carriers and operators are concerned. This impact is twofold. On the one hand, federal regulations help legitimize innovations and guide courts towards the appropriate threshold for liability of market participants. On the other hand, excessive and unreasonable regulations can stifle the market by expanding the bases for liability for persons and entities engaged in such activities. For example, it would be unlikely for courts to rule that commercial aviation is an unreasonably dangerous activity when the FAA has certified carriers and aircraft for such operations. At the same time, cumbersome regulations will discourage market participants from adopting innovations both in market practices and technology.

Products Liabilty Issues

As mentioned earlier, aviation manufacturers and resellers were traditionally liable for defects in the design, parts, or assembly of their aircraft under the American common law doctrine of strict product liability. In products liability litigation, there is no need to find fault to impose liability on a manufacturer or reseller (Restatement 2d. of Torts, 1977, § 402A). FBOs, operators, and maintenance companies can be subject to products liability claim, especially if they supply parts along with their services.

The rise of product liability lawsuits involving general aviation manufacturers prompted the passage of GARA. GARA sought to limit the liability of manufacturers for older aircraft by imposing a statute of ultimate repose on such claims. The goal was to protect the general aviation industry against liability arising from defects in older aircraft or parts without jeopardizing safety (General Accounting Office, 2001; General Aviation Manufacturing Association, 1999). GARA's policy goals are thus consistent with encouraging development in aviation technology. GARA also signals an area where federal laws are beginning to take hold in aviation law by pre-empting certain limited aspects of the states' tort law system.

In addition to strict liability claims, manufacturers are also held to the common law standard of negligence that generally applies to carriers and operators. Recall that the standard for common carriers is somewhat higher, however. In the context of commercial activities such as aviation, courts have applied a risk-utility analysis in determining whether a party is liable for adopting or not adopting a particular technology or operating procedure. Liability in such case is determined by weighing the probability of an injury against the cost of prevention as well as the general utility of the endeavor. In theory, an air carrier or operator, in deciding whether to use a particular technology, will compare the cost of the device or innovation against the probability and extent of possible damage (*United States v. Carroll Towing Co.,* 1947). Note that this risk-utility analysis provides little certainty because the probability of potential damage is often difficult, if not impossible to measure in aviation cases.

War and Terrorism Risk

One challenge that is facing the mass tort system in general is war and terrorism. Acts of terrorism are designed to inflict catastrophic loss of life and property damage. While such risks were thought to be generally associated with airline operations, new speculations have highlighted the vulnerability of many other industries in that regard.

In the wake of September 11, the federal government passed the Air Transportation Safety and Systems Stabilization Act (Air Transportation Safety and

Systems Stabilization Act, 2001). This unprecedented measure is designed to give potential litigants the option of settling their claims, which are calculated according to a pre-determined formula, and releasing commercial carriers and other entities from liability. The policy goals of this undertaking is to shield the airlines involved from the staggering cost of litigation, as well as provide the large number of victims with prompt compensation (Rapoport 2000, Krause and Swiger 2002). If nothing else, such measures highlight the need for a new solution for such risks for both general and commercial operations.

In addition to barring future litigation for claimants who opt to use it, recovery from the fund bars subsequent recovery for emotional injuries, such as pain and suffering. In this scheme, victims are compensated for both economic and non-economic injuries. Economic injuries take into account the present value of the victim's lost income, adjusted for tax liability. Non-economic losses are based on a pre-determined value applied consistently for all victims. Damages also take into account compensation from collateral sources, with the exception of certain charitable contributions (Federal Aviation Act, 2001).

The creation of the Victim Compensation Fund amounts to post facto tort reform that adds a federal no-fault layer to the state-based tort liability system (Rapoport 2000). In its efforts to deal with the impact of September 11, the federal government is also contemplating ways of making terrorism insurance more affordable to businesses. At the same time, some industries also considering possible self-insurance schemes to replace or supplement traditional insurance methods. Though it is too early to assess such efforts, it has been suggested that a fee could be charged to air travelers and other entities to create a fund to compensate companies and victims of terrorism if the insurance market fails to provide insurance coverage that bears reasonable returns on paid premiums.

Conclusion

Mass disaster litigation in the United States operates, for the most part, under the common law tort system. Under this regime, no amount of reform can make a party immune from liability. For one thing, the cost of litigating and settling claims can be high even if such claims are frivolous (Christie et al. 1997). Moreover, insurers have a duty to defend their insured regardless of the merits of the claim or damage claimed (Dobbs and Hayden 1997). In addition, the current insurance law regime cannot make any entity immune from over-exposure to liability. While courts and juries typically make rational decisions as to verdicts, studies have shown that tort liability verdicts can be exaggerated and unpredictable (Christie et al. 1997, p. 910).

In the short-run, the system is still coping with the problems that the insurance market is facing in the aftermath of September 11 as well as the global economic slowdown. We can also expect the insurance market to undergo a period of upheaval and major restructuring. Terrorism coverage is likely to be the subject of debate and reform on the federal level for years to come. The federal government has recognized this concern by enacting swift measures aimed at compensation victims promptly as well as protecting the aviation industry. These measures have already had an effect on liability arising from the September 11 events. Further measures are envisioned that specifically address the insurance market.

In the long-run, reform will depend more on issues of liability and the regulatory regime that affects liability in general. In this regard, laws and regulations at the federal, agency, and state level have undoubtedly had an impact on how aviation carriers operate today. Regulators, policymakers, and stakeholders are grappling with such issues as the regulatory rift between commercial and non-commercial risks, issues of products liability, and the immediate security concerns raised after September 11.

References

Air Transportation Safety and Systems Stabilization Act, 49 U.S.C. § 40101 et seq. (2001).

Boone, T., 1983. Florida's "Antitechnical" Statute: Should insurance exclusions be included? Florida State University Law Review 10, pp. 737-749.

Christie, G. et al., 1997. Cases and Materials on the Law of Torts. West Group, New York.

Dobbs, D. and Hayden, P., 1997. Torts and Compensation: Personal Accountability and Social Responsibility for Injury

Dombroff, M., 2002. Liability and the growth of fractional aircraft ownership programs. Air and Space Law 16, pp. 4-18.

Executive Jet Aviation, Inc., v. United States, 97-2 U.S. Tax Cas. (Fed.Cir.1997).

Federal Aviation Act of 1958, codified in 49 U.S.C. §§ 40101 et seq. (2001).

Federal Aviation Regulations, 14 C.F.R. pt. 135 (2001).

Gatenby v. Altoona Aviation Corp., 407 F.2d 443 (1968).

General Accounting Office, Aug, 31, 2002. General Aviation, Status of the Industry, Related Infrastructure, and Safety Issues, GAO-01-916.

General Aviation Manufacturing Association, 1999. Five year results: A report to the President and Congress on the General Aviation Revitalization Act.

General Aviation Revitalization Act, Pub. L. 103 - 298 (1994).

Gleimer, E., 1999. When less can be more: Fractional ownership of aircraft: The wings of the future. Journal of Air Law and Commerce 64, pp. 979-1032.

Gleimer, E., 1998. The convenience and confusion associated with corporate aircraft operations. Air and Space Law 12, pp. 3-25.

Gleimer, E., 1997. Corporate aircraft operations: The twilight zone of regulations. Journal of Air Law and Commerce 62, pp. 987-1035.

Griffith v. United Airlines, 416 Pa. 1, 203 A.2d 796 (1964).

Krause, K. and Swiger, J., Winter 2002. Analysis of Department of Justice regulations for September 11th Victim Compensation Fund. Journal of Air Law and Commerce 67, pp. 117-140.

Mamalis v. Atlas Van Lines, 552 Pa. 214, 560 A.2d 1380 (1989).

Margo, R., 1996. Aspects of insurance in aviation finance. Journal of Air Law & Commerce 62, pp. 423-478.

Margo, R., 1989. Aviation Insurance. Butterworths, London.

Mutual of ENUMCLAW Insurance CO. v. WISCOMB, 97 Wash.2d 203 (1982).

Palsgraf v. Long Island Railroad, 248 N.Y. 339, 162 N.E. 99 (1928).

Rapoport, D., 2000. The effect of tort litigation on the airline industry. DePaul Business Law Journal 14, pp. 303-318.

Restatement (Second) of Torts § 402A (1965).

Rolf, T., 2001. The coming of age of fractional aircraft ownership programs. Air and Space Law 15, pp. 11-34.

Stipcich v. Metropolitan Life Ins. Co., 277 U.S. 311, 316 (1928).

Tarry, S. and Truitt, L., 1995. Rhetoric and reality: Tort reform and the uncertain future of general aviation. Journal of Air Law and Commerce 61, pp. 164-201.

Teply, L. and Whitten, R., 1999. Cases and Problems on Civil Procedure: Basic and Advanced. Foundation Press, New York.

United States v. Carroll Towing Co., 159 F.2d 169 (1947).

Wells, A. and Chadbourne, B., 2000. Introduction to Aviation Insurance and Risk Management. Krieger, Florida.

Chapter 16

Recent Air Crashes in Nigeria: Legal Considerations

Roberta Chizoma Opara, Esq.

Introduction

Air transport is widely accepted as the safest means of transportation. However, the recent spate of air accidents in Nigeria has caused concern. It is recorded that the plane crashes that occurred in late 2005 accounted for over 20 percent of worldwide fatalities for that year and that historically Nigeria has accounted for 225 out of the 376 air fatalities recorded in Africa.[1]

The dire cause and consequence of these accidents have raised several issues of controversy, some of which are legal in nature.

Divergent views

While some aviation practitioners examine the arising legal issues from the point of contract—existing between the carrier/airline[2] and the manufacturers of the plane, between the carrier and the Aviation Authorities, and between the carrier and the passenger—other practitioners see the issues as arising from the benefits due their clients in the form of damages and compensation.

This chapter examines a few of such issues, with particular reference to the three most recent air crashes.[3]

Air Crash Details

- Bellview Airlines Flight 210 crashed on October 22, 2005, at Lisa Village, Ifo, Ogun State (some 30 km [20 miles] north of Lagos State in Nigeria). None of the 111 passengers and 6 crew members on board made it out alive.[4]
- Sosoliso Airlines DC-9 Flight 1145 from Abuja crashed in the Southern Nigerian city of Port Harcourt Saturday, December 10, 2005. 103 persons, including 60 children, died in the ensuing fire.[5]
- October 29, 2006, Sokoto-bound Aviation Development Company (ADC) Flight 053 barely made it off the ground, having lifted off from Nnamdi

295

Azikiwe International Airport, Abuja. The Boeing 737-200, registered as 5N-BFK, crashed a few kilometers from the Airport killing all but seven people on board.[6]

Before raising the considerations, it is pertinent to identify the relevant interest groups and applicable legislation.

Aviation Stakeholders

The Aviation Industry in Nigeria today has two main stakeholders: government and private investors.

Government

The country's aviation industry is principally regulated by the Federal Ministry of Aviation[7] and a plethora of agencies such as:

- The Nigerian Civil Aviation Authority (NCAA)—an autonomous body that regulates civil aviation in Nigeria.
- The Federal Airports Authority of Nigeria (FAAN)—a service organization statutorily charged with the development and management of all commercial airports in Nigeria.
- The Nigeria Airspace Management Agency (NAMA)—responsible for the provision of Air Traffic Management Services for local and international airline operations.
- Accident Investigations and Prevention Bureau (AIPB)[8]—an agency saddled with the task of unraveling the causes of air crashes and preventing same.
- The Nigerian Meteorological Agency (NIMET)—responsible for the provision of accurate and timely weather/climatic data used for airline operations.

Private Sector Stakeholders

These are the private airline operators in the industry. Currently operational are Arik Air, Virgin Nigeria Airlines, Bellview Airlines, Aero Contractors, and Chanchangi Airlines, amongst others.[9]

Aviation Laws

Aviation Law can generally be classified into:

i.   International Law which are the rules having effect between State Parties and are contained almost entirely in Treaties or Convention, such as The Warsaw Convention (1929), The Hague Protocol (1955), and The Montreal Agreement (1966),

ii.   National Law which are the rules applied by the Courts of a particular State to questions arising between the State and its subjects/citizens or between two subjects. In this case the Nigerian Civil Aviation Act (2006).[10]

A discussion of the relevant laws follows:

The Warsaw Convention of 1929
Signed at Warsaw on October 12, 1929, the Convention was ratified by signatory countries, of which Nigeria is one, and came into force on January 1, 1953. Its principal purpose was the unification of rules relating to Carriage by Air.[11]

It achieved uniformity in documentation[12] (tickets, waybills, etc.) and established substantive rules governing the rights and duties of carriers, passengers, consignors, consignees and the principles and limits of liability.[13]

The Carriage by Air Act of 1932
Great Britain ratified the Warsaw Convention in 1929 and, pursuant to Section 1 and 2 of the Carriage by Air Act, 1932, made it applicable to Nigeria.[14]

Nigeria then domesticated this Convention through two legal instruments, namely:

a.   The Carriage by Air (Colonies, Protectorates and Trust Territories) Order, 1953 No. 1474.[15] This focused on International Air Travel.
b.   The Carriage by Air (Non-International Carriage) (Colonies, Protectorates and Trust Territories) Order, 1953[a]. Focused on Domestic Air Travel. Hereon referred to as The 1953 Order.

The Montreal Convention of 1999
Also known as the Convention for the Unification of Certain Rules for International Carriage by Air, embodies the evolution of the liability regime (the carrier's) regulating Carriage by Air (International and Non-International). It incorporates the several Agreements and amendments from the Harbinger Warsaw Convention of 1929 and the Hague Protocol of 1955 to the Montreal Agreement of 1966 [Agreement Relating to Liability Limitations of the Warsaw Convention and the Hague Protocol].

Only recently domesticated[16] and incorporated into Nigerian Law, it is hereon referred to as The 1999 Convention.

The Civil Aviation Act of 2006[17]
Signed into Law November 2006, this Act granted autonomy to Nigerian Civil Aviation Authority and most importantly domesticated ALL international, bilat-

eral and regional conventions, protocols and agreements.[18] It also stipulated sustainable sources of funding for Aviation infrastructure.

The Law meets the ICAO statutory requirement, enforces safety guidelines, improves security checks, prescribes ministerial powers during emergencies, defines offences that endanger safety and enacts penalties for violations. It also, most importantly, addresses compensation for passengers and regulates licensing and permits of air transport.[19]

Unfortunately, this new enactment also came after the several incidents of air crashes in the country.

It is worth mentioning that there was an attempt to expunge the 1953 Order from the 1953 books (Federal Laws) on the grounds of "Irrelevance" through an Order acting on the powers conferred on the Attorney-General of the Federation by Section 3(1) of Decree No. 21 of 1990.[20]

However, it would appear that the decision of the Supreme Court in Ibidapo v. Lufthansa Airlines[21] made the 1953 Order a valid and subsisting law.[22]

For the purpose of this discourse, however, my attention is primarily on non-international carriage, as the accidents discussed herein involved non-international/domestic flights, regulated by the 1953 Order (and currently, the 2006 Civil Aviation Act which domesticated the 1999 Convention).

When the Crash Occurs

The common consequences occasioned by the three most recent plane crashes (involving Bellview, Sosoliso and ADC Airplanes) are:

1. Death
2. Bodily Injury
3. Loss of Luggage
4. Collateral Damage: damage to private property rights.

The first three are discussed together.

Death, Bodily Damage and Loss of Luggage

When an air crash results in death, injury, and/or loss of luggage, relatives of air crash victims are generally entitled to be paid some compensation for their loss.[23]

The three crashes caused substantial loss of lives, severe bodily injury to the very few that survived, and loss of the entire luggage on board the flights.[24]

We will now examine these in light of the applicable laws: the 1953 Order and 1999 Convention.

Chapter III (Articles 17-30) of the two laws[25] governs the liability of the Carrier, as it relates to Non-International Carriage by Air. Article 17 states:

"The Carrier is liable for damage sustained in the event of the death or wounding of a passenger or any other bodily injury suffered by the passenger, if the accident which caused the damage so sustained took place on board the aircraft or in the course of any of the operations of embarking or disembarking."

By the provisions of Article 18 of the 1953 Order,[26] the carrier is liable for damage in the event of the destruction, loss or damage to any luggage, so sustained during the carriage by air. "Carriage by Air" is to comprise the period during which the luggage (or cargo) is in charge of the carrier.[27]

The financial extent of liability, to which a carrier is liable, in the event of an accident is provided under Article 22 of the 1953 Order.[28] Its subsection (4) provides that:

"...... the carrier and the passenger,...... may by special contract in writing agree to a limit of liability higher than that specified in those paragraphs."

I will state at this juncture that although the article prescribes the lower cap limit, the rider in subsection (4) is to the effect that the carrier may enter into a separate contract increasing its liability. The Aviation Regulator (NCAA) required the airlines operatives in Nigeria to go beyond the reproduction of the standard terms and conditions (reflecting the 1953 Order) by entering into a private contract, between themselves (the airline operators), their insurers and the passengers, placing the liability limit at $100,000 (U.S. dollars).

This is in furtherance of the liability limit increase established with the Montreal Agreement. Section 48 (1) (2) and (3) of the 2006 Civil Aviation Act is also to that effect.

Article 23[29] prohibits a carrier from contracting on terms concerning liability more favourable to him than those provided for. It states:

"Any provision in a contract of carriage (ticket condition or special contract) tending to relieve the carrier of liability or to fix a lower limit than that which is laid down in this schedule....shall be null and void..."

This however, does not vitiate the contract in its entirety.

Nevertheless, once a claimant can establish willful misconduct on the part of the carrier, provisions of the Convention limiting or excluding the liability of the carrier are not available as a defence.

The provisions of Article 25 of the 1953 Order[30] create this exception wherein a claimant party[31] may be entitled to a sum for damages even higher than the limit prescribed by the Law.

Article 25(1) is to the effect that, "The Carrier shall not be entitled to avail himself of the provisions of this Schedule which exclude or limit his liability, if the damage is caused by willful misconduct."

Subsection (2) provides, "Similarly the carrier shall not be entitled to avail himself of the said provisions,[32] if the damage is caused as aforesaid by any servant or agent of the carrier acting within the scope of his employment......"

The Sosoliso Airplane's crash was reportedly caused by weather (the Wind Shear Phenomenon), negligence[33] (on the part of the airport authorities) and pilot error.[34]

The ADC plane crash was attributed to weather (stormy conditions), as well as pilot error.[35]

The cause of Bellview Flight 210 is, however, largely unknown.

Establishing the Exception

It is general knowledge that every action has a reaction and every accident, a cause. When a plane crash occurs, the information as to the "cause" of the crash, in most cases, is a fact within the knowledge of the Airline Authorities and Operators. Airplanes do not just take off and crash in the ordinary course of flying.

However, when knowledge of the cause of such crash is largely unknown to the victim's beneficiary (as is "Cause Unknown" with the Bellview crash), can a claim be brought under the exception created under Article 25(1)?[36]

[The cause of crash "Pilot Error" (for Sosoliso and ADC crashes) may arguably be qualified as "willful misconduct" bringing it under the exception.]

A submission has been put forward. It propounds that "cause unknown" may sustain a claim under the Article's exception if the doctrine of res ipsa loquitur is relied on.[37] This term is Latin for "the thing speaks for itself." It refers to situations when it is assumed that a person's injury was caused by the negligent action of another party because the accident was the sort that would not occur unless someone was negligent. The defendant is then required to "prove its case" by showing an absence of willful misconduct (negligence) on its part or that of its servants or agents.[38]

"Pilot Error" (qualified under willful misconduct[39]) seems a clear exception to bring a claim under the purview of Article 25. Could "Cause Unknown" be sufficient rationale to exclude the Carrier from claiming and insisting on the cap (for damages) placed by the 1953 Order/1999 Convention?

As it relates to the Bellview case, could the victims or his or her beneficiary, citing "Cause Unknown," rely on the doctrine res ipsa to claim further damages under Article 25?

It would seem, however, that the Carrier/Airline may deny culpability for the acts of its agents (the pilots/crew) under subsection (2) of Article 25, where it (the carrier) proves that, "...the willful misconduct of his servant or agent took place without his actual fault or privity."[40]

We should note, however, that where the Plaintiff is unable to prove willful misconduct by the Carrier or its Agents, she is only barred from claiming damages above the compensation cap of $100,000 (U.S. dollars). She is not barred from claiming the compensation limit itself, as provided by law.

Collateral Damage

Apart from the loss of life and baggage, the Bellview crash caused quite extensive collateral damage.

Areas of farmland used for growing cocoa and plantain bananas, among other crops,[41] were destroyed following the airplane's crash landing in the village of Lisa, in Ogun State. To have an idea of how extensive the area was, the Police Commissioner stated that it took about 100 policemen to cordon the place and block all routes that led to the area. The security restriction also denied the villagers access to their surrounding farms.[42]

The damage to private property and farmland was only worsened by the loss of a vital (formerly accessible) water source. These occasioned considerable hardship and loss to the villagers.

Pollution of Surface and Underground Waterways

The villagers of Lisa-Igbore Local Community of Ogun State were reported to have lost use/access to a major water source following the Bellview crash in their village. An interview with the Baale[43] (Chieftain/ Leader) of the village revealed this. According to him, members of the Red Cross and the Ogun State Environmental Protection Agency forbade his people from retrieving water from the Osun Water because it was polluted by the human remains and debris from the crash. The river was their only source of clean and constant water before the unfortunate accident.[44]

The airplane, on impact, created a 70 foot (20 meter) crater.[45] Underground water channels would invariably have been affected. Excavation activities also took a toll on the land. No doubt, the villagers suffered loss and resultant hardship.

Even though claims for damages could potentially lie—under the general Nigerian Laws—against the Carrier, I am not aware of any instituted by the indigenes of the village against Bellview. Perhaps because of the people's religious beliefs that such an accident was an act of fate.

Investigations

Investigations into the general and peculiar cause of the crashes are conducted by the Accidents Investigation and Prevention Bureau,[46] in certain instances with assistance from their American counterparts, NTSB.

Claiming Compensation

In practice, in the event of an air crash involving death,[47] the airlines usually require the Next of Kin ("the beneficiary") to obtain, from the Probate Division of the Federal or State High Court, a letter of Administration identifying the within-named/holder(s) as Administrator(s) to the estate of the deceased.

In agreement with the airline, the Administrators then execute a Deed of Release and Discharge acknowledging the payment of a settlement sum and discharging the airline, its agents and privies from further liability.

Following this, the airline communicates with and instructs the insurance company to pay the deceased's administrator/next-of-kin. The money is usually remitted through the airline to the family.[48]

The effect of Articles 21 and 23 of the 1999 Convention are that compensation paid must be at the prevailing exchange rate.

The Discharge and Release Form (format may differ slightly)

The deed of Release is usually in this format:

"We...............of the estate of ......who died in the ......Airlines incident of ...200_ ("the Deceased") for ourselves and on behalf of the estate, the Children, the dependants, the beneficiaries and the members of the Deceased[49] HEREBY AC-KNOWLEDGE due receipt from....... of the sum of.........consideration of which we, for ourselves and on behalf of the estate,........... of the Deceased.......release and discharge of all claims of whatsoever nature and howsoever arising whether now or in the future and whether known or unknown........from and against any and all future liability, ...however arising and by whomsoever brought arising from or in respect of the Deceased's involvement and death, and destruction of baggage...........we.............. without any reservation, waive forever our right of action against...... under the applicable law or any other law...."

From the Deed conditions, it would appear that the Administrator would totally exclude a right of action or claim for damages under any applicable law and/or Convention; for instance, when there is continuing/consequent damage as a result of the crash. The question is, how far should the signor/administrator go to release the carrier/airline from liability for matters arising "in the future" and of "whatsoever nature...known or unknown"?

Furthermore, there are other issues, such as:

- Who are the "Beneficiaries"?
  "Who comprise "....the estate...dependants, beneficiaries..."? How wide does the net spread?
  Does an "old friend" whom the deceased kept on a monthly allowance (prior to his/her death) qualify as a "dependant or beneficiary"?
  Reference to the 1953 Order would be in order.
  By Section 1, Schedule III, the expression "member of a family" means "wife or husband, parent, step-parent, grandparent, brother, sister, half-brother, half-sister, child, step-child, grandchild." Certainly, applying this in the Nigerian context this could be extended to include a whole community!

However, in light of the complexities of cultural practices in Nigeria, the definition raises further issues and considerations:

- Succession
  What would be the position of a woman married to the deceased under only customary law?
  If a child was not registered at birth, would an affidavit of birth suffice as proof if the paternity of such "child beneficiary" is suddenly in contest?

- "Wife"
  If the deceased was married to four wives and died intestate, which wife can rightfully claim compensation?

- Family Feuds, Contending Parties, Claimants
  Family members in court fight with themselves over compensation claims.

- Countless Court Injunctions
  Parties often forestall the judicial process by either failing to appear before the court, pleading insufficient notice/service or some contestable excuse, or appearing without proper representation and/or necessary documentation.

The Ticket

We must look at provisions of the ticket which forms the contract between the airline operator and the passenger.

Tickets of Nigerian domestic (non-international) carriers have endorsed on them Conditions of Contract/Notices limiting their liability. Incorporating the provisions of the 1953 Order (Warsaw Convention), and the Montreal Agreement of May 28, 1999, the Notices, so endorsed, are in line with Section 6.7.4.1 of the National Civil Aviation Policy December, 2001, i.e., prescribing the liability limit of $100,000 for damages on the occasion of death or bodily injury.[50]

The notice on one of the ticket reads:

"....if your carriage is wholly within Nigeria and does not form part of international carriage for the purpose of the Warsaw Convention or the Montreal Convention, the provisions of the limits of liability specified by Warsaw Convention apply by virtue of local law"[51]

Another is to the effect that,

"Carriage hereunder is subject to the rules and limitations relating to liability established by the Montreal Convention for the Unification of Certain Rules for International carriage by air. For carriage wholly within Nigeria, the provisions of the carriage by air of Montreal Protocol and the current National Aviation Policy made thereunder apply."[52]

"The provisions contained in the Convention for the Unification of Certain Rules Relating to International Carriage......shall from commencement of this Act have force of law and apply to non-international carriage by air within Nigeria, irrespective of the nationality of the aircraft performing the carriage, and shall....govern the rights and liabilities of carriers, passengers...and other persons."[53]

Section 48(3) of the 2006 Civil Aviation Act further requires the carrier to make an advance payment of at least $30,000 (U.S. dollars) to the beneficiaries of the victim, in any case of aircraft accident resulting in death or injury of passengers. Such payment is to be made within 30 days from the date of the accident.

The position then (of one of the airlines)[54] that beneficiaries collect an advance sum of only $10,000 on the condition that they sign a Discharge and Release Form is, therefore, totally at variance with provisions of the law.

Any carrier that has complied with the above directive may still refute liability by advancing the argument based on the same Sections' exclusion clause, which states, "...Such advance payments shall not constitute recognition of liability and may be offset against any amounts subsequently paid as damages by the carrier."

Further Considerations

Insurance

Under the Aviation regulations,[55] adequate insurance cover is one of the conditions for the issuance and sustenance of Air Operators Certificate.

> "Any carrier operating air transport services to, from or within Nigeria........shall maintain adequate insurance covering its liability under this Act....and also its liability towards compensation for damages that may be sustained by third parties......"

Furthermore, NCAA issued a directive requiring all airlines to enter into special contract with the passengers, raising the sum for damages to $100,000 (U.S. dollars), payable to each passenger in the event of an accident occasioning death/bodily injury. This agreement, endorsed on each ticket, is a special contract by which the airline agrees to pay the rate of compensation in the said policy.[56]

Thus the argument of one of the airlines' underwriters that it could not sanction payment of the different compensation sums — the total of which exceeds the amount paid (by the carrier) as its premium—is at variance with these requirements.[57]

Insurers' Delay

One of the three airlines blamed its delay in settling compensation claims on its underwriters who they claimed attributed the delay in resolving the passengers' claim to what they perceive as an ambiguity between the instructions given to the airline on the limit of liability as printed on the airlines' ticket, on the instructions of the NCAA, as against the position in the Aviation Laws at the time of the accident(s).

The management of the Aviation Development Company (ADC) Airlines stated in a newspaper advertorial that the underwriters still maintained that the position of the law at the date of the accident was provided under the "Carriage by Air (Non-International Carriage) (Colonies, Protectorates and Trust Territories) Order 1953" which provides for payment of $10,000 U.S. dollars (125,000 francs) per passenger.[58]

Contributory Negligence

When an air crash is a result of negligence on the part of the air field operators or oversight on the part of the maintenance and regulatory agency, an action may lie against such statutory body.

Case instance: The report by the Accidents Investigations and Prevention Board (AIPB) (with contribution from the United States National Transportation Safety Board, NTSB) on the Sosoliso crash in Port Hacourt stated "...some 60 metres further, the rear fuselage impacted on the exposed concrete drainage culvert on the runway..." The report further pointed out that the airfield lighting (of runway 21) not being turned on may have impaired the pilot from sighting the runway.

Further causes of the air crashes witnessed in the country include:

- Use of outdated planes and air navigational equipment,
- Obsolete equipment (communications, rescue and meteorological equipment),
- Dearth of (the much needed) highly trained aviation personnel, and
- Lack of a viable equipment replacement programme.

Legal Action Against a Statutory/Government Body— Issues for Consideration

Parties

For a claim to succeed in Court, claimants must include all the proper parties to the suit. In 2006, the Port Hacourt branch of the Parents Association of Loyola Jesuit College (parents of the children onboard the Sosoliso flight) sued Sosoliso Airline properly joining the National Aviation Authority and the Federal Government.[59]

Pre-action Notice

Section 25 of the NCAA Act,[60] is on the Limitation of suits against the Authority. It provides that subject to the provisions of the Public Officers Protection Act,[61] no suit shall be commenced against an officer or employee of the aviation authorities (NCAA, NAMA, or FAA) before the expiration of a period of one month after written notice of intention to commence the suit is served on the Authority by the intending plaintiff or his agent.

Limitation of Action

Against the Officers of the Aviation Authorities

According to law (at the time of the plane crashes and at present), a suit on the grounds of neglect or default cannot be instituted against such officer or employee of the Authority unless it is commenced within three months of the act, neglect or default complained of, or within six months if there is continued damage or injury.[62]

Against the Carrier

The Supreme Court decision in Ibinabo v. Lufthansa Airlines[63] also restated the provisions of Article 29(1) of the 1953 Order.[64] The Article states that the right to damages shall be extinguished if an action is not brought within two years, reckoned from the date of arrival at the destination, or from the date on which the aircraft ought to have arrived, or from the date on which the carriage stopped.

In light of the above, could some of the claims be argued to be time barred?

Jurisdiction

Section 251(k) of the 1999 Constitution of the Federal Republic of Nigeria,[65] vests the Federal High Court with exclusive jurisdiction to try aviation (and safety of aircraft) causes and matters.

Section 31 of the NCAA Act and Section 63 Civil Aviation Act accordingly provide that, "The Federal High Court shall have jurisdiction to try offences committed under this Act."[66]

The claimant may institute proceedings at the primary place of operation or business of the Carrier, or the victim, the take-off or destination State, or in the State where the incident occurred.[67]

Defences

Though the sustainability of a defence in a strict liability claim is debatable, claims contending unlimited liability of the Carrier(s) may give rise to defences as:

Act of God/ Nature

The AIPB report affirmed that the Sosoliso Aircraft encountered adverse weather conditions with the ingredients of wind shear activity. It stated that the reduced visibility in the thunderstorm and rain as at the time the aircraft came to land was also a contributory factor.[68]

Wind shear has been explained as "gusty-winds which can suddenly turn extreme and come accompanied by turbulence."

The Bellview plane was thought to have been struck by lightning. Whether this defence can be sustained is debatable.

Latent Defect

As defence, a Carrier may plead that the accident was caused by a latent defect that was undiscoverable upon the exercise of utmost due care by the airline. Also, that the fault was undiscoverable through the application of any known test.[69]

The defence is equally open to the manufacturer. The issues may, however, arise as to the Terms of the Aircraft Warranty.

Lack of Contract Privity

This is a tricky one. What happens when the victim's name is not as endorsed on the ticket? It is common to have persons exchange tickets or buy tickets in their names only to re-sell to someone else. Can the Carrier avail itself of this defence and argue that there was no contract between itself and victim (claimant) as the victim was not the one to purchase the ticket?

One may argue that although impersonation is a punishable offence, the death of, or injury to, any passenger while on board the aircraft caused as a result of an accident carries with it the strictest liability on the part of the carrier. The Contract of Carriage as endorsed on the ticket is governed by law and, as such, applies accordingly.

Authorities' Negligence

Whose responsibility is/was it to oversee installation and maintenance of instruments (weather and navigational)?

When the accident or subsequent damage is a result of the misconduct or oversight on the part of the Aviation Authorities, its officers and/or agents, a Carrier may accordingly shift the blame.[70]

However, when the claim (in Court) is for an Order compelling the Carrier to pay up the compensation sum, the following defence has been advanced: Delay by Partner or Insurer.[71]

On the other hand, the Aviation Authority may plead in its defence, Pilot Error.[72]

Conclusion

The smooth application of the Compensation Regime in Nigerian Aviation disasters certainly requires looking into. Nigerian Airlines should borrow a leaf from their Kenyan counterparts. Kenyan Airways Flight 507 crashed on May 5, 2007, causing the death of 105 passengers and nine crew members. By the 21st of May (barely two weeks later), the Airline had begun processing interim part payments to the next-of-kins' of the victims aboard its Flight KQ 507.

Nevertheless, with the Nigerian Aviation Act 2006 and the (ongoing) reforms in the aviation industry (covering Safety Oversight, Aviation Security, Air Traffic Forecasts, Airline Operations), efforts can be said to be underway to reposition the Nigerian Aviation Industry. The 2006 Civil Aviation Act also puts in place mechanisms to minimize incidents and accidents and to generally promote safety and security in the air transport sub-sector of the Nigerian economy.[73]

Audits by the International Civil Aviation Organization (ICAO) team and the International Safety Assessment Programme (IASA) have recently appraised the nation's air staff and facilities to ensure that they conform not only with

America's Federal Aviation Administration (FAA) standards, but with the world body/international regulations of the ICAO.[74]

Hopefully, with the implementation of the reforms and improvement of safety standards, the skies will indeed be a safer place in Nigeria.

Endnotes

1. And for 9.3 percent of the total air accidents that occurred in the continent from 1996-2005. Between October 2005 and November 2006, the country witnessed five fatal air crashes that resulted in the loss of over 300 lives. Source: Federal Ministry of Transportation (Air Transport) Monthly Journal, February 2007

2. Used interchangeably

3. Every other air crash in Nigeria, military or civilian fall within the ambit of the considerations discussed.

4. The twin-engine Boeing 737 left Murtala Muhammed Airport in Lagos at 7 p.m. (6 p.m. GMT) Saturday as Flight 210 en route to Abuja- a trip that should have taken about 50 minutes.

5. Research by the John Hopkins School of Medicine found that when aviation crashes do occur, aircraft fire is involved in 13 percent of general aviation crashes but contributes to 40 percent of the fatalities.

6. Odittah, C. "National Hospital Admits Seven Survivors" THISDAY Newspapers, Monday, October 30, Vol. 11, No.4209, Pg. 6.

7. http://www.ministryof aviation.org

8. Recently made autonomous and transferred to the Presidency.

9. Order not an indication of operational levels/ capacities.

10. Salu, A.O., "Rights To Compensation By The Relatives Of An Aircrash Victim", Quarterly Modern Practice: Justice-January 1998, Vol. 2, Page 93.

11. Chapter One (First Annex) of the Carriage of Air Law adopted the Convention for the Unification of Certain Rules relating to International Carriage by Air. *(This is because at that time, air transportation was a novelty coupled

with the fact that there existed in different countries different limits of liability for injury and wrongful death.

12. Chapters I and II of the Convention.

13. Chapter III Articles 17-30 of the Convention. Also Salu.A.O., Op cit.

14. Per Ogundare JCA, Oshevire .v. British Caledonia, [1990] NSL Vol. 3 at Page 666.

15. Annual Volume of the Laws of Nigeria, 1953. Pg. 617 and, Under Part I of the Schedule for The Carriage by Air (Parties to Convention) Order, 1958, Nigeria was set forth as one of the colonies/ protectorate "in respect of which they are respectively parties" since the 3rd of March 1935.
    "The provisions of the Convention[Warsaw]...so far as they relate to the rights and liabilities of carriers, passengers...and other persons and subject to the provisions of the Section, have the force of law in the Colony in relation to carriage by air to which the Convention applies, irrespective of the nationality of the aircraft performing that carriage." Section 1(1) First schedule Carriage by Air Order 1953.

16. This was in November of 2006, after the last three crashes had occurred.

17. Civil Aviation (Repeal and Re-Enactment) Act 2006.

18. Including the Montreal Agreement of 1966.

19. Aviation Journal, Ibid.

20. Revised Edition (Laws of the Federation of Nigeria) Decree 1990. Also, Schedule 1, Part II, No.6 of the Revised Edition (Authorized Omissions) Order 1990.

21. [1997] 4 Nigerian Weekly Law Report (NWLR) Part 498 at Pg. 124.

22. Aviation Lawyers argue that the Carriage by Air (Non-International Carriage) of 1953 has been repealed and that the Civil Aviation Act of 2006 which came into force on the 4th of November 2006 has overtaken that law. Per, Ukutt, V. Aviation Matters, THISDAY Newspaper, Monday May 21, 2007, Vol. 12, No. 4412, Pg. 32.

23. A lot of controversy has arisen over the issue of compensation and the Airlines ability to pay up. However, despite the airline mishaps, I am as yet not aware of any reported decision addressing the issues as it regards an aviation disaster in Nigeria.

24. Five of the seven survivors from the Sosoliso crash were reported to have died in hospital. THISDAY Newspaper, Friday, October, 2006, Vol. 11, No. 4199, Pg. 40.

25. The 1953 Order and The 1999 Convention.

26. Article 17(2) of the 1999 Convention

27. Subsection (2). The Carrier restricts its liability to about 20 US Dollars per kilo for loss of checked baggage and 500 US Dollars per passenger for unchecked baggage.

28. Article 21 of the 1999 Convention. Formerly placed at a limit of "125,000 francs", on the occasion of death or injury. It is currently set at $100,000.

29. Article 26 of the 1999 Convention.

30. Article 25 of the 1953 Order and Article 21 of the 1999 Convention.

31. The victim or his/her beneficiary.

32. Sub-section 1.

33. A concrete drainage culvert was left exposed on Runway 21 where the flight was given clearance to land.

34. Attributed to the Crew's decision to continue the approach beyond the 'Decision Altitude',without having the runway/ airport in sight. Accidents Investigations and Prevention Bureau (AIPB) Report on the Sosoliso Crash, THISDAY Newspaper, Friday, October, 2006, Vol. 11, No. 4199, Pg. 40. Also Edeaghe E., Ororo E., and Idiodi H., "Comparative Analysis of The Bellview and Sosoliso Air Crash: Matters Arising" The Internet Journal of Rescue and Disaster Medicine, ISSN: 1531-2992, ISPUB.com).

35. Ojeifo, S. and Muraina, F., "The ADC Plane Crash" THISDAY Newspapers, Moday, October 30, 2006, Vol. 11, No. 4209, Pg. 6.

36. Its counterpart provides that a carrier may stipulate that the contract of carriage shall be subject to higher limits of liability than those provided for in this convention or to no limit of liability whatsoever. S. 25 1999 Convention.

37. First formulated in the case of Byrne .v. Boadle [1863] in Great Britain. Res ipsa loquitur is a legal term from the Latin meaning literally, "The thing itself speaks" but is more often translated "The thing speaks for itself". It signifies that further details are unnecessary; the proof of the case is self-evident. http://en.wikipedia.org) Also upheld in the Nigerian cases of Okhai .v. C & C Construction Limited [1997] 3 NWLR (Pt. 543) 584 C.A and Ibeanu .v. Ogbeide [1998] 12 NWLQ (Pt. 576) 1 S.C.

38. http://www.lectlaw.com

39. Cited as "Volitional discourtesy/ guilty act" in the Roget's Thesaurus of English Words and Phrases.

40. Newspapers reported claims by the Aviation Authorities that the Pilot of the ADC Aircraft was warned of the stormy weather and advised to stall for a few minutes. He was however said to have ignored the warning.

41. These export farm produce/ products or cash crops formed a staple source of income for the villagers who had to transport it a further distance of about 10 Kilometers to the City Centres/ markets.

42. The Sunday Punch Newspaper of November 13, 2005, Pg. 7.

43. Chief Sadiku Odugbemi. Reported in the Sunday Punch Newspaper of November 13, 2005.

44. Ibid.

45. Reuters News report: http://cnn.worldnews.com.

46. Currently an autonomous body under the Presidency.

47. Where it involves bodily injury, the victims themselves make the claim(s).

48. In 2006, both Sosoliso and ADC had their Operating Licences revoked. An action, the Aviation Authority disclosed, was precipitated by the Airlines' inability to pay full compensation to families of the crash victims.

49. Raises issues which will be addressed below.

50. Currently reflected under Section 48(1) (2) and (3) of the 2006 Civil Aviation Act

51. Or summarily "Domestic carriage hereunder is subject to the rules and limitations relating to the carrier's liability regime for domestic airlines operations as provided for by Section 48(1)(2)and (3) of the 2006 Civil Aviation Act for carriage wholly within Nigeria." Terms and Conditions as printed on Arik Airlines e-ticket. (One of the several private airline operators in Nigeria.)

52. Conditions of Contract as set out in a Bellview Airlines Passenger Ticket.

53. Section 48(2) Civil Aviation Act 2006. Section 48(1) regulates International Carriage by Air.

54. Name withheld.

55. Section 74, 2006 Civil Aviation Act.

56. The Civil Aviation Policy 2001.

57. The Underwriters argued that the Carrier was insured up to a sum of $100 million, paid as premium, however that the payment of $100,000 to each family of the 105 passengers and crew that died, would exceed the amount paid up by the Carrier as premium. THISDAY Newspaper, Monday, May 21, 2007.

58. Refer to THISDAY Newspapers of Monday, 21st May, 2007. Op cit.

59. An out-of-court settlement was however agreed on.

60. Nigerian Civil Aviation Authority (Establishment E.T.C.) Act 2004, CAP N.94.

61. Contains identical provisions.

62. Section 25(2) (a and b) NCAA Act and Public Officers (Protection) Act. An article published in a National Daily, noted that the last three air crashes occurred over the weekends. The Author attributed such coincidence to laxity on the part of the Aviation personnel alleging "....non-committal attitude of

the best hands to man certain critical areas during the weekends....." Ndubuisi, F., "The Weekend Theory". THISDAY Newspapers, Monday, October 30, 2006, Vol.11, No. 4209, Pg.7.

63. Op cit.

64. Article 35 of the 1999 Convention.

65. 1999 Laws of the Federal Republic of Nigeria.

66. Laws of the Federal Republic of Nigeria. Also, Section 31 NAMA Act [2004].

67. High Court Civil Procedure Rules.

68. A storm was said to have been passing through Lagos on the night of the 22nd of October, 2005. Meteorological reports showed/ predicted widespread rains and thunderstorms around the Southwestern corner of Nigeria, particularly near Lagos to Ibadan. http://www.cnn.com/2005/WORLD/africa/10/23/nigeria.plane/index.html.

69. Salu. Op cit.

70. Op cit.

71. "...payment was in spite of the refusal of our former technical partner, ... which owned the aircraft that crashed, to honour its insurance obligations, to us and the passengers...". Statement in advertorial placed by Sosoliso Airlines, on cause of delay in compensation settlements.

72. Following the year-long investigation into the crash of the Sosoliso Airlines DC-9 late 2005 in bad weather, the AIPB listed Pilot Error as one of the causes of the crash.

73. Air Transport Update: Monthly Journal of the Federal Ministry of Transportation Air Transport, Vol.2, No.3, May 2007.

74. Nigeria was scored 93.1 percent during an Oversight Audit carried out between November 7 and 17 2006. www.businessdayonline.com/.

Bibliography

[1997] 3 NWLR (Pt. 543) 584 C.A

[1998] 12 NWLQ (Pt. 576) 1 S.C.

Air Transport Update: Monthly Journal of the Federal Ministry of Transportation Air Transport, Vol.2, No.3, May 2007.

Annual Volume of the Laws of Nigeria, 1953.

Civil Aviation (Repeal and Re-Enactment) Act 2006.

Civil Aviation Policy 2001.

Constitution of the Federal Republic of Nigeria 1999 (Promulgation Decree No. 24).

Edeaghe E., Ororo E., and Idiodi H., "Comparative Analysis of The Bellview and Sosoliso Air Crash: Matters Arising" The Internet Journal of Rescue and Disaster Medicine, ISSN: 1531-2992, ISPUB.com)

Federal Ministry of Transportation (Air Transport) Monthly Journal, February 2007.

High Court (Civil Procedure) Rules.

http://cnn.worldnews.com

http://en.wikipedia.org

http://www.cnn.com/2005/WORLD/africa/10/23/nigeria.plane/index.html

http://www.lectlaw.com.

http://www.ministryof aviation.org

Kirkpatrick, B. "Roget's Thesaurus of English Words and Phrases", Longman Group U.K Limited, 1987.

Nigerian Airspace Management Agency (Establishment, ETC) Act [2004].

Nigerian Civil Aviation Authority (Establishment E.T.C.) Act 1999 No. 49.

Nigerian Weekly Law Report (NWLR) Part 498 at Pg. 124.

Odittah, C. "National Hospital Admits Seven Survivors" THISDAY Newspapers, Monday, October 30, Vol. 11, No.4209, Pg. 6.

Ojeifo, S. and Muraina, F., "The ADC Plane Crash" THISDAY Newspapers, Monday, October 30, 2006, Vol. 11, No. 4209, Pg. 6.

Public Officers (Protection) Law, Cap, P.41.

Revised Edition (Laws of the Federation of Nigeria) Decree 1990.

Revised Edition (Authorized Omissions) Order 1990.

Salu, A.O., "Rights To Compensation By The Relatives Of An Air crash Victim", Quarterly Modern Practice: Justice-January 1998, Vol. 2, Page 93.

Sunday Punch Newspaper of November 13, 2005, Pg. 7.

THISDAY Newspaper, Friday, October 27, 2006, Vol. 11, No. 4199, Pg. 40.

THISDAY Newspaper, Monday, May 21, 2007.

THISDAY Newspapers, Monday, October 30, 2006, Vol.11, No. 4209, Pg.7.

Ukutt, V. "Aviation Matters", THISDAY Newspaper, Monday May 21, 2007, Vol. 12, No. 4412, Pg. 32.

Chapter 17

Recent Mass Disasters in West Africa: The Urgent Need for Training Forensic Experts in Africa

John O. Obafunwa, M.D., F.R.C. Path., L.L.B., Matthias I. Okoye, M.D., J.D., and E. J. C. Nwana, M.D., F.M.C. Path.

Introduction

Mass disaster is said to occur when the casualty overwhelms the available medical facility. The forensic pathologist is expected to deal with fatalities arising from these cases where the capacity of the local morgue is exceeded and the magnitude of the problem requires the collaborative effort of other specialists. In the African setting, there is the initial problem of a dearth of these specialists. Where one is available that specialist is unlikely to be involved in natural disasters such as famine. While he might have to deal with deaths resulting from human rights abuses, death penalty, violence against women and children, these cases will not necessarily overwhelm the available facility. Generally, mass disasters can result from explosions, plane crashes, rail derailments and terrorism involving the use of chemical, biologic or nuclear agents; others sources in Africa include flooding, collapse of buildings, stampedes in stadia, pipeline explosions with massive fires, asphyxial deaths from gas inhalation and genocides. There are no accurate figures of the magnitude of the problem in Africa for reasons ranging from the dearth of specialists in relevant fields to ignorance on the part of those involved in governance.

The role of the forensic team includes managing the scene for the purpose of gathering trace evidence that will assist with elucidating the causative factor,[1] identifying the decedents and, determining the cause of death.[1-3] The forensic team includes criminalists, forensic anthropologists, forensic entomologists, fingerprint experts, forensic toxicologists, forensic pathologists, forensic odontologists, forensic radiologists, forensic biologists (including DNA analysts), forensic engineers and forensic photographers. Others include members of the identification bureau, incident officers, control room officers and staff of the communications centre, records officers, supplies team, utility personnel, funeral directors, cleaners, Medical Examiner/Coroner and support staff, family support team, as well as psychologists. All these groups are detailed in the protocol prepared by the United Kingdom Police Chiefs and the National Association of Medical Examiners (NAME) for the Disaster Mortuary Operational Response Teams (DMORT).[1,3]

Recent Mass Disasters in the West African Sub-Region

The West African sub-region has witnessed a number of catastrophes recently. Emphasis will be laid on Nigeria, Cameroon and Ghana. Of course, parts of East Africa, has had its own share like the simultaneous bombings of the US Embassies in Dar es Salaam, Tanzania and Nairobi, Kenya, on August 7, 1998. The two attacks were linked to the *Al-Qaeda* network. A total of 213 died in Dar es Salaam with approximately 4,000 injured while 11 were killed and 85 got wounded in Nairobi.[4] About 800,000 Hutus were allegedly massacred in 1994 by the Tutsi-led Rwandan Army and the Alliance of Democratic Forces for the Liberation of Congo Zaire (AFDL).[5] The grave of the decedents were uncovered by the United Nations soldiers in 1996, near Rutshuru, located approximately 80 km north of Goma in the east of the Democratic Republic of Congo.

The National Population Commission of Nigeria projected the country's population to be 126,252,844 in 2003;[6] every fourth African is supposed to be a Nigerian. The implication of this is that Nigeria is the most populous African nation and any major catastrophe in Nigeria can potentially destabilize the rest of the continent. Events in Nigeria can to a large extent be extrapolated to give a picture of what is to be expected in the rest of underdeveloped Arica. The country, located in the West African sub-region, has played host to a number of mass disasters, some of which are itemized below:

October 18, 1998
Over 500 people died with about 100 wounded, when an oil pipeline exploded, as some economic saboteurs were trying to steal gasoline in Jesse, about 300 km southeast of Lagos.

May 2002
EAS Airline crashed in Kano, northern Nigeria, killing 148 people after crashing into a residential area with about half of the decedents actually being on the ground.

October 23, 2005
Bellview Flight 210 crashed at Lisa village, 400 km north of Lagos, killing all 117 aboard.

December 10, 2005
Sosoliso Airline crashed at Port Harcourt killing 108 school children returning home on vacation.

May 12, 2006
Pipeline explosion following vandalism with 200 people dead at Ilado fishing community on the outskirts of Lagos.

October 29, 2006
Boeing 737 of ADC Airlines Flight 53, crashed just after taking off from the nation's capital, killing 96 people including top medical personnel and the spiritual leader of Moslems in Nigeria, with 9 survivors.

December 26, 2006
Pipeline explosion in Abule-Egba area on the outskirts of Lagos following acts of vandalism and with hundreds of charred bodies, many of which were buried at the scene.

In May 2001 over 100 people died in Ghana when a stampede occurred at the Accra Stadium. Ghana is one of the rapidly developing African countries located west of Nigeria. That incident was about the deadliest soccer tragedy on the continent. It is noteworthy that in 2003, the United Nations estimated the population of Ghana to be 20.9m and, this figure is reportedly second to Nigeria.[7,8]

Located to the immediate east of Nigeria is Cameroon with a population estimated to be 16.0m by the United Nations in 2003 [9] It was here that the Lake Nyos gas disaster occurred in 1986.[10] That catastrophe witnessed the death of at least 1,700 victims, resulting from the sudden release of the rather dense carbon dioxide gas from the volcano-located lake. It is noteworthy that there was no volcanic activity at this time.

More recently, a Boeing 737, Flight KQ 507, belonging to Kenyan Airways, crashed in the south of Douala, Cameroon on May 5, 2007, killing all 114 people on board.[11] The flight had originated in Abidjan, Ivory Coast (another West African country), departed Douala at 0105 GMT and was due to arrive in Nairobi at 0315 GMT. That plane had on board persons from a minimum of 23 countries.

Another Kenyan Airways plane had crashed into the sea in January 2000, just after taking off from Abidjan Airport, Ivory Coast (Cote d'Ivoire) causing the death of 169 passengers with 10 survivors.

The wars in Sierra Leone and Liberia resulted in the dislocation of families and deaths of many people. Some warlords are currently being investigated and few are facing various charges of mass killings and other war atrocities. Of course all these will require forensic evidence and it would be appropriate to have validated forensic data, which are largely lacking on the continent.

These are some of the notable major mass disasters that recently occurred in the West Africa sub-region. The common denominator is that this part of the world was not adequately equipped and indeed prepared to personally handle the problem. These countries had to, in most cases, depend on foreign governments to send in recovery team and other forensic experts.

Dealing with Mass Disasters in the West African Sub-Region

The West African sub-region, as with most parts of Africa, does not have to regularly deal with such disasters like hurricanes or typhoons, earthquakes and eruptions. Perhaps the absence of these constantly challenging travails have encouraged the strikingly lackadaisical attitude on the part of the leadership towards being adequately prepared for other disasters earlier listed. Various Non-Governmental Organizations and the Red Cross have continued to concentrate preparedness for mass disasters on such things as drought with famine and the HIV/AIDS pandemic.

The typical mass disasters in West Africa itemized above require indigenous personnel who where possible need to be locally trained. Where they are trained abroad, there should be a mechanism that ensures that they practice in their local environment which they are expected to know better than expatriates. A dearth of forensic experts exists in the typical third world country. The availability of local experts will naturally make response time shorter because they can be dispatched quickly to places where needed and, blending with the local community should not be a problem. The basic problem though remains the non-availability of trained personnel and relevant tools.

The role of the forensic anthropologists cannot be underestimated,[11] but data that are specific for blacks of African descent are essential. Local physical anthropologists versed in the knowledge of societal peculiarities remain indispensable with regards to recovery and identification. There is a need to generate local data for easy comparison. These specialists would of course be armed with data from around the world because mass disasters cut across national boundaries with regards to victims.[2] The application of archeological grids when dealing with commingled bodies scattered over a rather large expanse of land as seen in various crashes requires a painstaking approach by the forensic anthropologist.[12]

The forensic anthropologist is best served by forensic botanist, forensic soil biologist and forensic geologist who know the terrain particularly where proper recovery and identification of artifacts are involved. When these specialists team up with forensic odontologists and forensic pathologists, they expectedly identify most of the scattered remains.[13,14]

West African governments have often acted ignorantly; the services of forensic teams have never been considered important and where these have been made available it is usually at the instance of more industrialized societies where these practices are routinely operational. This is particularly sad when it is realized that foreign nationals might be involved, particularly when dealing with airline crashes. In the case of the charred bodies of locals involved in the vandalisation of gasoline pipelines, those in government are often too quick to dispose of such bodies in mass graves, often at the scene of accident. Local funeral directors hasten to dispose of the bodies for economic gains and this approach means less headaches for the government. Nobody bothers about the identity of the dead, how many died and what actually caused death. Part of the governmental gains in the West African sub-region is premised on the fact that no compensation has to be paid to the affected families; nobody is asking relevant questions. The government does not have to explain to anyone, account for any missing person and consequently insurance companies themselves owe nobody no explanations. If these developing societies were to have more educationally and politically aware citizens, these individuals can falsely claim that a loved one was missing amidst the charred bodies and claim all accruing benefits.

Towards achieving the desired goal, particularly considering that mass disasters cut across nationalities, developed societies need to assist with the empowerment of these developing societies. The former have important roles to play with regards to training forensic specialists required to handle the investigation of mass disasters. Training can be partly done locally and emphasis should be placed on frequent rehearsals. These local experts should ideally constantly liaise with other experts overseas for purpose of self evaluation and improvement The activities at the locus of mass disasters can be summarized as below, thus identifying the needs of these developing societies.

The various rehearsals would have identified specific locations to be used as temporary morgues, power and water sources, sewage disposal, sites of temporary accommodation, mobile body storage facilities, regional health facilities, supply sources and coordinators, control room and communications centre among others. In many instances these disasters happen where none of these facilities are available and as such the forensic and support team must have identified ways of improvisation at remote locations, when conducting their rehearsals. A large number of supplies must be ready and there should be stand-by generators, heavy duty vehicles including earth movers to create access roads, refrigerated containers for storing bodies and body parts as well as prefabricated buildings for use as temporary morgues and accommodation facilities. In addition there should be stored water with pre-identified water tankers and possibly water-well diggers, tents for use by various experts, and mobile baths/toilets.

Once there is information that a catastrophe has occurred the various teams are required to assemble at the designated point and the team leader reminds all present of their roles. The team will then head to the disaster site and the command centre will be appropriately located as the recovery of survivors commences. Naturally the police will be expected to maintain law and order in these communities to prevent looting of properties of dying and dead victims; this is not an uncommon practice in developing societies. It is expected that the fatalities and properties will be left in-situ for the recovery team to handle. The scene will expectedly be treated in a grid manner by the recovery team while the communications centre will maintain appropriate links with the Coroner/Medical Examiner's Office, air/rail line operators, medical/dental offices, family bureau centre, media and others. The recovery team will include criminalists, photographers/video recorders, records officers, supplies officer armed with sit flags and body bags, forensic pathologists, forensic anthropologists, forensic entomologists and any other expert that might be considered appropriate. Of course there is a need to be cognizant of certain political visits but in handling this it must not interfere with the scientific activities. The scene visit by the political VIPs must thus be well managed by the Coroner/Chief Medical Examiner's Office.

The other forensic experts (pathologists, odontologists, radiologists, fingerprint experts and DNA specialist) responsible for the identification of victims and determining the cause of death will normally be located at the temporary morgue. The accompanying support staff will include documentation officers, records officers, radiographers, dental technicians and morgue technicians. While the forensic pathologist passes his report on each body to the Coroner/Chief Medical Director's Office, the bodies are passed on to the funeral directors for further processing. These include cleaning, embalming and encoffing of the victims.

It is the responsibility of the Coroner/Chief Medical Examiner to decide at what stage to release the bodies to the next-of-kin. This is a partly legal and quasi political decision and the decision will be disaster specific. An inquest would be expectedly held in these cases where the Coroner system is practiced. Should there be a suspicion of homicide the matter would have to be referred to the Office of the Director of Public Prosecution in jurisdictions practicing the Coroner system while the District Attorney would take up the case after the Medical Examiner makes the appropriate ruling. These established protocols are foreign to the West African sub-region and the various experts are lacking.

Considering that problems such as post-traumatic stress is a major problem following major disasters, psychiatrists on the continent have somewhat risen to the challenge, particularly following the bombings at the U.S. Embassies in East

Africa.[15-17] The post-disaster debriefing and counseling are essential components of mass disaster management that is still foreign to governments in West Africa.

Even where the relevant technology has been effectively transferred, these developing societies need to improve on transportation. Where such networks do not exist, there is a need for them to be developed. This must be done contemporaneously with the education of the populace. The latter must know what is required of them or the government. The provision and maintenance of basic utilities such as power and water supplies, disposal of wastes, good medical care and effective communication are mandatory. These are essential considering that they are required for the setting up of temporary morgues to be used in cases of mass disasters.

As part of the investments, these societies must provide for the establishment of proper forensic laboratories. The latter should expectedly provide for forensic toxicology, trace evidence analysis and DNA studies. The laboratory should have capabilities to accommodate the forensic entomologists, forensic anthropologists, forensic radiologists, forensic odontologists, and other specialists.

The decision makers need to be educated on the importance of investing in the training of forensic specialists and always remember that their society is part of a larger global village. It is for this reason that support services provided by the police, fire department and local hospitals must be enhanced. The corruption within the system must be reduced to the barest minimum if complete elimination is impossible, although the latter is ideal. Corruption is one of the biggest problems in developing societies and this has permeated all levels of the society thus making meaningful investigations difficult.

Conclusion

Mass disasters are fairly common occurrences in the West African sub-region but there is a dearth of trained personnel locally, to deal with the problems. The various national governments do not consider it to be an area of priority, apart from the intertwined corruption. Another political consideration is that the nation's available resources are considered to be better invested on the living as opposed to the dead. In view of the involvement of nationalities across the board with regards to victimology, developed nations have a duty to invest in the local development of forensic personnel. A state of the art forensic laboratory is essential in these developing jurisdictions. For most of them, there is the need to develop laws and medico-legal systems that ensure that correct practices are enshrined in these jurisdictions.

The forensic experts so trained and the support staff should be dispersed across the continent and must be capable of instantaneous dispatch to areas of need. The regional centers for their primary location should include Nigeria, Ghana, Cameroon, Cote d'Ivoire, Kenya, Namibia, Zimbabwe, Senegal and South Africa. Their training and activities should be developed along the lines of the DMORT as well as the U.S. Federal Emergency Management Agency. Overall all participants need to appreciate a multi-disciplinary nature of their task and act accordingly.

References

1. Vardon-Smith G. Mass Disaster Organization. In: Forensic Medicine: Clinical and Pathological Aspects. Payne-James J, Busuttil A and Smock W. (eds). Chp 37. Greenwich Medical Media Ltd. San Francisco, London. 2003: 565–578.

2. Lunetta P, Ranta H, Cattaneo C, Piccinini A, Niskanen R, Sajantila A and Penttila A. 2003. International collaboration in mass disasters involving foreign nationals within EU. Int. J. Leg. Med. 117: 4; 204–210.

3. NAME Mass Fatality Plan. In: Disaster Mortuary Operational Response Teams. http://www.dmort.org

4. 1998 United States embassy bombings. http://en.wikipedia.org/1998_United_States_embassy_bombings

5. Selva M 2005. Rwanda's army accused of killing civilians after mass grave of hundreds is uncovered in Congo. http://news.independent.co.uk/world/africa/article317216.ece

6. National Population Commission of Nigeria: Nigerian Population Facts and Figures. http://www.population.gov.ng/factsandfigures.htm

7. Ghana. In: Encyclopedia of the Nations. http://www.nationsencyclopedia.com/Africa/Ghana-POPULATION.html

8. Adlakha A. International Briefs. Population Trends: Ghana. In: U.S. Department of Commerce Economics and Statistics Administration. Bureau of Census. July 1996.

9. Cameroon. In: Encyclopedia of the Nations. http://www.nationsencyclopedia.com/Africa/Cameroon-POPULATION.html

10. Kling GW, Clarke MA, Wagner GN, Compton HR, Humphrey AM, Devine JD, Evans WC, Lockwood JP, Tuttle ML and Koenigsberg EJ. 1987. The 1986 Lake Nyos Gas Disaster in Cameroon, West Africa. Science. 236: 4798; 169–175.

11. Finegan M. 1995. Killed in Action - Body Not Recovered: Forensic Anthropology and Archeology Applied to the Recovery of U.S. Military Remains in Vietnam. In: Proceedings of the American Academy of Forensic Sciences. Vol. 1, p. 175. American Academy of Forensic Sciences, Colorado Springs, CO.

12. Dirkmaat DC and Adovasio JM. The role of Archeology in the Recovery and Interpretation of Human Remains from an Outdoor Forensic Setting. In: Forensic Taphonomy: The Postmortem Fate of Human Remains. Haglund WD and Sorg MH (eds). Ch. 3 CRC Press. New York, London. 1996: 39–64.

13. Berryman HE, Potter JO and Oliver S. 1988. The Ill-Fated Passenger Steamer "Sultana:" An Inland Maritime Mass Disaster of Unparalleled Magnitude. J. For. Sci. 33: 842–850.

14. Sledzik P and Hunt D. 1995. When the Dead Return, Part 1: The Hardin Cemetry Disaster. In: Proceedings of the American Academy of forensic Sciences. Vol.1, p. 154–155. American Academy of Forensic Sciences, Colorado Springs, CO.

15. Nyamai CM and Njega FG. 2000. Post-traumatic stress disorder: case report. East Africa. Med. J. 77; 4: 228–230.

16. Njega FG, Nichols PJ, Nyamai C, Kigamwa P and Davidson JRT. 2004. Post-traumatic stress after terrorist attack: psychological reactions following the US bombing in Nairobi: naturalistic study. Brit. J Psych. 185: 328–333.

17. Bryant RA and Njega FG. 2006. Cultural sensitivity: making trauma assessment and treatment plans culturally relevant. J. Clin. Psych. 67; Suppl. 2: 74–79.

Chapter 18

Forensic Toxicology in Mass Disasters: From Specimen Preservation to Toxic Truth

Christopher Long, Ph.D.

Toxicology of Mass Disasters

The toxicology in mass disasters can help in causation identification. There are several examples where the toxicology explains what happened. The Jonestown mass suicide where over 100 people drank cyanide laced beverage and died. This was repeated in Fresno California where a group of people believed they would be taken aboard a space ship that trailed Halley's Comet. Other examples involve plane crashes and while the cause of death may appear as trauma, toxicology may provide a different one. The cushions used in the airplane seats have been made of a urethane, that when exposed to fire releases cyanide not to mention the carbon monoxide release during the fire.

In a mass disaster, such as plane crash, it is difficult to identify the deceased. The impact of the crash may cause a "splattering" of body parts and people may be co-mingled. Therefore, proper partitioning of the site in order to properly identify and collect samples is crucial. Once the specimens are collected and labeled properly they can be transferred to the toxicology laboratory.

The laboratory must identify the exhibits individually or grouped according to the method of specimen collection. In disasters involving only 2 or 3 people it is reasonable to tests multiple specimens, however, with larger numbers it may not be possible.

The first question for the toxicologist is the method of exposure. This will help identify the type of compound(s) involved. While there are exceptions, generally toxins leave a trail as to how they entered the human body. The defining factor for the route of exposure depends upon how much toxin is required for producing harmful effects. If a material is very toxic then inhalation is an acceptable route of administration. If more toxin is required then oral, or via the gastrointestinal tract is the choice. Dermal absorption is not a reasonable route because of the protective nature of the skin and it's multiple layers. The shin, eyes and mucosal membranes will demonstrate irritation and ulceration if the exposure is of a caustic nature.

Chemical weapons are in actuality directed against the civilian population. The reasons are two fold. The first is that the military have the protective apparel, antidotes and training to survive the chemical attack. The civilian population does not. The second is that attacks at "home" are demoralizing for the military troops. The worry about their loved ones back home. Compounds such as "Mustard Gas" produces severe damage to the skin and mucosal membranes producing a very ugly, painful picture.

Anthrax is similar in producing dermal lesions and can be spread by a single individual. The Ebola virus is also transmitted from person to person with a fatal result. The problem with these biological weapons is to produce a significant quantity without indiscriminant killing.

The biggest problem for those attacking with chemical weapons is the delivery system. That is, how do they get the toxic material to the target group? The second biggest problem is to manufacture and transport the toxin without dying, as this would "tip off" the intended targets, not that life their life would be important.

In this evaluation it becomes possible to determine what type chemical agent was used based on the method of delivery, the observations of toxicity and the pathology. Pathology demonstrates the change in tissue structures as a result of toxic injury. Whether or not the toxin remains in the tissue is not as important as the identification of the injury.

Several poisons produce toxic metabolites while the parent compound is virtually non-toxic. One such example is ethylene glycol (antifreeze). This chemical is fatal as a result of it's metabolites, or breakdown products. The parent chemical is metabolized and may not be detected, but the pathology of the oxalate and acidosis remains. Ethylene glycol requires oral administration of approximately 100 milliliters for a potential fatality. This is generally not a problem because ethylene glycol is sweet tasting and can be added to any number of beverages. Part of the effect is acidosis with nausea, and vomiting. Without proper treatment the individual expires with a slow prolonged painful death.

Chemical inhalants produce a much faster death. Sarin, an anticholinesterase, produces death by over stimulation of the cholinergic nervous system. The immediate effects produce stimulation followed by blockade of that part of the nervous system.

Certain toxins act on the energy generating system of the body, that is, oxidative phosphorolation. When this sequential process involving cytochromes is stopped, there is no energy for the body. Oxygen cannot be utilized by the body and death results. Cyanide generally produces a blue-ish color to the body and potentially a smell of almonds (or amaretto liquor). Unfortunately, 1 in 5 people cannot smell the almond odor.

If pesticides are suspected then chemistries, especially cholinesterase inhibition, are required. These type compounds, or at least the more toxic, produce effects similar to Sarin. This test requires a quick sampling and testing as it is checking for an enzyme that will breakdown providing a false negative. In cases where the toxin produces an allergic reaction, such as anaphylaxis, then a tryptase level would be an appropriate test in postmortem blood.

In mass disasters there are several categories of potentially toxic material or drug that should be prioritized for analysis. This is a screening technique for multiple compounds and classes of compounds in order to test for as many potential toxins as possible.

The first category is volatile components. This would include the usual ethanol, methanol, acetone acetaldehyde. Other organics, such as benzene, hexanes, ketones and toluene require a longer analytical analysis time and higher temperatures. These components would be from a potential fire accelerant contamination or an explosion.

Gaseous toxins must also be considered. These would include carbon monoxide and cyanide at a minimum. Other potential volatiles could be from leaking Freon condenser coils. The best analysis is a longer chromatographic analysis to insure proper separation of the components. Misidentification of acetaldehyde as methanol and decompositionase as toluene have occurred. Highly volatile compounds, such as ethyl ether would not generally be expected in blood testing because they evaporate too rapidly. If a compound is inhaled then the brain, being lipid, would be an excellent specimen in volatile determination as it would retain the volatile. The lung would be next as lipids coat the inside of alveoli and they would trap the volatiles.

Certain compounds are not reasonably identified. Nitrogen and helium are two such compounds. The major problem with these two elemental gases is atmospheric contamination. Once a sample is exposed to the air, these gases can be solublized and retained by the sample making any differentiation between toxic and normal exposure impossible.

Carbon monoxide can determine if the person was alive during the fire. However, a CO-Oximeter may not provide the correct result such as in the Waco standoff. Carbon monoxide (CO) saturation concentrations were reported to contain 20% using a CO-Oximeter. This does support that it was the fire that was responsible for the deaths. However, individuals that had died 6 months earlier also were reported at 20% saturation. The conclusion is that something is interfering with the CO testing, possibly sulfoxy-hemoglobin from sulfur in the drinking water. A better test would have been the traditional ultra-violet-visible scan. With this test the scan of the wavelengths is printed and it is clearly discernable if the result is carbon monoxide or something else.

In other cases where blood is available testing can follow a normal routine. The better analytical techniques depend on immunoassays and chromatography. The immunoassays are an allergic type reaction in a test tube. This is a test where an antibody is developed for a drug or drug class and if allergic there is reaction which identifies the class or drug. The problem with this type assay is that the test is only available for major classes of drugs (amphetamines, opiates, cannabinoids, phencyclidine, cocaine, etc.) and is too complicated to develop a single assay. Once positive with an immunoassay, further testing is required. This generally is gas chromatography mass spectroscopy (GCMS).

The term chromatography refers to separation, gas chromatography means separation in a gas phase. One test that is excellent for screening is gas chromatography with a nitrogen-phosphorous detector (GC-NPD). This detector is 5000 times more sensitive to nitrogen containing compounds than carbon. Fortunately, most drugs and toxins have a nitrogen group and can be detected by this instrument.

The "gold standard" for chromatography is GC-MS. While not as sensitive as the GC-NPD it has the advantage of providing molecular structure identification. This is of particular benefit when the results get challenged. Newer types of mass spectrometers include liquid chromatography mass spectroscopy and tandem mass spectroscopy. Each of these has specific benefits and liabilities.

With the screening using the prior instrumentation many of the potential toxins can be identified. One exception is metals. Arsenic, lead and thallium are potential poisons. The amounts required for toxicity would generally mandate oral administration. Arsenic can be made into a gas as arsine gas. This is quite fatal, requiring only a few breaths and inhalation is the route of administration.

Once the analytical testing has been completed the results must paired to the pathology of the body and the circumstances of death. In this way can mass disasters be better understood for the future. The disasters can be avoided because of past experiences and investigations of this type can serve as an early warning to potential disasters.

References

Armdur, Mary et al. (ed.) Casarett and Doull's Toxicology 4th Edition. New York: Pergammon Press, 1991

Ellenhorn, Matthew et al. (ed.) Medical Toxicology. New York: Elsevier, 1988.

Goldfrank, Lewis R. et al. (ed.) *Goldfrank's Toxiclogic Emergencies, 4th Edition*. Norwalk, Conn.: Appleton & Lange, 1990.

Hardman, Joel et al. (ed.) Goodman and Gilman's The Pharmacologic Basis of Therapeutics 10th Edition. New York: McGraw Hill, 2001.

Chapter 19

Survival Time and Activity Prior to Death in Fatal Head Trauma: Part I

Erin H. Kimmerle, Ph.D., Matthias Okoye, M.D., J.D. and Sue
Gabriel, B.S.N., M.S.S., M.S.N.

Introduction

Being aware of the length of time that elapses between fatal cranio-cerebral injuries and death, as well as the level of activity the injured person was capable of, is important for scene reconstructions in police investigations and in courtroom testimony. Victims of these types of injuries are often found dead. The lack of witnesses or subsequent medical intervention leaves investigators with unanswered questions regarding the circumstances surrounding the death.

Since the brain regulates motor activities and vital functions, we would expect direct injuries to it to differ from those to other aspects of the body and that immediate death or at least immediate collapse without the ability for activity to occur. Yet numerous studies such as, Spitz and colleagues in 1961 and Karger 1995, have reported cases of suicide involving multiple gunshot injuries, and numerous examples of delayed incapacitation following fatal cranio-cerebral injuries (refer also to Elkin 1936, Clyne 1955, Halpern and Aldrete 1979, Mandal et al. 1979, Ahoa nd Vuori 1980, Demetriades and van der Veen 1983, Moar 1984, Thoresen and Rognum 1986, Levy and Rao 1988, Betz et al. 1997, Karger and Brinkman 1997, Karger and DuChesne 1997, Webb et al. 1999, Oehmichen et al. 2001). In this review, we found that 41.0 percent of individuals survived for a short period of time and that 6.0 percent of those individuals were able to perform some level of activity such as carry on a conversation, fight back, or walk a short distance. Therefore, a number of variables are investigated to determine what set these cases apart from the rest.

Methods

Beginning in 1998, we initiated a comprehensive study of gunfire and deeply penetrating sharp force injuries, and blunt force trauma. The mechanism of injury within the blunt force trauma category includes Motor Vehicle Accidents (MVA), Assault, Child Abuse, Falling or Crushing Injuries, and Explosions (Table 19.1). We reviewed autopsy cases, dating 1987-2000, from the Lancaster County Coroner's Office in Lincoln, Nebraska; the Cook County Medical Examiner's Office in Chicago, Illinois; and the Knox County Medical Examiner's Office in Knoxville, Tennessee. Over 6,250 autopsies were performed during this time frame, however only a portion of those qualified for this study (n=213). Preliminary findings and methods have been previously addressed (Okoye and Kimmerle 2000, Kimmerle et al. 2002).

Strict criteria were followed to determine whether cases were applicable to this study. The mechanism of death was central respiratory failure secondary to cerebral edema and compression of the midbrain. The time of injury and the time of biological death had to be known. This is an important point because often the time of death listed represents the time the individual was pronounced dead rather than the actual time of biological death. Therefore, the death of each individual was witnessed. Data for this study was retrieved from death certificates, emergency medical records, and autopsy, coroner, and police reports.

Table 19.1
Classification of Cranio-Cerebral Injuries (n=213)

Type of Injury	Sample Size
Gunfire Injury	76
Blunt Force Trauma (n=131):	
Motor Vehicle Accident	105
Assault	5
Child Abuse	5
Falling, Crushing, Explosions	16
Sharp Force Trauma	6

Five categories were created to explain and group the activities present following injury:

Activity Level = 1: Immediate death.

Activity Level = 2: Immediate collapse.
Vital signs present but low, meaning the person was alive, but exhibited no physical activity.

Activity Level = 3: Minimal physical activity.
Activities included pulling out medical intravenous lines and is mostly characterized by agitated behavior, confused verbal responses, or other signs of shock.

Activity Level = 4: Moderate activity.
In this category individuals were fully alert, they knew what happened, often asked for help, and occasionally walked a short distance, such as staggering across the room.

Activity Level = 5: Maximum activity.
This category consisted of cases where victims walked a substantial distance and even drove a car.

Descriptive statistics were compiled to generalize trends in the data, test for normalcy, and describe the characteristics of each injury. Second, the data were quantified for linear, stepwise regression analysis, using dummy variables for categorical data, with the use of the statistical package, SPSS for Windows, Rel. 11.0.1. (2001. Chicago: SPSS Inc.). The logarithmic transformations of time, internal blood loss, and number of wounds were used in order to decrease the variance and normalize the distributions and were used to investigate the statistical power of estimating influential variables in survival time and level of activity. The variables we investigated have been discussed in the survival time literature as important determining factors. They include: the type of weapon; location of injuries; number, size, and track of the wound(s); amount of blood loss; presence of alcohol or drugs, amount of activity from time of injury to death. Additional variables specific to gunfire injuries include: the distance of the shot and the caliber of the weapon. Finally, the position of the deceased in fatal motor vehicle accidents with resulting blunt force trauma and the use of safety belts are assessed.

Results

Our test results show that the presence of alcohol and drugs (56.8 percent) does not directly influence survival time or activity per se, however, they do affect blood loss, which in turn influences survival time and therefore activity. In gunfire and sharp force injuries, internal blood loss measured less than 500 ml, in 60.0 percent of cases. Further, 55.3 percent of gunfire injuries are single deeply penetrating gunshot injuries to the head, which means that in a small majority of cases, the bullet does not exit the cranium. The most commonly used firearms were .22 and .45 caliber weapons; each occurring in 23.8 percent of cases. The majority of gunfire and sharp force trauma victims are male, 85.0 percent (35/41) of cases, and nearly 70.0 percent (29/41) of all victims are under the age of thirty years old.

Gunfire Injuries

In one example of a single gunshot wound to the forehead of a 13 year old girl, the frontal bone exhibited a 6 x 4.2 cm circular defect, with a 4.1 cm fracture extending anterior-posteriorly. A subgaleal hemorrhage was present. Further, there is an 8cm wide separation between the parietals, along the sagittal suture, which is a common occurrence among juveniles whose sutures are not yet fused. There is a 6 x 7 cm frontal lobe laceration with an extensive subdural hematoma throughout. The falx cerebellum and sagittal sinus are also lacerated. The bullet did not exit. Instead it ricocheted off the wall of the occipital bone, lodging in the left cerebral hemisphere. This victim was immediately incapacitated but survived 9 hours and 15 minutes, with medical intervention.

Overall, among the single gun shot cases we reviewed, 52.5 percent (33/61) survived for 12 minutes to 4 and 1/2 days (98/45 hr/min). The amount of activity among those short term survivors ranged from immediate collapse with life but no activity, to a minimal amount of activity meaning the individual was agitated, capable of verbal responses or slight involuntary movements.

Cases of multiple gunshot wounds tended to be more varied. Overall, there were fewer short term survivors, however, those who did tended to live for a slightly longer period of time, ranging from 14 minutes to 4 and 1/2 days (111/54 hr/min). The amount of activity among those short term survivors ranged from immediate collapse, to a maximum amount of activity (phase 5) including one individual who was able to continue driving his car a short distance after receiving one shot to the occipital region of his skull, and two through and through shots to his mid back and upper right arm.

Cranio-cerebral injuries are unique due to the anatomy of the brain being enclosed by the skull that is a rigid, fixed structure. As a result, there is a limited amount of space for bleeding and edema to accumulate. Increased intracranial pressure leads to swelling and eventually herniation. Time is needed for bleeding and the development of hematomas and cerebral edema. These delayed events may themselves lead to death. The hemorrhages listed in Table 19.2 serve as a measure of the amount and location of bleeding. Their differential prevalence is suggestive of the wound trajectory and track. Subarachnoid hemorrhages were the most common type among gunfire cases. Few victims survived long enough for the formation of subdural hematomas or the development of cerebral edema.

Survival time is regressed on the type of injury, blood loss, presence of alcohol or drugs of abuse (Cocaine, Ecgonine Methyl Ester, Marijuana, THC

Metabolite), number of wounds, and range of fire (Table 19.3). Non-significant variables were excluded through the stepwise process, where as, range of fire is shown to have the only significant influence on decreasing survival time (t=1.901, p=.061). This verifies that survival time is shorter with contact injuries due to the amount of damage caused by contact injuries which significantly exceeds that by shots fired from a distance.

Table 19.2
Percentage of Cases with Cranio-Cerebral Hemorrhages and Edema: Gunfire Injuries (GSW)

	Single GSW	Multiple GSW	Total GSW
Cerebral Edema	11.8%	11.8%	11.0%
Subarachnoid	55.9%	35.3%	59.1%
Subgaleal	30.3%	11.7%	18.4%
Subdural Hemorrhage	32.0%	0	25.0%
Subdural Hematoma	3.4%	6.0%	4.0%

Table 19.3
Survival Time—Gunfire Injuries

R	R Square	df	F	p
.223	.050	1	3.614	0.061
Model 1	b	Std. Error	t	p
Range of Fire	9.285	4.884	1.901	0.061
Predictors: Type of Injury, No. Wounds, Drugs/Alcohol, Blood Loss				

Blunt Force Trauma

Within the category blunt force trauma, motor vehicle accidents (MVA), assult, child abuse, falls, explosions, and crushing injuries were reviewed. Among MVA, over half of the individuals (57.1 percent) survived for a short time period ranging from 1 minute to 75 hours and 32 minutes. The pattern of activity after injury extends beyond that of single gunshot wound cases, ranging from immediate collapse to a moderate amount of activity including victims who where fully alert, able to ask for help, or walk a short distance. Compared to single gunfire cases, fewer individuals died immediately. However, unlike gunfire injuries, all MVA victims had multiple injuries throughout the body, including severe injuries to the chest in 93.3 percent of cases and to the abdomen in 82.9 percent of cases. MVA fatalities most commonly involved the drivers and front passengers, followed by pedestrians (Table 19.4). In one case, an 88 year old female was struck by a garbage truck. She suffered a 7.5 by 4.5 cm left parietal subgaleal hemorrhage and several contusions and fractures to the lower extremities. Immediately following the accident she exhibited high levels of activity such as walking and talking, however, she died 13 days later. Her medical chart indicated that she died upon "just giving up".

Interestingly, 45.0 percent of people involved in MVA's who were located inside the vehicle did not use seatbelts (37/82). Survival time was regressed on the usage of seatbelts and on the location of the victim within the vehicle, or as a pedestrian (Tables 19.4–6) and both are statistically significant for predicting survival time. Pedestrians survived significantly longer than victims who were located in vehicles, but were generally capable of less activity and were less likely to remain conscious. The location of the victim, within the vehicle did not significantly correlate to survival time.

Table 19.4
Motor Vehicle Accidents

Position	n	Safety Belts Used	Alcohol/Drugs Present
Driver	42.0%	25.0%	39.0%
Front Passenger	26.8%	21.0%	44.4%
Rear Passenger	7.1%	0	37.5%
Pedestrian	23.2%	0	34.6%

Table 19.5
Survival Time—Use of Safety Belts

R	R Square	df	F	p
.266	.071	1	3.515	0.067
Model 1	b	Std. Error	t	p
Safety Belt Used	38.364	20.464	1.875	0.067

Table 19.6
Survival Time—Position of Victim

R	R Square	df	F	p
.214	.046	1	5.213	0.024
Model 1	b	Std. Error	t	P
Pedestrian	50.924	22.303	2.283	0.024
Predictors: Driver, Front Passenger, Rear Passenger				

Among drivers involved in MVA's, 39.0 percent tested positive for alcohol and/or other drugs of abuse. Survival time was regressed on the presence of these drugs. Alcohol was shown to be a marginally significant predictor of whether a person with fatal cranio-cerebral injuries was capable of any level of activity. However, there appears to be no significant relationship between alcohol usage and survival time (Table 19.7).

Note that like gunfire injuries, the prevalence of subdural hematomas was low, just under 4.0 percent (Table 19.8). However, cerebral edema was present in 28.6 percent of cases. This is more than double what was observed among gunfire victims. Further, the overall prevalence of cerebral hemorrhaging was high and exceeded that of gunfire cases. This is explained in part by the overall longer survival time of victims of blunt force trauma. Further, it is clear that measurement of the grade of edema at the time of autopsy would be more useful than the descriptive terms usually applied, such as mild or moderate. All cases exhibited subdural and subarachnoid hemorrhages. Further, 80.0 percent (5/6) of individuals survived for a minimum of 45 minutes to 117/45 (hr/min). Finally, cerebral edema was present in 40.0 percent of cases. However, despite the overall tendency for short term survival, all of these individuals immediately collapsed and were rendered unconscious.

Table 19.7
Cranio-Cerebral Hemorrhages and Edema—MVA

Type of Hemorrhage	Frequency
Cerebral Hemorrhage	28.6%
Subarachnoid Hemorrhage	74.3%
Subgaleal Hemorrhage	63.8%
Subdural Hemorrhage	65.7%
Subdural Hematoma	3.8%

Table 19.8
Sharp Force Injuries to the Head (n=6)

Case	Profile	Blood Loss	Survival Time	Activity
Case 1	35 year, Male	1000 cc	35 minutes	4
Case 2	23 year, Male	500 cc	17 minutes	5
Case 3	35 year, Female	300 cc	0 minutes	1
Case 4	38 year, Female	960 cc	2 hours, 50 minutes	2
Case 5	63 year, Male	200 cc	0 minutes	1
Case 6	33 year, Male	640 cc	10 hours, 45 minutes	2

We reviewed five adult cases of assault and five cases of child abuse, all of whom were under the age of 3 years old. Among cases of child abuse, the location and severity of injury to the brain varied but they all survived a minimum of 27 minutes. Findings pertaining to activity level were consistent with the assault cases reviewed among adults in that death was not immediate however, each of the children immediately collapsed and were rendered unconscious.

Other types of blunt force trauma included in our review resulted from crushing, falls, and explosions. The majority of these victims survived a minimum of 25 minutes. Activities ranged from agitated behavior to walking around and asking for help.

Table 19.9
Cranio-Cerebral Hemorrhages and Edema: Sharp Force Injury (SFT)

Variable	n	Survival Time
Cerebral Edema	1	10 hour, 45 minutes
Subarachnoid	1	No time
Subgaleal	3	Cases range: 0 survival time to 10 hours, 45 minutes
Subdural Hemorrhage	0	No time
Subdural Hematoma	1	No time

Sharp Force Trauma

Table 19.8 lists the six cases of fatal cranio-cerebral injuries due to sharp force injuries. In all six cases the manner of death was homicide. In two cases, both blunt force injuries and sharp force injuries to the head and body were present. In both of these cases, the activity level of the victims was either immediate collapse or incapacitation, however, one survived for 10 hours and 45 minutes, whereas in the other case, death was immediately fatal. The cases with the shortest survival time, suffered less blood loss and less activity. Activity levels can be summarized as the following: 1) among two cases there was no survival time, 2) among the two victims who immediately collapsed, they survived the longest amount of time (2 hours and 50 minutes; and 10 hours and 45 minutes), 3) the two cases in the middle, survived 17 and 35 minutes respectively and performed high levels of activity (stages 5 and 4, respectively).

Summary

We reviewed 213 cases of fatal cranio-cerebral injuries resulting from numerous causes in order to account for the variation in survival time and levels of activity. Overall, the type of injury and presence of alcohol or drugs of abuse significantly influenced both survival time and activity. If we look at gunfire wounds separately from blunt force trauma, interesting patterns emerge. Immediate death was less likely among cases of assault, child abuse, and injuries due to falls, than that associated with gunfire wounds, motor vehicle accidents or explosions because of a lower amount of force dispersed when the wound is inflicted, resulting in less tissue damage.

Second, activity and time are not in and of themselves correlated. Victims of MVA's tend to be more active than those with GSW's, although victims tend to survive for a shorter amount of time. Finally, the use of seatbelts, location of the victim as pedestrian rather than in a vehicle, and the presence of alcohol or drugs are significant variables, accounting for 46.0 percent of the variation among MVA victims. In other words, the variables investigated illustrate patterns in the levels of activity and time, however neither can be predicted. The extreme variation in these cases may be explained by further analysis of the specific region of the brain or blood vessels damaged, or may be secondary to intangible elements such as a person's will to live, general constitution, or preexisting health conditions.

Acknowledgments

Accomplishing this research would not have possible without Drs. Mitra Kalelkar, Sandra Elkins, and William McCormick who made their case work available. We would also like to thank Dr. Kathy Haden, Dr. Richard Jantz, Dr. Lee Medows Jantz, Dr. Lyle Konigsberg, and Ms. Tami Ruth for their assistance throughout the research and analytical processes.

References

Aho AJ and J Vuori. 1980 Penetrating Abdominal Injuries with Special Reference to Knife Wounds. Acta Chir Scand 146:47-54

Betz, P, D Stiefel, R Hausmann, W Eisenmenger. Fractures at the base of the skull in gunshots to the head. Forensic Science International, 1997 86(3), 155-161

CLYNE AJ. The wounding and killing power of small-arms fire in jungle operations. J R Army Med Corps. 1955 Jan;101(1):33-8.

Demetriades D and van der Veen BW. 1983 Penetrating Injuries of the Heart: Experience over Two Years in South Africa. Journal of Trauma 23(12):1034-1041

Elkin DC. 1936 Wounds of the Heart: Report of Thirteen Cases. Journal of Thoracic Surgery. Nineteenth Annual Meeting of the American Association for Thoracic Surgery at Rochester, Minnesota. May pp. 590-603

Halpern NB and Aldrete JS. 1979 Factors Influencing Mortality and Morbidity form Injuries to the Abdominal Aorta and Inferior Vena Cava. American Journal of Surgery 137:384-388

Karger, B. Penetrating gunshots to the head and lack of immediate incapacitation. II. Review of case reports. INTERNATIONAL JOURNAL OF LEGAL MEDICINE. 1995, VOL 108; NUMBER 3, pages 117-126

Karger, B. Brinkman, B. Multiple gunshot suicides: potential for physical activity and medico-legal aspects. INTERNATIONAL JOURNAL OF LEGAL MEDICINE. 1997, VOL 110; NUMBER 4, pages 188-192

Karger, B. DuChesne, A. Who fired the gun? A casuistic contribution to the differentiation between self-inflicted and non-self-inflicted gunshot wounds. INTERNATIONAL JOURNAL OF LEGAL MEDICINE. 1997, VOL 110; NUMBER 1, pages 33-35

Kimmerle EH, Okoye M, Gabriel S (2002) Characteristics of Different Types of Fatal Head Trauma and the Factors that Influence Survival Time and Activity Prior to Death. American Academy of Forensic Sciences, Academy's 54th Annual Meeting, February, Atlanta, GA.

Levy V and Rao V. 1988   Survival Time in Gunshot and Stab Wound Victims. American Journal of Forensic Medicine and Pathology 9(3):215-217

Mandal AK, Awariefe AO, Oparah SS. 1979 Experience in the management of 50 consecutive penetrating wounds of the heart. Br. J. Surg. 66:565-568

Moar JJ. 1984 Homicidal penetrating incised wounds of the thorax. SA MEDIESE TYDSKRIF DEEL 65(10):385-389

Oehmichen, M, C Meissner, HG König Brain injury after survived gunshot to the head: reactive alterations at sites remote from the missile track. Forensic Science International, 2001 Forensic Science International, Volume 115, Issue 3, Pages 189-197

Okoye M, Kimmerle EH (2000) Survival Time in Fatal Penetrating Sharp Force and Gunfire Injuries. American Academy of Forensic Sciences, Academy's 52nd Annual Meeting, Reno, Nevada.

Spitz WU, Petty CS, Fisher RS (1961) Physical activity until collapse following fatal injury by firearms and sharp pointed weapons. Journal of Forensic Science 6(3):290-300.

SPSS for Windows, Rel. 11.0.1. (2001. Chicago: SPSS Inc.).

Thoresen SO and Rognum TO. 1986 Survival Time and Acting Capability After Fatal Injury by Sharp Weapons. Forensic Science International 31:181-187

Webb, E, JP Wyatt, J Henry, A Busuttil. A comparison of fatal with non-fatal knife injuries in Edinburgh. Forensic Science International, 99 (1999), pp. 179-187.

Chapter 20

Survival Time and Activity Prior to Death in Fatal Trauma to the Body and Limbs: Part II

Erin H. Kimmerle, Ph.D. and Matthias Okoye, M.D., J.D.

Introduction

As discussed in the preceding chapter, the time a person survives following a fatal injury and the level of activity for which they are capable during that time has important legal and medical implications. The purpose of this chapter is to expand the discussion of survival time and activity level in cases of fatal injury to the body and limbs. The amount of time and activity between gunfire or deeply penetrating sharp force injuries and death are important for scene reconstructions in police investigations and in court room testimony. Victims of these types of injuries are often found dead. The lack of witnesses or subsequent medical intervention means that investigators are left with unanswered questions regarding the circumstances surrounding the death. Furthermore, studies on this topic have been largely qualitative in nature, providing descriptive statistics and examples of extreme variation. Patterns are not easily predicted, even in cases with the same types of injuries. Consequently, these studies have lead to conflicting results in the published record.

In our own experience, we have seen considerable variation in survival time and activity. In one case, a fifty-six year old male, shot twice with a 12-gauge shotgun in the anterior thorax, was immediately incapacitated. He suffered seventeen wounds, bilateral hemothoraces, hemopericardium, and pulmonary edema. In a second case, a twenty-four year old male was shot with a .38 caliber pistol, also in the anterior thorax. He survived thirty-five minutes and was able to run out of the apartment and down the street one-half block prior to collapsing. There, the paramedics recovered him in full cardiac arrest. He suffered a wound to the heart, massive hemopericardium, cardiac tamponade, and a massive left hemothorax. Further, 1,440 milliliters of blood was recovered from the left pleural cavity.

What explains this variation? Numerous researchers have reported similar findings of unusual activity following fatal injuries or offered analyses of variables likely to be contributing factors (refer also to Elkin 1936, Clyne 1955, Halpern and Aldrete 1979, Mandal et al. 1979, Ahoa nd Vuori 1980, Demetriades and van der Veen 1983, Moar 1984, Thoresen and Rognum 1986, Levy and Rao 1988, Betz et al. 1997, Karger and Brinkman 1997, Karger and DuChesne 1997, Webb et al. 1999, Oehmichen et al. 2001, Okoye and Kimmerle 2000, Kimmerle et al. 2002). Factors discussed in the literature as variables in survival time and activity such as the role of alcohol and drugs of abuse; the particular structures and blood vessels damaged; the amount of blood loss; the wound type, number, and location; and the caliber of the weapon and range of fire in gunfire cases are explored in this chapter. Further, the different regions of the body and particular location of injury are further investigated for gunfire and deeply penetrating sharp force injuries.

Materials and Methods

Quantitative analyses were used to determine the statistical power of estimating influential variables in survival time and activity. The data for this study come from death certificates, emergency medical records, and autopsy, coroner, and police reports. Cases dating 1980–1999, from the Lancaster County Coroner's Office in Lincoln, Nebraska; from 1995–1999 at the Cook County Medical Examiner's Office in Chicago, Illinois; and the Knox County Medical Examiner's Office in Knoxville, Tennessee, were reviewed.

Over 6,250 autopsies were preformed during this time frame. Gunfire or deeply penetrating sharp force trauma was the cause of death in over 615 cases. However, only n=120 or approximately 20 percent of these cases qualified for this analysis. Strict criteria were followed to determine whether cases were applicable to this study. First, the cause of death was gunfire injury or deeply penetrating sharp force injury. Second, the mechanism of death was cardio-respiratory failure from bleeding. Cases with complications, such as pneumonia, were omitted. Third, the time of injury and the time of biological death had to be known. This is an important point because often the time of death listed is the time the individual was pronounced dead. This may differ by minutes, hours, or even days from the actual time of biological death. This meant that the death of each individual was witnessed by a police officer, civilian, or medical personal.

Descriptive statistics were compiled to generalize trends in the data, test for normalcy, and describe the characteristics of each injury. Second, the data were quantified for linear, stepwise regression analysis, using dummy variables for categorical data, with the use of the statistical package, SPSS for Windows, Rel. 11.0.1. (2001. Chicago: SPSS Inc.). The logarithmic transformations of time, internal blood loss, and number of wounds were used in order to decrease the variance and normalize the distributions. Five categories were created to explain and group the activities present following injury:

Activity Level = 1: Immediate death.

Activity Level = 2: Immediate collapse.
Vital signs present but low, meaning the person was alive, but exhibited no physical activity.

Activity Level = 3: Minimal physical activity.
Activities included pulling out medical intravenous lines and is mostly characterized by agitated behavior, confused verbal responses, or other signs of shock.

Activity Level = 4: Moderate activity.
In this category individuals were fully alert, they knew what happened, often asked for help, and occasionally walked a short distance, such as staggering across the room.

Activity Level = 5: Maximum activity.
This category consisted of cases where victims walked a substantial distance and even drove a car.

Results

The demographic profile of this sample includes 105 males and 15 females. Ages ranged from 5 to 63 years old. Of the cases investigated here, 80.0 percent were homicide. The remaining 20 percent included suicides, accidents and indeterminate cases. Approximately 57.0 percent of cases (n=68) were single gunfire injuries, 35.0 percent (n=42) were multiple gunfire injuries and 8.3 percent (n=10) were stab wounds. The number of wounds in single gunfire injuries ranged from 1 to 5. This was due to exit and re-entry of a single missile into the body. The average number of wounds in multiple gunfire injuries was seven (n=7), although the number of wounds ranged from 1 to 30. Whereas, the number of wounds in sharp force trauma range from 1 to 3.

Among gunfire cases, 90.0 percent of injuries resulted from handguns and just under 19.5 percent of cases were contact range. 3.9 percent of gunfire cases were multiple gunshot injuries that included cases with both contact and non-contact injuries. The only known weapons used in sharp force trauma cases were standard kitchen knives and butcher knives. In most cases these injuries were associated with superficial cuts and defense wounds on the hands and forearms. Alcohol or drugs of abuse (Cocaine, Ecgonine Methyl Ester, Marijuana, THC Metabolite) were present in 38.0 percent of cases.

Figure 20.1 illustrates a bi-modal activity distribution, which suggests there are really two categories at work, not five. Essentially, persons either sustained injuries that cause immediate death or which allow them to live a short while but with no activity, or, they sustain injuries that allow them minimal to extended activity for a given period of time. Consequently, for the regression analyses, the data were re-grouped into a dicotomous variable separating "no activity" (based on categorical levels 1 and 2) from "activity present" (categories 3-5).

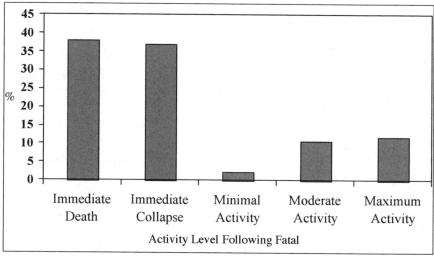

Figure 20.1 Bar graph depicting percentage of cases within each activity level, following fatal injuries. Notice the bimodal distribution, where cases tend to result in immediate death or incapacitation verses a small number of cases where individuals exhibit varying levels of activity.

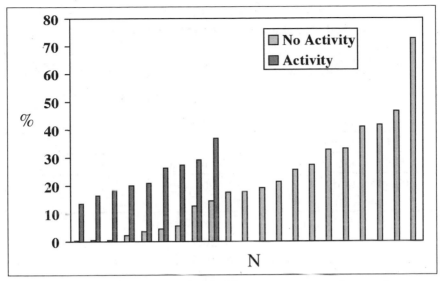

Figure 20.2 *Individuals were divided into two groups, those who exhibited activity, and those who did not. The amount of blood loss for each group is represented by the percentage of cases, within each group.*

If survival time and activity are broken down by anatomical region of the body injured, we find that overall 25.0 percent (n=21) of post-cranial cases engaged in some type of physical activity following injuries (Table 20.1). Injuries to the abdomen resulted in survival time of at least 28 minutes and to up to 13 hours and 48 minutes. Further, activity was present in 100 percent (n=4) of injuries to the abdomen. Injuries to the posterior thorax resulted in survival time that ranged from 0 time to 1 hour and 18 minutes. Injuries to the anterior thorax ranged from 0 time to 41 hours and 38 minutes. Activity was present in 40.0 percent (n=2) of cases with injuries to either the anterior or posterior thorax. Whereas, injuries to the extremities resulted in survival time that ranged from a minimum survival time of 51 minutes up to 14 hours. Activity is present in 50.0 percent (n=1) of these cases. Ironically, the longest survival time occurred in individuals with a combination of these regions injured, ranging from 0 time to 89 hours and 45 minutes. Activity was present in 21.4 percent (n=6) cases. Finally, injuries to the neck resulted in no survival time.

Table 20.1
Survival time and activity level by anatomical region

Anatomical Region	Survival Time Range	Activity Present
Neck	0 survival time	None
Abdomen	28 min–13 hours, 48 minutes	100% Cases
Posterior Thorax	0–1 hour, 18 minutes	40% Cases
Extremities	51 minutes–14 hours	50% Cases
Combination of Multiple Regions	0–89 hours, 45 minutes	21.4% Cases

Table 20.2
Regression Model for Survival Time (n=111)

R	R Square	df	F	p
.519	.270	1	17.355	<0.001
Model 1	b	Std. Error	t	p
No. Wounds	-1.292	.310	-4.166	<0.001
Predictors: Location of Wound, Type of Injury, Number of Wounds, Drugs/Alcohol Present, Blood Loss				

Table 20.3
Regression Model for Activity (n=41)

R	R Square	df	F	p
.511	.261	2	6.175	0.005
Model 1	b	Std. Error	t	p
Time	0.202	.0.067	3.029	0.005
Blood Loss	0.314	.0116	2.709	0.010
Predictors: Location of Wound, Type of Injury, Number of Wounds, Drugs/Alcohol Present, Blood Loss, Time				

Survival time was regressed on the location of the injury, type of injury, blood loss, presence of alcohol and drugs, and number of wounds. Non-significant variables were excluded through the stepwise process. Table 20.2 shows the increased number of wounds has the greatest influence on decreasing survival time. Injury to the abdomen, compared with other regions of the body, correlated highest to greater survival time with a r=0.122 correlation. However, this is a weak correlation and there is not a significant relationship between any the anatomical regions/structures injured or the type of injury with survival time. When the same model is applied to the dependent variable, activity, we find that both time and blood loss significantly influence whether or not there is activity following injury (Table 20.3).

If immediate death, verses short term survival is investigated, in the same manner as activity, the result varies. The number of wounds is the only significant factor influencing short term survival (Table 20.4).

When the same model is applied, but the dependent variable is changed to blood loss, there are several variables that in fact predict the amount of bleeding, and therefore have an indirect effect on activity and survival time (Table 20.5). The presence of alcohol or drugs and the number of wounds most greatly influences the amount of blood loss. Generally, more wounds are expected in multiple gunfire cases, however, the number of wounds in single cases of gunfire averaged greater than 1 and ranged from of 1 to 5. As each of these models demonstrates, it is misleading to discuss these cases in terms of single or multiple gunfire. It is more accurate to discuss them in terms of the specific number of injuries.

Table 20.4
Regression Model for Survival Time (n=110)

R	R Square	df	F	p
.570	.325	1	22.171	<0.001
Model 1	b	Std. Error	t	p
No. Wounds	-0.610	0.130	-4.709	<0.001
Predictors: Location of Wound, Type of Injury, Number of Wounds, Drugs/Alcohol Present, Blood Loss				

Table 20.5
Regression Model for Survival Time (n=49)

R	R Square	df	F	p
.519	.269	2	8.471	<0.001
Model 1	b	Std. Error	t	p
No. Wounds	0.554	0.176	3.139	0.003
Drugs/Alcohol	0.447	0.148	3.018	0.004
Predictors: Location of Wound, Type of Injury, Number of Wounds, Drugs/Alcohol Present, Blood Loss				

Conclusion

Research on gunfire injuries by Karger and Brinkman (1997) describe incapacitation following gunfire injuries as resulting from a disruption of the central nervous system (CNS), through either direct disruption of the brain tissue or cerebral hypoxia due to bleeding. DiMiao (1985) also discussed oxygen to the brain as the limiting factor in survival and cites cases where individuals were able to live 10-15 seconds after occlusion of a carotid artery. He further states that blood loss interferes with activity when it surpasses 20-25 percent of the total volume and that over 40 percent is life threatening. We found internal blood loss ranged from 10 to 4000 ml. Assuming the average adult male has 5.5 liters of blood, individuals lost an average of 19.0 percent of their body's blood volume. Among individuals who exhibited some activity, blood loss ranged from 13.6 percent to 37 percent. This compares with individuals who were immediately incapacitated. Their blood loss ranged from <1 percent to 73 percent.

Through this investigation, we found that gunfire injuries and deeply penetrating sharp force injuries resulted in a short survival interval with no activity, or victims survived short to long intervals with activity. In other words, the particular type of activities were not relevant. The question was whether or not someone could perform some type of activity following fatal injuries. Neither survival time nor activity is shown to be predictable once a victim suffers these types of wounds. In only 27.0 percent of cases, can the number of wounds and blood loss explain the variation among cases. The most variation that any of the regression models presented could explain is 12.0-33.0 percent of the variation in survival time, activity, and blood loss. The extreme variation in these factors may be attributed to the specific organs and blood vessels damaged, or may be intangible such as a person's will to live, general constitution, or preexisting health conditions. Importantly, we found that the number of wounds and the presence of alcohol or drugs did influence the amount of blood loss. And that, blood loss coupled with survival time are the only statistically significant determining factors regarding the activity of victims. Likewise, the number of wounds is the only significant factor in whether or not a person is immediately incapacitated and for what period of time they are able to survive.

Injury to the neck resulted in no survival time, whereas, 100 percent of cases with injury to the abdomen, did exhibit activity. Injury to the anterior or posterior thorax resulted in no difference in amount of activity, although survival was longer in injuries to the posterior thorax. Moreover, the longest survival time and range of survival time occurred in individuals with a combination of regions of the body injured. We found that despite noted patterns in survival time and activity, based on the structures injured - these trends are not statistically significant, and tell us little about what to expect in the greater population.

It is further interesting to note, that medical intervention occurred in 71.0 percent of cases (n=85). We found that whether or not medical intervention was present, was of little use in this analysis because all cases eventually ended with death. Further investigation into the question of the effectiveness of various medical treatments would be insightful for this discussion. However, the issue of medical intervention cannot be ignored because of the tremendous improvements made by emergency response units in quickly reaching victims, particularly in recent years. Much of the early literature on this subject was completed in prior to 1980s when the average response time was approximately 1.5 hours, according to Halpern and Aldrete (1979). Today's average is less than thirty minutes, depending on geographical location.

Acknowledgements

Accomplishing this research would not have possible without the work of Drs. Sandra Elkins, Mitra Kalelkar, and William McCormick who made available their case work. We would also like to acknowledge everyone who contributed insight and assistance to this project; Dr. Richard Jantz, Dr. Lee Meadows Jantz, and Mrs. Tami Ruth.

References

Aho AJ and J Vuori. 1980 Penetrating Abdominal Injuries with Special Reference to Knife Wounds. Acta Chir Scand 146:47-54

Betz, P, D Stiefel, R Hausmann, W Eisenmenger. Fractures at the base of the skull in gunshots to the head. Forensic Science International, 1997 86(3), 155-161

CLYNE AJ. The wounding and killing power of small-arms fire in jungle operations. J R Army Med Corps. 1955 Jan;101(1):33-8.

Demetriades D and van der Veen BW. 1983 Penetrating Injuries of the Heart: Experience over Two Years in South Africa. Journal of Trauma 23(12):1034-1041

Elkin DC. 1936 Wounds of the Heart: Report of Thirteen Cases. Journal of Thoracic Surgery. Nineteenth Annual Meeting of the American Association for Thoracic Surgery at Rochester, Minnesota. May pp. 590-603

Halpern NB and Aldrete JS. 1979 Factors Influencing Mortality and Morbidity form Injuries to the Abdominal Aorta and Inferior Vena Cava. American Journal of Surgery 137:384-388

Karger, B. Penetrating gunshots to the head and lack of immediate incapacitation. II. Review of case reports. INTERNATIONAL JOURNAL OF LEGAL MEDICINE. 1995, VOL 108; NUMBER 3, pages 117-126

Karger, B. Brinkman, B. Multiple gunshot suicides: potential for physical activity and medico-legal aspects. INTERNATIONAL JOURNAL OF LEGAL MEDICINE. 1997, VOL 110; NUMBER 4, pages 188-192

Karger, B. DuChesne, A. Who fired the gun? A casuistic contribution to the differentiation between self-inflicted and non-self-inflicted gunshot wounds. INTERNATIONAL JOURNAL OF LEGAL MEDICINE. 1997, VOL 110; NUMBER 1, pages 33-35

Kimmerle EH, Okoye M, Gabriel S (2002) Characteristics of Different Types of Fatal Head Trauma and the Factors that Influence Survival Time and Activity Prior to Death. American Academy of Forensic Sciences, Academy's 54th Annual Meeting, February, Atlanta, GA.

Levy V and Rao V. 1988 Survival Time in Gunshot and Stab Wound Victims. American Journal of Forensic Medicine and Pathology 9(3):215-217

Mandal AK, Awariefe AO, Oparah SS. 1979 Experience in the management of 50 consecutive penetrating wounds of the heart. Br. J. Surg. 66:565-568

Moar JJ. 1984 Homicidal penetrating incised wounds of the thorax. SA MEDIESE TYDSKRIF DEEL 65(10):385-389

Oehmichen, M, C Meissner, HG König Brain injury after survived gunshot to the head: reactive alterations at sites remote from the missile track. Forensic Science International, 2001 Forensic Science International, Volume 115, Issue 3, Pages 189-197

Okoye M, Kimmerle EH (2000) Survival Time in Fatal Penetrating Sharp Force and Gunfire Injuries. American Academy of Forensic Sciences, Academy's 52nd Annual Meeting, Reno, Nevada.

Spitz WU, Petty CS, Fisher RS (1961) Physical activity until collapse following fatal injury by firearms and sharp pointed weapons. Journal of Forensic Science 6(3):290-300.

SPSS for Windows, Rel. 11.0.1. (2001. Chicago. SPSS Inc.).

Thoresen SO and Rognum TO. 1986 Survival Time and Acting Capability After Fatal Injury by Sharp Weapons. Forensic Science International 31:181-187

Webb, E, JP Wyatt, J Henry, A Busuttil. A comparison of fatal with non-fatal knife injuries in Edinburgh. Forensic Science International, 99 (1999), pp. 179-187.

Chapter 21

Florida's Disaster Fatality Management Team

Larry R. Bedore, M.S., C.J.

Introduction

All disasters are local by their very nature. This truism applies more so to Medical Examiners and Coroners than to any other agent of public service. Regardless of the magnitude of the event, only the Medical Examiner or Coroner can establish the identity, cause and manner of death of each victim by issuing a death certificate. Regardless of the level of aid provided to the Medical Examiner or Coroner, the mission of every assisting element is to support, not supplant, their efforts. They are the only officials who, by law, are responsible for a disaster in their jurisdiction, and may not "hand it off" to those who arrive to help.

Disaster Fatality Management Response Background

The world of emergency management, including fatality management, changed radically following the multiple events of September 11, 2001. Prior to that moment only a few states had organized teams to assist Medical Examiners or Coroners with mass fatality events. When there were major disasters most communities looked to the surrounding areas and to the state to aid them when floods, fires, crashes, earthquakes or other incidents occurred and surpassed their local capabilities. For the most part these local resources consisted of fingerprint technicians, forensic dentists and funeral directors. More recently in our country's history, communities began to rely on the federal Disaster Mortuary Operational Response Team (DMORT) an arm of the National Disaster Medical System (NDMS). DMORT/NDMS reported through the US Public Health Service at the time of 9/11. Following that event the entire NDMS system was realigned under FEMA in the new Department of Homeland Security. Then, as of January 2007, mostly as a result of lessons learned from Hurricane Katrina, NDMS was again moved back under the Department of Health and Human Services (DHHS) and its Office of the Assistant Secretary for Preparedness and Response (ASPR).

DMORT (www.dmort.org) started out as a dedicated committee of the National Funeral Directors Association (NFDA) back in the 1980s under the vision and motivation of Tom Shepardson (a funeral director in upstate New York) and a core of like minded volunteers. It evolved by the early 1990s to offer a full spectrum forensic approach to managing multiple deaths since no single discipline could accomplish all the tasks needed to identify victims. By 1992, DMORT was incorporated into the NDMS family of response teams under DHHS. Its members were divided into 10 multi-state regional teams mirroring the 10 federal FEMA regions. DMORT's first mission came with the flooding and washout of a Hardin Missouri cemetery in 1993 and was followed by response to the Oklahoma City Murrah Building bombing in April 1995. DMORT assembled the first federal Disaster Portable Morgue Unit (DPMU) capable of being delivered to any event by plane or truck. Its first use came about for the Korean Air crash in Guam in August, 1997. DMORT has been deployed to numerous airline accidents including the 1999 Egypt Air, the 2000 Alaskan Air and many more.

By the time the World Trade Center disaster occurred, DMORT had grown to over 1,000 members with two portable morgue caches (both of which were sent to New York City although they were not fully utilized). Over a nine month period, DMORT provided equipment and staff assistance to the Office of Chief Medical Examiner in Manhattan (while also fielding a teams to Shanksville, Pennsylvania and to the November, 2001 American Airlines Airbus A-300 crash in Queens, N.Y.). However, it was Hurricane Katrina that resulted in the largest ever deployment of DMORT assets including both portable morgues and most of its by then 1,200 responders to aid in the recovery and identification of the approximately 1,200 dead in both Louisiana and Mississippi.

Florida's State Level Awareness Following 9/11

The attacks of 9/11 shook the foundations of Florida's confidence in being prepared to prevent and respond to terrorist events. While Florida had become a de facto recognized leader in natural disaster response organization (owing to its untoward destiny of being positioned in the path of recurrent hurricanes), then Governor Jeb Bush wasted no time in marshalling forces across the state. On September 14, 2001, he formally directed the Florida Department of Law Enforcement (FDLE) and the Florida Division of Emergency Management to immediately complete (within 10 days!) a comprehensive assessment of Florida's capability to prevent, mitigate, and respond to a terrorist attack. That report was completed by October 1st and was followed shortly by a subsequent report to lay out a funding strategy. Among the myriad issues identified was a need to develop a mortuary response capability to assist the local medical examiners in the state under the Health and Human Services umbrella. Florida's Department of Health (FDOH) was designated the lead agency during emergencies for the Health and Medical Emergency Support Function 8 (ESF8). As a result of the reports' findings the FDOH was tasked to implement the recommendations.

Strengthening Domestic Security in Florida
Funding Strategy

GOAL III. – HEALTH AND HUMAN SERVICES

STRATEGY 2 – Equipment

<u>Identify and obtain appropriate equipment for all response efforts</u>

Funding Requirements (Human)   **$2,787,371**
➢ Enhance statewide Department of Health laboratory capacity $389,786
➢ <u>Medical stockpiles - supplies - mass casualty capability</u> $420,000
➢ | Develop Disaster Mortuary Response Team capabilities $400,000 |
➢ Systems to support collection, analysis, reporting, and sharing of biological and
  chemical threats to public health.. $928,000
➢ State epidemiological intelligence service $640,585

Figure 21.1 Domestic Security Strategic Plan October 2001 Report FDLE

Ostensibly, an observation was rendered that multiple, simultaneous disaster events across the nation could overtax existing federal DMORT resources to such an extent that, should another event occur in Florida, the state would have to manage on its own. (DMORT now has three portable morgues as a result of lessons learned from Hurricane Katrina). Added to this is the response time issue of holding on for 24-48 hours during those initial chaotic times following an event as federal teams are mobilized to get boots on the ground. Even without media pressure, the task of recovering the dead and managing a sudden influx of phone calls from families to the Medical Examiner or Coroner begins almost immediately. For hurricanes there is advance warning and often advance placement of federal assets. But for sudden, unexpected catastrophes, ramp up time can be a challenge. Having a state level asset close by for doing a strike team assessment of need reduces the time it takes to set up command and control of fatality management operations.

There is another, perhaps more important fundamental reason for establishing a state level team. Who will pay? Some events do not rise to the level of being declared federal disasters. Two examples illustrate this well:

1. Tri-State Crematorium Incident, Nobel, Georgia, February, 2002
   - More than 300 decomposing bodies that should have been cremated were found scattered about a wooded area.
   - DMORT responded and spent over a month helping to gather and "re-identify" these remains.
   - While technically not a Medical Examiner/Coroner problem (because these were previously certified deaths), logically the Medical Examiner was placed in charge of the investigation.

2. "The Station" Nightclub Fire, West Warwick, Rhode Island, February, 2003
- 100 victims died overnight from one fire
- DMORT responded with dental and "Family Assistance" teams to coordinate missing person interviews and make dental identifications.

Because no federal disaster declarations had been issued, these events resulted in both Georgia and Rhode Island reimbursing the federal government for the cost ($ millions) of deploying the DMORT assets.

It is only when a federal disaster declaration is issued that states may be reimbursed by federal agencies for costs associated with responding to and mitigating a disaster event. (Transportation accidents are different. The Aviation Disaster Family Assistance Act of 1996 requires that air carriers prepare Family Assistance Plans and, through their underwriters, assume all responsibility for covering costs of response.)

FEMORS Evolution

Florida's Department of Health (FDOH) initiated contact in the Fall of 2001 with the Maples Center for Forensic Medicine at the University of Florida under its College of Medicine. The request was to explore methods of developing a state level team to respond to the needs of Florida's 24 Medical Examiner Districts. It is worthwhile to note that the first medical examiner's office was opened in 1954, in Broward County. Shortly thereafter, other counties began to establish offices throughout the state. Eventually the Florida Legislature established Florida Statute 406, The Medical Examiner Law in 1970, and also created a commission to establish rule making capability for the entire state. The statute establishes the jurisdiction, qualifications, and other general practices for the 24 Medical Examiner Districts in the state. Florida is the only state that has a unified death investigation system.

The directors of the Maples Center, Bruce A Goldberger, Ph.D. and Anthony B. Falsetti, Ph.D. collaborated with experienced forensic and disaster mortuary response individuals to serve as an advisory panel in developing a state level program. A number of DMORT experienced individuals were involved in that charter group. The Maples Center drafted a proposal for starting the team and a contract was issued by FDOH to proceed. With a seed grant of $150,000 from the Centers for Disease Control (CDC), the Maples Center inaugurated the Florida Emergency Mortuary Operations Response System (FEMORS) on July 1, 2002. It established a web site (www.FEMORS.org), attracted interested individuals from across the state through word of mouth among the forensic community, and began preparing materials for a training program.

From its inception, FEMORS was designed to mirror the DMORT model of full spectrum forensic service. Numerous disciplines contribute to effecting identification of disaster victims including: pathology, anthropology, odontology, radiology, fingerprint, DNA, and evidence specialties. Specialists, however, cannot do it alone; an infrastructure of support staff is needed to manage, support and service those laboring with the remains.

By the spring of 2003, FEMORS hosted its first annual training session and more than 100 members attended. This fledgling group began the process of fleshing out the numerous organizational issues required to create a truly functional state level response team. FDOH renewed its contract with FEMORS over the ensuing years using CDC funding derived from the original 1998 Bioterrorism Grant program. CDC funding (Figure 21.2), however, was limited in use to program development and training and excluded equipment for a portable morgue. Thus, FEMORS' organizational development, membership and training efforts continued to grow to the point where the personnel side of a response capability was fairly robust but the equipment side to augment a compromised Medical Examiner facility was lacking.

Program development funding also provided partial payroll costs for the Program Director at 5% Full Time Equivalent (FTE), Commander at 100% FTE for the first two years (now at 40% FTE), Finance Director at 75% FTE, and Logistics Chief at 100% FTE for the two years of DPMU procurement (now at 40% FTE). The labor and time commitment required to coordinate FDOH human resource issues, pay scales, membership requirements and classification, create and implement the written procedures needed, create and host training programs, and stage meaningful field exercises was, and continues to be, significant. To be realistically effective in starting up a state team, at least one full-time individual is essential. While volunteers are a great asset when the next grant application has to be written (often with only a few days notice) it is the full time person who must be there to get the task accomplished.

Portable Morgue Equipment

Since 9/11 Florida has adopted a unified approach to maximize all disaster preparedness grant opportunities on a yearly basis by establishing a priority ranking of all requests from response agencies competing for the same funds. As a result, FEMORS was allocated $350,000 for FY 05-06 to procure a cache of equipment to establish a Disaster Portable Morgue Unit (DPMU).

DMORT's list of equipment being stocked in its then two morgues served as the basis for the FEMORS' morgue. Although the procurement process was delayed until the Spring of 2006 the portable morgue cache was essentially complete by January, 2007 with the exception of a body x-ray unit and a few other items sacrificed due to funding limitations. (Recommendation: initial cost for creating a portable morgue should be not less than $600,000 for a state level team.) A subsequent funding allocation for FY 07-08 will enable FEMORS to add the digital body x-ray unit to the cache.

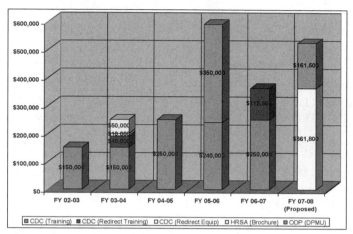

Figure 21.2 *Funding History*

The Concept of "Volunteers" Under Florida's Rules

During its first five years of existence, FEMORS continued to attract many "volunteers". Similar to the Federal model, FEMORS members are not true volunteers but become temporary employees of FDOH upon activation. They do this by being authorized to take leave from their primary employer and receive State compensation (without fringe benefits such as retirement or insurance) based on a pay plan consistent with similar positions within state government. Because most disaster responses result in working 12-hour days during the typical 2 week rotation of a deployment, overtime is paid to these temporary employees.

Flexibility of the FEMORS members' primary employers is the driving factor in being able to muster a team when the need arises. In some cases, FEMORS has provided educational awareness assistance to help employers understand the nature of the employee's desire to help and the human resources consequences for the employer. Often a bereavement or sick leave analogy is applicable - like a sudden absence of an employee due to bereavement for the death of a family member or unforeseeable sick leave, the employer typically finds a way to fill the temporary absence. Permitting the FEMORS member to respond to a deployment can be viewed in much the same vein.

In the Federal DMORT system all members are deemed "federal employees" and members of the "uniformed services". When deployed they are afforded certain job protections under the Uniformed Services Employment and Reemployment Rights Act (USERRA). Florida's response teams do not have such protections. Perhaps most states are in a similar situation with regard to job protection. Thus, it is the willingness and support of the member's primary employer that determines whether or not they may participate.

Perhaps of more importance from an employer risk management standpoint, however, is that worker's compensation and liability insurance coverages are provided by FDOH - the primary employer is not at risk for work related injuries occurring while responding to or resulting from the deployment. This alleviates one of the most troubling aspects of many of the "mutual aid agreements" among volunteer agencies who have no worker's compensation coverage. Unlike police, fire, and search an rescue squads of municipalities that essentially remain on-duty with their primary employer under well executed mutual aid agreements, FEMORS professionals come from a diverse background of private practice, government and the retired sectors.

Sending an employee to participate in training or an actual disaster deployment also generates tangible benefits to the employer. Responder participation delivers knowledge and hands-on experience unavailable through any other medium. Upon return to work, that employee brings back practical knowledge that can aid in refining the agency's disaster response awareness planning efforts. Should a major event impact the agency, having experienced staff on hand from the start aids in establishing effective command and control. It also demonstrates that employer's commitment to the larger Medical Examiner/Coroner community and, ultimately, families of victims - an appropriate, justifiable and laudable philosophy for any public service sector provider.

"Active" Status

From is beginning, FEMORS recognized the importance of training to develop skill sets adapted to the sometimes austere response environment and the sense of camaraderie it takes to make a team effective. From the first moment the disaster occurs, countless issues and time demands impact the ability to set up an effective operational response. It is a well recognized managerial fact that it is unwise to spend precious start up time trying to bring untrained volunteers up to speed during the early stages of response. (Volunteer participation in non-critical areas can be phased in later.)

For that reason one of the requirements for continuing active status on the state team is active participation, i.e., attendance at least once every two years at a FEMORS, DMORT or similar disaster preparedness training session, or experience from an actual fatality focused response.

To date, 479 people have registered with FEMORS and 190 remain in active status (Figure 21.2) having satisfied the continuing education requirement. Thus, when a deployment mission is issued by FDOH to activate the FEMORS Team, those in active status are requested first. Should the need for additional staff continue beyond the first wave of response, inactive members could'then be polled for their availability to respond.

Field Operations Guide (FOG)

Response to an unpredictable event on a moment's notice results in displacing the day-to-day comfort of office settings and replacing it with field operating conditions that are far different. It is unrealistic to expect professionals who rarely get to exercise the unique nature of disaster response to remember training that is provided once yearly. For that reason, FEMORS developed its Field Operations Guide (FOG) to serve as a ready reference and refresher for members. The FOG (http://femors.org/docs/FEMORS_FOG_3rd_Edition_Final_010507.pdf) is a compilation and summary of important general information, developed procedures, and reference material. In addition, position description summaries and operational checklists are outlined for each of the positions that comprise a FEMORS response.

Standard Incident Command System (ICS) terminology is used throughout the FOG to ensure consistency with all ICS response elements and the National Incident Management System (NIMS). Redefinition, refinement and adoption of NIMS followed 9/11. This was a consequence of the Homeland Security Act of 2002 and Homeland Security Presidential Directives 5 and 8 in 2003 and resulted in mandating the use of the Incident Management System (ICS) across all response efforts nationwide. Briefly stated, all programs receiving federal funding were required to adopt the ICS system into their operating plans as a condition for continued funding.

The FOG is a living document and the 4th Edition is currently being prepared. As an educational tool for members, it lays out all of the membership, classification, travel and employment issues. It also identifies reporting responsibilities of every position to which a member might be assigned especially if the position requires a specific forensic skill set as well as some supervisory responsibility. For example, a forensic pathologist may need a reference guide if he/she is to perform not only typical forensic medicine but also serve as the Pathology Team Leader in the temporary morgue.

Standardized forensic protocols for various processing tasks are also included. There are procedures for dental, photography, personal effects, evidence chain of custody, records management and embalming to name just a few. Templates are included for morgue station log books, administrative tracking forms, daily Incident Action Plans and a variety of others. These may be used in Florida if the local medical examiner requests them.

NIMS and ICS depend heavily on limiting effective "span of control" so that no person is supervising more than 7 subordinates. It also emphasizes "unity of command" which means that each person reports to only one supervisor. These factors are fully incorporated into the various tables of organization that illustrate FEMORS staffing and functions in a field deployment.

Deployment Response Structure

For the benefit of those not conversant in NIMS/ICS procedures, Unified Command of the overall incident is managed under a combination of local, state and federal partners from emergency management agencies, law enforcement, fire rescue, public works and many others. The ICS structure used for that process involves Command and 4 "Sections" of function: Operations, Planning, Logistics and Administration/Finance.

When ESF8 deploys FEMORS, it is actually operating as an element of the Operations Section and, in line with NIMS, adopts its own internal ICS structure to accomplish its mission.

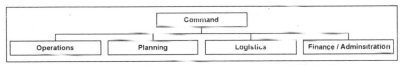

Figure 21.3 ICS Core Structure

By the use of organizational charts strictly adhering to the ICS model and terminology, the FOG illustrates both the simplicity and complexity of managing over 100 personnel in a worst case scenario (Figures 21.4–6). While most events may only utilize some of the services available, the system must be flexible and able to provide any assistance level from small individual teams (dental, pathology, etc.) to a full array of services if the event dictates the need.

It does require a bit of understanding of ICS to make sense of these charts and the terminology used. Fortunately, courses in ICS basics are required for participating in response programs so FEMORS members have little difficulty in understanding the inter relationship of all positions. In a nutshell, for those not educated in the ICS concept:

- Operations Section is where the work gets done.
- Planning Section is where event documentation and long range decisions are developed.

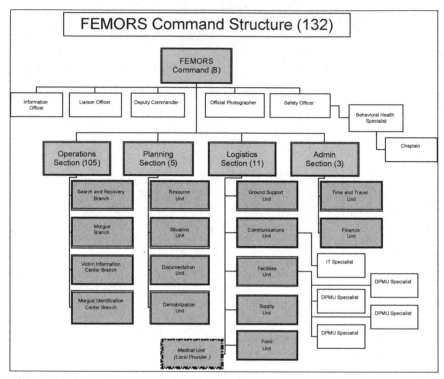

Figure 21.4 *FEMORS ICS Overview*

- Administration Section takes care of human resource and financial issues.
- Logistics Section is the equipment and supplies element, the infrastructure so to speak, that allows the whole system to get the tasks accomplished.

An expanded view of the Operation Section reveals the range of specialty teams needed in each of its four functional branches.

ICS has been called scalable meaning that, as an example with the Search & Recovery Branch, a need might arise to create many additional Remains Collection Teams for the first few days. In the early days of a response, while the temporary morgue is being established, body processing is just beginning or the Morgue Identification Center has not yet become operational, staff can be assigned to such teams. As the rate of recovery slows down, team sizes and numbers can be reduced and staff reassigned to other functional areas (assuming they are qualified for the new assignment).

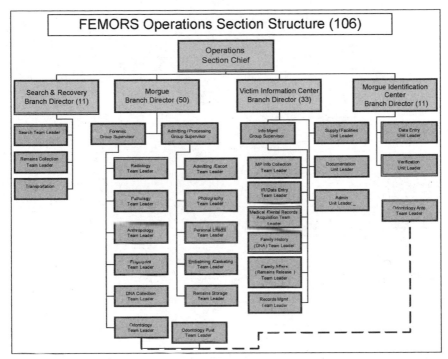

Figure 21.5 *Operations Section Overview*

It is important to remember that this illustrates a full contingent (worst case scenario). Larger Medical Examiner offices may need only limited assistance so only those elements requested would be activated. It does little good to overwhelm a disaster site or Medical Examiner office with well-intentioned responders if they are not needed - they become part of the problem to solve rather than the solution. That initial strike team assessment, and subsequent adjustment as conditions change, is critical to providing the most appropriate level of response.

An expanded view of the Morgue Branch of the Operation Section reveals the detail of each specialty team and the number of positions required for optimal effect.

In an actual deployment each member's name is placed on the appropriate organizational chart so that all of the team can understand reporting relationships and the chain of command.

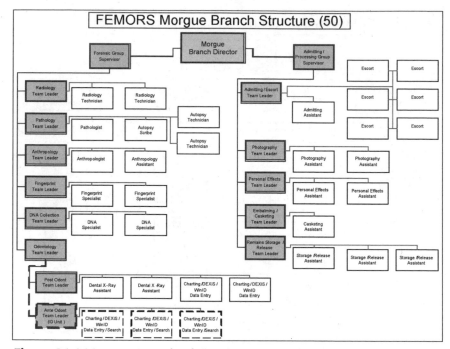

Figure 21.6 *Morgue Branch of Operations Section Detailed*

Morgue Work Flow

FEMORS coordinates with the Medical Examiner, local officials, local EOC, State DOH/ESF-8, and others to establish a temporary morgue facility if the primary facility has been compromised or incapacitated. Defining the "ideal" morgue set up is next to impossible, however when establishing the morgue, the following issues are evaluated:

- Facility availability for the time frame necessary.
  - ◊ Fixed structure (e.g., warehouse) vs. temporary tents.
  - ◊ Retrofit capability and cost.
  - ◊ Hard weather tight structure with concrete floors (optimal)
  - ◊ Accessibility from event site.
- Space Requirement: 10,000 sq. ft.
  - ◊ Parking area for refrigerated trailers
  - ◊ Site Security
- Electrical capabilities (minimum 600 amp service).
- Drainage (sanitary sewer floor drains in operational areas is optimal).
- Heating/cooling (HVAC/power supply-rental).

- Communications services (e.g., telephones, internet, etc.).
- Water supply.
- Sanitation services.

The DPMU cache contains equipment and supplies for processing stations (as well as for Command Post, Victim Information Center, and Morgue Identification Center) for the first 72 hours of operation. Victim processing is accomplished in an assembly line fashion to maximize the use of resources.

The order of processing is flexible and often adjusted to suit the needs of the event and the space limitations present. For example, embalming and casketing may be needed only in rare situations because final arrangements and disposition options are normally decided by the next-of-kin.

Likewise, for a potentially criminal event (terrorist or otherwise) the Personal Effects and Evidence collection functions take on added importance and may need to accommodate additional staff.

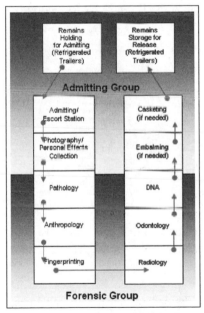

Figure 21.7 *Morgue Processing Overview*

Figure 21.8 *Portable Morgue at 2007 Training/Exercise*

How It All Works—Tiered Response

Medical Examiners in Florida, under NIMS and ICS guidelines, actually report resource needs (personnel or equipment) through the local Emergency Operations Center to the Law Enforcement Emergency Support Function (ESF16 in Florida).

However, when a Medical Examiner requests fatality management assistance, that request is transferred from ESF16 to the ESF8 Desk for action because it is a Health and Medical issue.

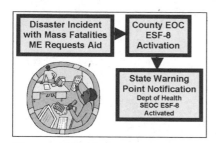

Figure 21.9 *Typical Activation Sequence*

When any disaster event involving deaths occurs, the local Medical Examiner is (or at least should be!) notified immediately for response. Tiered support response means that:

- if the event exceeds local capability, regional or state assets are requested to assist, and
- if the event exceeds state capability, federal resources are requested to assist.

In all cases however, the Medical Examiner remains in charge; all of the resources responding are there to support the Medical Examiner.

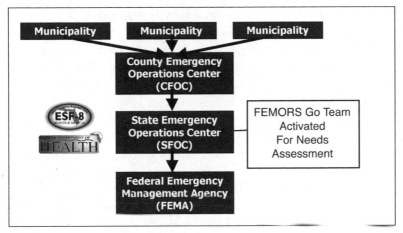

Figure 21.10 *Tiered Response of Support*

ESF8 (at the State EOC) assigns FEMORS to a mission when a request is received from a Medical Examiner. This authorizes the FDOH temporary employment status and initiates the liability coverage issues. FEMORS first sends an assessment Go Team to meet with the Medical Examiner to assess the scope of the event and explain the range of resources available.

In Florida, FEMORS has members located across the state, and a small Go Team can be activated within hours to make contact with the Medical Examiner. The Go Team is made up of a core group that has received advanced training and is capable of explaining the resources and options available. It is the Go Team that reports back to ESF8 on which assets need to be activated, whether they be facilities, personnel, equipment, supplies or special needs.

The large Florida metropolitan Medical Examiner offices may require far less support than some of the more rural, less populated areas, so the process will always adapt to the uniqueness of the event and its demands.

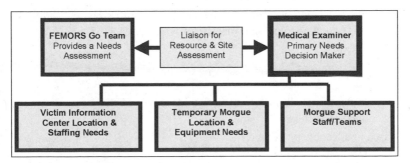

Figure 21.11 *Go Team Assessment*

Transition from State to Federal Level Support

Like any state level team with a limited membership, FEMORS recognizes the basic fact that the magnitude of the event may require a longer time commitment than its personnel resources can sustain. FEMORS does not have the 1,200 member base that DMORT has to draw from. In spite of the fact that Florida's population is approaching 18 million, the number of FEMORS members remains in the low hundreds. (Less populous states may be even more constrained to muster sizeable fatality management teams.) For this reason, the fundamental planning assumption for state teams is that any event that would require support longer than a month will likely require requesting the federal DMORT team assistance.

The Planning Section's role in tracking daily activities and laying out the future course of response needs is critical in recognizing when the request for federal support should begin. Fortunately, time is not quite as critical by this point (3-4 weeks into the response) since the portable morgue and basic operations will be well underway by the time DMORT reinforcements arrive.

The primary reason for having used the DMORT model in designing the Florida state team now becomes self-evident. With a portable morgue, administrative centers, and equipment fully deployed and operational the resource needed most from DMORT will be on the personnel side. FEMORS' role is to support the Medical Examiner's needs and DMORT's role is to support FEMORS in that effort. Because all the equipment can continue to operate even with most of the original team members demobilized, DMORT team members can step in to fill the staffing gaps and use the existing system with little ramp-up training time.

In the event of a non-federally declared disaster, Emergency Management Assistance Compact (EMAC) agreements between Governors can also be used to permit states to assist each other in the same fashion. Again, transition of staffing needs creates minimal disruption provided that the DMORT model was used by both state teams from the beginning.

Functional Area Assessment

While all disasters are unique, there are common basic functions that apply to any disaster fatality management and identification process.

1. Medical Examiner/Command
   - Directs resources
   - Makes final decision on victim identity and the issuance of the death certificate
2. Search and Recovery Center
   - Documents field recovery of victims
   - Preserves identifying personal effects
   - Transports victims to morgue

3. Victim Information Center
  • Establishes victim information and Call Center
  • Receives missing person reports
  • Interviews families for ante mortem details of potential victims
4. Morgue Operations
  • Processes remains for identifying features and injuries
  • Preserves evidence for criminal investigations
5. Morgue Identification Center
  • Compares ante and post mortem data
  • Performs dental and fingerprint matching
  • Presents potential matches to Medical Examiner

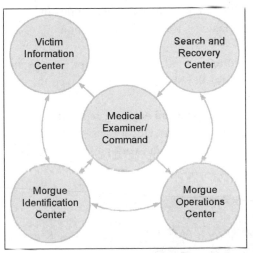

Figure 21.12 Functional Area Assessment

Identifying Victims and Data Management

A tremendous amount of data and facts are gathered throughout the recovery time. In addition to the paper files inevitably generated in large quantities, FEMORS manages data by means of a Fatality Response Emergency Database (FRED). It is an adaptation of the original Victim Identification Program (VIP) used by DMORT. The adaptation was made based on the lessons learned from Hurricane Katrina. In Katrina, being able to manage the tremendous influx of phone calls reporting missing persons proved to be a most challenging and difficult task.

Briefly summarized, FRED focuses on three major phases to manage data:

1. It incorporates a Call Center module to take initial contact information about potential victims. This is followed up by Victim Information Center (VIC) specialists who return the calls and are able to meet with families to conduct in-depth interviews. Family interviews provide potentially identifying information such as dental and medical records, clothing and jewelry descriptions and the like.
2. During morgue processing, examination of the remains documents all identifying features such as scars, marks and tattoos, dental charting, personal effects including jewelry, medical device implants, and the like.
3. It is in the Morgue Identification Center where the data mining in FRED takes place to yield potential matches for closer examination.

Other parts of the program track field recovery data, body receipt, storage and release information, statistical reports for the Medical Examiner, even the supplies consumed and in need of replenishment.

FRED is developed on the FileMaker platform enabling rapid adjustments in the field for the unique conditions of that event. History has shown that this flexibility to adjust is essential and has happened in every previous disaster to some extent.

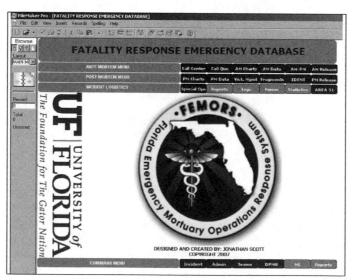

Figure 21.13 *FRED Program*

Winding Down

Disaster response teams are designed to pitch in quickly to help with caseload surge conditions. Offices still need to be able to process the daily caseloads that would have occurred even without the mass fatality event. This can be a contributing factor in deciding if an off-site temporary morgue is even needed.

The need for support teams begins to diminish over time because victims are identified and released to funeral homes. It is the volume of unidentified cases and the flow of new missing person reports that determine long range support planning needs. Demobilization plans are instituted to manage the downsizing aspects of the operation and to help the District Medical Examiner return to normal operations. Field recovery and morgue processing teams eventually complete their tasks leaving only the unidentified remains and the stack of missing person reports to be sorted out.

By the time FEMORS ends its mission and the Medical Examiner's office returns to more routine daily operation, transition of the disaster data can be made to the data system used by the office. A full runtime version of all event data contained in FRED is transferred to the Medical Examiner (and FEMORS wipes its computers clean of all Medical Examiner data and photos). Although a runtime version prevents altering the basic program further, it remains fully functional for as long as the need exists to effect identifications. The Medical Examiner is and remains the custodian of all records regardless of how much support is on hand.

So, the original truism comes full circle—the Medical Examiner can't give his/her disaster away. All disasters are local.

Chapter 22

Public Health Aspects and Preventive Measures

Bruce W. Dixon, M.D.

22.1 Introduction

Public health has a key role in biological and chemical terrorism response and works closely with law enforcement agencies and emergency response agencies at the local, state, and federal levels. Public health is an over-arching term that includes not only government agencies but private individuals and institutions whose unifying purpose in the event of a terrorist attack is to contain, control, to educate people at risk or perceived to be at risk, and to educate people who have fears of being affected by such an event. These activities are a part of the core functions of public health as defined by the Institute of Medicine, and include assessment and assurance functions as well as policy development to maximize safety by reducing hazards. Public health's role in responding to biological and chemical terrorism is part of a larger role as a support agency in disaster response, whether naturally occurring or man made. It may include issues beyond the scope of this chapter, such as building collapse, possibly from structural deficiency; natural disaster, such as a fire, or a man-made disaster such as a bomb; and may include radiological accidents such as occurred at Three Mile Island, near Harrisburg, Pennsylvania, and more recently at Chernobyl in the Ukraine.

Although beyond the scope of this chapter, it is important to recognize that combinations of terrorist events may occur so that biological or chemical weapons disseminated by a bomb could result in building collapse and radiation release as well. The initial response must look at the latter two situations in order to assure the safety of first responders. Building integrity and lack of radiation threat must be rapidly ascertained and assured before the assessment of biological or chemical risk begins. It is only within the last decade that attention has been paid to the potential for biological or chemical terrorism so concepts for identification, response, and public health intervention are in their infancy and are constantly changing. For purposes of defining public health response, it is convenient to think of public health activities in two broad categories; those activities that occur prior to any terrorist event and which are ongoing as part of the overall mission of public health, and those specific activities that would occur post-terrorist event which are targeted specifically to that event.

22.2 Pre-Event Activities

Pre-event activities on the part of public health that relate to biological or chemical terrorism fall in three general categories (1) surveillance, (2) laboratory capabilities, and (3) education and training. All three activities are core functions of public health at the local, state, and federal level and have a long and distinguished history. However, the threat of terrorism has caused a rethinking of all of these activities and further clarification and definition of their role.

A. Surveillance

Traditional infectious disease surveillance has been a public health activity since at least the eighteenth century and has been responsible for major breakthroughs in disease recognition and intervention. Throughout much of its history, however, disease surveillance has been a passive process. Physicians and, more recently, hospitals, laboratories, and infection-control nurses have reported definitive diagnoses of disease to a health authority that, by virtue of its legal mandate, has then taken some action to control, stop the spread, and eventually eliminate the infectious disease process. Regardless of the circumstances—whether the control of cholera in nineteenth-century England by eliminating contamination of the city well by sewage or, more recently, the limitation of cases of paralytic polio by vaccination or the elimination of smallpox from the globe by vaccination—the principles have remained the same. Traditional surveillance has been called into question, however, by the threat of terrorism. For many years, this system has been a passive one that depended on voluntary reporting of disease states. Today, that process is being supplanted by active surveillance systems that go out and search for disease by a variety of mechanisms, with the goal of reducing the time between occurrence and recognition of illness. The scope of individuals involved in active surveillance has been increased as well, so that nurses, pharmacists, laboratory directors and technicians, and other health care-related personnel are actively surveyed for potential biological disease. The process is labor intensive, however, and requires personal interactions to achieve reporting of a significant number of conditions of interest. The surveyor must establish personal communications with the reporting entity and survey them regularly and repetitively.

As a result, there are growing initiatives to create automated surveillance systems. Electronic surveillance systems capable of managing large and redundant amounts of data are being developed, especially at the federal and state levels. The National Electronic Disease Surveillance System (NEDSS), presently under development and deployment by the Centers for Disease Control, is one such system designed to facilitate surveillance. There have been various state revisions to this system to accommodate special interests and needs, but the overall intent is to have a variety of healthcare professionals enter data suggestive of, or confirmatory of, an infectious disease or other condition and to allow public health practitioners wide access to that data so that they can associate disparate bits of information and begin to see patterns of disease occurrence and spread. Such a system allows a local jurisdiction to see patterns of spread within their own area of concern, allows a larger entity, such as a state, to see patterns of spread between jurisdictions, and has the potential for a government agency such as the CDC to see potential spread on a much wider area involving multiple states or territories. Most present-day surveillance (whether active or passive) has been disease specific and has depended on either laboratory or clinical confirmation before reporting occurs. In order to be better prepared to respond to a biological event, it is necessary to shorten the time that elapses between the event and its detection, and for that reason, syndromic reporting of illness becomes desirable. Since most biological terrorist agents, and indeed, most chemical terrorist agents, will result in a fairly limited number of clinical manifestations, looking at clinical syndromes of respiratory disease, gastrointestinal disease, neurologic disease, and dermatologic conditions should result in the detection of virtually all chemical and biological terrorist agents. By their training, physicians and other health professionals have been accustomed to think in terms of clearly defined disease entities; retraining to think in terms of broad clinical presentations has proven to be difficult to achieve. In addition, most of the potential biological or chemical agents that would be considered terrorist threats result in rare diseases. As a result, health professionals do not recognize them or may ascribe them to some more common illness and miss the opportunity for early intervention. One researcher, in 2000, showed photographs of smallpox to physicians involved in family practice, internal medicine, and infectious disease. The infectious disease specialists suggested smallpox to a greater degree than did the internists or family practitioners. But the overall identification rate was poor and resulted in a positive diagnosis far less than 50 percent of the time. Indeed, the tendency of health practitioners to ascribe a rare event to a common occurrence is common behavior. For instance, in the early cases of anthrax which occurred in 2001, which were subsequently shown to be spread by the mail service, the index case was thought to have been acquired by natural means in central Florida, although the septic form of that illness had not been seen there for at least two decades. All efforts of disease surveillance have been largely concentrated thus far on hospitals and large, freestanding clinics. The reality is, however, when looking for unusual disease, that it will probably show up in an individual physician's office; thus the need for continuing education of the practice community and the continued need to reassure physicians that they do not need to have a specific diagnosis in order to report an infectious disease. Indeed, simply recognizing that a patient seems to have an unusual illness should be sufficient cause to report and then allow others to help with the diagnosis and solution. Frequently, practitioners and other health professionals will raise the issue of confidentiality in failing to report a potential infectious disease. Every state has reporting laws that give public health broad authority to receive and protect such reported disease information. HIPAA requirements recently enacted by the Department of Health and Human Services have a major exception for public health reporting which is not confined to an illness for which there is a specific reporting provision or statute. Because of the uncertainties and inexact nature of disease surveillance, even with active surveillance, a variety of surrogate reporting systems have been developed or are in development. The United States Postal Service has recently deployed a biological detection system (BDS) in thirteen facilities, that depends on scanning mail in stamping machines and sampling the surrounding air at frequent intervals with PCR (polymerase chain reaction) for anthrax. Although conceivably, this automated process could be expanded to other pathogens, the specific antigen must be loaded into the BDS and so its applicability for unusual disease or unrecognized disease is quite limited. The University of Pittsburgh has embarked on a project known as "RODS" (reactive outbreak and disease surveillance) that depends on a variety of direct and surrogate indicators of health conditions including emergency room visits, pharmaceutical purchases, absences from schools and other workplaces. The difficulty with RODS is that it is unlikely to pick up a single occurrence of a rare disease and, although it may pick up large concentrations of individuals who may be afflicted with one or another syndromic conditions, it is not specific enough to distinguish naturally occurring illness from unusual and perhaps, terrorist-related illness. Further refinement may reveal that there is some use, however, for this data mining process. In addition to these human health surveillance efforts, a variety of environmental efforts have recently been deployed. Funded by the Environmental Protection Agency, several cities have a bioshield project that samples the air at a variety of sites and rapidly performs an analysis, in most instances, by PCR for pathogens. While there is some theoretic likelihood for success with such a system, the small amount of air sampled, the limited geographic area from which a sample is obtained, and the need to compare it with known pathogen standards make it unlikely that it will have a significant impact on detecting biological agents that may be generally released into the environment. Similarly, although issues around food safety have been raised and the Rajneesh cult in Oregon placed salmonella in foodstuffs, routine surveillance is not likely to pick up any food contamination.

B. Laboratory capabilities

As a result of the inexact nature of surveillance, laboratory identification of organisms of particular concern for bioterrorism has remained the standard. While the reporting system from laboratories has generally been quite good, there is an obvious time delay between obtaining an environmental specimen or a specimen from a potential victim of bioterrorism, having it processed in the laboratory, and obtaining a result. There is, in addition, a dynamic tension between law enforcement and public health, as far as laboratory determinations are concerned. Although the FBI has been designated as the primary response agency for acts of bioterrorism, its focus is largely criminal prosecution, where the interest of public health is to rapidly ascertain whether or not a pathological agent is present and to intervene. While a laboratory which processes specimens from a variety of medical providers may occasionally find an organism suggestive of bioterrorism, specimens obtained from a suspected site of terrorism must be handled in such a way that a chain of custody is maintained to be useful for prosecution. For that reason, laboratories processing specimens from a suspected terrorist scene, in general, are laboratories under the control of government, either at the local, state, or federal level who can use and attest to the chain of custody. Such laboratories must be close enough to the site of potential terrorism that long delays in transportation do not hinder the rapid identification of a pathogen by the laboratory. For instance, in many parts of the country, a public health laboratory is several hours' distance, even by plane, from the site and although today, the technology exists to identify an organism in as short a time as forty minutes, the long delays in getting the specimen to the laboratory make the rapid identification of lesser value. To deal with these concerns, several laboratories, including those of state and local health departments and CDC, have been certified as parts of the Laboratory Response Network, to allow for specimens to be rapidly identified using newer antigens and techniques and to be sent on to other more specialized facilities for diagnostic confirmation. Laboratories processing such specimens should at the very minimum, meet the qualifications of Biosafety Level III, as promulgated by the Centers for Disease Control, to allow the identification of pathogens with safety for the laboratory technicians. When used for bioterrorism, many of the organisms will be weaponized—that is, in sufficient size that it results in a greater infectivity than would occur in nature. Laboratory safety is therefore of paramount concern. Similarly, within the laboratory network, there needs to be sufficient redundancy so that if the capabilities of one laboratory are exceeded or are rendered inoperable, other laboratories are able to rapidly provide the capabilities necessary. More specialized laboratories able to perform genetic fingerprinting are part of the network so that one can associate infections disassociated in time or space with a common source. Determination of chemical agents, like bacteriological agents, requires specialized laboratory equipment and specialized safety measures for staff. Many of the potential chemical agents, including a variety of neurotoxins, represent gases that must be collected safely and analyzed either by mass spectroscopy or infrared chromatography in equipment that doesn't expose the laboratory technicians to undue risk. Because of the unique nature of chemical agents and their rapid onset, many emergency response units have been equipped with portable gas chromatography-mass spectroscopy units to identify the agent, at least preliminarily, in the field.

C. Training

Public health training is another pre-event function important to the overall bioterrorism effort. Continued training of health professionals and related staff is vital to transmit not only new knowledge, but to refresh principles of disease surveillance and response among health practitioners who have had relatively little training during their formal education. Since it is likely, should an event occur, that people with specialized skills would be needed to care for injured or affected individuals, collaboration and sharing of resources is once again important. The Medical Reserve Corps grants, funded by the Department of Health and Human Services, have allowed jurisdictions to recruit a variety of health practitioners, including physicians, nurses, and pharmacists to assist should a terrorist event occur. Training of those individuals in not only disease recognition but also triage and dispensation of medications, including vaccines and technical knowledge, is imperative. It is felt to be prudent that a small number of individuals who represent this level of health practitioners should be immunized against common pathogens for which vaccines exist so that they can be used as immediate responders or to help vaccinate other individuals. Vaccines for smallpox have been deployed by the federal government with questionable success. Small groups of people appear to be available in most regions of the country with sufficient

protection either from former or revaccination to allow them to be first responders if a smallpox outbreak does occur. Similarly, although there is controversy
around the use and potential side effects from anthrax vaccine, a small but diverse group of people have been immunized for anthrax and could serve as first
responders from a public health point of view. Specialized knowledge continues
to advance and it is important that ongoing training and education be available.
For consistency, many jurisdictions have adopted Internet-based training so that
the training is not only comprehensive, but allows one to receive training at their
own pace and with similar content. This becomes more important if some sort of
a mass hazardous event occurs which will require people to come to an area to
assist not only with public health, but also with patient care.

The Metropolitan Medical Response System has been a preparedness system initially deployed in many of the larger cities throughout the United States
and gradually expanded to cities and regions of more moderate size. This is a
planning effort to ensure that those jurisdictions most at risk for some type of
man-made or natural disaster have begun the planning process to ensure there is
coordination between healthcare providers, local and state health systems, and
emergency management personnel and systems.

22.3 Post-Event Activities

There have been relatively few events that have tested the post-event response to
large scale public health emergencies. The radiation emergencies at Three Mile
Island and Chernobyl were several years ago and the capacity to detect and respond has improved significantly since those two events. A sarin gas release
in a Japanese subway is often cited as an example of a chemical release and
the release of methylisocyanate at Bhopal, India, also provided experience with
the release of a chemical agent. Again, both events occurred long enough ago
that significant improvement in knowledge has occurred since then. More recently, the dissemination of anthrax in multiple areas by U.S. mail has provided
an opportunity to study response to a biological agent in which person-to-person
spread and secondary cases does not occur. While there has been no purposeful
release of an agent in which person-to-person spread occurs, there are clearly
naturally occurring examples which can be used as models of such an event.
These range from such conditions as pulmonary tuberculosis to the more-re-
cently described, severe acute respiratory syndrome (SARS) and the latter served
as an excellent model for post-event planning. The areas of interest and concern
for public health in a post-event situation again can conveniently be grouped in
a series of initiatives:

- surveillance and epidemiology
- communication
- interaction with hospitals and health professionals to accomplish treatment and risk reduction
- deployment of medical materials, including vaccines and medications to both treat affected individuals and prophylactically treat individuals at risk
- removal of individuals from areas of risk
- segregation of individuals known to be affected or at risk to reduce further spread
- mental health issues
- other considerations

A. Surveillance

Surveillance in a post-event situation is somewhat distinct from pre-event surveillance in that a known agent has been recognized and the emphasis shifts from detection of an unusual event to detection of individuals who exhibit the symptom complexes characteristic of the agent known to have been released. Epidemiologic investigation begun by questioning individuals who have the symptoms becomes extremely important in identifying other individuals who may either be incubating disease or who may have been put at risk. This activity must be coordinated since individuals have a tendency to travel large distances in a relatively short period of time and multiple sites may be infected simultaneously or in succession by a noxious agent. It is necessary that surveillance activities be available twenty-four hours daily, seven days a week, to not only receive information but to respond in a rapid fashion. Complementing an active surveillance system, it is necessary to have a responsive laboratory, which is equipped with the latest technologies for infectious diseases and to a lesser degree, chemical identification. A level-A hospital laboratory or other freestanding laboratories should have agreements in place to forward specimens to a laboratory of level-B or C capability and ideally, one that is a member of the Laboratory Response Network which can handle not only hazardous pathogens but do so in a way that preserves chain of custody for potential future legal prosecution. As previously noted, it is necessary that those laboratories, in the Laboratory Response Network, have surge capacity so that, in the event they become overwhelmed by specimen acceptance, they can have additional resources available for the quick turnaround of results. Efforts are presently underway to facilitate electronic data reporting and sharing. The laboratory component of the National Electronic Disease Surveillance System (NEDSS) has been made operational to a variable degree in many states.

B. Communication

A unified command and an incident command system is critical to any emergency response. While public health is a key component, many of the direct response functions are the responsibility of a local or regional emergency management agency and the close working between those two entities as well as the private healthcare system is key to any emergency response. In order to facilitate coordination, it is necessary that communication devices be available which are compatible and optimally redundant means of communication be available. Ideally, a senior public health official is part of the incident command and emergency operation center to receive information from the field and to help formulate a cohesive plan for response. While it has been common for various groups such as police, fire, emergency management, and public health to deploy radio systems, in many instances the frequencies have not been compatible and such lack of consistency has led to fragmentation of effort, on occasion with serious or fatal consequence. Cell phone and land line phones are other means of communication and are useful for communication with agencies at a distance from an event that may not be reachable by radio transmission. Electronic computer-based communication with partners at both state and federal levels provides additional redundancy for the transmission of information. The Centers for Disease Control has recently deployed a Health Alert Network; this electronic form of data exchange is being used regularly to disseminate information of health importance with the goal of having people become comfortable enough with its use that it could be rapidly switched over in an emergency situation to disseminate important information to health providers and field personnel. In addition to communication between various health practitioners, health providers, and responders, communication with the public and at-risk communities becomes extremely important. It is necessary that this be done in a coordinated way, to avoid misinformation, and be presented by someone with known credibility. The goal should be to identify individuals who have been at risk, as well as to avoid panic among a larger number of individuals who have no actual risk but who may, because of lack of information, unnecessarily clog the healthcare delivery system or jam roadways by trying to avoid an area, thus making it difficult for responders to reach an area of concern. Such actions put more people at risk. By properly informing the public about potential health events, the electronic and print media are important allies and participants. The electronic media has the advantage of being able to rapidly transmit information and radio networks, in particular, have demonstrated their abilities to remain active in a wide variety of environmental conditions. The print media, although a somewhat slower avenue to disseminate information, has the advantage of covering facts in much greater detail and providing a written document to which people can repetitively refer for instructions. In some cities, local telephone companies have made use of supplements to their telephone directories to have generic information about emergency response. This, again, is an important avenue to reduce panic. It is clear that, in almost every incidence of both naturally occurring and man-made disaster, panic is the single biggest event. Clearly, a prime goal of terrorist activity is to produce panic and fears of the unknown as evidenced by the large number of people collecting dust and powders for analysis during the recent anthrax events.

C. Interaction with hospitals and health professionals to accomplish treatment and risk reduction

Hospitals and other acute-care facilities play an obvious central role in any public health response to natural or man-made disasters. Not only are the most seriously ill patients hospitalized, but hospital emergency rooms are apt to be jammed with self-referred individuals either because of risk or perceived risk. The ability to communicate that risk and delay the concerns of those individuals who are not at risk has a direct relationship to the number of people seeking emergency room evaluation. Good communication keeps a hospital emergency room from being unnecessarily congested. Central to any mass casualty event is field triage and, depending on the circumstances, it may be carried out by paramedics and other emergency response personnel, by nurses, in some instances by physicians and, in situations of extreme emergency, by other allied health practitioners. Surveillance information obtained soon after an event is of extreme importance to the triage personnel because they themselves may be exposed as part of this activity to either a biological or chemical agent. In order to err on the side of caution until the exact nature of an event is known, it is prudent in most instances that those individuals use protective garments and, occasionally, self-contained breathing apparatus. Triage needs to occur in proximity to the location of an event, particularly when there are multiple victims. But also, it needs to be far enough away to reduce the risk of further injury. There needs to be a close interaction with law enforcement personnel to ensure that the boundaries of a triage area are not violated and that casual onlookers do not have ready access to the area. It is anticipated in those areas, particularly those that have a Medical Reserve Corps, that people from the Corps would serve as the triage staff. It makes no sense that skilled and tertiary care physicians are asked to leave their hospital in order to accomplish field triage when there is a greater need for them to care for the most seriously ill patients who are apt to be transported to their institution for care. Similarly, as part of the triage activities, those tertiary-care hospitals close to an event would probably become the hospitals for the most critically ill patients. Those with less severe needs but requiring evaluation would be taken to institutions at greater distances. In the event of a large-scale disaster with multiple victims, if the capacities of a Reserve Corps were exhausted, triage individuals would need to come from contiguous jurisdictions and surrounding institutions that did not have the critical need for inpatient staffing. Depending on the nature of the event, it may be necessary for individuals to be decontaminated either in the field or on arrival at the hospital emergency room. Many large hospitals have established decontamination facilities and procedures in the event that decontamination is necessary. Decontamination, in some instances, may be as simple as removing clothing and showering, but may be complicated if exposure to vesicant agents or inhalational toxins has occurred. Should an infectious agent be implicated, particularly one that is spread person-to-person, such as smallpox, it is prudent that appropriately immunized staff be available to care for that individual and minimize risk to the caregivers. Similarly, many hospitals have either built negative-pressure emergency rooms or have been retrofitted with negative air pressure, at least in portions of the emergency room, and installed air handling systems which separate the emergency room from the main hospital system to reduce the potential spread of infectious agents to the at-large hospital population. Included in hospital contingency plans are schema to identify the least seriously ill patients and discharge them to provide beds for victims of a widespread catastrophe. Elective procedures, from radiology to surgery, would be curtailed so that such facilities would be at the ready. Mortuary facilities need to be established off site to tend to those who have died at a scene, and in the hospital to care for victims that expire in the hospital, and to allow for the rapid examination of remains to further define causative agents under the direction of the appropriate coroner or medical examiner. Depending on the nature and size of the event, and if the ordinary means of postmortem holding are exhausted, this may require the use of refrigerated trucks or warehouses or in the event of an extreme emergency, the use of large facilities, such as an airport hangar with the need to bring in refrigeration equipment. Depending on the nature of the contagion, the medical examiner may order cremation of the remains to control and reduce the contagion. Such issues are discussed in greater detail in other chapters.

D. Deployment of medical materials

Many regions have accumulated local stockpiles of emergency medications, vaccines, and equipment to use in the event of a natural or man-made emergency. These range from such measures as equipping firemen, paramedics, emergency medical technicians and other first responders with self-contained breathing apparatus and protective clothing to equipping paramedics and field personnel with agents such as atropine or 2-PAM (pralidoxime) to treat cholinesterase inhibitor poisonings. Most hospitals have at least small quantities of ciprofloxicin available to treat individuals who may have been exposed to anthrax or to begin prophylactic treatment of individuals who may be at risk. Larger public health agencies may have additional supplies of ciprofloxicin and in many instances, have small quantities of smallpox vaccine to begin immunization of healthcare workers and individuals at risk, should smallpox exposure occur. Although large numbers of healthcare workers did not volunteer to receive smallpox immunization, most areas have a small contingent of people who are appropriately immunized who could begin both epidemiologic investigation and treatment. It is reassuring to note that many individuals who previously had been immunized for smallpox and were re-immunized had an accelerated reaction, which would suggest that they have some residual immunity from the previous immunization. Based on the nature and size of a disaster, it may be necessary to mobilize the Strategic National Stockpile of pharmaceuticals and equipment, which are maintained at sites throughout the United States. The mobilization of the SNS is on request of a governor, after consultation with the Secretary of Health and. occurs at a statewide level. Multiple sites for acceptance of the SNS have been determined and the supplies, along with a minimal staff of expert consultants, can be made available within forty-eight hours of request. The dissemination of materials from the accepting site is, however, a local responsibility and requires appropriate numbers of pharmacists, pharmacy technicians, and couriers at the acceptance site to break down packaging and disseminate the materials to hospitals or predetermined community sites, for instance, for the administration of vaccines or medications. Such sites, in general, would be staffed with public health workers supplemented by nurses and physicians from the Medical Reserve Corps. Clerical staff and security staff needs to be obtained from the local workforce. Most areas have planned and practiced to be able to provide medications including immunizations to the entire population of an affected area within 100 hours using multiple sites.

E. Segregation of individuals known to be affected or at risk to reduce further spread

A general evacuation of an area affected by some type of disaster may be necessary because of continued hazard or the potential for further damage. In general, individuals affected by such an evacuation tend to be well or minimally affected by the initial event and would be temporarily housed in shelters such as schools, auditoria, or a combination of private and public facilities, including those already equipped for domiciliary care such as hotels and motels and those that can be converted with minimal effort to house individuals. The large numbers of people cohabiting leads to the potential spread of common infectious diseases such as respiratory illnesses as well as psychological unrest due to the sudden change of environment. At-risk individuals, such as the elderly, may be disproportionately impacted by any evacuation exercise and public health has a role to ensure that the mental anguish is minimized, that the unrelated infectious diseases are evaluated and treated as necessary to reduce spread, and that ongoing medical conditions present in the individuals so evacuated such as hypertension, diabetes, and other common but chronic illnesses are cared for, particularly when medications may not be readily available. Individuals on dialysis or respirators may pose special challenges as may prisoners. A second and more important public health initiative is the segregation of individuals known to be at risk or minimally affected with a potentially infectious condition in order to reduce spread. The isolation of people with person-to-person spread infectious diseases in either hospitals or at home has been a long-standing public health practice and has been widely used in the past to reduce the spread of infectious disease; it has become less common as potent antimicrobials have been developed so that the periods of infectivity of disease have become much shorter. There are still, however, times when such isolation is necessary. A good example is tuberculosis, where it is commonplace to restrict the movement of an individual with infectious disease until they are rendered noninfectious. More recently, it was the practice to restrict individuals with sudden acute respiratory syndrome (SARS) to their home during their period of infectivity. This endeavor proved effective when used to reduce person-to-person spread of that illness. The authority to restrict peoples' movement is well established by law and although the exact conditions of that restriction vary from region to region, in some instances requiring review in a timely fashion with the courts, the authority of public health to do so is a well established principle in all areas. Federal legislation has been enacted to allow for the emergency isolation of individuals and those areas with weak statutory authority have adopted that federal regulation and others have used it as a model to improve their existing regulatory authority. One of the goals of the federal regulation and always one of the goals of public health is to balance the individual's needs against the needs of society to protect itself and the federal regulation allows for the rapid isolation of individuals if, on review, it is found to be necessary. Such isolation or quarantine may extend to a forced isolation either in a home or institution equipped to restrict the movement of an individual and may require close coordination with law enforcement to ensure that the terms of that isolation are being met.

F. Mental health issues

Some of the mental health issues resulting from a disaster have been mentioned above and are more fully described in other chapters. However, since mental health programs in many jurisdictions are a part of the public health system and in others are closely aligned with public health, the public health system has a major role in providing mental health services. Those services must be in place not only for the workers, who in many instances are exposed to conditions and situations with which they are not familiar, or are not comfortable and that have at times resulted in long-term posttraumatic stress syndromes, but also include mental health services for victims who may be displaced from their usual domicile, are rendered unemployed, are unable to locate close family members and loved ones, or who may be overwhelmed by the enormity of the situation. Just as in every other area of public health, sharing of responsibilities is important. Many times, pastoral care is a useful adjunct included in pre-established mental health teams.

G. Other considerations

The public health system has operated on a principle, in general, that events confined to a single jurisdiction are handled by that jurisdiction so long as they are able. If more than one jurisdiction is involved, then there is a sharing of responsibility with the next highest level, which may be either a state or a region. The federal government has teams in place to assist in instances of severe disaster and although they have tremendous expertise, mobilizing them takes a reasonable amount of time and often, they are not familiar with local conditions that must be considered. Teams such as National Disaster Medical Assistance Team (ND-MATS), Veterinary Medical Assistance Teams (VMATS), and Mortician Teams (DMORTS) are available for consultation and help in a large disaster. Other skills and other agencies may be involved, depending on the unique nature of a particular incident. In the case of a zoonotic illness, teams of veterinarians may be mobilized to help with investigation and control. Food safety public health experts, including members of the FDA and Department of Agriculture, may be useful in the event of a food-borne illness. The unique nature of every public-health-related disaster requires constant re-evaluation of the circumstances, consultation with individuals who can share expertise, and a scaling up or scaling down of interventions and resources as the situation evolves.

Appendix A

National Association of Medical Examiners Mass Fatality Plan

NATIONAL ASSOCIATION OF MEDICAL EXAMINERS
MASS FATALITY PLAN

SECTION I - INTRODUCTION

I. Definition

Any situation in which there are more human bodies to be recovered and examined than can be handled by the usual local resources. Local teams should define the terms of disaster, personnel, equipment, and resources BEFORE the disaster hits.

II. Evaluation Team

   A. Should consist of at a minimum the CME/Coroner, the Operations Director, and the Chief Investigator who proceed together to the disaster site. The safety of the scene must be assessed and clearance issued by the appropriate agency before the evaluation team enters.

   B. Evaluate

      1. Potential or real number of fatalities

      2. Condition of the bodies

      3. Level of difficulty in recovery – types and numbers of personnel and equipment needed.

      4. Accessibility of the incident scene

      5. Possible biological, chemical, physical, or radiological hazards

   C. Begin the formulation of a plan for documentation, body recovery, and transportation

   D. Select a site for a Temporary Morgue – estimate personnel needs. This morgue can be used as a holding area until the examination center is prepared to receive additional bodies.

   E. Select a site for the Morgue Examination Center – estimate personnel needs

   F. Select a site for the Family Assistance Center- estimate personnel needs

   G. DMORT (Disaster Mortuary Operational Response Team) – If it appears advisable, DMORT can provide a Multidisciplinary Assistance Team to aid the evaluation of the need for additional personnel and equipment. The team should be available and on site in less than 24 hours. During an emergency response, DMORT works to support local authorities and provide technical assistance and personnel to recover, identify, and process deceased victims. The main unit may be preceded by a DMORT evaluation team. A part of National Disaster Medical Services (NDMS), DMORT may be activated under several legal authorities including the Federal Response Plan (FRP), the Public Health Services Act, the Aviation Disaster Family Assistance Act, Presidential Mandate, and Federal and State existing agreements. DMORT is accessed by the local medical examiner/coroner through a request to their Emergency Management Agency. DMORT also has temporary portable morgue facilities available.

III. Sites of Operation Under the Direction of the ME/Coroner

    A. The Scene(s): Body and initial evidence recovery; site of a temporary morgue if indicated.

    B. The Morgue Examination Center: Body identification and processing

    C. The Family Assistance Center:

        1. Acquisition of antemortem information

        2. Care of the families

        3. Media information

        4. Positive identification notification

    D. The Long Term Examination Site: Processing biological specimens and evidence not originally accessed at the Scene or Morgue/Examination Center.

SECTION II – SCENE RESPONSIBILITIES

I. Develop a plan in conjunction with police, fire, and rescue personnel. Incident Command System (ICS) will be instituted. This assures a unified command center with a specific individual in charge through which all activities are coordinated. It follows the standard military model.

II. Equipment: Getting things organized before attempting to move bodies.

    A. Designate an Equipment/Supply Officer(s)

    B. Protective Clothing: gloves, boots, coats, hard hats, rain suits, and respirators (etc) as dictated by the situation.

    C. Substantial Body Bags; number and type.

    D. Refrigerated Trucks with metal floors which allow decontamination: 20 bodies per 40 foot trailer at 35 - 38"F

2

  E. Transportation: Personnel, equipment, and bodies (military, other government, contract services, funeral homes)

  F. Tents & Storage

  G. Paint for numbering (1,2,3; P1, P2, P3; E1, E2, E3…)

  H. Flags for marking locations

  I. Plastic toe tags; Sharpie permanent pens

  J. Biohazard bags & boxes

  K. Photography equipment

  L. Gridding, laser survey, GPS systems

  M. Critical incident stress debriefing

  N. Rest stations and food

  O. Worker Safety – health provisions in place (includes having appropriate immunizations – Tetanus, Hepatitis B – up to date)

  P. Communication devices: radio, cell phones

  Q. Writing or computer equipment for scene log maintenance

III. Body Recovery Teams – Evaluation

  A. ME/Coroner Investigator

  B. ME/Coroner Assistant(s) – Police, fire, military

  C. Scribe

  D. Photographer: Separately badged. Personal cameras are not allowed at the site or scene of mortuary operations.

  E. Physical Anthropologist

  F. Evidence Technician

  G. Scene Registrar

IV. Body Recovery Teams – Removal & Transfer

  A. Recovery Evaluation Teams

  B. Up to 4 transport personnel/body to move a deceased from the site to the temporary morgue

3

C. Scene Log required in addition to individual case records and paperwork

V. Search and Body Recovery (document, document, document)

    A. Appoint a Body Recovery Team supervisor

    B. Assure overall security of the area

    C. Establish and execute an adequate search pattern

    D. Grid and consider the use of aids such as global positioning devices for each body or body part discovered EARLY in the discovery process.

    E. Utilize engineering/surveying consultants as indicated

    F. Document, process, and recover bodies, fragments and associated evidence (Scribe and photographer)

    G. Transport to and storage in temporary morgue and refrigerated truck pending transportation to the Examination Center

VI. Role of the Scene Registrar

    A. Arrange for scene data entry into the total record system

        1. Have a system in place to electronically track used supplies throughout your system

        2. Assure replenishment and billing information.

        3. NDMS can have acquisition programs rapidly in place to assist.

SECTION III - MORGUE/EXAMINATION CENTER

This material applies in part to both the Temporary Morgue and the Morgue/Examination Center. The DMORT web site (www.DMORT.org) contains suggestions for equipment and supplies.

I. Equipment: Early considerations

    A. Site selection based on the findings of the Evaluation Team

    B. Security/ID badges; different colors reference function and access.

    C. Unique numbering system separate from your usual case numeric system.

    D. Refrigerated trucks with ramps to allow access and egress

E. Protective clothing - gloves, scrubs, aprons, shoes, shoe covers, masks, coveralls, headwear, respirators

F. Communications - telephones, radios, fax, PA (paging systems); local cell operators may designate a specific reserved air wave.

G. Computers – programs and operators – all electronic files (including WIN ID, supplies, tracking, etc.) should be backed up daily.

H. Records

1. Personnel log including name, agency, SSN & in and out time.

2. Morgue/Examination Center Registrar

3. Antemortem and postmortem formats and forms

4. Entry operators/Data analysts

I. Office equipment and supplies – copiers, typewriters, log books, etc…

J. Disaster Victim Packet – should contain all forms and paperwork necessary for every examination station

K. Station Processing Plan – flexible to fit the situation

L. Worker Safety and Comfort Supplies

1. Healthcare provisions in place

2. Immunization records

3. Rest areas including toilet facilities

4. Nutrition needs

5. Critical Incident Stress Debriefing

II. Station System and Personnel (suggested procedure – local adaptation will be necessary)

A. Registration in Body Receiving Area

1. Receipt of DMORT Transportation Log or like document completed at the Temporary Morgue

2. Log in documentation from Temporary Morgue: date, time, and numbering (from the scene)

3. Assignment of permanent body tracker

4. Transfer of chart and all required documentation (Disaster Victim Packet) to the individual tracker.

B. Screening Station: Personal effects and clothing documentation/anatomic charting/further evidence collection. This is the point at which a decision can be made for a specimen (body part, fragmentary

5

remains, partial body) to take a long path through all subsequent stations or a shorter path with an examination at the morphology station and DNA only retrieved. Criteria for long or short path need to be established before the disaster.

1. Medical Examiner/Coroner's officer

2. Medical Examiner/Coroner's officer assistant

3. Scribe

4. Photographer and assistant

5. Personal Effects Technician

6. Evidence Technician

7   Anthropology consultant

8. Bomb Tech or other specialist as indicated

9. Complete necessary forms and return to tracker

N.B.: All paperwork generated at this station (Disaster Victim Packet) must be placed in the case file to go with the tracker and body to the next station. This procedure is repeated at every station.

10. Option of DNA or other convenient specimen procurement (requires lab tech for transmission)

C. Print Station (finger, palm, foot)

1. Print Specialist – Local Law Enforcement, FBI Disaster Squad

2. Print all bodies

3. Complete proper documentary form

4. Fingers or hands removed only at the discretion of the Chief Medical Examiner/Coroner. If removed – place in a properly identified container and place them back with the body after processing.

D. Radiology/X-ray Station

1. Radiologist

2. X-ray technician/assistant

3. Portable x-ray units, film and developers

4. Full body x-rays are mandatory

5. Dental x-rays may be a part of this operation or are often a part of the Dental Station operation as

6

dictated the Chief Odontologist. A bomb technician or other specialist as indicated may be needed here.

6. Log all films

- Morgue ID #

- Date/time

- Radiograph #

- # of films taken

- Initials or signature of technician

E. Dental Station

1. Odontologist

2. Dental assistant

3. Photographer

4. Evidence technician

5. Scribe

6. X-rays – if not previously performed

7. Charting – The universal numbering system, 1-32 with the upper right 3rd molar as #1, upper central incisors as #8 & #9, upper let 3rd molar as #16, lower leg 3rd molar as #17 and lower right 3rd molar as #32 is usually preferred. There is also a FDI numbering system available.

8. Immediately enter data into WIN ID II (2002)

9. Jaws are only removed on non-viewable bodies (the funeral director is an excellent consultant) at the discretion of the CME/Coroner at the request of the Chief Odontologist. If removed – place in a properly identified container and place them back with the body after processing. Many medical examiners feel that jaw removal is antiquated and unnecessary with modern dental technology.

F. Autopsy Station

1. The decision to do complete or partial autopsies resides with the Medical Examiner/Coroner authority locally responsible for body processing and death certification. Some reasons for complete autopsies:

- Homicides – terrorism

- Indeterminate manner of death

- Flight crews – the same pathologist should do all members

- Unidentified remains

- Federal request

- Local ME/Coroner request

2. Forensic pathologist

3. Autopsy assistant

4. Evidence technician

5. Bomb tech or other specialist as indicated

6. Scribe

7. Photographer

8. Lab technician

9. DNA (4 mL blood in a purple top tube; 5 – 10 gm skeletal muscle, spleen, liver, bone, and/or teeth), toxicology and other specimen procurement. Some may have already be obtained at the initial screening station in some operations – requires lab tech for proper documentation and transmission.

10. Evidence collection continues

11. Completion of form designating preliminary autopsy findings Victim Identification Profile (VIP)/DMORT Program, Pathology examination of partial or complete remains)

12. Documentary forms to the tracker

13. Histology specimens to the lab tech

14. Toxicology specimens to lab tech for transmission

G. Anthropology/Morphology Station

1. Personnel needed:

- Anthropologist

- Anthropology assistant

- Scribe

8

- Evidence Technician

- Photographer

- Radiographer

- Forensic pathologist

2. Fragmented, incomplete, charred, commingled remains

3. Documentation to the tracker with the remains

4. If a bone section or the like is retained, place in a properly identified container and place it back with the body after processing. If it is a specimen for DNA, for example, it is to be properly documented and transmitted to a laboratory technician.

H. Body Storage

1. Individual tracker returns the body to the receiving area.

2. The body or part, with the direction of the receiving registrar is transferred to the appropriate secure designated "processed" refrigerated area and documented. The refrigerated area must be fully staffed with receivers and security.

3. The Examination Center Registrar receives the Victim Disaster Packet from the tracker and assures proper transfer to the Records Management Team.

4. Special storage sites should be designated for specimens such as DNA & Toxicology.

I. Records Management Team

1. Personnel needed:

- Supervisor/Registrar

- Computer entry clerks

- Data clerks

- File clerks

- Security

- Communication clerks – telephone, e-mail and fax (one member made an entry here – I was unable to read) from other sites (scene, family assistance center, command post)

2. Establish tracking procedures for files

3. Establish back-up protocols for computer files

SECTION IV - LONG TERM EXAMINATION/"SIFTING" SITE

In any mass fatality event in which there is extensive property destruction, the need for a long term off-site examination center will exist.

I. Site Selection

The site should be secure, accessible, and well away from the other sites of operation.

II. Equipment

A. Storage for evidence

B. Refrigeration

C. Communication

D. Protective gear

E. Worker safety and comfort supplies

1. Health care

2. Rest areas including toilet facilities

3. Nutrition needs

4. Critical incident stress debriefing

5. Tent

F. Heavy duty equipment for debris removal and disposition

G. Transportation services for body parts and evidence (to the examination center)

H. Transportation services for personnel

I. Sifting grids, tools, wheelbarrows, etc.

III. Personnel

A. Anthropologist

10

B. Anthropology assistant

C. Evidence technicians

D. Scribe

E. Registrar – proper transmission and overall entry of data

F. Photographer

G. Bomb tech or other specialist as indicated

H. Supply officer

I. Pathology, radiology and odontology services remain available at the Examination Center and , if needed, at any long term sifting site.

J. Security – 24 hour for as long as operational

K. Workers capable of assisting with significant physical labor demands

IV. This site will likely remain functional well after the scene, Examination Center, and Family Assistance Center are closed. It is the responsibility of the ME/Coroner to assure proper support and operation of this site as long as it is required.

SECTION V - FAMILY ASSISTANCE CENTER

A representative of the Medical Examiner's office should be in charge during the initial setting up of the Family Assistance Center (FAC). Personnel may be recruited from the local Funeral Directors Association. The Family Assistance Center is a multi-agency organization and can not be handled by the Medical Examiner alone. In the case of aviation disasters, the National Transportation Safety Board (NTSB) requires the airline involved to set up the FAC. DMORT has members assigned to this "go team".

I. Site Selection

A. Functional for the specific incident.

B. Close to the actual scene.

C. Easily accessible for families.

D. Adequate parking.

II. Security

A. Sheltering families from possible media intrusion.

B. Secure parking lot, inside, and outside the FAC.

C. Use of military personnel as well as police.

III. Transportation Services

    A. Secure, sensitive, and professional.

    B. Knowledgeable of the area.

    C. Serve family, friends, and staff needs.

IV. Administrative Staff

    A. Family Assistance Center Team Leader/Coordinator

        1. Overall operation supervisor

        2. Establishes antemortem data acquisition and entry plan

        3. Coordinates operation with Registrar/Records Supervisor

        4. Conducts daily briefings with families before media briefings.

        5. Conducts daily briefings with media in a secure area away from friends & family.

        6. Establishes and supervises death notification procedures with medical, psychological, and religious personnel

        7. Coordinates Center transportation and security plans

        8. Coordinates roles of family assistance team members

        9. Coordinates relations with outside agencies

        10. Serves as a member of the death notification team

        11. Provide for critical incident stress debriefing

    B. Medical Examiner/Coroner Representatives

    Function in liaison and general inquiry needs. Outside staff such as funeral directors familiar with ME/Coroner operations are desirable.

    C. Family interview personnel for antemortem data acquisition

    D. Computer specialists for antemortem data entry and transfer to the Morgue/Examination Center

E. Communication Specialists

    1. Telephone services for the Center

    2. Referring media inquiries to the FAC Team Leader from addressing at the daily briefings

F. Support Services

    1. Red Cross/Salvation Army/other service organizations

    2. Communication companies

    3. Food services

    4. Religious services

    5. Mental health support

    6. Physical health support

    7. Massage therapy/chiropractic

    8. Therapy animals

    9. Site support – Janitorial/Plumbing/Electrical

    10. Translators and Embassy and Consulate representatives when international victims are involved.

G. Death Notification Procedure/Release of Body, Identified Parts, and Effects

    1. All families should be counseled with regard to their wishes for disposal should additional body parts be identified. Their decision must be recorded on an appropriate form.

    2. After positive identification has been established by the ID Team and approved by the CME/Coroner.

    3. Conducted preferably by the staff of the Family Assistance Center according to an established protocol.

    4. A release authorization form should be completed and placed in the Victim Disaster Packet.

    5. Associated personal effects not deemed to be evidence should be released with the body and documented according to the standard operating procedure of the ME/Coroner jurisdiction involved.

    6. Unassociated personal effects will be handled through a contract with a recovered property company (i.e. Kenyon International)

    7. Unidentified body parts will be documented and stored as "common tissue". Subsequent disposal will be the responsibility of the ME/Coroner. This procedure will likely be established through consultation with victims groups and establishing a group consensus consistent with local regulations

and resources.

8. A death certificate should be released to the funeral home with any remains. (See also Section VII – Death Certificates)

9. A release log will be kept separately to document the overall process.

SECTION VI - LOGISTICS

I. Logistics Team

Responsible for the operation of the logistics section, including the acquisition, storage, issue, and accountability of all supplies and equipment necessary to support the operation. NDMS has supplemental programs which can be put in place.

A. Team Leader

➤ Will monitor the status of all procurement actions.

➤ Will hand-carry, as necessary, all high-priority supply actions.

➤ Will maintain expense data, accountability documents, procurement documents, and other information pertaining to the logistics operation.

➤ Will insure that the logistics section is staffed at all times during operating hours.

➤ Will insure that personnel logs including name, agency, SSN and in and out times are maintained at all sites of operation.

B. Supply Clerks

➤ Will perform duties assigned by the team leader to include, but not limited to, staffing the logistics section of the morgue, making supply runs, preparing supply documents, issuing supplies and equipment etc.

SECTION VII - IDENTIFICATION/DEATH CERTIFICATION

I. The final determination of body or body parts positive identification is the sole responsibility of the local ME/Coroner in which the disaster occurs.

II. I.D. Team

    A. Composition: Pathologist, dentist, anthropologist, radiologist, print technician, investigative staff, and family counselor.

    B. Must meet at the end of each working day.

    C. Review all proposed positive identifications.

    D. Make recommendations daily to the ME/Coroner.

III. Positive identifications should be transferred to the Family Assistance Center for action by the Death Notification Team.

IV. All notification procedures are the responsibility of the ME/Coroner.

V. Possible identification methods may include:

    A. DNA

    B. Prints

    C. Dental

    D. Medical radiography

    E. Distinctive physical characteristics

    F. Serial numbers on permanently installed medical devices

    G. Visual in some cases (N.B. – personal effects do not constitute a true means of identification).

VI. Death Certificates

    A. Issued according to procedures normally in place and as directed by the local ME/Coroner jurisdiction.

    B. The administrative or judicial issuance of death certificates in situations in which there is an absence of positive physical forensic scientific identification is a responsibility solely of the local ME/Coroner in conjunction with local legal and public health authorities.

SECTION VIII – MASS FATALITIES RESOURCE LIST

It is recommended that 24/7 contact methods be available and kept up to date by quarterly review for local and federal resources necessary for the successful management of a mass fatality incident. This is a major planning responsibility for the local ME/Coroner.

Although any consultants such as DMORT or USAR are ultimately under the supervision of the local medicolegal authority, it is the responsibility of that authority to see that all necessary logistical support services for them are put in place.

- Adjutant General
- Airlines
- Ambulance
- American Red Cross
- Architects
- Attorney General
- Automobile rental
- Barriers
- Batteries
- Biohazard disposal and supplies
- Body bags
- Body handlers
  - Local police and fire auxiliary
  - National Guard
  - Funeral Directors Association
- Boots and Footwear – steel toe/shank
- CDC
  - Bioterrorism
  - www.bt.cd.gov
  - 770-488-7100
- Chairs
- Chiropractic

- Cleaning supplies
- Clergy/Religious resources
- Coats
- Contractors
  - Commercial
  - Kenyon International – Personal effects
- Communications
- Computers and software programs
- Copiers
- Dental technicians
- Dentist (Odontologist)
- Disaster Mortuary Team (DMORT)
  - State Emergency Management
  - 1-800-USA-NDMS
- Day Care
- Dogs, cadaver
- Domestic Preparedness
  - Hotline 1-800-424-8802
  - Helpline 1-800-368-6498
- Electrician
- Emergency management
- Engineers

16

- Environmental Protection Agency
  1-201-321-6765
- Fax machines
- Film
- Fingerprint technicians
  - FBI Disaster Squad
  - Local and State Law Enforcement
- FAA 1-718-553-1919
- Fire service
- Flags and stakes
- Flashlights
- Food and beverage
  - Restaurant Association
- Funeral Directors Association
- Generators
- Governor
- Gridding and laser surveying equipment
- Hard hats
- Hazmat
- Health and Human Services
- Health Department
- Helicopters
- Hotels and motels
- ID badges
- Insurance, State Dept of

- Laundry service
- Maintenance supplies
- Maps
- Massage therapy
- Media
- Medical supplies
- Medical societies
- Mental health
- Military
- Mobile morgue   1-800-USA-NDMS
- Morgue supplies
- NTSB 1-202-314-6100
- National Guard
- Osteopathic society
- Office supplies
- Pathologists
  - AFIP 1-301-319-0000
- Portable x-ray services
- Photographers
- Police services
- Protective clothing
- Radiation health
- Radiologist
- Radiologic technicians
- Rain gear
- Refrigerated trucks

17

- Secret Service   1-315-448-0304
- Salvation Army
- Security
- Search dogs
- Signs
- Spray paint
- Tables
- Telecommunication
- Tents
- Toe tags
  - Plastic (Kinko's for example)
- Trackers
  - DMORT
  - Funeral Directors
  - National Guard
- Trailers (supply storage)
- Translation Services
- Transportation
  - Body
  - Personnel
- Transportation workers
  - Motor Pool
  - Signs
  - Barriers
- Turnpike Authority
- Travel services

- Typewriters
- Urban Search & Rescue
  - 1-800-USA-NDMS
  - 1-703-222-6277
- Volunteer organizations
- Weather services
- Websites
- X-ray supplies and equipment

SECTION IX – APPENDIX (FORMS AND REFERENCES)

18

Disaster Scene
Death Investigation Record

Date/Time: _____   Body Number: _____

Possible Name of Deceased: _____

Race: _____   Sex: _____   Approximate Age: _____

Physical Investigation: _____   Photos Taken: Yes ____ No ____

Clothing/Personal Effects:

Position and Location of Body: (Grid location, GPS, etc./Note type of surface the body is on, covering, etc.)

| Rigor Mortis: | Livor: | Body Temperature: |

| Observations/Trauma (NOTE MISSING PARTS) | Decomposition and Artifacts: |

Identifying Marks: (i.e scars. tattoo. etc)

Comments/Summary

Team Leader: _____

Recovery Team: _____

Notification of Mass Disaster

Medical Examiner's Office Notified by _____
NAME OF CALLER

from _____ at _____
AGENCY   DATE AND TIME

Call back number(s) _____

Type of Incident (i.e. aircraft crash, train derailment)

_____

Agency handing scene _____
                                                          TELEPHONE #

Approximately Number of Fatalities _____

Date and Time of Occurrence _____

Exact Location of Incident

_____

Access Route to Use

_____

Noteworthy Conditions (i.e. Hazards to responders, terrain, chemical/biological exposure)

_____

Exact Location of Command Post _____
                                                          TELEPHONE
Exact Location of Staging Area _____

Need a Representative Now? _____

When do you anticipate needing a disaster response? _____

    Pathologist on duty notified. _____   Date and Time _____
    By: _____   Comments: _____

    Chief Medical Examiner notified: _____ Date and Time _____
    By: _____   Comments: _____

    Director of Operations notified: _____ Date and Time _____
    By: _____   Comments: _____

Transportation Log

ALL of the following fields must be completed before the transfer vehicle is released to the morgue. The driver of the transfer vehicle is responsible for the log sheet until he/she releases it to the admitting section leader at the morgue. Additional sheets may be added depending on the number of body bags that are being transferred.

Total Number of Body Bags: _____

License Number of the Vehicle: _____

_____   _____
Driver's Name (Print)   Driver's Signature

_____
Date and Time Leaving Crash Site

_____   _____
Admitting Section Leader (Print)   Admitting Section Leader's Signature

_____
Date and Time Vehicle Arrived at Morgue

Morgue Admission Log

Body Bag Number	Admitting Section Leader	Date & Time of Admission	Body Escort Name	Destination of Remains

Anthropology Log

Anthropologist	Morgue Number	Date/Time Arrived	Gender	Age	Race	Stature	General Description

Photography Log

Photographer	Film Roll & Picture No.	Morgue Number	Description of Photograph

Pathology Log

Pathologist	Morgue Number	Date & Time Arrived	General Description	Date & Time Left	Path Initials

Radiology Log

Requested by:	Morgue No.	Date & Time Arrived	Radiograph No.	No. of Radiographs Taken	Radiology Technician

Release Log

Decedent Name	Morgue Number	Date & Time Released	Removal Person's Name	Removal Vehicle License No.	Funeral Home

Release Authorization

Name of Deceased _____ MRN-_____

Please be advised unidentified human tissue will be buried in an appropriate manner.

In the event any additional tissue(s) are recovered in the future and are identified as belonging to the above named deceased. I/We request the following:

1.   ( )   I/We do not wish to be notified. I/We are authorizing the appropriate officials to disposal of said tissue(s) by methods deemed appropriate by said officials.

2.   ( )   I/We wish to be notified and will make a decision regarding disposition at that time.

I/We the undersigned hereby authorize the _____Office to release the

(Name of ME / Coroner)

Remains of _____ to the designated Disaster Mortuary Team or

(Name of Deceased)

other authorized agent.

I/We further authorize the designated Disaster Mortuary Team or another authorized agent to embalm, and perform post mortem reconstructive surgery techniques, and otherwise prepare, as they deem necessary and upon completion to release said remains to:

_____

_____

_____

(Name, address & phone of Funeral Home or Agent)

I/We certify that I/We have read and understand this document. I/We further state that I/We are all of the next of kin, or represent all of the next of kin and am/are legally authorized, and/or charged with the responsibility of burial and/or final disposition of above said deceased.

Signed: _____ Relationship to Deceased: _____

Print Name: _____ Date Signed: _____ Time: _____

Complete Address: _____

Telephone Number. _____

Signed: _____ Relationship to Deceased: _____

Print Name: _____ Date Signed: _____ Time: _____

Complete Address: _____

Telephone Number: _____

Witness: _____

Printed Name of Witness   Signature of Witness

Requested Records List

Case Number	Victim: Last Name	First Name	Middle Name

Informant Last/First/Middle Name:
Informant Address:
Informant Phone:

Location	Contact	Phone	Date Ordered	Date Received
Dental				
Fingerprints				
Radiographs				
Medical Records				
Photo Requests				
Notes				

Policy on Release of <u>Incomplete</u> Human Remains

Incomplete is defined as a body with any missing structure due to the disaster incident.

When Positive identification is made by the Medical Examiner / Coroner of a disaster victim classified as Incomplete Human Remains the "Declaration of Positive Identification of Disaster Victim". Following the completion of said form, the next of kin will be notified through established procedures by designated staff at the Family Assistance Center. Release Authorization Form shall be used for "Incomplete Human Remains". This form must be signed by the next of kin or person acting as such and returned to the Mortuary Operations Center.

If, after release of the "Incomplete Human Remains", additional tissue(s) or structure(s) are recovered and positively identified as belonging to the released "Incomplete Human Remains" appropriate next of kin wishes will be followed as designated on the "Incomplete Human Remains Form".

The Incomplete Human Remains Form outlines two options for the next of kin. They are:

1.   I/We **do not** wish to be notified. I/We are authorizing the appropriate officials to dispose of said tissue(s) by methods deemed appropriate by said officials.

2.   I/We wish to be notified and will make a decision regarding disposition at the time.

The policy is agreed upon and adopted this date: _____

Signed: _____   Signed: _____
                Medical Examiner / Corner   DMORT Incident Commander

Print Name: _____   Print Name: _____

SAMPLE / LETTER

Official Notification to Next of Kin Regarding Positive Identification of Victim

(The following is a suggested format, which should be created on the official letterhead of the Office Medical Examiner / Coroner of jurisdiction)

Date

Name of Next of Kin
Address

Dear   ,

      Please consider this letter official notification to you and your family that the body of your   .... Enter relationship ....., ... Enter full name or deceased......, has been positively identified.   Identification was accomplished as a result of forensic examinations correlated with ante-mortem records. On behalf of the entire mortuary disaster team, please accept our heartfelt condolences regarding the loss of your loved one.

      I appreciate your patience and cooperation during this most trying time. It is necessary for you and your family to make certain decisions regarding disposition. Please carefully read the following information and complete where necessary.

      Our official will arrange for your ......enter relationship... to be transferred to a funeral home or agent of your designation. Please sign and return the attached RELEASE FORM to the official who delivered this form to you.

Sincerely,

Name of Medical Examiner / Coroner or designee:

NOTE:
(Attach to this letter DMORT Form 320A "Release Authorization" if remains are classified as "Incomplete Human Remains" INC/HR or DMORT Form 320B "Release Authorization" if the remains are classified as "Complete Human Remains" C/HR.)

VIP Personal Information
Page 1 of 8

Name _____ / _____ / _____   Gender ○ Male ○ Female
    Last   First   Middle   Maiden/Birth name _____

Address _____   Phone (H) _____
   City _____ State _____ Zip _____   Phone (W) _____
Res County _____ Res Country _____ USA _____   Phone (O) _____

Live Inside City Limits ○ Yes ○ No   Race: ○ African American ○ Hispanic   ○ Asian/Pacific Islander
                          ○ Caucasian ○ Native American ○ Other _____

Social Security # / Other _____   Age _____   Date of Birth _____
                                           (MMDD/YYYY)
   Citizenship (1 or more) _____
Naturalization Card ○ Yes ○ No   Religion _____
   Alias   1 _____   2 _____
           Last   First   Middle   Last   First   Middle

    Birth Hospital   Birth City   State/Country

Group Status: ○ Traveling Alone ○ Group   such as family, company, sports team or school
   Group Type: _____   Fam/Grp Name _____
If family group, please list other family members below:
Related to _____

Marital Status ☐ Never Married ☐ Widowed ☐ Divorced ☐ Separated ☐ Unknown   Wedding Date _____
                                                  (MMDD/YYYY)
Spouse _____   ☐ Living ☐ Deceased ☐ Unknown
     Last   Maiden/Birth name   First   Middle
Father _____   ☐ Living ☐ Deceased ☐ Unknown
     Last   First   Middle
Mother _____   ☐ Living ☐ Deceased ☐ Unknown
     Last Maiden/Birth name First   Middle
Legal Next of Kin _____   Phone _____
          Last   First   Middle
Address: _____   On Site Phone _____
   City _____ State _____ Zip _____
        ☐ Wife   ☐ Father ☐ Brother ☐ Son   ☐ Employer ☐ Other _____
Relationship: ☐ Husband ☐ Mother ☐ Sister ☐ Daughter ☐ Friend

Informant 1: Name _____   Phone _____
          Last   First
Address _____   On Site Phone _____
City _____ State _____ Zip _____
Relationship ○ Wife   ○ Father ○ Brother ○ Son   ○ Employer ○ Other
         ○ Husband ○ Mother ○ Sister ○ Daughter ○ Friend   Please place other here

Informant 2: Name _____
          Last   First
Address _____   Phone _____
   City _____ State _____ Zip _____   On Site Phone _____
Relationship ○ Wife   ○ Father ○ Brother ○ Son   ○ Employer ○ Other
         ○ Husband ○ Mother ○ Sister ○ Daughter ○ Friend   Please place other relationship here

V9.2002

VIP Personal Information
Page 2 of 8

Name _____ / _____ / _____   ○ Male
                    Last   First   Middle   ○ Female

Dentist Name _____

Address _____   ☐ Extensive Dental Work   ☐ Most/all teeth
                                ☐ Lower dentures   ☐ Dental Films
City _____ State ____ Zip _____ ☐ Upper dentures   ☐ Bridge
                                ☐ Upper & Lower   ☐ Other
Phone _____   ☐ Partial Plate

Dentist 2 _____   ☐ Braces
                                ☐ No teeth
Address _____

City _____ State ____ Zip _____

Phone _____

Medical Radiographs?   **Physican(s)** _____

○ Yes
○ No   **Address**

Medical Radiographs Location	Potential Type of Radiographs - and dates taken if known

---

Objects in   ☐ Pacemaker ☐ Steel plate ☐ Shrapnel
Body: ☐ Bullets   ☐ Needles   ☐ Other _____

Old Fractures: Description: _____   Please place other objects here
○ Yes ○ No   _____

Surgery ☐ Gall Bladder   ☐ Laparotomy   ☐ Breast Implants
           ☐ Appendectomy   ☐ Caesarean   ☐ Open heart
           ☐ Tracheotomy   ☐ Mastectomy   ☐ Other _____
                                              Please place other surgery here

Unique   Description of: Scars, Operations, birthmarks, burns, missing organs, amputations, other special characteristics
Characteristics
○ Yes ○ No   _____
                   _____

Prosthetic   **Prosthetic Location/Description**
○ Yes   _____
○ No   _____

Prints on File: **Prints Located**
○ Yes ○ No
☐ Fingerprints   _____
☐ Footprints   _____

Employer & Address Please list last employer if retired - Information on additional employers should be placed on page 6

_____
_____

Type of Business _____

Occupation _____   V9.2002

VIP Personal Information
Page 3 of 8

Name _____ / _____ / _____   ○ Male
       Last   First   Middle   ○ Female

Height inches ○ Less than 24 ○ 24-36" ○ 37-48" ○ 49-60" ○ 61-72" ○ 73-84" ○ 85-96" ○ Over 96"

Weight in ○ less than 10 ○ 41-60   ○ 101-120 ○ 161-180 ○ 221-240 ○ 281-300
Pounds   ○   11-20   ○ 61-80   ○ 121-140 ○ 181-200 ○ 241-260 ○ Greater than 300
               ○   21-40   ○ 81-100 ○ 141-160 ○ 201-220 ○ 261-280

Eye   ☐ Blue   ☐ Green ☐ Grey   **Eye**   ☐ Missing R ☐ Glass R ☐ Cataract R ☐ Blind R
Color ☐ Brown ☐ Hazel   **Status** ☐ Missing L ☐ Glass L ☐ Cataract L ☐ Blind L

Optical ☐ Glasses   **Description**
            ☐ Contacts   _____
            ☐ None   _____

Hair Color ☐ Auburn ☐ Brown ☐ Gray ☐ Salt & Pepper ☐ Other _____
               ☐ Blonde ☐ Black ☐ Red   ☐ White   Please place other here

Hair Colored ○ Yes ○ No ○ Unknown   **Color** _____   **Hair Style** _____

Hair Accessory ☐ Wig ☐ Toupee ☐ Hair Piece ☐ Hair Transplant

Hair Length ○ Short 1-3" ○ Medium 4-8" ○ Long 8-12" ○ Very Long 10-24" ○ Over 24" ○ Bald

Hair Description _____

Facial Hair Color ○ Blonde ○ Brown ○ Black ○ Gray ○ Red ○ Salt & Pepper ○ White ○ N/Applicable

Facial Hair Type ○ Beard ○ Beard & Moustache ○ Moustache ○ Clean Shaven ○ Goatee ○ N/Applicable

Facial Hair Style ○ Fu Manchu   ○ Mutton Chops
                      ○ Handle Bar   ○ Pencil Thin Upper Lip
                      ○ Whiskers Under Lower Lip ○ Full Upper Lip

Facial Hair Notes _____

Ear Lobes ○ Attached ○ Unattached ○ Unknown   **Circumcision** ○ Yes ○ No ○ Unknown ○ NA

Fingernail Type ○ Natural ○ Artificial ○ Unknown   **Length** ○ Extremely Long ○ Long ○ Medium ○ Short
Fingernail Color _____ **Fingernail Charactersitics** ☐ Bites ☐ Mishapen ☐ Decorated ☐ Stained
Description
Toenail Color _____ **Toenail Characteristics** ☐ Bites ☐ Mishapen ☐ Decorated ☐ Stained
Toenail description

Complexion: ○ Light ○ Medium ○ Dark ○ Acne ○ Tanned ○ Olive ○ Ruddy

Tan Mark Description _____

Tatoo(s) ○ Yes **Description/** _____
             ○ No   **Body Location** _____

Can family draw a picture? _____

Tatoo   ○ Yes ○ Unknown **Tatoo**
Photos ○ No   ○ NA   **Photo Location** _____

        Body Piercing(s)? ☐ Yes ☐ No

Body Piercing Location(s) _____
Body Piercing Description _____

V9.2002

VIP Personal Information
Page 4 of 8

Name _____ / _____ / _____   ○ Male   ○ Female
            Last   First   Middle

A= Data not available   B= Photo   C= Further information available on page 6

#	Clothing Items	Material	Color	Description	Size	A	B	C
01	Hat					☐ A	☐ B	☐ C
02	Overcoat					☐ A	☐ B	☐ C
03	Scarf					☐ A	☐ B	☐ C
04	Gloves					☐ A	☐ B	☐ C
05	Jacket					☐ A	☐ B	☐ C
26	Suspenders/Braces					☐ A	☐ B	☐ C
14	Sweater					☐ A	☐ B	☐ C
09	Vest					☐ A	☐ B	☐ C
07	Tie					☐ A	☐ B	☐ C
08	Shirt					☐ A	☐ B	☐ C
15	Blouse					☐ A	☐ B	☐ C
06	Undershirt					☐ A	☐ B	☐ C
18	Chemise/Camisole					☐ A	☐ B	☐ C
19	Bra					☐ A	☐ B	☐ C
11	Underpants					☐ A	☐ B	☐ C
20	Girdle					☐ A	☐ B	☐ C
17	Slip					☐ A	☐ B	☐ C
10	Trousers/Slacks					☐ A	☐ B	☐ C
23	Shorts/walking					☐ A	☐ B	☐ C
13	Dress					☐ A	☐ B	☐ C
16	Skirt					☐ A	☐ B	☐ C
12	Socks					☐ A	☐ B	☐ C
21	Hose/Stockings					☐ A	☐ B	☐ C
22	Tights					☐ A	☐ B	☐ C
24	Belt					☐ A	☐ B	☐ C
25	Belt Buckle					☐ A	☐ B	☐ C
27	Other 1					☐ A	☐ B	☐ C
28	Other 2					☐ A	☐ B	☐ C
29	Other 3					☐ A	☐ B	☐ C
30	Other 4					☐ A	☐ B	☐ C

V9.2002

VIP Personal Information

Page 5 of 8

Name _____ / _____ / _____ ○ Male ○ Female
Last   First   Middle

Shoes

A= Data not available B= Photo C= Further information available on page 6

#	Material	Color	Description	Label	Size US	Size cm	A	B	C
01 Shoes							□A	□B	□C

Watch

A= Data not available B= Photo C= Further information available on page 6

#	Type	Material	Color	Description	Make	Inscription	A	B	C
01	Digital						□A	□B	□C
02	Analog						□A	□B	□C
03	Other						□A	□B	□C

04 Worn □ Right Wrist □ Left Wrist □ Finger □ Pin On □ Pocket Watch

05 Band □ Leather □ Metal □ Other   Specify Other _____   Band Color _____

A= Data not available B= Photo C= Further information available on page 6

#	Jewelry	Material Color	Stone Color	Description	Inscription	Where Worn	A	B	C
01	Wedding Ring						□A	□B	□C
02	Finger Rings						□A	□B	□C
03	Ear Rings						□A	□B	□C
04	Earclips						□A	□B	□C
05	Neck Chains						□A	□B	□C
06	Pendant Chain						□A	□B	□C
07	Other Chains						□A	□B	□C
08	Bracelets						□A	□B	□C
09	Medic Alert						□A	□B	□C
10	Other2						□A	□B	□C
11	Other3						□A	□B	□C
12	Other4						□A	□B	□C
13	Other5						□A	□B	□C

Use this space for more info regarding jewelry:

V9.2002

VIP Personal Information
Page 6 of 8

| Name | _____ / _____ / _____ | ○ Male |
| | Last   First   Middle | ○ Female |

Wallet: Description _____

       Contents _____

Purse: Description _____

       Contents

**Other Personal
Effects**

Ever in Armed Forces?   ○ Yes   ○ No   ○ Unknown   Military Branch _____

Military Service Number _____   Nation Served _____

Approximate Service Date _____

Highest Education Level: Elem/Second (0-12)   _____   Or   College (1-5+)   _____

Additional Data

V9.2002

VIP Personal Information

Page 7 of 8

Name		/		/		SS#	
	Last		First		Middle		○ Male ○ Female

Potential Living Biological Donors

Mother/Father of Missing Individual

Name	Age	Address	Phone	DNA Collected	Consent Form Signed
				○ Yes ○ No	○ Yes ○ No
				○ Yes ○ No	○ Yes ○ No

Brother and Sisters of Missing Individual

Name	Age	Address	Phone		
				○ Yes ○ No	○ Yes ○ No
				○ Yes ○ No	○ Yes ○ No
				○ Yes ○ No	○ Yes ○ No
				○ Yes ○ No	○ Yes ○ No
				○ Yes ○ No	○ Yes ○ No
				○ Yes ○ No	○ Yes ○ No
				○ Yes ○ No	○ Yes ○ No
				○ Yes ○ No	○ Yes ○ No

Spouse of Missing Individual

Name	Age	Address	Phone		
				○ Yes ○ No	○ Yes ○ No

Children of Missing Individual

Name	Age	Address	Phone		
				○ Yes ○ No	○ Yes ○ No
				○ Yes ○ No	○ Yes ○ No
				○ Yes ○ No	○ Yes ○ No
				○ Yes ○ No	○ Yes ○ No
				○ Yes ○ No	○ Yes ○ No
				○ Yes ○ No	○ Yes ○ No
				○ Yes ○ No	○ Yes ○ No
				○ Yes ○ No	○ Yes ○ No

Primary donor for Nuclear DNA Analysis

An "appropriate family member" for nuclear DNA Analysis is someone that is biologically related to and only one generation removed from the deceased. The following are the family members who are appropriate donors to provide reference specimens, and in the order of preference (family memers highlighted in bold print are the most desirable):

1. Natural (Biological) **Mother and Father**, OR
2. **Spouse** and Natural (Biological) **Children**, OR
3. A Natural (Biological) Mother or Father and victim's biological children, OR
4. Multiple Full Siblings of the Victim (i.e., children from the same Mother and Father

V9.2002

VIP Personal Information
Page 8 of 8

Name _____ / _____ / _____
Last   First   Middle

Interview Location _____ Interview Date _____ Interview Time _____
                                                (MM/DD/YYYY)

Interviewer Info:
       Interviewer Name _____ _____
                                 First   Last
      Interviewing Organization _____

Interviewer **Home** Information
Interviewer Address _____
                      Street, City State, Zip
    Interviewer home phone _____
      Interviewer cell phone _____
     interviewer work phone _____

Interviewer **On-Site** Information
interviewer onsite address _____
                     Street, Hotel, Room #

interviewer onsite phone _____
     interviewer onsite cell _____

       Reviewer Info:
        Reviewer Name _____
      Reviewer Signature _____
        Reviewing agency _____

V9.2002

VIP/DMORT Program
To be attached to the front of each Disaster Victim Packet

Tracking Form

Incident Location _____

Incident Name _____

Body Bag # _____

Coroner Case # _____

First/Middle/Last Name:

Person performing station function must check and sign below when completed. "No" represents that this station function <u>could not be performed</u>.

Processing Station:	Section Rep. Signature:
Admitting ○ Yes ○ No	
Personal Effects ○ Yes ○ No	
Photography ○ Yes ○ No	
Body Radiography ○ Yes ○ No	
Fingerprint ○ Yes ○ No	
Anthropology ○ Yes ○ No	
Pathology ○ Yes ○ No	
Embalming ○ Yes ○ No	
DNA ○ Yes ○ No	
Dental Examination ○ Yes ○ No	
Dental Photography ○ Yes ○ No	
Dental Radiology ○ Yes ○ No	

Tracker's Name

_____

After Processing Location

_____

Identification Method

○ Anthropology
○ Radiographic
○ Dental Records
○ Fingerprints
○ Pathology
○ Personal Effects
○ Photography
○ DNA

Comments

This bag produced bag #'s:

Photo's:

_____ NUMBER OF DENTAL PHOTOS _____ NUMBER OF SPECIMAN PHOTOS

_____ NUMBER OF PERSONAL EFFECTS PHOTOS

Also included in this file:

4/10/2002

AFIP/DNA SPECIMEN TAKEN

Incident Location ▨▨▨▨▨▨▨▨   Incident Name ▨▨▨▨▨▨

Body Bag # _____ DATE OF SPECIMEN PROCUREMENT _____

EXAMINER1 ....

EXAMINER 2 ....

☐ NOT SUITABLE FOR TYPING - NO SPECIMEN TAKEN

If not, why? ....

☐ ENTIRE SPECIMEN TAKEN

☐ PORTION OF SPECIMEN TAKEN -   DESCRIPTION OF SPECIMEN TAKEN (INCLUDE SIZE)

☐ HOLD   (NOTES ON HOLD)

ADDITIONAL INFORMATION

<Field Missing>   4/10/2002

VIP/DMORT Program
Morphology Examination Form
FRAGMENTED REMAINS

Bag #   Location #   DNA Taken   Date of Exam

○ Yes ○ No ○ Unk

Case # _____   Seat Assignment

Decedent: _____
                          (First, middle, last)

Sex _____   Age _____   Race _____   _____
                          (Confirmed info in this box DO NOT enter info)

Condition of Remains

☐ Fresh   ☐ Charred   ☐ Specific Trauma   ☐ Scavenger Activity
☐ Decomposing   ☐ Cremains   ☐ Floating (GPS)
☐ Burned   ☐ Distinct Marks   ☐ Submerged (Grid #)

Associated   ○ Aircraft Parts   Sex ○ Not Determined   Size ○ Less than 1" (2.5cm)
with Material: ○ Non Aircraft Parts   ○ Male   ○ 1-2" (2.5-5cm)
                  ○ Unknown Source   ○ Female   ○ 2"-6" (6-15cm)
                                                                       ○ 6"-12" (16-32cm)
Shape ○ Piece (Fairly symmetrical)   ○ Strand (Linear)   ○ 1'-2 Feet (33-64cm)
                                                                       ○ Larger than 2 Feet
Recognizable ☐ Tissue ☐ Organ ☐ Bone ☐ Teeth
                                                                       (Greatest Dimensions)

Descriptions of Fragmented Remains in Full Detail :

Pathology   Additional Information Available?   ○ Yes ○ No

_____
_____
_____
_____
_____
_____
_____
_____
_____
_____

Dental   Additional Information Available?   ○ Yes ○ No   Anthropology   Additional Information Available?   ○ Yes ○ No

Pathologist signature: _____   Anthropologist signature _____

4/10/2002

VIP/DMORT Program
FINGERPRINT EXAM FORM

Incident Location　　　　　　　　　　　　　　　　　**Incident Name**

Body # _____   Date of Exam _____

Examiner 1	
Examiner 2	
Condition of Body Burned, mutilated, etc	
Finger Printed (LIST FINGERS PRINTED)	
If not, why?	

Footprint available　☐ Yes ☐ No

4/10/2002

<Field Missing>

VIP/DMORT Program
Pathology Report
Recovered Clothing Description
Incident Name _____

AK Body #	Coroner Case #	First Name	MI	Last Name	Location

Item	Color	Size	Style	Material	Manufacturer
Dress					
Blouse					
Hose					
Slip					
Girdle					
Bra					
Skirt					
Shirt					
Tie					
Undershirt					
Hat					
Jacket					
Gloves					
Sweatshirt					
Coat					
Sweater					
Blazer					
Suit Jacket					
Vest					
Slacks					
Shorts					
Shoes					
Boots					
Socks					
Underpants					
Belt					

Belt Buckle Description

Belt Buckle Inscription

Other Clothing: (List significant descriptions)

Dry Cleaning Marks Description	Laundry Marks Description

Tobacco Smoker Tobacco Product	Tobacco Brand	What Fingers Stained
○ Yes ○ No		

4/10/2002

VIP/DMORT Program

Pathology Report
Personal Effects

Body Bag# _____

		Rings			Stone Color _____				

Size |_____ ⚬ None ⚬ 2 ⚬ 4 ☐ Clear ☐ Blue ☐ Gray ☐ Green ☐ Red ☐ Turquoise
⚬ 1 ⚬ 3 ⚬ 5 ☐ White ☐ Lt Blue ☐ Lt Green ☐ Black ☐ Yellow ☐ Jade ☐ Garnet

Wedding Ring **Number of Stones** ☐ None ☐ 1 ☐ 2 ☐ 3 ☐ 4 ☐ 5

Description on Tracking Form _____

Inscription _____

Additional Rings Description _____

Additional Rings Inscription _____

Misc Jewlery Description _____

Misc Jewlery Description _____

Watch Brand ⚬ Yes ⚬ No **Band Color** _____

Description on Tracking Form _____

Inscription _____

Necklace Description on Tracking Form _____

Inscription _____

Religious Medal Description on Tracking Form _____

Inscription _____

Wallet Description on Tracking Form _____

Contents _____

Purse Description o _____

Yes No Contents _____

CURRENCY: _____

MISC ITEMS FOUND: _____

Currency found _____

Misc personal effects _____

4/10/2002

VIP/DMORT Program
Jewelry Recovered Description

Post Mortem Records

Body #

Location

	Description on Tracking Form	Inscription
Ankle Bracelet		
Belt Buckle		
Bracelet		
Cuff Links		
Necklace		
Religious Medal		
Misc Jewelry		
Tie Clip		

Ear Ring Location   ○ Both   ○ Right   ○ Left   ○ More than one right   ○ More than one left

Ear Ring Description

<Field Missing>

4/10/2002

VIP/DMORT Program

AK Body #   **Anthropology Examination Form**

	Date of Exam	5/9/2003

Coroner # _____   Decedent: _____

(First, middle, last)

Sex _____   Age _____   Race _____

(Do not enter info in this box)

Estimate age   Anthropology estimated information in this area.

Age narrow lower _____   **Age narrow upper** _____   **95% Lower limits:** _____   **95%Upper limits:** _____

Stature _____ (in inches)   **Anthro sex** ☐ Male ☐ Female ☐ Unknown ☐ Male possible ☐ Female possible

Ancestry Skeletal   **Skeletal Robusticity**

○ Caucasoid ○ Asian ○ Hispanic ○ Other	○ Gracile ○ Robust
○ Negroid ○ American Indian ○ Unknown	○ Intermediate ○ Indeterminate

Present Parts

☐ Cranium   ☐ Partial R Upper Arm   ☐ L Forearm   ☐ Partial R Lower Leg   ☐ L Foot
☐ Partial Cranium   ☐ R Forearm   ☐ Partial L Forearm ☐ R Foot   ☐ Partial L Foot
☐ Mandible   ☐ Partial R Forearm   ☐ L Hand   ☐ Partial R Foot
☐ Partial Mandible   ☐ R Hand   ☐ Partial L Hand   ☐ L Upper Leg
☐ Torso   ☐ Partial R Hand   ☐ R Upper Leg   ☐ Partial L Upper Leg
☐ Partial Torso   ☐ L Upper Arm   ☐ Partial R Upper Leg ☐ L Lower Leg
☐ R Upper Arm   ☐ Partial L Upper Arm   ☐ R Lower Leg   ☐ Partial L Lower Leg

Unique Skeletal Features (Pathology, Healed Trauma, Non-metric Traits, Etc.)

☐ Cranium   ☐ Partial R Upper Arm   ☐ L Forearm   ☐ Partial R Lower Leg   ☐ L Foot
☐ Partial Cranium   ☐ R Forearm   ☐ Partial L Forearm ☐ R Foot   ☐ Partial L Foot
☐ Mandible   ☐ Partial R Forearm   ☐ L Hand   ☐ Partial R Foot
☐ Partial Mandible   ☐ R Hand   ☐ Partial L Hand   ☐ L Upper Leg
☐ Torso   ☐ Partial R Hand   ☐ R Upper Leg   ☐ Partial L Upper Leg
☐ Partial Torso   ☐ L Upper Arm   ☐ Partial R Upper Leg ☐ L Lower Leg
☐ R Upper Arm   ☐ Partial L Upper Arm   ☐ R Lower Leg   ☐ Partial L Lower Leg

Anthro sex based on _____

Anthro age based on _____

Anthro Ancestry based on _____

Anthro Stature based on _____

Anthro UniqueSkeletal _____

Anthro Cond of Remains _____

Examining Anthropologist _____

VIP/DMORT Program

Pathology Report
Physical Characteristics

Incident Name

Bag # _____   **Sex** ○ Male ○ Female ○ Unk

First/MI/Last Name _____   **Grid Location**

Race ○ African American ○ Caucasion ○ Hispanic ○ Native American ○ Asian/Pacific Islander ○ Other

Build ○ Gracile   ○ Robust   **Height cm** _____ **Inches** _____
         ○ Intermediate ○ Indeterminate   **Weight kg** _____ **Pounds** _____

Complexion ○ Light ○ Medium ○ Dark ○ Acne ○ Tanned ○ Olive ○ Ruddy

Eyes ○ Blue   ○ Green ○ Grey ○ Missing R ○ Glass R ○ Cataract R   **Ear Lobes** ○ Attached   ○ Unknown
       ○ Brown ○ Hazel ○ Blind ○ Missing L ○ Glass L ○ Cataract L   ○ Unattached

Facial Hair   ○ Beard ○ Beard & Moustache ○ Moustache ○ Clean Shaven ○ Goatee

Facial Hair Color   ○ Blonde ○ Brown ○ Black ○ Gray ○ Red ○ Salt & Pepper ○ White

Facial Hair Style   ○ Bushy   ○ Full Upper Lip ○ Whiskers Under Lower Lip ○ Pencil Thin Upper Lip
                       ○ Fu Manchu ○ Handle Bar   ○   Mutton Chops   ○   Very long

Hair Color ○ Auburn ○ Blonde ○ Brown ○ Black ○ Gray ○ Red ○ Salt & Pepper ○ White ○ Other

Hair Length ○ Ex Short less than 1" ○ Medium 4-8" ○ Very Long 12-24"   ○ Shaved
               ○ Short 1-3"   ○ Long 8-12"   ○ Ex Long more than 24"

Hair Colored ○ Yes ○ No ○ Unk   **Hair Accessory** ○ Wig ○ Toupee ○ Hair Piece ○ Hair Transplant

Finger Nail Type ○ Natural ○ Artificial ○ Unknown   **Length** ○ Extremely Long ○ Long ○ Medium ○ Short

Characteristics ○ Bites ○ Deformed ○ Dirty ○ Mishapen ○ Decorated ○ Tobacco Stain

Polish Color _____

Toenail Length ○ Extremely Long ○ Long ○ Medium ○ Short

Characteristics ○ Deformed ○ Dirty ○ Mishapen ○ Decorated   **Toenail Color** _____

Optical   ○ Glasses ○ Contacts

Objects in Body ○ Pacemaker ○ Bullete ○ Prosthetic Devices ○ Orthopedic devices ○ Other _____

Prothestics ....

Circumsion ○ Yes ○ No ○ Unk ○ NA

**Scars,
birthmarks,
deformities** ....

Surgery ○ Thoracotomy   ○ Choleoystectomy ○ Other laparotomy ○ Laminect
           ○ Coronary Artery Bypass ○ Appendectomy ○   Mastectomy

Smoker ○ Yes ○ No

Tatoos ....
....

**Other
Personal
Effects** ....
....

<Field Missing>   4/10/2002

VIP/DMORT Program

Radiology Report

Incident Name

Body #   Incident Location   Coroner Case #

Date of Exam

Decedent:
(LAST, FIRST, MIDDLE)

Radiology Team
From :

Sex _____   Age _____

Healed   ☐ Cranium   ☐ R Forearm   ☐ L Hand   ☐ L Upper Leg
fractures   ☐ Mandible   ☐ R Hand   ☐ R Upper Leg   ☐ L Lower Leg
             ☐ Torso   ☐ L Upper Arm   ☐ R Lower Leg   ☐ L Foot
             ☐ R Upper Arm   ☐ L Forearm   ☐ R Foot

Radiology Parts X-Rayed

Radiology Per Effects

<Field Missing>

VIP/DMORT Program
Pathology Report
Recovered Clothing Description
Incident Name _____

AK Body #	Coroner Case #	First Name		MI	Last Name	Location

Item	Color	Size	Style	Material	Manufacturer
Dress					
Blouse					
Hose					
Slip					
Girdle					
Bra					
Skirt					
Shirt					
Tie					
Undershirt					
Hat					
Jacket					
Gloves					
Sweatshirt					
Coat					
Sweater					
Blazer					
Suit Jacket					
Vest					
Slacks					
Shorts					
Shoes					
Boots					
Socks					
Underpants					
Belt					

Belt Buckle Description

Belt Buckle Inscription

Other Clothing: (List significant descriptions)

Dry Cleaning Marks Description	Laundry Marks Description

Tobacco Smoker	Tobacco Product	Tobacco Brand	What Fingers Stained
○ Yes ○ No			

4/10/2002

VIP/DMORT Program
Pathology Examination of Partial or Complete Remains

Bag #　　　　Coroner Case #　　Sex:　　　　　　　　　　Date of Exam

○ Male　○ Female　○ Unknown

Examining
Pathologist

Morgue # _____
Coroner Case # _____

General Description
Est Race

○ Caucasoid　○ Negroid　○ Asian　○ American Indian　○ Hispanic　○ Unknown　○ Other

Est Height Inches _____
Est Wt Pounds _____

Consists Of:　　　Specimen Wt _____　　　Dimensions _____

Head

Scalp Hair
□ Black　□ Lt Brown　□ Gray　□ Red /Auburn　□ Other
□ Dk Brown　□ Blonde　□ White　□ Gray/White

Hair Length Style
○ >24"　○ 8-12"　○ 1-3"　○ Straight　○ Curly
○ 12-24"　○ 4-8"　○ <1"　○ Wavy　○ Tightly curled
Other

Facial Hair Color
□ Black　□ Lt Brown　□ Gray　□ Red /Auburn　□ Other
□ Dk Brown　□ Blonde　□ White　□ Gray/White

Facial Hair Type
□ Beard　　　□ Other (describe)
□ Moustache
□ Clean Shaven

Ears ○ Left Ear　Pierced　Yes　No #_____　○ Right Ear　Pierced ○ Yes ○ No #_____

Pierced other: _____

Teeth Present?　○ Yes ○ No

Additional head and neck exam remarks:

Torso

○ Viscera Identifiable

<Field Missing>

4/10/2002

Pathology Exam Form Page 2 0f 2

Bag #   Sex

○ Male ○ Female ○ Unknown   Date of Exam

Genitalia

Ext ☐ Male ☐ Female ☐ Indeterminate ☐ Penis Circumcised ☐ Penis Uncircumcised ☐ Penis Indeterminate

Internal ☐ Testis Left ☐ Testis Right ☐ Uterus ☐ Tubes Left ☐ Tubes Right ☐ Ovaries Left ☐ Ovaries Right

Extremities

○ Rt Upper	○ Arm ○ Forearm ○ Hand	# Fingers	Fingernails/Polish
○ Left Upper	○ Arm ○ Forearm ○ Hand	# Fingers	Fingernails/Polish
○ Rt Lower	○ Thigh ○ Leg ○ Foot	# Toes	Toenails/Polish
○ Left Lower	○ Thigh ○ Leg ○ Foot	# Toes	Toenails/Polish

Extremity
Remarks

○ Scars (other than surgical)
○ Birthmarks
○ Deformities (non peri-mortem)

○ Tattoos

Objects in Body   ○ Pacemaker ○ Bullets ○ Prosthetic Devices ○ Orthopedic devices ○ Other

Prothestics   List manufacturer, serial numbers, and other identifying features:

Surgery   ○ Thoracotomy   ○ Cholerystectomy ○ Other laparotomy ○ Laminectomy
        ○ Coronary Artery Bypass ○ Appendectomy ○ Mastectomy

Personal Effects   Brief
○ Yes ○ No   Description

Optical   ○ Glasses ○ Contacts   ○ Clothing   (See Clothing Form)

Additional Information

CASE NO. ———————————— NAME ————————————

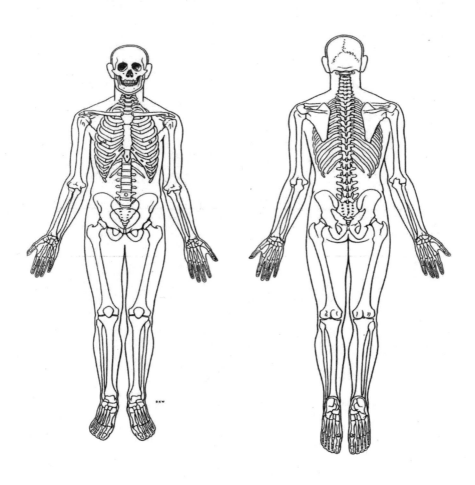

FORM C

CASE NO. ——————————— NAME ————————————————

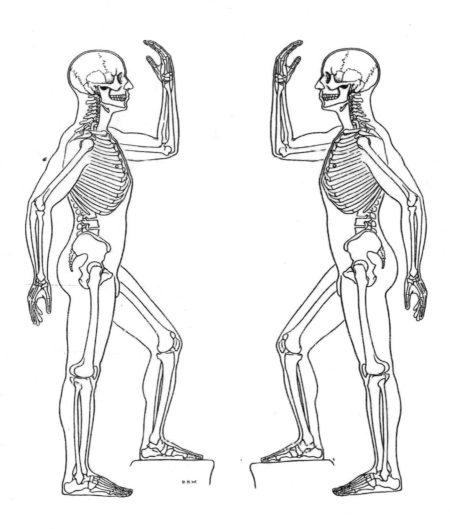

FORM D

CASE NO. _____ NAME _____

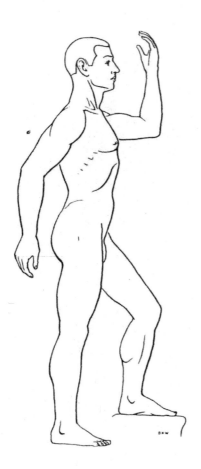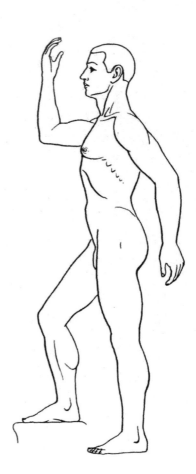

FORM B

CASE NO. ——————————— NAME ———————————

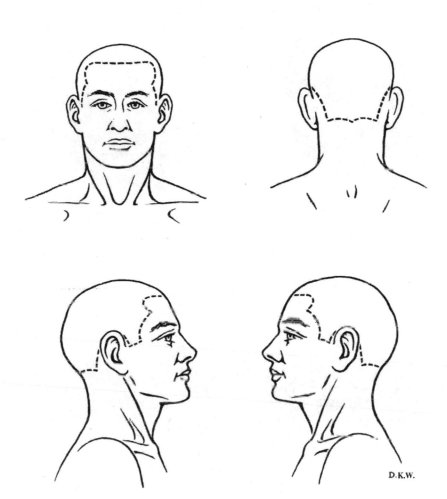

D.K.W.

FORM E

CASE NO. _____ NAME _____

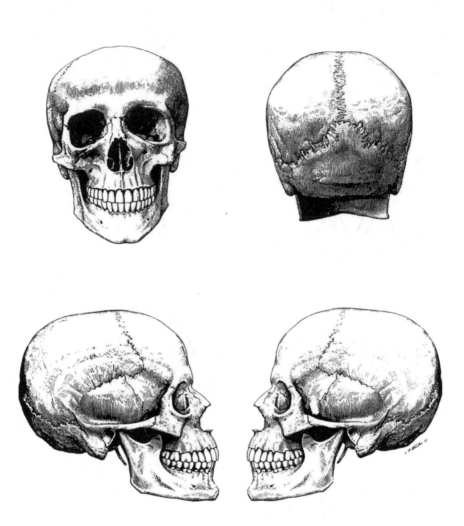

FORM G

About the Editors

Dr. Matthias I. Okoye, M.D., J.D. is a practicing physician and lawyer, and the Director of the Nebraska Institute of Forensic Sciences, Inc., and Nebraska Forensic Medical Services, P.C. He is Clinical Associate Professor of forensic pathology at Creighton University School of Medicine, Omaha, Nebraska. He is also an adjunct professor of forensic medicine and pathology at several universities abroad. He was formerly the Chief Medical Examiner for the District of Columbia, Washington, D.C. He is a consultant forensic pathologist with the State of Nebraska's Office of the Attorney General, and serves as a coroner's physician and forensic pathologist for several Nebraska counties. Dr. Okoye is a member of the bars of Pennsylvania, U.S. Supreme Court, and several federal courts. He is also a member of the Board of Governors of the American College of Legal Medicine and the American Board of Legal Medicine. He is a member of the National Association of Medical Examiners and a Fellow of the College of American Pathologists. He has lectured and published extensively in the fields of forensic sciences, legal medicine, forensic medicine and pathology.

Dr. Cyril H. Wecht, M.D., J.D. is the former Coroner of Allegheny County, and one of the world's leading experts in forensic pathology. He has been consulted in numerous high profile cases. As a medical-legal expert, Dr. Wecht has performed approximately 16,000 autopsies and has supervised, reviewed or been consulted on approximately 36,000 additional postmortem examinations. Dr. Wecht is the Past President of the American Academy of Forensic Sciences and the American College of Legal Medicine. He is the author of more than 475 professional publications, along with the popular non-fiction books *Cause of Death*, *Grave Secrets*, *Who Killed JonBenet Ramsey?*, *Mortal Evidence* and *Tales from the Morgue*.

447

About the Authors

Dr. Steven C. Batterman, Ph.D. was the first engineer in the world to be elected president of the American Academy of Forensic Sciences. Dr. Batterman's areas of expertise include accident reconstruction, occupant kinematics, vehicle dynamics, biomechanics, mechanics of human injury, crash worthiness, restraint systems, products liability, safety engineering and human factors. Additional expertise is in mechanics of solids and structures, including stress analysis, buckling and stability, failure analysis, structural dynamics, impact, mechanical and structural design. Dr. Batterman holds numerous academic honors and awards, has published extensively and enjoys international recognition as an engineering consultant and one of the leading forensic engineers of our time.

Larry R. Bedore, M.S. CJ. earned his Bachelor's degree in Biology at the Franciscan University of Steubenville (Ohio) and he completed his Master's Degree in Criminal Justice with Nova University. Mr. Bedore has been a member of the federal DMORT program since 1994 and assisted the Office of the Chief Medical Examiner during the World Trade Center Disaster response. He served as Planning Chief for the Mississippi DMORT response to Hurricane Katrina in 2005. Mr. Bedore was part of the original working group to establish the Florida Emergency Mortuary Operations Response System (FEMORS) in 2002 and became its first Commander in 2003.

Major John J. Buturla, Director, State of Connecticut, Department of Public Safety, Division of Homeland Security.

Bruce W. Dixon, M.D., received his B.S. in chemistry from the University of Pittsburgh and his M.D. from the University of Pittsburgh School of Medicine. He completed his residency at Duke University and served in Professional and Academic capacities there before returning to the University of Pittsburgh in 1975. Currently, Dr. Dixon is an Associate Professor of Medicine at the University of Pittsburgh School of Medicine, a position he has held since 1979.

Since 1992, in addition to his teaching duties, Dr. Dixon has been the Director of the Allegheny County Health Department. Dr. Dixon manages all Health

Department programs, which impact air quality, environmental quality, and human health areas. He personally directs the Sexually Transmitted Diseases/HIV/ AIDS Program, which provides diagnosis, treatment, and patient care, including social services case management, to residents of Allegheny County.

In October 2000, Dr. Dixon was instrumental in forming a new nonprofit corporation, Allegheny Correctional Health Services, Inc., which is responsible for inmate medical services at the Allegheny County Jail. Dr. Dixon is serving as Chief Executive Officer and Chair of the Board of Directors.

Annette Doying is currently a full-time graduate student in the Applied Anthropology program (bio-medical track) at the University of South Florida (Tampa, Florida USA). She received her undergraduate degree in Anthropology from the University of South Florida (B.A.). She has been a professional emergency manager since 1993 and is credentialed in a wide range of roles to include field-based incident commander, liaison officer, planning section chief, hazardous materials technician, emergency medical technician, GIS specialist, operations coordinator, instructor, and domestic security task force responder. Ms. Doying was instrumental in securing and managing approximately $3 million in federal grant funds to assist homeowners suffering from catastrophic real property losses (1996–2000) and was a major contributor to the Florida Department of Community Affairs, Division of Emergency Management's Handbook for Floodplain Acquisition and Elevation Projects (2001). Most recently, Ms. Doying served on the Tampa Bay (Florida) Incident Management Team deployed as the first-in resource to Hurricane Katrina's landfall in Hancock County, Mississippi, where she directly established the foundation to one of the largest disaster relief efforts in U.S. history. Her current interests include forensic anthropology in mass disasters, resolution of missing and unidentified person cases through the application of anthropological identification techniques, and U.S. disaster response systems.

Bassel El-Kasaby, Esq. As Senior partner of the law firm of Kasaby & Nicholls, Mr. El-Kasaby practices in the areas of immigration law, employment law, civil rights, and aviation law. He received his B.S., his M.S., with distinction, and his J.D., with distinction, from the University of Iowa. He is a former faculty member at the University of Nebraska at Omaha Aviation Institute, involved in teaching and research on aviation law, policy, and regulation. He has published on issues involving aviation law, insurance, and passenger rights.

Dr. John Filippi, D.D.S., A.B.F.O. is a forensic dentist and dental consultant for the State of Nebraska. Dr. Filippi's first involvement in mass disaster dental identifications was in 1989 with United Flight 232, in Sioux City, Iowa. Since 1991, and his affiliation with the NDMS/DMORT System, he has been actively involved with multiple cemetery desecrations as well as six commercial airline disasters. His experiences also include two tours of service at the World Trade Center/ 911 and Hurricane Katrina in New Orleans. Dr. Filippi is a member of the Board of Governors for the American Society of Forensic Odontology.

L. Sue Gabriel, B.S.N., M.S.N., M.F.S. is the Assistant Professor at BryanLGH College of Health Sciences, School of Nursing and co-developer of the first Senior Forensic Nursing Elective which has a 90-hour clinical component in an undergraduate program. She is a national and international speaker and workshop presenter on Forensic Nursing, Child Abuse, Sexual Assault, and Intimate Partner Violence. Sue is a guest faculty and University of Nebraska and Nebraska Wesleyan University in the undergraduate and Masters Programs in Forensic Science. Sue is a member of International Association of Forensic Nurses, American Academy of Forensic Sciences, Disaster Mortuary Response Team Region VII, The American College of Forensic Examiners, and the Commission on Forensic Education. A graduate of University of Nebraska Medical Center College of Nursing and is a practicing Sexual Assault Nurse Examiner. Sue is also co-author of an entry level Forensic Nursing text that will be available in 2009.

Timothy E. Huntington, M.S., is a board certified forensic entomologist and Member of the American Board of Forensic Entomology. Currently, he is a Ph.D. candidate in the Department of Entomology at the University of Nebraska-Lincoln, where his area of research is in the ecology and physiology of forensically important blow flies. His publications in the area of forensic entomology focus on the use of insects for the estimation of postmortem intervals.

Mr. Huntington is a forensic entomology consultant for several law enforcement agencies, and has consulted on more than thirty death investigations in seven states and four countries. He is a member of the Entomological Society of America, American Academy of Forensic Sciences, North American Forensic Entomology Association, and Nebraska Chapter of the International Association for Identification.

Dr. Erin Kimmerle, Ph.D. is an Assistant Professor of Anthropology at the University of South Florida. She earned her M.A. in Anthropology at the University of Nebraska and her Ph.D. in Anthropology from the University of Tennessee. Dr. Kimmerle served as Forensic Anthropologist in Kosovo and as the Chief Anthropologist in Croatia and Bosnia-Herzegovina for the United Nations, International Criminal Tribunal for the Former Yugoslavia (ICTY). Kimmerle has worked as a forensic consultant on cases throughout the United States, Bermuda and the Balkans.

Dr. Henry C. Lee, Ph.D. is the Chief Emeritus Director of the Connecticut State Police Forensic Laboratory. He is professor of the Forensic Science program at the University of New Haven, a program which he created in 1975. He has served on national and international committees in forensic science, criminal justice, education, and training. Dr. Lee has over 800 workshops/seminars to his credit, has investigated over 6,000 major cases worldwide, and has testified over 1,000 times in criminal and civil cases. He serves more than 3,000 agencies as a consultant.

Dr. Chris Long, Ph.D. is the Chief Forensic Toxicologist and Associate Professor at St. Louis University School of Medicine, St. Louis, Missoui, where he directs the toxicology laboratories of several counties for the State of Missouri. He is a Fellow of the American Academy of Forensic Sciences and has published and lectured extensively in forensic Toxicology. He has been involved in the toxicologic analyses of specimens in several mass disasters.

Dr. David McCann, M.D. was appointed chief medical officer of the Florida One Disaster Medical Assistance Team in the U.S. Department of Homeland Security in 2004, and is the newly elected chair of the American Board of Disaster Medicine. Dr. McCann is also an instructor at the Department of Homeland Security's Center for Domestic Preparedness at Fort McClellan, as well as a National Disaster Life Support Instructor. He is also an Advanced HAZMAT Life Support Instructor and a VA Decontamination Course Instructor. Dr. McCann is an accomplished professional speaker and teacher, and a co-founder of Disaster Life Support of North America, Inc., a corporation dedicated to disaster preparation, planning response and recovery education for businesses and communities nationwide.

Professor Edmund Joseph Chukwueloka Nwana, M.D., F.M.C. Path., is the professor and head of the department of morbid anatomy at the University of Ilorin College of Medicine, Ilorin, Nigeria. Professor Nwana obtained his M.D. degree from the University of Ibadan, Nigeria, and took his residency in anatomic pathology at the University of Jos Teaching Hospital, Jos, Nigeria. He obtained his fellowship of the medical council of Nigeria (Pathology) from the Nigerian National Post Graduate Medical College. He is adjunct professor and consultant pathologist to several medical schools in Nigeria. Professor Nwana is also a fellow of the International College of Surgeons and has lectured extensively in the area of pathology. He is also a consultant pathologist for the Nigerian police and the coroner for Lagos State, Nigeria.

Professor John O. Obafunwa, M.D., F.R.C. Path, L.L.B. is the Professor and Head of Department of Morbid Anatomy and the Provost of the Lagos State University College of Medicine, Ikeja, Lagos, Nigeria. Professor Obafunwa was the State Pathologist for Cayman Islands and the Republic of Bermuda. He is a member of the American Academy of Forensic Sciences and also a delegate to the International Academy of Legal Medicine. He is a member of the British Association of Forensic Pathologists and the World Association of Police Surgeons.

Ms. Chizoma R. Opara, Esq. is a Staff Attorney with the American Bar Association (ABA-Africa), Abuja, Nigeria—an implementing partner for the Anti-Trafficking in Persons (TIP) project of U.S. Agency for International Development (USAID). She is responsible for conducting extensive legal research for various TIP projects, drafting and presenting case studies for educational materials on human trafficking and child abuse and exploitation, maintained and distributed to various law enforcement agencies.

Major Timothy Palmbach, M.S., J.D., received his M.S. in forensic science from the University of New Haven in New Haven, CT and his J.D. from the University of Connecticut School of Law in Hartford, CT. He is the director of the Connecticut Division of Scientific Services and works with Dr. Henry Lee in crime scene reconstruction. He is an adjunct instructor at the University of New Haven and Central Connecticut State University and has been a guest lecturer at University of Connecticut School of Law, Western Connecticut University, Saint Joseph College and Northwestern Connecticut Community College.

He has processed more than 200 crime scenes and is a qualified expert witness in crime scene processing, blood spatter pattern interpretation and digital enhancement of forensic photographs.

Mark W. Perlin, M.D., Ph.D. develops biomedical information and automation technologies. He has been working in the area of computational genetics for over 15 years. Dr. Perlin invented linear mixture analysis and deconvolution-based STR genotyping technologies for forensic DNA interpretation. At Cybergenetics, the firm of which he is the founder and CEO, he directs the development of the TrueAllele® system for automated computer review of casework and databank DNA data. Dr. Perlin also invented the inner product mapping method for rapidly building genome clone maps, and led the project that produced the first genome map for human chromosome 11. Currently, he is using TrueAllele® computers to reanalyze the DNA data from the World Trade Center mass disaster. Dr. Perlin actively collaborates with researchers at Carnegie Mellon University, the University of Pittsburgh and Duquesene University. He received a B.A. in chemistry from State University of New York at Binhamton; a Ph.D. in mathematics from City University of New York Graduate School; an M.D. from the University of Chicago Pritzker School of Medicine; and a Ph.D. in computer science from Carnegie Mellon University. Dr. Perlin also completed a transitional residency at mercy Hospital in Pittsburgh and was a fellow at IBM's Watson research facility in Yorktown Heights, New York.

Mr. Mark Roper is a fouth generation funeral director at Roper & Sons Funeral Home in Lincoln, Nebraska. He has been a mortuary officer member of DMORT, the Disaster Mortuary Operational Response Team, since 1995 and has been activated on responses to Guam Korean Airline disaster in 1997, World Trade Center 2001, Kirksville Missouri American Airlines accident in 2004, and Hurricane Katrina 2005. He is a graduate of the Fountain National Academy for Advanced Post Mortem Reconstructive Surgery.

Dr. Michael Welner, M.D. As chairman of The Forensic Panel, he founded the first and only peer review forensic expert consultation practice in the country. Most recently, he developed The Depravity Scale, a device currently being validated for the psychological determination of evil. Dr. Welner specializes in violent patients and those who fail to respond to treatment. He has consulted in a number of high profile cases, including the death of heiress Doris Duke, the Wyoming homicide of Matthew Shepard and the mass murders at a Xerox facility in Hawaii.

Dr. Thomas Young, M.D. As the Jackson County Medical Examiner for 11.5 years, Dr. Young served as the chief death investigator for metropolitan Kansas City on the Missouri side of the state line. He obtained for the office full accreditation by the National Association of Medical Examiners. The office remains the only nationally accredited death investigation agency in Missouri. Dr. Young has assisted in several mass disasters and is the former director of a nationally accredited forensic pathology training program.

Index

A

affidavit, 303
Afghanistan, 210
Al-qaeda, 216, 218, 318
American Academy of Forensic Sciences (AAFS), 40, 169, 270, 272, 325, 341, 352-353
American Board of Entomology (ABFE), 270-271
antemortem, 39, 46, 49, 56, 64, 67-68, 73-76, 94-95, 102, 148, 180, 221, 224, 226-229, 237, 242, 245-247, 258, 260
autopsy, 13, 16, 49, 81-84, 87, 93, 95-97, 101, 103-104, 107, 113, 115-118, 120, 128, 130, 132, 134-136, 140-143, 145-148, 152-153, 158-159, 167-168, 283, 332, 337, 344
aviation law, 289, 296

B

biohazard, 10, 146, 166
biological profile, 23, 224, 243
bioterrorism, 1, 21, 56, 121, 154, 161-163, 167, 169-170, 268-269, 359, 379-380
bioweapons, 118
blowflies, 271-273
body escorts, 171, 179-180
body identification, 56, 88

C

cemetery, 155, 243, 245, 356
Center for Disease Control (CDC), 18, 56, 114-115, 120-121, 124, 126-129, 131-138, 140, 143, 145, 151, 154, 160-163, 165-170, 281, 358-359, 377, 379
cerebellum, 334
cerebral, 332, 334-335, 337-339, 350
chain-of-custody, 7, 153
coagulation, 129, 131, 163
counterterrorism, 21
courtroom, 84, 331

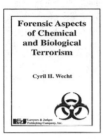

#6028 Terrorism Law: Materials, Cases, Comments, Fourth Edition
by Jeffrey Addicott

Over the past few years, the United States has faced many changes and challenges pertaining to the War on Terror, and continues to do so today. The biggest challenges have become fighting and winning the War on Terror under a democratically based rule of law, and protecting human rights and civil liberties in an ongoing wartime situation.

The fourth edition has been updated to include new developments in this war as well as some of our nation's and the world's biggest challenges while fighting it. This new edition includes many appendices containing important American and international documents pertaining to the War on Terror as well as discussion questions, citations of legal cases pertaining to terrorism, and bibliographic information for further reference.

8.5" x 11" • Hardcover • ISBN: 1-933264-21-7 • Pages: 557

#5563/5564 Physical Evidence in Forensic Science, Second Edition
by Henry C. Lee, Howard A. Harris

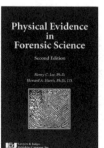

This new edition of the classic by America's leading forensic scientists gives you an insider's understanding of physical evidence at the crime scene.

Written in an easy-to-understand format, this outstanding guide, by the nation's foremost forensic scientists, introduces you to the basics of crime scene evaluation. This extensive resource is packed with valuable information about the details of collecting, storing, and analyzing all types of physical evidence. You'll learn how to connect the victim(s) and suspect(s) to the crime scene, and to the physical evidence left behind.

**6" x 9" • Softcover/Hardcover •
ISBN: 1-930056-01-X (soft) 1-930056-00-1 (hard) • Pages: 346**